The Mountains Call My Name

THE MOUNTAINS CALL MY NAME

Cover photo copyright 2009 by Ryan C. Harmening, http://www.ryancharlesphotography.com/. Limited usage rights obtained. Cover design, Eric St. Clair

The Mountains Call My Name

Terri Thomas St. Clair

Edited by Stan St. Clair

Final Proofing by Rhonda St. Clair

THE MOUNTAINS CALL MY NAME

© 2009 by Terri Thomas St. Clair,
St. Clair Publications

All rights reserved. No part of this publication may be reproduced or transmitted in any form by any means electronic or mechanical, including telecopy, recording, or any information storage and retrieval system now known or invented, without permission in writing from the publisher, except by a reviewer who wishes to quote brief passages in connection with a review written for inclusion in a magazine, newspaper or broadcast.

ISBN 978-0-9801704-2-9

Printed in the United States of America by
St. Clair Publications
P. O. Box 726
Mc Minnville, TN 37111-0726

http://stan.stclair.net

Contents

Dedication

9

Introduction

11

Part One – The Mountains Call My Name

13

Chapter One

14

Chapter Two

21

Chapter Three

47

Chapter Four

152

Chapter Five

168

Chapter Six

175

Chapter Seven

191

Chapter Eight

241

Chapter Nine

275

Chapter Ten

288

Chapter Eleven

314

Chapter Twelve

331

Chapter Thirteen

369

Chapter Fourteen

399

Chapter Fifteen

416

Chapter Sixteen

457

Chapter Seventeen

492

Part Two – Searching for My Mountain

525

Chapter One

526

Chapter Two

551

Chapter Three

571

Chapter Four

616

Chapter Five

625

Chapter Six

637

Chapter Seven

708

Dedication

I dedicate this book, first of all, to my Lord and Savior, Jesus Christ, for giving me my artistic talents.

I dedicate this to my husband, Roger, who adores me and lets me know this. His encouragement to me is priceless.

I dedicate this to my two children, Melissa and Eric, and to their spouses, Jonathan Weaver and Katie Estes St.Clair.

I dedicate this to my perfect grandchildren, Jonathan 2nd, who is already heartily working on his first book and Abigail St. Clair Weaver, who is a work of art in her own rights.

And I want to take this time to tell Geneva St. Clair how very much I love her for making me feel like her child.

I want to thank my son for using his talents to produce the cover of this book. He, also, is writing a book.

I dedicate this to my sister-in-law, Barbara Thomas. She labored hard and long hours with my creation in its embryonic stage, and to her granddaughter, Mary-Beth, the first to weep through the sad parts. Barbara was my initial cheerleader, and encouraged me to continue in the birthing process.

I especially want to thank Lori Gamble Edmisten and Quiet Expressions Gallery for working wonders with the beautiful talents God has given her in photography. www.quietexpression.net

I especially want to thank Stanley St. Clair for the many long hours he spent preparing my book for publication. Without him it would still be on my bookshelf. I thank the providence of God for bring together these people at just the right time to make my dream come true: Stan, Lori and Eric.

The tithe from the profits of this book will go for the furthering of the Gospel in Reykjavík Iceland where my son, Eric, and his wife, Katie, labor for the Lord.

THE MOUNTAINS CALL MY NAME

Introduction

Editorial note: though no dates are given in the text, events herein flash back to the period beginning in the 1960s, but the major part of this saga takes place in the early 1980s.

A peaceful sleep finally spread over the restless Elizabeth. It had become increasingly difficult to find the deep dreamless sleep that her mind and body longed for. At last, the slow steady breathing indicated that she would be able to escape the pain in which she lived. Her loving husband, the one that filled her life with joy, was gone. A car full of drunken teenagers, out for a New Year's Eve party, had run head long into David's car. He had been on his way to the emergency room where she worked as an R.N. to take her a special New Year's Eve supper. It was not to be, for as fate would have it, he had had another appointment he couldn't miss. Elizabeth was headed into a lonely and isolated time in her life. A time without the one who had led her from the poverty of the mountains to the fast-paced life of the medical world.

What would she do now? The foreboding feeling she had of the mountains = she had never quite explained that away. The times she did go were periodic visits to see her dear mother. Since David's death, she had withdrawn to the sanctuary of her home, bound by grief and loneliness and the remnants of her life with David: roses long dead in a vase from her anniversary, Christmas pictures, albums of wedding photos, his housecoat which she wrapped herself in pretending he was near her. The scent of his cologne was so faded now she could barely smell it. Each day the vividness of him slipped a little more, easing further and further away. The more his image dimmed, the deeper the depression became, slowly pulling her into the depth of the blackness. The sleep she longed for was the blessed sleep of the eternal. Then the pain would be gone.

Part One:

The Mountains Call My Name

Chapter One

"Hello..."

"Miss 'Lis'beth, this is Anna Belle callin'."

"Oh, hi Anna Belle. You're calling awfully early, is something wrong?"

"It's yer Mama, she ain't doin' so well."

"How come?"

"Miss Bessie died late last night. She be needin' fo' ya to come home. She just sits and cries, and I cain't do nothin' fer her. She just keeps a sayin' she wish you was here."

"I'm so sorry, Anna Belle. I know that Bessie was just like a sister. As soon as I make arrangements here I'll head home. I should be there by nightfall."

"I was a hopin' you'd make it. You know yer Mama, she don't want to be no bother. The funeral's in two or three days. Soon as Sharon gets home."

Why didn't Mama call?"

"Sompthin's been wrong with her phone. They cain't fix it today."

THE MOUNTAINS CALL MY NAME

"Be sure and tell her I'm on my way and not to worry."

"Thanks so much, Ms. 'Lis'beth, I's so lookin' forward to seein' ya."

I threw a few things together and grabbed some outfits from my closet. I didn't know exactly what I was going to wear, so I just picked up the first ones I saw. I arranged for my neighbor to feed my cat.

It had started raining when I pulled out of the driveway. I knew from having lived in the mountains of Virginia that this could easily turn to snow before I reached Mama's.

I headed up the interstate toward home. I couldn't help but think back to the early days when I first left there.

I'm not sure what bothered me most about living in the mountains, the oppression of the people, or the depressed area itself.

The few friends I had were already planning weddings, or had married. Some didn't even wait for graduation before tying the knot. I'm not even sure why they bothered with getting a diploma. Only a few went on to college. Maybe it was just the idea of graduating.

The thought of working in the mills and factories was not one of the things I relished. Even worse was trying to raise a family on welfare. Because of the lack of work and layoffs, that happened quite often.

My parents didn't have a lot of money, so I knew I was going to need scholarships to pay for education. I worked hard toward that goal. There wasn't much time for extracurricular activities. Every spare moment was used to make sure my grades were on top.

Mama canned everything she could get her hands on. Food was one thing we had plenty of. Daddy would go to turkey shoots to get us our bird for Thanksgiving, or a ham for Christmas. He was a good shot with a gun and rarely came home empty handed.

A lot of my dresses were made from cotton feed sacks. Daddy would let me pick the print the sacks were made of. After he had the corn and wheat ground at the mill. They would put the flour and cornmeal in the sack I picked out. Mama was a good seamstress and made me pretty skirts and dresses. She would have me pick dresses I liked out of the catalog. Then she would make a pattern out of brown paper bags. You barely could tell the difference in the catalog dresses and the feed sack dresses. I don't think I truly appreciated her talents until I was older. I just took for granted that she could magically make clothes appear for me. One thing about our area, we all dressed pretty much alike. Oh, there were some kids in school that flaunted what they had, but they were the minority.

The summer of my graduation will be one I will never forget. Daniel Scott was my closest friend. Even though he was a boy, we couldn't have been closer as friends. I didn't have many close girl friends; I just didn't make time for them. Daniel and I were racing for Valedictorian. We studied together, planned projects together; what one did, the other one did. That made the hard work for a grant a little more fun. He wanted out of

THE MOUNTAINS CALL MY NAME

the hills as bad as I did. The big difference between Daniel and me, other than the obvious, was he didn't need a scholarship to go to college. His parents owned a lot of the land around Scott's Corner, so he didn't lack funds to go to school. He loved a challenge and I sure gave him one.

Daniel and I roamed the "hills and hollers" from the time we first became friends around five or six years old. We would dissect frogs, worms, and anything else that would hold still.

He always made me be the nurse. He said, "Only men can be doctors." He was a brother and a confidant. Neither one of us considered ourselves as dating each other. Unless you called going to the library to study a date. He sure was cute though. The girls at school were ga-ga over him. They were jealous because we were together a lot. We both dated some, but our main focus was on leaving the hills of Virginia. Good study habits paid off, I got a scholarship to nursing school at Duke University in North Carolina. Daniel ended up getting accepted at the University of Virginia. He didn't quite make it out of the hills, but he was on his way. We both got exactly what we had worked so hard for, a way out.

It was the hottest summer I could remember. June was already as hot as a normal August. Mama and I had been canning peas all day. I hated working with peas the worst, because it took so long to get enough to can. It was late afternoon and we were sitting in the porch swing. When the sun went down behind the mountain you could catch a breeze coming down the hollow. The kitchen was still hot from canning, and mama wasn't ready to tackle supper. We sat quietly, to tired to carry on a conversation. My body was sticky with sweat and my blouse clung to my skin. I had my long brunette hair pulled up in a ponytail to keep it out of my face.

The swirl of dust rising up from around the curve down the road caught my eye. We lived on a dirt road with a spattering of gravel. State trucks dumped them on there from time to time. Sometimes they would oil the road to keep down the dust. There were four or five houses up the hollow, and so I figured it was one of our neighbors. As the car approached our driveway, it turned ever so slowly into our lane. I had never seen it before. I sat up in the swing and absent-mindedly ran my fingers through my hair to catch the loose strands. My focus sharpened as I looked at the car, trying to decide if it was indeed someone I knew.

There was a large dent in the right front fender. It was an older make of car. The once bright blue was faded with a lot of rust spots showing through. A tall young man got out with a satchel in hand. He walked up the sidewalk toward us with a confident stride, and a smile spread across his face. He introduced himself to us as David Mason, his hand outstretched to shake Mama's.

He said he was selling magazines to help pay for his graduate work. He went on to explain that he lived on campus at Duke University. His summers were spent making money for the next year of studies. He had to make up the difference from what scholarships didn't pay. I told him I was going there in the fall. Mama explained that we didn't have any need for magazines, but he was welcome to stay and have a nice cold glass of tea.

Our conversation came easy. We talked about everything but magazines. Our visit continued until the sun was setting. Mama invited him to have a bite of

THE MOUNTAINS CALL MY NAME

supper with us, which he readily accepted. He seemed so comfortable at our modest table. He even helped with the dinner dishes.

We went back to the porch swing and talked long into the evening. With each word he spoke, I became more mesmerized. We talked of our dreams and hopes for the future. It seemed as if I had known him all my life. My heart had never felt so light. I felt giddy with him as we talked. How could I let myself act so foolish? I wasn't prepared for the onslaught of feelings. I had guarded my heart so closely. I dared not let anyone draw me away from my pathway to freedom, and here I was, actually not wanting him to leave. I was hungry to learn everything I could about the school I would be attending.

As he left, he asked if he could come back again, so we could talk further about school. I asked Mama if he could come back on the weekend and help me with my list for college. After all, he knew what dorm life was like and what I would need.

Needless to say, he came back again and again. We shared many hours on that front porch swing. I'm not sure when it dawned on us that we were in love. Over the summer we grew closer and closer. The heart that I had guarded so closely was stolen away by this handsome, blue-eyed, blond salesman. At summers end he asked my daddy for my hand in marriage. He and I both accepted.

We were married in the little white chapel down the lane from my house. The church was decorated with flowers from Mama's garden. I wore the wedding dress her mother so lovingly made for her. The intricate stitching was beautiful. There was little that had to be done to make it fit me. Daddy walked me down the aisle. I had never

THE MOUNTAINS CALL MY NAME

seen him look so handsome. With tears in his eyes, he gently placed me in the care of this stranger, David Mason. I couldn't believe that I had fallen in love so easily, after fighting so hard to keep from doing so in school. So it was, I began my life away from the hills of Virginia with a new husband and on my way to achieving my dream of becoming a nurse. From that day forward I would not look back. Finally I was headed to a place I had worked toward my whole life. Could I dare hope and dream for more?

Chapter Two

The closer I got to the Virginia state line, the colder it became. The rain had turned to a wet snow. Big fat flakes were dotting my windshield. By the time I topped Fancy Gap Mountain the fog was as thick as pea soup. The traffic was traveling at a snail's pace. I sure hoped I reached Scott's Corner before dark. It wasn't too far from the Virginia state line that I would have to turn. That exit was so hard to see. I would have to watch closely so I wouldn't miss it. I remember missing it once and driving all the way to Hillsville before I realized it. Trying to watch other cars, the road, and the exits was no easy task with the fog so thick.

I turned on an easy listening radio station. The soft music filled the car, soothing my spirit. If only my heart could feel as peaceful as the music.

The last three years had been filled with sadness, since my David went to be with the Lord. How my heart longed to share one more Christmas with him. I yearned to feel the warmth of his body as he held me. To see that dazzling smile again would be wonderful. I remembered the scent of his body fresh from a shower, as he lay close to me. My joy left with him the night he went to be with Jesus.

Finally, the exit I was looking for was just in front of me. I slowly turned the car off the interstate onto the two lane road that would take me home. Home.... the place I've tried so desperately to run from; my birthplace, the place I took David as my husband. Home...the hills that time had somehow forgotten, and I had tried so desperately to forget. *The hills and hollows are just as I left them*, I thought. Why is it then that I felt such dread coming back to them?

Generation after generation followed in the footsteps of the ones that went before them. Each in succession scratching in the same dirt as their fathers, a place they called home. Being born and dying on the same property as their mother and father. They, in turn, left it to their children and their children's children. The oppression was just the same. Factories and welfare were the major way of income. Education put somewhere on the list of things that one had to tolerate. That is, if they got far enough to graduate. Then the cycle began over.

Healthcare was a little better, but old ways were hard to overcome. People only went to see a doctor after all other herbs, and cures passed down from generation to generation didn't do their work. Many times it was far too late. When they finally went to the doctor, questions were rarely asked and little information was given. Nothing was volunteered except the obvious reason they were there. If a sore throat was the problem, the fact that you had bleeding from the bowels was never mentioned. The doctor had to be a mind reader as well as a physician. I've asked Mama many times after she had seen the doctor if she had told him certain things. Her reply was, I forgot, or they didn't ask.

THE MOUNTAINS CALL MY NAME

The big water tank that supplied the town with water was just coming into view. It wouldn't be long before I would see the lights of home. The road was narrow and twisted like a snake slithering along among the mountain terrain. The local people called them switchbacks. This was because you're constantly switching back and forth over hills and valleys. A few more twists and I would be in the small town of Scott's Corners.

I noticed the town seemed to be growing. There seemed to be new streets and new houses. A theater was a new addition. They had a new drive-in restaurant. My eyes drank in all the familiar sights. It was a warm feeling that started to thaw the coldness in my soul. It was good to see the little town growing. I noticed that they were building a new store on the outskirts of town.

The store I was looking for was Scott's. It had been here as long as the town had. As a matter of fact, it used to *be* the town. I saw that a Laundromat had been added and a Kroger store. The feed and seed store, also run by the Scotts, stood at the end of the street. A gun shop was sandwiched in between. The feed store was added when Mr. Scott ran out of room in his store for the farming supplies. Julie's home style café was also a new addition. I'm sure Mr. Scott liked the change of places to eat.

I pulled into the parking lot, glad to see the lights on inside. I thought I had better get a few things in case Mama was out of essentials. It looked like the storm was going to be a bad one.

There was and old Sun Drop sign dangling by one corner at the end of the building. There were old fence posts that lined the back of the parking lot. The wire that once connected the fence posts was long gone. "Scott's" was printed in large white letters across the big picture window. There were handwritten signs pasted here and there of things on sale.

The porch was large and adorned with big rockers. The wood was a weather-beaten brown, aged from hours of being in the elements. They were worn smooth from the many hands that held them.

They rocked slowly as the wind danced around them. It pushed them backward and forward as if ghosts from the past stopped to set awhile. The howling of the wind sounded like their trapped voices waiting to tell their stories to all who would listen.

It was a place where people gathered to share the latest news from the hills and hollows, or "hollers", as they were fondly called here. By the time you drank your cola and headed home, you knew who was having babies, died, getting married, divorced, having affairs etc... Scott's was the social center of this quaint little town.

The Scotts were wonderful people. They treated the folks that visited their store like family. Charge accounts were common, and were allowed to be paid in a timely fashion. Many were forgiven in times of crises.

I noticed that they had installed new gas pumps. The old ones sat over beside the store. They served as a reminder of the very old days. The glass on top of the tank allowed you to see the gas bubble as it was making its way to the hose to be pumped. It would probably bring a handsome price from some antique dealer. A crude sign sat in front of it. "Not for Sale" was painted in big black letters on a white background. They probably had been asked one too many times.

As I walked up the wooden steps onto the porch I could see Grandma Scott with her white hair showing above the checkout counter. She had the same familiar braids wrapped around her head. As I opened the door, a jingle of bells rang, announcing my arrival.

"Hello...Grandmother Scott, do you remember me?" I asked as I approached the counter.

"Glory be! It's my little 'Lis'beth. Come here, child, and give me a hug. I always love it when ya come home."

"It's good to see you too, Grandma. I can't believe you're still working the counter," I said, smiling at her.

I saw her wheeling her way around the corner to meet me. She was so tiny sitting there, but still seemed to be her perky little self.

"How have you been feeling?" I asked.

"Tolerable well, I don't do much 'round here no more. Daniel fusses over me all the time. Checkin' this and listin' to that. I told him it was just the 'tism got a holt o' me and won't let go. I keep on a pushin'. I come out when June or George needs to eat supper or somethin'. I still love to hear the gossip from the hollers. I don't hear quiet as good as I used to. I'm gonna' have to get some of 'em plugs you put in yer ears to hear better. I don't want to miss nothin'."

"I bet you don't miss much," I said teasingly.

THE MOUNTAINS CALL MY NAME

"You'd be surprised the things these old ears have heared. Did ya come fer Bessie's funeral?" she asked.

"Yes, Anna Belle called early this morning. She said my mom needed me. I threw a few things together and here I am."

"Ya better hurry, sweetie, the weathers a gettin' purty bad. You know how those hollers get."

"I wanted to get a few things in case Mama is out of something," I said, heading down the aisle with a cart.

"Daniel, that doctor grandson of mine, said he asks yer mom about you when he sees her."

"Oh my, it been years since I've seen Daniel. How is he?" I asked.

"He's a doin' purty good. You knowed he'd took over old Doc Adam's practice, didn't you?"

"No, I didn't. What happened to Dr. Adams? He's been here a long time."

He jest plum tuckered out, couldn't keep up with all the new fangled stuff. He said we needed new young blood to take over."

"How did Daniel end up being the new young blood?" I asked.

"Well, he'd been a doctrin' in one of 'em big cities up north somewher'. The more he visited here, the more he complained about the lack of good doctrin'. So I jest told him one day, 'quit complainin' and do it yerself'. He just kinda' shook his head and laughed at me. 'afore I could say Jack Sprat, he done left 'at doctrin' place in the city and took over here," she said with a chuckle.

"I would love to see him. Tell him I can't believe he came back."

"I tell 'im you're here. Maybe ifen he ain't too awful busy he will see ya 'for ya go home," she said, giving me a toothless grin.

"What does his wife think about these hills?" I asked.

"Oh, he ain't got none. He said he didn't have time to take care of a wife and a practice too."

"How old are you now Grandma?" I asked.

"Now you know a lady don't tell her age, but I'm proud to be 97 years old. I don't know why the good Lord done left me here this long. I don't him ask and he don't tell," she chuckled.

"Well Grandma, I have to scoot. You take care; I'll see you before I go back," I said, stooping to give her a hug.

"You better get on up the holler 'fore it gets real bad. It can get nasty purty quick. Don't ferget to come back and visit," she called after me.

"We'll have a long visit soon, I promise," I said as I jangled my way out the door.

THE MOUNTAINS CALL MY NAME

The wind had picked up considerably, blowing the heavy wet snow in all directions. I pulled my hood up close around my face and tied the tie to the hood, then proceeded to load the groceries.

The road out of town to my house was two lanes, but hardly wide enough for one car. I wound round and round the twisting little road. We were only about five miles from town, but with the bad weather it seemed much farther. I was glad the snow plow had already gone before me.

The road was now just a track down the middle, packed down from being run over by the heavy snow plow. I hoped I didn't meet anyone going in the opposite direction. We wouldn't have any place to go. It was hard to see the ditch because it was already filled with snow. I felt the car slip a little as I turned a curve, and it gave me a queasy feeling in the pit of my stomach. I knew this was the last curve before the turn, up the hollow. *Just a few more feet*, I thought, *just a few more feet*.

"Please keep me safe, Lord, please keep me safe." I prayed out loud.

Suddenly, before me in grand beauty, stood the little white chapel where David and I started our life together. It stood at the entrance to the road going up the hollow. The headlights of my car illumined the sacred structure. The red door starkly contrasted the blanket of white, and stretching up into the night was the steeple. Tightly tucked within its bosom were the bells. They were silent in their hibernation of winter, waiting their next call to announce to all who could hear the tolling of joy or sadness. The silence would end in two days with the announcement of the home-going of my mother's dear friend.

Across the road, mailboxes lined up in a row. I could tell you every name that was written on them. No one ever moved from here. Their children just took over when their parents died. Well, this was one child that would not carry on the tradition. I escaped once, and no one would bring me back. I loved the people here and didn't consider myself better than they were, but I had put a lot of time and distance between me and this hollow and I doubted that I could come back again. Visits were sweet here in this hollow with my mother, but I was always glad to get back to the city. In the city we were rushing headlong into the future that we had planned so carefully, and enjoying all the things it afforded us. When David was alive we would retreat to the sanctity of the mountains or the beach, and once rested, we jumped back on the fast train. We thought we had it all. Except for the one thing we desired so badly: a child. The faster we ran, the less we thought of it. Somewhere in there we made time for church. When our busy life gave us a free Sunday, we were there. God was definitely not our first priority, sadly to say. When David died, it made me realize the distance I had put between me and my Savior. If only I could go back and take life a little slower. I would take more time with my David, but that was not to be, I thought wistfully, not to be.

The turn up the hollow would be a tricky one. I had to have enough speed to make a turn, but not spin into the fence that framed its entrance. I would be stuck for sure if that happened.

"Lord, help me get home, please."

THE MOUNTAINS CALL MY NAME

I gave the gas pedal a strong push and turned the wheels hard to the right, aiming for the driveway. With just a little slipping and sliding, I was headed up the lane. As I rounded the curve in the road I could finally make out the lights of home.

The little girl in me longed for the warmth of my mother's arms. Just a little more, just a few more feet and I could finally stop. It seemed the car couldn't get there fast enough. Our drive was already deep with snow, I observed, as I tried to make the turn. I got the car almost all the way to the house.

"Thank you, Lord. Thank you so much," I said aloud.

I turned off the engine of my car, thankful to be home. As much as I wanted to get inside to the warmth of the potbellied stove, I was all but hypnotized with the scene that lay before me. The roof of the house was already covered with snow. The windows were ablaze with light, a beacon for a weary traveler. The wind was pushing the swing to and fro, rocking ever so slowly, as if propelled by unseen legs.

The branches of the tall pines that dotted our yard were already bending with the weight of their heavy burden. The evergreen bushes where hugging the side of the house, pulling their branches close to protect the house from the wind. The snow was already piling a blanket of white on their green shoulders.

The old iron water pump rose starkly from its base. Its goose-like neck was gracefully curved, waiting to hold the next bucket for it's offering of water. I couldn't begin to count the gallons of water I had pumped over the years. It was our only source of water, and were we ever thankful for it. Even in the heat of summer the water ran icy cold because it flowed down from inside the mountain, unheated, sheltered from the sun.

I especially hated wash days. By the time I carried enough to fill the tubs with wash and rinse water, my arms ached from shoulder to fingertip. I was also responsible to keep the water well filled in our wood cook stove. The heat from the fire warmed the water. We used this for dishwashing and bathing. There was nothing worse than finding it empty, because cold baths in winter weren't very pleasant.

I saw the silhouette of the outhouse down the path behind the house. David and I had running water installed in the house, along with a new bathroom. Still, the old outhouse stood sentry, ever ready for someone in need of its service. The well-worn path never had grass to grow on it.

Daddy had our house built close to the base of the mountain to protect it as much as possible from the winter winds. We were never surprised to see animals wander down to our yard. I saw the dilapidated wire fence that once protected our large garden from the wildlife that loved to come down to eat. It had been a long time since it had been used for produce. Mama's health had been on the decline for years, and Daddy was with Jesus. There was no one left to plant and take care of it.

I got out of the car, gathered the few groceries and made my way up to the house. The new snow was scrunching beneath my feet and coming up the calf of my legs. I walked up the steps, my heart racing with the anticipation of seeing Mama. I was kicking the snow off my feet when the door opened.

"I'm so glad ya finally here!" the little voice said.

"You and me both," I answered.

"Here's a broom to sweep the snow off yer feet and legs," she said, offering it to me.

"I still have to get my luggage out of the car. Here are some things I picked up at Scott's. Let me set these inside the door. I'll be right back. Thanks for the broom," I called back to her over my shoulder.

It wasn't long until I had everything inside.

"Come here, child, and give me a big hug. I've missed ya so," she said, wrapping her frail arms around me.

"I've missed you too, and I'm so sorry about Bessie dying. I know she meant a lot to you."

"She was always there for me, sunshine or rain night or day. I didn't know she was 'at sick," she said, with tears in her eyes.

"Come, Mama, sit by the fire with me a little, while I get warm. Tell me how you've been lately," I said.

"Well, I have good days and bad days. I get right swimmy-headed at times. Daniel says it's something getting hard in my head," she said with a laugh.

I couldn't help laughing at the description of her illness.

"Mama, I think he probably meant hardening of the arteries," I said, laughing.

"I told him I always had a hard head," she said with a chuckle.

"Grandma Scott told me that Daniel had become the local doctor," I said.

"He's a good 'n' too," she replied.

"I remember when we were trying so hard to outdo each other in school. He told me when he left here he would never come back," I told her.

"Well, you know how the old sayin' goes, 'bout the thing you vow you won't ever do, you end up doin' it."

Strange how things come to pass, isn't it, Mama?" Who would have thought Bessie would have been this close to meeting Jesus. I thought the same about David, too," I said.

"I 'member when David took you away from us; at first it was like someone ya love died. Me and Daddy both grieved fer ya. It nigh broke your daddy's heart. You always had him wrapped around yer finger. I kind a knowed in my heart you weren't a comin' back. Not to live anyway, but yer daddy always was a lookin' fer ya. You were his sunshine. The one that brought him life again after baby Jonathan died. I wish I coulda' done fer him what you did," she said wistfully.

"I just wanted more than these hills could give me," I said.

"These hills been mighty good to me, and to you," she said,

"I know, I just had a rainbow that I had to go chase. Then David came and swept me off my feet. It's like God gave him to me, to take care of me when I went off into the world. He already was at the school I was going to, plus he made me happy. Why do things have to end the way they do Mama?" I asked.

"God's the giver and the taker, sweetie. He orders our footsteps and we never know where they might take us. I 'member the day God took yer little brother, Jonathan, home to be with him. That mornin' was just like any other. I went in to wake him up fer breakfast and his little body was already stiff and cold. His little smile would light up this whole house. My, how yer daddy loved that little feller," she said, as dampness welled in her eyes.

I saw tears rolling down the cheeks of her tired, wrinkled face. I put my arm around her and pulled her close to me.

"The death angel come sometime while I was sleepin'. We never knowed what took him. Somethin' died in your daddy that day too. I didn't see him smile again fer a long time. He jest shut me out. We bore our grief in silence. It was like I lost 'em both that day. We both hurt so bad we couldn't help one another. Then we got you, and life changed ferever," she said, smiling at me.

"I'm so sorry, Mama. You never told me much about that time. It must have been so hard," I said.

THE MOUNTAINS CALL MY NAME

"But Bessie, bless her heart, and Anna Belle made it so much easier fer me. They came ever' day for the longest time. Bessie was the one what he'ped me lay him out."

"What's laying out?" I asked.

"Well, back then people didn't always use funeral homes like today. So we would wash the body and dress it up, and put it in a special made pine box. Then people would come by fer the wake. We'd set up all night with the body. Jest 'memberin' and tellin' stories about who ever it was that died."

"It gives me the creeps just thinking about staying in the house with a body all night," I said.

"Ain't no use bein' scared of the dead. They cain't hurt ya'."

"Well, it just sounds so….so barbaric," I answered.

"I don't 'xactly know what 'at is, but it was done with so much love. Bessie he'ped me wash little Jonny's body. We put a white gown on him, and a little white bonnet. He jest looked like he was a sleepin'. Next day we carried him up to the cemetery on top of the mountain and buried him under the weepin' willer tree. A good place, I guess, since there was lot a weepin' goin' on, everbody 'cept yer daddy. Have ya hurt so bad you couldn't cry?" she asked.

"When David died, I cried until there was only emptiness. Then there were no more tears to come, just the awful pain that no one can take away. If I hadn't had Jesus, I think I might have taken my own life, but he wouldn't let me. He would always send someone to me, or a card would come in the mail. Times like these bring a lot of painful memories back. If you hadn't needed me I wouldn't have come today. As much as I love Bessie, I wouldn't have come," I answered.

"Yer daddy, he just held it all inside. He never would a let me see 'im cry. When he come home and heared about his boy he ran out the door. He went up into the mountains and stayed fer hours. I was so worried. When he came back, he pulled his cher up beside the fire and jest sat there and rocked. The legs of the straight back cher pounded heavy into the wooden boards of the floor. It echoed the heavy pounding of my heart. He never would look at Jonny, jest said he couldn't. The day of the funeral he held me close to him as we stood there beside that little hole in the ground, but his body was all stiff and ridged as he tried to comfort me. Bless his heart; I guess 'ats all he had to give. I cried so hard I couldn't hardly see 'em as they lowered his little body in the ground," she went on.

I just let her talk. It seemed as if she needed to.

"I couldn't watch 'em throw the dirt on, I jest couldn't."

"I remember you showing me the markers where Jonathan and Daddy were buried.

"I forgot, how many years were between mine and Jonathan's ages?" I asked.

"It was about two and a half years. Your daddy went to West Virginia to work in the coal mine right after Jonny died. He started a drinkin' after that. I guess he let the bottle be his comfort instead of Jesus. He was always drunk by the time he made it home on the weekend. When it was time for him to go back, he would sober up. I was so lonely then. If it weren't fer Bessie and Anna Belle I don't think I could a made it. I'm sure gonna miss her," she said,

I pulled her into my arms and let her cry for her friend, for the friendship she had lost, and for her sweet companion all these years.

"Well, let me dry these tears. Yer probably starved to death," she said, hurrying into the kitchen.

"Don't go to any trouble for me," I called after her.

"You ain't no trouble, child. I made an apple pie today. The kind ya like, warm with a little ice cream on top," she called from the kitchen.

I followed her into the brightly lit room, and again I thought how good it was to be home. She was always a giver, a lot of times to the exclusion of herself. She could never say "no" to anyone. A servant, a true servant, of God. Her gift from him was a servant's heart.

"I'll just have a piece of pie. I don't feel like a heavy dinner, but you go ahead. I'll sit with you while you eat," I told her.

"That's jest what I'm gonna have to. Let me fix our plates and we'll take them into the livin' room. It'll feel good to sit by the fire," she said, cutting the pie.

"You always make such beautiful pies, Mama. I never could do that. The lattice work on top is so perfect. How do they always turn out so good?" I asked.

THE MOUNTAINS CALL MY NAME

"Go on now; you'll make this hard head big too," she laughed, cutting us each a slice.

"I wonder why people work so hard on something they're just going to eat," I said.

"God gave me the love of cookin' the way he gave you a love fer nursin'. We do it 'cause we love to do fer people. When ya see people enjoyin' what they do it jest makes ya feel good."

"I guess I never looked at it that way. It's true isn't it? When God give us our gifts for life, what we do is a labor of love," I said.

"It also takes my mind off my aches and pains fer a few minutes. Thinkin' about you a comin' home always fills my heart with joy. If you'll get the ice cream for me we'll be all set," she said.

I got the ice cream out and put a big scoop on each plate.

"I'll carry these, you go make yerself comfortable," I said.

"There's two T.V. trays in the pantry. We can use those," she called after me.

"You've had these for years," I said.

"And they still hold a plate of pie," she cajoled.

"The fire is dying down. I'll put some more wood on before it goes out," I said, making my way to the wood box on the back porch.

THE MOUNTAINS CALL MY NAME

I filled the stove and the box behind it, and we settled back on the soft, cozy sofa to enjoy our supper.

"You haven't lost your touch, Mama. This is the best pie I've ever eaten."

"Ya always say that."

"And it's always true," I answered.

I took the plates into the kitchen, and put the trays away.

"I'll do these few dishes. You just rest a little. You can watch me from where you sit."

"Please don't do those," she said, "I'll do them in the mornin'."

I was already running the dish water by then.

"I'll just be a minute," I said.

I saw her head lean back on the sofa.

"I might jest rest my eyes minute," she said,

I loved the way Daddy built the new kitchen for Mama. The walls were a pale, creamy yellow. He put double windows over the sink. She always wanted big windows to set her flowers in front of. That's where they would get the morning sun. He built a long shelf that set behind the sink that could hold lots of flowers. For Christmas one year, he had the man down by the saw mill build her some dark oak cabinets. She had everything fixed up so cute.

I noticed the things she used to do so meticulously have been let go. I could tell she had tried, but it wasn't like it used to be. I'm sure it bothered her. She had always been a spotless house keeper. I guess she hurts too badly to do much. I need to talk to Daniel before I leave, and find out more about what is happening with her health. I think she's been holding things back. I noticed a walker in the corner of the living room. She hadn't mentioned it, but she hadn't concealed it either.

I need to pay more attention to what is going on with her and less about what's going on with me. I finished cleaning up and sat down beside her once again.

"I wasn't sleepin'," she said, rubbing her eyes. "I was just restin' my eyes."

"I think I'm about ready to go to bed, how about you?" I asked

"I was just thinkin' the same thing," she answered.

"I'll make something tomorrow to take up to Bessie's," I told her, helping her to her feet.

"I don't think I'll be able go, the weather bein' so bad. I don't want to see her all laid out in her funeral stuff, I just cain't bear seein' her dead. Is that bein' a bad friend?" she asked me.

"Of course that isn't being a bad friend. You just remember the good things and the way you last saw her," I told her.

THE MOUNTAINS CALL MY NAME

"Old John's probably takin' things awful hard. And Sharon, she's due to have her baby soon," she said, talking to herself as much as to me.

"What funeral home is she at?" I asked.

"She ain't, she's gonna be at her house. They bringin' her up tomorrow after they do whatever they do to the bodies. Old John wanted her brought home. They gonna bury her up on top of the mountain where ya daddy and Jonny is buried."

"What?" I asked in astonishment. "In this day and time I can't believe they would allow that."

"Well, Old John, he can't get out too good, so him and the kids agreed on bringin' her home."

"I'm not sure I want to go for that visit after all. Where in the world would they put her?" I asked. "Their house is so small."

"I think Anna Belle told me they were layin' her out in the livin' room."

"Maybe I'll feel better about all this tomorrow. Right now I'm going to bed."

"I'm glad yer home. It's been mighty lonely since yer daddy died. I don't think I will ever get over needin' him and missin' him," she said.

"I know, I feel the same way about David, That's one thing we have in common that I wish we didn't."

THE MOUNTAINS CALL MY NAME

"Time, that's what you need, 'Lis'beth, you just need some time. Yer young enough to get another man to love ya," she said.

"I don't want any one else, I can't see myself with any one but David. Time hasn't done much for my pain," I said.

"Time is a great healer, but the thing about that is, when yer in pain time is a slow movin' thing. How long has it been since David passed?" she asked.

"It will be three years December 31st. I haven't celebrated Christmas since he died. I don't even put up a tree now. David loved everything about Christmas. There wasn't one thing he didn't like about it. I cringe at the thought of another Christmas season," I said.

"That's a few weeks away. You have some time," she said.

We walked down the hall toward my bedroom. This room had always been mine, and she always tried to make it beautiful. I was so proud of the quilt she made for me. "The Little Dutch Boy" was what she called the pattern. Everything was done in pink and lavender, with frilly white curtains hung at the double windows. The way they were pulled back, moonlight would flood the room. When the moon was full it would bathe the room in a beautiful light. A lamp sat on the table beside my bed. It was made of glass with one ball sitting on the other. It had pail pink roses on a background of cream, and it gave the room a soft warm glow.

THE MOUNTAINS CALL MY NAME

"Let me turn on the electric blanket. It still gets awful cold in the back part of the house," she said, reaching over to turn the dial.

"I'll see you in the morning," I said, reaching to give her a goodnight hug. "Sleep well."

"You too, sweetie, I'm so glad yer home. I hate Bessie was the reason, but I'm so glad ya came."

She walked slowly toward her room. She seemed a little unsteady on her feet. I'll talk to her about the walker in the morning, I thought.

I put on my gown and climbed into bed. It had started to warm, but still had some chill. I lay there waiting for the warmth to spread over my chilled bones. I turned out the light and listened to the familiar sounds of the night. I heard the tick-tock of the grandfather clock that still kept guard in the hall. I remember Daddy winding it every night before he would go to bed. A single winding was supposed to last about a month, but he chose to do it every night. He said he didn't want it to run down. There was a key hole on each side of the clock face. He took the key and gently wound until it would halt, and then do the same on the other side. He would put the key in a little drawer inside the clock until he needed it again. It chimed every hour and half hour. It never missed a tick-tock or a chime as long as I could remember.

I heard the creaking of the old boards as Mama was getting ready for bed. My room smelled of sweet lavender sachet, mixing with the scent of wood smoke floating in from the living room. It was soothing to my spirit.

THE MOUNTAINS CALL MY NAME

I remembered that I had forgotten to put wood in the stove for the night. I dreaded putting my warm feet on the cold wood floor. I ran on tiptoe, keeping as much of my foot as possible off the cold floor. I hurried quickly down the hall, and was glad when my feet touched the living room carpet. I hoped I wouldn't disturb Mama. I opened the door of the old iron stove as quietly as I could. I picked through the wood in the dimness of the night light to find some that was greener so it would burn more slowly. I wished I could remember how Daddy used to bank the coals so it would burn throughout the night. I checked the furnace setting and moved it up to kick in just in case the fire went out.

Hurrying back down the hall, I thought I heard soft crying coming from Mama's room. I stopped and listened for a moment, but didn't hear it again.

It must have been the wind blowing through the cracks of the old house, I thought. I opened the door and tiptoed to the side of her bed.

"Are you okay?" I whispered, laying my hand on her head.

"I'm fine, jest tryin' to settle in," she answered. "I wind round and round like a cat sometimes before I can find a comfortable spot. And by the time I get snuggled in, my bones hurt and I have to turn over," she said, with a little laugh.

"I thought we might pray together," I said.

"Come, child," she said, reaching for my hand. "Hop under the covers where it's warm."

THE MOUNTAINS CALL MY NAME

I crawled in beside her and taking her hand began to pray....

"Dear Lord," I started, "thank you for bringing me home safely. We pray for Daddy John, Sharon and the boys. Be with them in a mighty way. Give them peace and rest tonight. Send your angels to surround them and comfort them. Touch Mama with your love and healing touch. Give her grace and comfort in this time of loss. Lord, thank you for taking Bessie quickly and not letting her linger in pain. Bless Sharon, and give her strength to bear this. I'm sure she really needs her mama with her, since her baby is due now. Only you, Lord, can heal a broken heart. Bless the twins. They're just like children in their minds. They need you to help them understand what has happened. Give Daddy John the strength he needs to adjust to losing Bessie. Again, thank you for your love. Give us rest as we go to bed. We love you so much. In your precious and holy name we pray. Amen.

"Goodnight Mama," I said. "Sleep well."

I reached over and pulled the cover up close around her shoulders, and gave her a kiss on her forehead. Then I hurried down the hall to the warm cover of my bed. I snuggled way down underneath its warmth.

Sleep is an elusive thing sometimes. As hard as I tried I couldn't shut down my mind. I slipped on my bedroom shoes and walked to the window to see if it was still snowing. There were still big fat flakes falling.

I wished that I could get rid of the darkness that shrouded my heart. I couldn't make it go away. I felt it was more than the loss of David. Something just wasn't right. I felt this way a lot when I went home. There isn't a

THE MOUNTAINS CALL MY NAME

definition I can place on what I feel. Whatever it was, it wasn't a good emotion. Then again, it's probably just this grief thing. I've got to let it go and get on with life. Tomorrow I would have to call Daniel and talk to him about Mama's health.

I crawled back into bed hoping I could fall asleep quickly. I prayed that God would take away the remainder of sorrow that I held so tightly. "Lord, show me your way and I will follow. Put me in the center of your will, not mine. I release it all to you. Fix my heart and make it whole again. It's been so long since I've felt peace. Lord, I beg you for this one thing, peace, I have to have peace.

At last, I could feel myself drifting into an exhausted and welcomed sleep.

Chapter Three

I woke to the aroma of breakfast cooking. I felt almost as weary as I had before sleeping. I pulled the covers up close around my ears and snuggled under the warm blanket. I don't know how long I lay there drifting in and out of sleep. After awhile I pulled myself from my warm nest and made my way to the window. I pulled back the curtain and looked at the wonderland before me. The sun was brilliant reflecting off the snow. I had to shield my eyes from the brightness. It looked as if we had gotten about five or six inches of snow.

I was getting out of the shower when I heard a light knock on the bathroom door.

"Yes?" I said.

"Breakfast is ready whenever yer ready to eat," she answered.

I finished dressing and went into the kitchen.

"It smells wonderful in here, and I'm so hungry."

"I have the pancake batter all ready. I 'membered how ya' used to love 'em. How many would you like?" she asked.

"I think two will be plenty."

THE MOUNTAINS CALL MY NAME

"I fixed some bacon, too. Mr. Rankin still brings me ham and bacon from his farm. Yer daddy used to do some tradin' fer meat. When he died I thought sure he'd quit bringin' it, but he still does. I told him he didn't have to, but wouldn't take 'no' fer an answer."

"Mama, breakfast was just wonderful. You shouldn't have done so much."

"It weren't nothin', I feel my best in the mornin' time."

"I don't remember you using a walker before. When did you start?"

"Well the last time I saw Daniel I told him I get a little dizzy sometimes. He said I should keep one around just in case I felt wobbly. He even brought me one. I still can't believe he's an honest to goodness doctor. Some people like him, some don't."

"Why wouldn't they like Daniel? He's one of the sweetest and gentlest men I know. At least the one I knew ten years ago. I can't imagine people not liking him."

"Well he's young and good lookin'. I guess they think ya' have to be old to know stuff like doctoren'. Maybe they a little embarrassed. Don't ferget, they watched him grow up in these hollers."

"He'll just have to win them over," I said. "It will take time."

"He's been talkin' about bringin' some new fangled doctors up here. I think he called them 'specialists'."

"That's really needed here. Right now you have to go to the city for special treatment," I said.

"Well, it just seemed to me Doc Adams didn't need 'em," she answered.

"That's probably why he quit. He knew the medical field had by passed him, and he wanted more for all his patients. There have been many new treatments and procedures that people could benefit from. Daniel just wants the people here to have the best care possible," I said.

"If ya don't mind, I'm gonna go sit in the livin' room by the winder and read my Bible a little."

"You go ahead, and I will clean up the kitchen," I answered.

After cleaning up, I started a couple of dishes to take up to Bessie's. While I was waiting for food to finish cooking, I decided to call Daniel. I found his number on a notepad by the phone. I felt a little excited about talking to my friend again.

"Good morning, Dr. Scott's office. May I help you?"

"Hello," I said to the lady that answered. "Could I speak with Dr. Scott please?"

"He's in with a patient right now. Is there anything I can help you with?"

THE MOUNTAINS CALL MY NAME

"My name is Elizabeth Mason. My mother is Mary Edwards. I live out of town, and I wanted to discuss her health. I'm at her house now, so he can call me here."

"As soon as I see him I'll give him your message."

"Thank you," I said. giving her my number.

It wasn't long before the phone rang.

"Hello," I said.

"Hi, is this my best friend in the whole world?" a male voice said.

"You will always be my best friend," I said. "Long time no see."

"Lets see if I remember correctly it's been about ten years. It seems that every time you were in town, I wasn't. I did keep up with you through Grandma, and now your mom," I said,

"I saw her yesterday when I came in. She's as cute as a button. She still is very informative."

"As a matter of fact, she told me you were here," he said. "She called me last night. She said you had just been in the store."

"I still can't imagine you being a real doctor," I said, laughing.

"Well gee, thanks. Don't tell my patients that. I'm having a hard enough time making them trust me. I am making some headway. I think Grandma threatens them."

THE MOUNTAINS CALL MY NAME

"Do I have to call you 'Dr. Scott', or can I still call you Daniel?"

"Since it's you, you can call me Dr. Daniel," he said with a laugh. "I thought you would become a doctor yourself. I fought tooth and nail to keep up with you when we were in high school."

"Well, I would have been, except you told me only men could be doctors."

"And you believed me?" he said, laughing.

"Not really. It was too much work, and I'm lazy."

"What can I do for you?" he asked.

"Well Mama doesn't look like she's feeling very well. She mentioned you were her new doctor. I was wondering if we might get together and talk."

"Sure thing. I've been needing to talk to you, too. Your mom's health is declining some, as you've observed. Are you going up to Bessie's tonight?"

"Yes, are you?"

"I plan on it. Why don't I pick you up, and we can go up together. There isn't a lot of room for cars to park up there."

"What time are you going?"

"Just as soon as I get out of the office. Baring any unforeseen emergencies, about 6:00?"

THE MOUNTAINS CALL MY NAME

"That's sounds good to me. I fixed some food to take. Did you know that Sharon's expecting a baby?"

"No, I didn't. I lost track of the kids when I was away at school. When is she due?"

"Mama said, 'any day now'. I think it's sad that her mom won't be able to see her first grandchild."

"It sure is. Well, I have to run. I have a room full of sick people waiting for me to make them better. I'll see you a little after 6:00, if that's okay."

"I'll see you then," I said, hanging up the phone.

Mama had been sleeping in her recliner. Her Bible lay open on her lap. She was such a soldier of the cross. She was the one that taught me to pray, and also the one that led me to the saving knowledge of Jesus.

Her hair was chestnut brown when she still had color. Now, it was white as snow. It lay in soft, silky waves all over her head. She said that God gave her curls. I was not blessed with Mama's curls. My hair is straight as an arrow. She told me many times that she wished she had my brunette hair. Her skin has always been a beautiful olive color. She always claimed it was her Indian heritage. She was told her great, great grandmother was Cherokee. She had the tan everyone longed for, and didn't even try. By the time mine looked good, it was time for winter.

Her face was heavily lined with wrinkles from working in the hot summer sun and the freezing winter wind. Her knuckles were large and swollen from arthritis. The knots looked even larger because her hands where so skinny. A slight hump rounded her shoulders. Her body was frail now, broken down from years of hard labor. Daddy worked away from home for such a long time and she had no choice. The work had to be done by someone, and she was the only one here, other than me.

It was hard for her to admit that keeping up with the smallest of chores was difficult.

She stretched and turned to look at me.

"How long have I been sleepin'?" She asked.

"Not too long," I answered.

"Readin' makes me sleepy. I cain't hardly make it through my chapter fer the day without fallin' right a sleep," she chuckled.

"I heard you tossing and turning last night. Didn't you sleep well?" I asked.

"I was hurtin' right much. Some nights I just can't find the right place to get comfortable. I know when the weather's actin' up, the pain in my joints is worse. The colder it gets, the more it hurts."

"Where does it hurt the most?"

"Just about ever'where. The old 'tism done got the best of me, I guess."

"While you were doing your devotions, I cooked some food to take up to Bessie's tonight. Daniel is going to pick me up, since there isn't much parking space up there."

THE MOUNTAINS CALL MY NAME

"That's nice of him," she said,

"It will be good to see him again. I haven't seen him since he became a doctor."

"He just looks like he al'ays did, 'cept he's just bigger. He still has that beautiful smile. I 'member when he was little he could flash that little grin of his and melt yer heart." She laughed.

"I asked Anna Belle to come over and stay with you while I'm gone."

"I don't need no babysitter," she said,

"Well, having a friend over isn't like having a babysitter. Anyway, you're just a little too old to be called a baby," I said, laughing.

"You know, I'm well into my second childhood," she answered, echoing my laugh.

"That means Anna Belle is, too. So I guess I'll have to get you both a sitter," I said, smiling at the thought.

"Now wouldn't that be cute," she chuckled.

It was good to hear her laugh. For just a few minutes, her sadness had lifted.

The rest of the afternoon we spent looking at pictures and catching up on days gone by. Before we realized it, it was time for supper. I made extra when I cooked earlier in the day, so all I had to do was warm it up.

THE MOUNTAINS CALL MY NAME

After supper I took a long hot bath, letting the heat from the water warm my cold body. By the time I was dressed, it was time for Daniel. I looked forward to seeing him after all these years, but I was a little nervous. I don't know why I was anxious; we never had any problems communicating.

Mama called back to the bedroom and told me Daniel had arrived. I took one last look in the mirror to make sure everything looked right, and then I headed down the hall to meet my friend.

Mama was right. He still had that beautiful smile.

"Hi, beautiful," he said, reaching to give me a hug.

"Hi yourself," I said, hugging him back.

"I took the food out to the car while you were getting ready. Your mom and I even had a little time to chat," he said,

"My goodness, I must be hard of hearing. Why didn't you call me?"

"Well, I wanted Daniel a little to myself before you got him," she said,

"I'm secretly dating your mom. We've been trying to keep it under wraps. Grandma doesn't even know."

"Well, if Grandmother Scott doesn't know, then you two are mighty good. She knows everything about everybody, and she loves it. She is so cute."

THE MOUNTAINS CALL MY NAME

"She'll be the first to let you know, too," Daniel said, laughing.

"Well, I guess we better go if you two have finished your date," I said.

"We'll catch up later won't we, sweetie?" he asked, leaning over to give her a kiss on the cheek.

I got my coat from the closet. Daniel was quick to help me into it. He held the door open for me to exit in front of him.

"Here, hold my hand. I don't want to have to set any bones tonight. My work day is over."

"Just let me know when you switch from friend to doctor. Okay?" I asked.

"Sure thing," he said. "I can't imagine you ever calling me 'doctor', even when we were kids you wouldn't call me 'doctor'."

"It made me mad because you would never let me be the doctor. You were quick to remind me you had never seen a woman doctor. I remember just as plain as if it were yesterday you saying 'they don't even make women doctors, Libby'."

"And what is your calling?" he asked.

"A nurse, and a very good one at that."

"You would have made a very good doctor, Libby," he said,

THE MOUNTAINS CALL MY NAME

"Doggone it! Now you tell me."

We stepped on the slick spot at the same time. We grappled for each other as we tumbled downward into the snow.

We were laughing so hard we couldn't get up.

"We look like snow angels," I said, taking inventory of the situation.

"Ohhh," I moaned. "Is there a doctor in the house?"

"Are you hurt?" he asked, suddenly becoming more serious.

"Just my pride. I don't think a doctor can fix that. Thanks for holding my hand, though. It sure helped." I said, still laughing.

He got to his feet and pulled me to mine.

"Are you sure you're okay?"

"Very sure, and you?" I asked him.

"The snow was a soft landing," he returned.

He held the door of his van open for me to climb into.

"You're positive you're okay?" he asked again.

"Daniel! The doctor in you is taking over. Switch back to friend, I'm okay."

57

THE MOUNTAINS CALL MY NAME

"I was just kidding about your breaking a bone," he said,

"I know that. It would be funny if it happened though."

"I would never live it down. Breaking the bones of the only girlfriend I ever had"

"Daniel Scott! I was never your girlfriend, we were just best friends."

"Didn't you know I had a major crush on you when we were little?"

"No, I thought you liked me for my brain?"

"I had dreams of us going off to save the world, doctor and nurse. Preserving the frogs and worms of the universe."

"Never doctor and doctor? I asked.

"Sorry, I never did imagine you being a doctor. I just couldn't get past that woman thing, I guess."

"It's a man thing, isn't it, not a woman thing?" I said.

"You're probably right. I could never picture a man being a nurse either. It was the era we lived in. The feminist movement never quite made it up the hollow. You have to realize I had never seen a woman doctor. Anyway, being a nurse is a high calling. Where would we doctors be without nurses?

THE MOUNTAINS CALL MY NAME

"Forever lost!" I said.

"You're so right," he replied. "I learned early on in medical school, you'd better treat the nurses right or your life would be a living hell."

There was a pensive pause. We just looked into each other's eyes.

"I can't believe I finally get to see you again," he said, finally breaking the silence.

"My life compared to yours probably has been a boring one," I said.

"I don't think my life has slowed down since the last time I saw you on your wedding day."

"You went one way, I went the other," I commented.

"I took classes all summer, trying to get ahead a little so I could get through early. It seems like all I've ever done is go to school. Actually there wasn't anytime for serious relationships. I wouldn't do that to a girl. Medical school consisted of long, long hours."

"I didn't have it quite that bad. I did get my Masters Degree. I specialized in emergency medicine. It was very exciting, but the burnout came fast."

"Are you still doing that?"

"I haven't been back since David died."

"I'm sorry; I meant to ask you how you've been doing since he died. I was going to try to come to the funeral, but was at a medical convention. Grandma told me about it."

"That's okay; I'm doing pretty good, I guess."

"I'm sorry I haven't been in contact with you. I meant to send a card. So is everything going good now?"

"Yes, it's been three years now. It's about time don't you think?"

"I don't know, Libby. I've never grieved for anyone before. I don't think there is an appropriate time frame."

"How did we get on this subject anyway? Tell me about your practice," I said.

"I'm trying to get some new doctors in the area. We need specialists of all kinds. I've got some friends from med school that I'm thinking about contacting. Doctors don't especially like coming to the mountains. The money is better in larger places."

"Speaking of which, I remember your saying you would never come back to this place," I said.

"I was warned about that 'never say never' thing."

"Or, you'll end up doing just that," I added.

"You're next," he said,

THE MOUNTAINS CALL MY NAME

"Me? No way! Not me. You'll never get me back here. My vow is still in tact. You don't see me here, do you?"

"Well, actually I do. Right here before my eyes," he said, teasing me.

"You know what I mean."

"We'll see, you'll be back. I might even let you be my nurse," he said, laughing at the thought.

"That'll be the day. Anyway, you couldn't possibly afford me. My price tag is too high for you," I said.

"If the quality is there, I'll pay the price," he said, smiling at me.

I saw the lights of Bessie's house coming into view. He was still so charming, I thought to myself.

The night was breathtaking. The moon was full on the new-fallen snow. The mountain ridge that surrounded the hollow was a silhouette against the brilliant sky. I could see the lights flickering in the windows of the cabins. They were flitting like fireflies on a summer evening. The ice clung to the branches of the trees. When the moon hit them just right they glistened like crystal on a chandelier. The breeze clinked the hanging branches together. It sounded forth Mother Nature's chimes, ringing through the stillness of the night.

"A penny for your thoughts," Daniel said.

"I was just taking in the beauty of the evening. I forgot how gorgeous it can be."

THE MOUNTAINS CALL MY NAME

"I see the tide turning," he said with a grin.

"My mother warned me about that smile of yours, and how charming you can be. I was just commenting on how gorgeous it is here."

"Okay, we'll leave it at that," he said, smiling from ear to ear.

We pulled up in front of Bessie's house to the sound of Old Blue and Tucker howling. They were Darrell and David's dogs. Those boys have always loved their dogs. Darrell and David were Bessie's twin boys. They were slow of mind and gentle as lambs. I called them boys, but they were almost as old as I. They've always been very tall, muscular boys. Probably from all the hard work they did. They live in a cabin up the hollow at the end of the road. They seemed content and happy there with their dogs and each other.

They were on the porch as we pulled up. Daniel rolled down the window and asked Darrell if the dogs would bite.

"No, they don't 'less I tell 'em to," Darrell said, smiling at Daniel.

"You're not going to tell them to, are you?" he asked.

"I'll chain 'em up," he called back.

Daniel got the basket of food out of the car and we headed up the path to the back porch.

"Is that you, 'Lis'beth?" David asked.

THE MOUNTAINS CALL MY NAME

"Yes, it's me, David. How are you doing?"

"I'm doin' fine as I can. You knowed Mama died?"

"That's why we came. So we could see you all."

"Sharon's in the kitchen, she ain't feelin' so good."

Daniel and I headed around the house to the kitchen door. The porch light was so dim we could hardly see where we were going.

"I can't hold on to you Libby, so be careful," Daniel said.

"I think we're better off not holding on to each other," I said, laughing.

Sharon opened the door, and was in my arms before I was barely inside the door.

"Mama died, 'Lis'beth. I don't know what I'm gonna' do. I don't know what I'm gonna' do."

"I know," I said, holding her close to me.

"Everything happened so fast. She was here, then gone. The baby's comin' and I don't know what I'm gonna' do," she said, with tears streaming down her dark cheeks.

"You'll do fine. I'll be here for you. It won't be like your mama, but I'll be close by."

"Have you moved back?" she asked, pulling back and looking at me.

THE MOUNTAINS CALL MY NAME

"Well, not exactly, but I'll be here for a little while. When is your baby due?" I asked, releasing her.

I led her to a chair at the kitchen table. She sat down and wiped her eyes.

"Mrs. Wilson said it would be real soon."

"Who is Mrs. Wilson?' I asked.

"She the midwife that Mama found for me. Mama said she the best."

"Don't you have a doctor?" I asked her.

"Well, Mama said they's not need fer one. Babies come the same way they always do. Ain't that right, 'Lis'beth?"

Daniel was standing behind her chair with his hands on her shoulders. He looked at me, closed his eyes and shook his head. He came around to the front of her chair and knelt down in front of her.

"You haven't seen a doctor at all?" he asked her gently.

His trained fingers were on her pulse. I could tell he was looking for signs of trouble.

"Daniel, I fergot you was one," she said, smiling at him. "No. I ain't, but I've been doin' good. I been swellin' some, but Mama said that's just normal in 'spectin' women."

"How do you feel now?" he asked.

THE MOUNTAINS CALL MY NAME

"Well, not too good today with ever'thing goin' on. I haven't been able to eat nothin' all day. I just cain't do it. You know, I just feel sick in my belly."

"You've got to eat something," Daniel said. "Libby, would you see if you could find something that she might be able to keep down."

"Sure," I said.

I checked the food people had brought. I filled her small plate and carried it to the table.

"Thank you, 'Lis'beth. You so sweet," she said, smiling at me.

"Try to eat something for the baby."

Daniel turned to Darrell and asked him to go to the van and bring him his doctor's bag on the back seat.

"Sharon, would you trust me to check you?" he asked, looking gently into her face.

"Sure, Daniel, you and 'Lis'beth always been my friend," she said, looking from one to the other. "I hear from people yer good. Do you think there's somethin' wrong?"

"Well, I was just thinking you've been under a lot of stress today and I wanted to check and see if you and the baby are handling everything okay. I would like to check and see if the baby's heartbeat is strong."

"If you think I should, then I don't see no harm."

THE MOUNTAINS CALL MY NAME

"Good," he said taking a deep breath and letting it out slowly. "Libby, would you take Sharon into the bedroom and help her get ready for me to examine her?"

"I ain't gonna walk by Mama's coffin. I just cain't see her dead," she said, starting to break down again.

"We'll go into the bedroom off the kitchen. Okay? I asked.

Without waiting for an answer, I led her to the bed. You don't have to undress, just let me pull up your top so Daniel can listen to the heartbeat. He cares about you, Sharon, and he just wants to make sure you're okay."

"I know."

"Come in, we're ready." I said, peeking out at Daniel.

I had a sheet over her so she wouldn't feel so exposed.

"My hands are cold, so bear with me," he said,

I watched him feel all around her exposed belly.

"Did you know your baby has dropped down?"

"What's does 'dropped down' mean?" she said, looking up at Daniel.

"What that means is, you're really ready to have this baby."

"Oh, Lord," she said, putting her hand to her head.

THE MOUNTAINS CALL MY NAME

He checked her ankles for swelling. I tried to continue the small talk to keep her mind occupied.

"Would you hand me my stethoscope and blood pressure cuff out of my bag, Libby?"

I did as he had asked. I was seeing first hand the doctor that Daniel had become. He was transformed before my very eyes from my childhood play doctor to a real one. I watched his gentleness and thoroughness as he checked Sharon.

"The baby's heartbeat sounds strong and fast. I bet it's going to be a boy," he said, smiling at Sharon.

He handed me the stethoscope in exchange for the cuff.

"Don't hold me to it. I know I'm fifty percent right," he said, as he placed the cuff around her arm.

"You think so?" she asked.

"I'm all done. That wasn't very bad, was it? When you get yourself back together, come back into the kitchen," he said, smiling down at her.

"No, you just as good as they said," she said, returning his smile.

I followed Daniel into the kitchen and we sat down at the table to wait for Sharon to get dressed.

"You look concerned. Is she okay?" I asked.

He leaned back in the chair and ran his fingers through his black curly hair, a look of concern crossing his face.

"She doesn't look well. Her pulse is fast and her blood pressure is sky high. If she were my patient, I would already have her in the hospital. I suspect she might have toxemia. I'm going to try to get her to let me admit her so I can take care of her and the baby."

"What do you think about this midwife thing?" I asked.

I don't think she's a very good candidate for a midwife. I think midwifery is a great thing if they are well trained. I find a lot of times around here, if they have been present at a birth, that makes them as good as a doctor. You just pray to God there are no problems. Sharon definitely will be a high risk delivery."

"Well, am I gonna' make it?" she asked with a little laugh, walking into the kitchen.

"You're going to be fine. Your blood pressure's on the high side. I would feel better if you would go to the hospital so we can keep and eye on it. This would just be for precaution. Do you think you could do that?"

"Mama was countin' on Mrs. Wilson doin' all that. You know, havin' the baby here and all."

"Sharon, you told me awhile ago that you trusted me. Is that true?"

"Well, yes, but...."

THE MOUNTAINS CALL MY NAME

"You and your baby might be in danger. I don't want to scare you, but if your blood pressure stays up like it is now, you and the baby could be in a lot of trouble. We have to try to get it down. Will you let me and Libby take you to the hospital? We won't leave you by yourself, I promise."

"I guess, after I go see Mama. I just don't know if I can do all this. I'm scared of the dead. Even if it is my mama. I just don't know if I can go in the front room."

"If it's upsetting you this much, then maybe you could just pass."

"No, I gotta do it. If I don't, the twins won't, and I know they need to see Mama."

"What if Libby and I go with you? I'll be on one side and Libby on the other. How about that?"

"Okay. I guess I better go see her," she said, slowly getting to her feet.

I got on one side of Sharon and Daniel on the other; the twins were right behind us. As we entered the living room, the heat from the wood stove hit me fully in the face. The scent of the flowers along with the intense heat made me feel nauseated. We walked slowly to the coffin, our little train of mourners.

Bessie looked beautiful in her pastel pink dress. Her ebony skin shone against the white satin of the coffin. My mind wandered back to the sweet times I had spent with this lovely lady. She had loved Daniel and me just like her own children. We spent many summer days playing with her kids. Suddenly I was jarred from my

THE MOUNTAINS CALL MY NAME

thoughts by a loud cry from Sharon. It seemed to start from deep within her and rose to a shrill wail. I felt her sway toward me, leaning heavier by the second. I knew she was going down. Her hands were firmly planted on the side of the coffin. I felt it rock as we went down. I tried to grab something to hold to, but there was only emptiness. I tried to catch her, but both of us ended up on the floor. The last thing I remember is the thud of my head when we hit the wooden floor. The next thing I heard was someone calling my name.

"Libby, are you okay?" he asked.

"I think so," I said, dazed. "What happened?"

"Sharon fainted and fell on top of you. You hit pretty hard," he said, helping me into a sitting position.

"Ouch, I said, rubbing my head. I must have hit it when I fell."

I shook my head to clear it some. My clothing felt wet and cold. I couldn't imagine for the life of me why. Then it dawned on me; it must be from Sharon.

"Daniel! I exclaimed, with an urgent whisper. Either her water has broken or I wet myself, and I don't think it's the latter."

"Oh, great! Let me help you up. The boys have taken her into the bedroom to lie down. She didn't say anything about being wet."

"She was probably embarrassed. I bet she doesn't know what's happened. She probably thinks she wet herself when she fell."

THE MOUNTAINS CALL MY NAME

"We just might be having a baby. Do you think you are well enough to help me with her?"

"I think so. Just let me sit here a minute and clear the cobwebs. Other than a terrific headache, I think I'm okay."

We heard Darrel call out to Daniel, "Come quick, Dr. Daniel, Sharon ain't doin' so good. She say she hurtin' sumpthin' awful."

I noticed Daddy John sitting in the rocker behind the stove, rocking back and forth in the wooden rocker with his eyes closed. I thought he was asleep until he spoke.

"Take care of the children, 'Lis'beth."

"I'll be right with you, Daniel. Let me speak to Daddy John and let him know everything is okay."

"You hope everything is okay," Daniel called over his shoulder as he went to Sharon.

I went over to him and knelt down by his chair and put my arms around him.

"Are you okay?" I asked.

"I probably should be asking you that question," he said, hugging me back.

"I'm fine, just a little knot on my head. I'm so sorry about Bessie. She meant so much to me. She treated me like her own. I'm sure going to miss her. She looks so beautiful."

THE MOUNTAINS CALL MY NAME

"She always was beautiful. The death angel came quick, 'Lis'beth. I just weren't ready to let her go. I know the good Lord knows best. I just wondern' if he knows what a hole it done put in my heart."

Tears were slowly running down his cheek.

"Of course he does. He promises to be close to them that mourn. So he's very close to you right now," I said, patting his bony little hand.

"Go take care of the children. I worry about my little girl. Her mama spoiled her rotten. Our only girl you know. Course I spoiled her a little too," he said, smiling. I heard Daniel calling for me.

"I have to go help Daniel, she's in good hands," I told him, as I headed out of the room. "I'll keep you updated."

When I entered the room, Daniel had just finished examining Sharon. He motioned for me to meet him outside her room.

"We're having a baby," he said, looking directly into my eyes.

"You're sure?" I asked, looking intently at him.

"Oh yeah, I'm positive."

"Shouldn't we call …?"

"A doctor," he said, finishing my sentence.

"I was going to say 'an ambulance'."

THE MOUNTAINS CALL MY NAME

"I called one, but there's no way it will get here before the baby's born. Are you up to a delivery?"

About that time we heard a shriek come from Sharon.

"See if you can find some large trash bags to put under her. And get something warm to wrap the baby in. Clean off the kitchen table so you will have a place to work with the baby. Make sure the kitchen is really warm."

I asked David and Darrel to get me some clean sheets and towels. I put some water on the stove to boil for sterile water. My mind was traveling in fast forward. I found some large leaf bags in the pantry and cut them up the side to make them wider.

"Here are the bags, Daniel."

"Sharon, can you lift up your bottom so Libby can slip these bags under you?" he asked.

"Here it come again. Help me, Jesus, please help me," she wailed.

"The baby's head is just about out. Give me a big push, big push... good girl. With your next contraction the baby will be here. Take a deep breath and give me another push just like that one," Daniel said.

"I cain't, it hurts too bad. Oh, God, make the pain stop! I cain't breathe, it hurts too bad."

"Sharon, listen to me. Take a deep breath and push. Put your chin to your chest and push," I told her.

THE MOUNTAINS CALL MY NAME

"Okay, I'll try."

I got up at the top of the bed and helped her lift her head and shoulders.

"Now, take your hands and pull your knees up toward your chest," I instructed.

"Heads out, heads out, don't push until I tell you to," Daniel instructed.

Daniel had a bulb syringe cleaning the baby's mouth and nose.

"Okay, sweetie, give me one last push and you're going to have a baby."

"Tuck your head down and use everything you've got and push," I said.

She pushed and moaned as the contraction increased. She gave one last scream as the baby emerged.

"And here she is. She's perfect, Sharon, just perfect. I'm going to cut the cord and I'll give her to you. Libby, in my bag is some suturing cord; if you could cut two pieces about six inches long, that would be great," he said, concentrating on cleaning out her mouth and nose. Would you like to cut the cord?"

"Sure, doctor, I'll be happy to."

He held the tied cords between his gloved fingers and handed me the scissors. With tears blinding my vision, he guided my hand with his and we cut her cord together.

"It's not exactly frogs and worms, but close, huh?" he asked, beaming up at me.

I handed Daniel the large towel to lay her on and one to clean her with. He rubbed her vigorously, and she began to cry.

"No prettier sound. Get some air in those new little lungs," Daniel said, crooning to her. "She's singing for her mama."

He wrapped her up and placed her in Sharon's arms at just the right angle so she could look at her beautiful little face.

"Thank God, thank God, thank God...." she said, with tears of relief, reaching out for her new baby.

Daniel was starting to massage Sharon's uterus so the bleeding would slow, when suddenly he looked up at us, eyes wide with surprise.

"Sharon, I don't know if this is good news or not, but if I'm not mistaken you've got another baby coming. It won't be as long as before. Hang in a little longer, okay?"

"Oh my God, Don't tell me that Daniel. Ain't no way they can be two, ain't no way. Oh! Jesus, Jesus, here it come again," she yelled out with the pain of another contraction.

I took the little girl and placed her on the bed behind Sharon, and ran to get some more towels, excited about witnessing a twin birth. Daniel was handling everything with such confidence. He made everything so much easier for me and Sharon.

THE MOUNTAINS CALL MY NAME

"Hurry, Libby, I see the head, it won't be long. This one is coming fast," he yelled after me.

I entered the bedroom just as Daniel was delivering the baby. He was trying to unwrap the cord from around the baby's neck. I could see from where I was standing that the baby was very blue and limp. I cut the sutures and had them ready to hand to Daniel. This time I knew there would be no lingering. He cut the cord and hurried into the kitchen with the limp little baby. He laid the baby on the table I had set up for him.

"Oh God, Daniel, he's so blue. What do you want me to do?"

"Pray, just pray."

He was working feverishly to clean his airway, but there was no sound. He did C P R, but to no avail.

"Libby... Daniel, what's happening? Is it okay? Sharon called from the bedroom.

"Go to her, I'm afraid there's nothing you or I can do can do here," he said to me.

"Hi, sweetie," I said, going to her bedside.

"I don't hear him cry. Is he okay?" she said, with a look of panic across her face.

"Daniel is working with him, but it doesn't look good right now."

I picked up her little girl and placed her in Sharon's arms.

"She looks like her daddy. He should be here tomorrow. He's comin' from the army base in North Carolina. I came up to spend some time with Mama. The midwife was here that was gonna' deliver the baby. I knew it was close."

"I'm sorry; I forgot to even ask about your husband. What is his name?"

"Ralph Wiggins. His mama and papa live down by the saw mill. They work there. Him, his daddy and his two brothers"

"What are you going to name her?"

"Ralph and I ain't decided yet."

Daniel came into the room carrying the little bundle in his arms.

"I'm so sorry. I never could get him to breathe. I did everything I knew to do. The cord was wrapped so tightly around his neck I could hardly get it off. He never took a breath. Would you like to hold him?"

Through tears she held out her arms to take her little boy. I took the little girl and held her close to me. She was wide-eyed and content.

Her crying accelerated as Daniel placed the boy in her arms.

"Libby, would you keep Sharon company? I need to give this little angel a once-over," he said, reaching for the precious newborn girl.

THE MOUNTAINS CALL MY NAME

"Sure," I said, handing her to him.

"He's so pretty," Sharon said, unwrapping his blanket. He look just like he's sleepin'. The death angel done visited this house again. I hope he's done gatherin'."

"You know what? I believe he's in the arms of your mama. She'll take good care of him until you see him in heaven."

"I know. It's just so hard lettin' him go. I never knew I had him, and now I miss him so much. Ever'thing happened so fast. I'm so glad you was here."

"Daniel?" I said, walking to the kitchen. "Is that a siren I hear?"

"Yeah, I guess it is. I called when I knew she was in labor. Have Darrell and David go out and tell them where we are. At least turn on the front porch light."

Darrell and David were in the living room with Daddy John, so I turned the light on myself. I could see it the ambulance lights flashing down the hollow road, casting an eerie red glow over the white snow.

Mama and Anna Belle will be worried when they see the light, I thought. I need to call them before we leave for the hospital.

I went over to where the three were sitting near the fire to tell them what had happened.

"Is the baby here, 'Lis'beth Anne?" Daddy John asked.

THE MOUNTAINS CALL MY NAME

"I need to talk to you about that. You have a beautiful little granddaughter, and she is doing great. The bad news is she also had a little boy that didn't make it. He never took his first breath. Daniel worked hard to get him to breathe. I'm so sorry."

Tears were rolling down his leathery cheeks.

"'Lis'beth, the good Lord gives, and the good Lord takes. He done took two and left one. He knows best, but it don't help the pain none. Is my baby girl okay?"

"Sharon?" I asked.

"Yes, my only baby girl."

"You have two now. A big one and a little one. She's doing well. Of course she is heartbroken over her little boy, but she is cooing over her little daughter."

"Don't leave her alone, 'Lis'beth, her mama's gone, ya' know. She be needin' a woman folk right now."

Daniel was showing the ambulance workers to the bedroom where Sharon was.

"Daddy John, would you like to go see her and the babies before they go to the hospital?"

"I sho' would!"

I went to his side and helped him to his feet. I placed his cane in his arthritic hand, drawn and knotty for such a long time now. His whole body was filled with this painful disease. It was difficult for him to put one foot in front of the other. He kind of shuffled as he walked. Daniel mentioned to the paramedics to let him have some time with Sharon and the babies before removing them. As we passed by Bessie, he reached down and placed his loving lips on hers.

"It looks like God gave me one and you one. You take care o' yours and I take care o' mine." He said, patting her folded hands.

I led him to the bedside and set him in a chair close to her. I left them to rejoice and grieve as a family.

Daniel was in conversation with the paramedics, giving them instructions for Sharon when they transported her. I went into the living room and sat in the rocker that Daddy John had vacated. The fire was still warm and enveloped me as I sat there trying to absorb all that had happened in the previous hours. My head throbbed from the fall. I ran my hand through my hair to the spot that hurt. I felt crustiness and realized it was from dried blood. I hadn't realized in the furor that I had a cut. I gingerly leaned my head back to rest it. I had my eyes closed trying to ease my headache. I felt a hand on mine and opened my eyes to see Daniel kneeling beside me.

"You okay?"

"Yeah, I just have a terrific headache. I think I got a little cut. My hair feels a little yucky back there."

"Lean up and let me see."

I brushed him away with my hand.

"It's nothing. Go take care of Sharon."

THE MOUNTAINS CALL MY NAME

He was already on his feet pulling me forward.

"Let Dr. Daniel see," he said, parting my hair.

"Be careful back there, my pain threshold is low. Don't hurt me."

"Hold still so I can see. It looks like you might need a stitch or two."

"Just put a butterfly on it." I said.

"Maybe three. That's not bad," he said,

"Is it still bleeding? I pass out at the sight of blood."

"After what we've been through tonight, I hardly think so."

"But it wasn't mine. That makes a difference."

"You can ride to the hospital with me. I'll stitch you up there. I want to check you just a little bit closer. I'm not so sure you don't have a mild concussion."

The attendants came through with Sharon. She held the little girl close to her body. The little boy was in the arms of one of the paramedics. Daddy John was following close behind with Darrel and David on either side. He walked to the coffin and stood quietly, gazing at the empty shell of his love.

He lowered his crooked little body and placed another kiss on the lips that were once warm and sweet. He took the little girl from Sharon's arms and lowered her down into the coffin. It was as if he felt Bessie could see the treasure he held before her. The wonder of it all. I think she actually might have been able to see her first little granddaughter.

"Look, precious, what God done gave us tonight. Sharon's little girl. I think she looks a little like you. Look at her little turned-up nose. Just like her grandma's."

He turned and carefully handed the bundle to Sharon. He motioned to the paramedic to hand him the little boy. He went through the same procedure of laying the baby in Bessie's arms. He carefully drew the blanket back from his little lifeless face.

"This one is already with you. I bet you thinkin' he look just like me," he said, with a smile on his face. "You take good care of him. Hear? I'll look after this angel, and you look after the other one. We'll all be together before you know it."

He handed the little boy back to the paramedic.

"I just couldn't stand to cover his little face up again," he told the man.

It was then that all the strength he had mustered seemed to drain from him. His body shook as tears of grief overtook him. Darrel and David each had an arm around his skinny little shoulders. The boys had been so strong tonight. God had surely given them sufficient grace. I thought they would be the ones that wouldn't be able to handle their mother's passing. I'm so glad they have each other. They seem to speak to one another without uttering a word. The way they look at each other and the body language they use never ceases to amaze me.

THE MOUNTAINS CALL MY NAME

Daniel was coming toward me with my coat and purse.

"Here, let me help you with this. We need to follow pretty close behind the ambulance. I promised Sharon we would be there when she got there."

The boys where standing on the porch where they were when the evening started, the light illuminating them. As Daniel and I started down the snowy slope to his car, I called over my shoulder for them to take care of things until Ralph got there later tonight.

"Okay, they called back in overlapping trio."

Daniel held the door open for me. I felt a sudden wave of nausea and my head began to spin.

"I don't feel so well all of a sudden," I said, grabbing hold of the door frame. I pushed him to the side and promptly threw up. He held my head and supported me while I finished. He pulled a handkerchief from his pocket and wiped my face.

"I'm sorry. I tried hard not to do that. I'm so sorry, so sorry," I said, as tears began trailing down my cheeks.

"You can't cry; your tears will freeze. And don't be sorry, things like this happen to me all the time. Do you feel better?"

"I'm okay; I just had a weak moment there. I think we'd better try to catch Sharon. Just pray I don't throw up in your van. I reached down and got a handful of snow and held it to my forehead. I hoped it would still my swimming head. After he had me seated and buckled in, he handed me a bag.

"Just in case," he said, smiling at me.

Because of the icy conditions, the ambulance took its time getting Sharon to the hospital. Since she was stable, I guess they saw no need to put everyone at risk. We were able to catch up by the time they arrived.

The paramedics had radioed ahead, and they were ready for us. They took the baby straight to the nursery just to make sure she was okay. Then they proceeded to have Sharon admitted.

Daniel walked me to a small room with a bed, and removed my coat.

"I want you to lay down right here and rest," he said, patting the bed.

I'll have a nurse come and help you get undressed, and into a gown."

"I really don't need to undress," I said, looking at Daniel. Then I happened to look down at my clothing. "On second thought, I'm a real mess. Guess a gown sounds pretty good."

Without any hesitation on my part, I promptly threw up again. This time I happened to get part in the trash can; the rest splattered on the floor. After what seemed like an eternity of dry heaves, Daniel helped me lie down onto the stretcher.

"I'll be right back. Don't go anywhere."

THE MOUNTAINS CALL MY NAME

"As if I could," I replied weakly.

"Just relax. You are in competent hands," he said, winking at me.

"Okay, I just hope I don't live to regret this."

The nurse appeared quickly with a gown in one hand and a syringe in the other.

"After I get you into this, I have an injection for nausea. Dr. Scott didn't think you could keep a pill down."

"I've made such a mess. I'm so sorry."

"Don't worry; people get paid to clean it up. It gives them something to do."

I remember saying those exact words to patients embarrassed by what they had done. She helped me out of my soiled clothing and offered me a pan of warm water and soap. The steaming, wet cloth felt good on my face. After finishing my sponge bath the nurse helped me into the gown she had proffered.

"If you will turn over on your side, I'll give you something to help your nausea. Dr. Scott said to tell you he would be in shortly. He had to get the new arrival checked in."

"Okay." I answered.

The needle was painless, but the medicine was a killer. I let out a little moan.

THE MOUNTAINS CALL MY NAME

"Sorry, they always hurt. We'll let that shot work a little before he gets here," she said, walking out the door.

The shot made me drowsy and the nausea was already receding. Not a bad tradeoff. Now if they could make my head stop hurting, everything would be just fine. I closed my eyes, willing my queasy stomach not to act up anymore. I heard someone enter the room.

"Wake up my friend. We're not sleeping are we? It's time for Dr. D. to sew up the holes in your head. I hope you like what I picked out for you in the boutique."

"We've been separated all these years and you still know my taste in clothing. Wow! I wish I had a nickel for all the ones I've put on other people."

"Now, since you're all cozy, I'll have a little look see at the head," he said, reaching for the overhead surgical light.

He pulled the bright light over me to illuminate the wound.

"I'm going to clean this up a little before I stitch it. I might have to shave a little of your hair off. Sorry," he said,

"I hope you have my sucker handy," I said.

I heard him rummaging around in the drawers in my room.

He took a square of gauze, put alcohol on it and started to clean some of the blood off.

THE MOUNTAINS CALL MY NAME

"The blood came out of your hair pretty well," he said, swabbing the area.

"I guess my red roots are showing," I said.

"Okay, little girl, you're going to feel a little stick, well, actually a big one. We have to lie a little."

"Ouch! Where did you pick up your skills doctor?"

"Come on now, be nice to me. I'm the one with the needle. Seriously, are you okay?"

"I'm just great, but I'm not a good patient though."

"I finally get to practice medicine on you. You never would let me when we were kids."

"If you mess this up, at least it will be covered up by hair."

"Eventually," he said with a chuckle.

"Remember who your friends are," I said.

"I do beautiful suture work. Don't I, Karen?"

"The best," she replied, handing him the scissors to cut the suture cord.

"You said that just like I taught you to," he said, laughing.

In no time he was finished, and Karen cleaned up the room.

THE MOUNTAINS CALL MY NAME

"I'm done. I only put four in. If it had been in a different place, I would have done the butterfly stitches. But with all the hair, I thought I would suture it."

"You just wanted to hurt me."

"We all have to go through a little pain sometimes. By the way, I called your mom and told her what happened so she wouldn't worry."

"I'm glad they got the phone working. She would have been so worried if I couldn't call her. Thanks, for calling, I was concerned about her. She knew I should have been home long ago. I'm sure she saw the ambulance lights."

"Anna Belle is spending the night with her. I told her not to wait up. You might not make it home tonight."

"And why did you tell her that?"

"Because I want to monitor you for a little while."

"I'm feeling better," I said.

"How's your nausea? Did the shot help?"

"Yeah, it did. I feel kinda' sleepy."

"But you can't go to sleep."

"How are you going to keep me awake? Please, Daniel, just a five minute nap. I'm so tired."

I closed my eyes and he immediately opened them with his fingers and shown a light in each.

THE MOUNTAINS CALL MY NAME

"You have to stay awake. You have a slight concussion. That's why you were nauseated."

He placed a cold wash cloth on my face and kept talking to me to keep me awake.

"Don't you have anything to do other than keep me awake?"

"You are my one and only patient. Talk to me."

"Okay, can I have something for my headache?"

"Sure, I'll be right back."

Soon, he was back in with a syringe for the injection.

"You like those needles, don't you?"

"I'm going to do it myself to show you I can, but first I'll give you this joy medicine. Roll over on your side."

"Don't nurses usually do the shots?" I asked, slowly starting to turn.

He was pushing me as he talked. "Usually, but I want to show you how good I am. Trust me, it's going to hurt you more than it does me," he said, slipping the needle into my flesh. "I promise, before I can count to ten, you'll feel better. At least you won't care if your head hurts or not."

"Is there anything else you've learned to do that you feel you need to practice on?"

"I have a lot of things to show you later and they all aren't about medicine."

"You've raised my interest. I didn't think there was anything about you I hadn't seen, or heard."

"You'd be surprised," he said,

Karen appeared at the door with the IV bag, pulling the monitor behind her. Daniel deftly put the needle in with one try, taped the area securely and set the drip speed.

"Not an IV! Come on, Daniel, do you have to? I believe you can start the best IV in the world. There, you don't have to show me."

"Sorry, you need the hydration. Why am I telling you this? You're a trauma nurse, you know why."

"You just wanted to show off," I said coolly.

"That's the last boo-boo, I promise."

He reached up and turned off the surgical light.

"We're going to move you to a more comfortable room. You'll have a little more privacy there," he said, pushing the bed as he talked.

They rolled me down the hall to an elevator. I'm not sure where we went from there. I do know he kept his promise about the room. It was small, but cozy. He and Karen helped me from the stretcher to the bed.

THE MOUNTAINS CALL MY NAME

"Do you need anything else, Dr. Scott? Karen asked.

"I think that's all for now. I'll call if I need you," he said.

"Goodnight, Dr. Scott, Mrs. Mason, I hope you feel better soon," she said, leaving the room.

As Karen left, she turned out the overhead light. The shot had really taken affect and I could hardly keep my eyes open.

"Daniel, I hate to tell you this, but I'm not going to be able to stay awake," I said, closing my eyes. "What did you give me in that shot?"

"Are you warm enough?" he said, pulling the cover up over me?"

I nodded my head, keeping my eyes closed.

"I put some morphine in your shot. Is your headache better?"

"Much," I answered. "I feel so good I'm going to sleep any minute.

"Go ahead, I'll just wake you up every little bit. Sweet dreams, my little friend."

"Daniel?"

"Yeah?"

"I can't remember…"

THE MOUNTAINS CALL MY NAME

"Go to sleep," he said, chuckling at me.

He woke me up several times during the night. The morphine put me into a wonderful sleep. The best I'd had in such a long time. I woke to find him dozing in the chair beside my bed. I lay there for several minutes, studying his face. He hadn't changed much over the years. My little friend had turned into a very handsome man. It seemed we picked up right where we left off when we were children. The same ease in which we communicated, and to think I was worried that we wouldn't have anything in common. It's hard to believe he made it this far without someone capturing his heart. He stretched his tall, lanky frame full length in the chair. When he opened his eyes he was startled to see me staring at him.

"You caught me," he said, yawning. "I was supposed to be watching you, not you watching me."

"You've got to be tired," I said.

"One thing that is still fresh in my mind is how little sleep I can get by on. I'm not that far out of medical school. That's one of the main reasons I didn't have a serious relationship. I was too tired. How in the world could you make time for a family and be on your feet for days at a time? I learned to sleep anywhere I could lay my head. Speaking of which, how is yours?"

He reached for my hand to take my pulse, and then took my blood pressure.

"You did well during the night. I told you that shot would make you feel good."

"I feel great, no headache or nausea. As a matter of fact, I'm starved."

"Try setting up on the side of the bed and see if you feel woozy."

He took my hand and helped me sit up.

"I feel absolutely wonderful. Would you mind if I went to the bathroom?"

"I'll get a nurse."

"Daniel! I'm just going to the bathroom, I don't need a nurse."

"Well, just let me help you stand up."

"Okay."

He took my hand and pushed the stool over for me to step down on. I reached behind me to pull the gown together.

"How do you feel? Do you have any dizziness at all?"

"Nope," I said, slowly shaking my head... Do you show all your patients this much attention?"

"I reserve this treatment for important people. Plus I wanted to show you what a good doctor I turned out to be. How am I doing so far?"

THE MOUNTAINS CALL MY NAME

"Well, I would have given you an A plus, except you didn't give me my sucker. Now get out and let me go to the potty."

He walked me to the door, pushing the IV pole behind me. Having deposited me safely in the bathroom, he waited patiently by my door. When I was finished, he helped me back to the bed.

"Let me take your IV out. I'm sure that will feel better."

"You could have done that before my potty excursion," I said.

"I just wanted to watch you use the bathroom," he said, laughing.

He gently loosed the tape and pulled out the IV needle.

"I have something for you," he said, going to the closet. "I stole these from the surgical suite last night. I thought you might feel a little more comfortable in these. Look, I even found you a lab coat."

"If you would step out, doctor, I'll change."

"I need to make a phone call. I'll be right back."

I changed out of my gown into the teal scrubs. Now, if he can find my shoes, I'll be all set, I thought.

I heard a light tap at my door.

"Come in," I said.

THE MOUNTAINS CALL MY NAME

"You look cute. There isn't another one like it for at least fifty feet outside your door. I managed to get some things for you to freshen up with. If you need anything else, I'll beg, borrow or steal them from somewhere. Then we'll go see Sharon and the baby."

"I think I'll need some shoes," I said, wiggling my toes.

He got two bags out of the closet and handed them to me.

"Your clothes from last night and shoes too. This one you don't want to open," he said, holding up the clothing bag.

"Thank you, Daniel. I'll be ready in just a little bit."

"About your hunger, after we see Sharon I'll take you for some real food. I've got to make some calls to the office, but I promise I won't be long. You go ahead and do whatever it is you do to freshen up. I'll be right back."

He left to make his calls and I went into the bathroom. The image that faced me in the mirror was not a pretty sight. I felt a little weak, but I didn't dare tell Daniel.

On the vanity in the bathroom he had laid out a hairbrush, some moisturizing cream, a wash cloth, toothbrush, toothpaste, soap and a towel. I had just finished when I heard a tapping at the door.

"Libby? Daniel...just checking to see if you're okay."

THE MOUNTAINS CALL MY NAME

I opened the door as he was maneuvering a wheelchair toward me.

"No, no, no, I'm not riding in a wheelchair."

"Well, the reason is, it's a long way to Sharon's room."

"I can walk. I'm not helpless."

"You are as stubborn as you were when you were young."

"I remember you being stubborn, too. So who wins?"

He pushed the chair to the corner and took me by the arm.

"I'll let you win this time. Next time it's my turn."

"Maybe, maybe not," I said, smiling at him.

It was a long walk to Sharon's room and I was getting pretty tired. I dared not let Daniel know he was right. We made our way to the seventh floor, where labor and delivery was.

"I want to check the baby before I go see Sharon. The first thing she's going to ask me is how the baby's doing. If you go down that hallway and turn right, she's in the first room on the right. The room number is 727. If you want to go on down, I'll catch up."

I found the room with no problem. I knocked lightly on the door and she beckoned me to come in. As I entered the room, I saw a man sitting beside her, holding her hand. I assumed it was her husband, Ralph.

"Hello, it's just me, Sharon," I said, tapping lightly on the door.

"Come in, come in. Ralph this is 'Lis'beth, one of the ones that helped me last night."

"Hello, Ralph, it's my pleasure," I said, extending my hand to him.

"Thank you so much for bein' there fer Sharon. I don't know what woulda' happened if you hadn't been there."

"Well, God put me and Daniel right where he wanted us to be. I'm really sorry about your little boy. Daniel did everything he could to save him."

"I know. It just wasn't meant to be. At least we got our little girl. She's so beautiful."

Daniel came into the room, pushing the bassinette before him.

"Who belongs to this little girl?" he asked.

He picked her up and brought her to Sharon and Ralph.

"She's perfect, Daniel said," kissing her on the cheek.

THE MOUNTAINS CALL MY NAME

"Ralph and I have decided to name her 'Lizbeth Rose, after her grandmother and my friend here. And we have named our son, John Daniel after you and daddy."

"I don't know what to say, except 'thank you'. It's such an honor," I said.

"It's the first baby I've had named after me," Daniel said.

"I know you want to know what happened to him. At this point I'm almost sure it was the cord being wrapped around his neck. If you want us to do an autopsy, we will," Daniel said.

"We just want his little body to rest. God knows, that's all that matters. So we don't want one," Ralph said.

"We want him buried in the coffin with Mama," Sharon said.

"I didn't have him taken to the funeral home last night, just in case Ralph wanted to see him before then."

"I would like to if I could. Could you show me?" His voice was choked with emotion.

"I'll take you. We'll let the girls visit."

Sharon and I visited while the guys were downstairs.

"Lisbeth, are you goin' to the funeral tomorrow?"

"Yes, Daniel and I were going to go together."

"It will mean so much to me and Ralph to have you there."

"We had already planned to go to Bessie's funeral. Are you going to be able to go?" I asked.

"I'm fine. I'm goin' by to see daddy. I think we spendin' the night with Ralph's mama 'cause I need help with baby Rose, and I don't think I can stay up there with Mama. That is, if Dr. Daniel lets me go."

Daniel and Ralph entered the room. Are you ready to go home?" Daniel asked.

"Yeah, I don't like hospitals."

"If you two would step out for just a minute I want to examine Sharon and make sure she's doing okay."

Ralph and I stepped into the hallway.

"Are you doing alright?" I asked Ralph.

"I think I'm still in shock. Ever'thing just happened so fast. 'Spectin' one baby and gettin' two then havin' one again. Then losin' Mama Bessie. I don't know if I should be happy or sad. I want to be happy for the one we have, but feel guilty 'cause little John Daniel died."

"I'm sure you're reeling from it all. Your little boy was so cute."

"It was hard just now lookin' at him dead, and all. I'm glad I got to be out here for a minute 'fore I had to face Sharon. Get collected an' all."

THE MOUNTAINS CALL MY NAME

"Don't be afraid to cry with Sharon. It's not a sign of weakness to cry. You need to do what you feel like doing."

"Our baby girl is a beautiful little thing, ain't she?"

"Very."

"Do you think she's gonna' be okay?"

"Sharon, or the baby?"

"Both."

"I can answer that," Daniel said, coming out of the room. "She is doing wonderfully. Both your girls are doing well. You are free to go home anytime you want to. But as soon as you get them back to base, you need to get both of them to the doctor for follow-up care. That's really important. You need to get the baby a pediatrician and make sure she gets all her shots. I'll call the front desk to bring the papers for you to sign."

"Thank you, Dr. Daniel and 'Lis'beth, for bein' there fer Sharon."

"Thank God, he's the one that had everything in place," Daniel said.

"We're glad we were there. Take care of the boys and Daddy John, Daniel, and I will be there to help, too."

I gave Sharon a hug and kiss. I picked up little Rose and gave her a squeeze.

"That was for your Grandma Bessie," I said, holding her close.

I laid her back in the bassinette and covered her with the blanket.

"We'll see you guys tomorrow," Daniel said as we left the room.

We walked quietly down the hall to the elevator.

"As soon as I take care of Sharon's paper work, we're out of here."

"Not too soon for me," I answered.

It was a cold, sunny day as we pulled from the parking lot toward home. Traffic was light because of the early hour.

"You ready for breakfast?" Daniel said.

"I'm more than ready."

"You're in for a real treat. This place has a big sausage gravy breakfast."

"You still eat gravy, Dr. Scott?"

"Yep, I eat there most every day on the way to the office or the hospital. They see me coming and start fixing my plate."

He saw the place and turned into the lot. It wasn't hard to find a spot to park. He came around to my side of the van and opened my door. The blast of cold air caught me by surprise.

"It's freezing; the wind seems to cut straight through me," I said, pulling my coat close to me.

"It's going to take a long time for the snow to melt unless it gets a lot warmer than this," Daniel said, closing the door behind me.

"Hey, Dr. D., you want the regular?" the waitress asked as we entered.

"Make that two," he said.

"How did you know that's what I wanted?" I asked.

"Trust me."

"I keep hearing you say that, just trust me," I said, smiling at him.

"We want a quiet place away from traffic," Daniel told the hostess.

"No problem, right this way."

Daniel helped me off with my coat, and I slid into the booth.

"You really look cute," he said, looking at me.

"I'm sure I do," I said sarcastically.

"No, really. Have I ever lied to you?"

THE MOUNTAINS CALL MY NAME

"Only when it was convenient," I said.

"How do you feel?" he asked.

"I'm tired, but other than that I'm fine. My head is really sore where someone put big long sharp needles in it."

"Better sharp than dull, I might add, and the quality of the work couldn't be better."

The waitress brought the steaming plates of food and set them before us.

"What can I get you two to drink?"

"I'll take some coffee with all the caffeine in it," I said.

"Same here," Daniel said.

"This is so good," I said, delving into the gravy biscuits, and fried eggs.

"I thought you would like it. Isn't it the best you've ever had?"

"It's right up there, I said.

I ate until I was overly full. The waitress had taken our plates and brought us another cup of coffee.

"Now that we've taken care of our bodily needs, lets set awhile and relax. That is, if you're up to it."

THE MOUNTAINS CALL MY NAME

"I'm fine. Let's just hope all this stays down," I said, settling back into the booth.

"Here we are after all these years, together again. Brought together because of death. Who could have imagined?" Daniel said.

"Before you picked me up, I was wondering if we would have anything to talk about. I guess that kind of took care of itself, didn't it."

"I was worried about having to work last night. And pulled an all-nighter anyway. I was excited to get to see you again."

"You look so tired," I said, looking at him.

"I'm fine. I slept in that monster chair bedside you. You don't even remember my waking you up during the night, do you?"

"Vaguely. The bright light anyway."

"Those chairs stretch out and make a fair bed. You just can't roll over."

"I didn't roll over, either."

"You looked so beautiful lying there asleep."

"You make me blush."

"You always were. I forgot how much until I saw you again last night."

"You've never told me. All the time we spent together in high school and you never said that to me."

"I didn't want you to know that I thought so."

"Why?" I implored.

"I didn't want to ruin our friendship. I thought if I told you, you wouldn't want to hang out with me anymore."

"Well, if it makes you feel any better, I thought you were really cute. The girls at school were green with jealousy because we were always together."

"You think so?" he asked, smiling at me. "You never told me I was handsome. Did you really think so?"

"We sound like two goofy teenagers. I think we're punchy." I said, laughing. "How did we get on this conversation?"

"I told you that you looked beautiful as you slept."

"Okay, I remember now. On to bigger and brighter subjects."

"Tell me about your life after Scott's Corner," Daniel said.

"Do you have time?" I asked, looking at my watch. "It's a long story."

"This is my day off. You're my only patient, and date, I might add. I haven't seen you safely home yet."

THE MOUNTAINS CALL MY NAME

"The luxury of being a doctor," I laughed.

"It's good to hear you laugh," he said.

"It feels good to laugh; it's been such a long time since I had a good laugh."

"Where has your joy gone, Elizabeth Mason?" he asked, frowning at me.

"I lost it a long time ago. I quit looking for it. Joy has been an elusive thing for me. It left when David died."

"When I found out he died, I didn't have much information about what happened. I felt badly for you. I did pray for you. What happened, do you mind telling me?" he asked, looking tenderly at me.

"It happened on New Year's Eve three years ago. I worked the night shift. I was working in trauma that night when we got a call that they were bringing in multiple injured from a bad car wreck. I remember running to the helicopter to get this patient. I knew it was a male in pretty bad shape. I couldn't see his face very well because they had him on life support and his head was in this support thing with tape around it. He also had a lot of bandages on his face. I got the vitals from the paramedic as we were pushing him into the trauma bay. He'd already had one cardiac arrest.

I was into the protocol I had done a million times. His face had been smashed into the windshield. I didn't know at first that it was him." I took a long, deep breath before I continued. "Then..." I struggled a little before going on. "I'm sorry, this is the first time I've told this story to anyone since right after it happened, and it's a little hard."

"Take your time," he said, still looking intently at me.

"I picked up his hand and turned it over to start another cath line..." I felt the tears start to well in my eyes. I fought to keep Daniel from seeing them. He squeezed my hand, letting me know he had seen them, but didn't try to stop me.

"That's when I saw his wedding ring. We had matching bands ..." I said barely above a whisper. I paused for a moment before continuing.

"Then I knew it was David. His body was so broken and bloody. His face looked really bad. Like a meat grinder got a hold of it. It would have been impossible to recognize him from his face."

I looked at Daniel for the first time since I started my story. He looked at me and held my gaze, not once looking away, but didn't speak. He waited patiently for me to continue.

"They did start his heart beating again, but he wasn't breathing on his own. I felt numb, like I was moving in slow motion. I was screaming at the doctor to help him, to stop the bleeding. Blood was pouring out of so many places. Right before his heart stopped for the last time, he opened his eyes really wide and looked straight into mine. Just briefly, I think he knew I was there. Then his heart had stopped again. There was nothing more they could do. It was as if I were in suspended animation. Everything went silent, totally silent. I remember looking into my friend Mitch's face when he called the time of death. It was 11:59. There was still one minute left of his thirtieth birthday. I don't remember much after that. My life changed forever on that night, December 31st, the night David died, I died too. You ask where my joy went. It's frozen somewhere in time"

"I'm sorry...so sorry," he said softly. "I thought that after all this time you would..." He let his sentence drop.

"I know, be over it?" I said, finishing his sentence. I played with the ring my coffee cup made in the saucer.

"Well, maybe a little more than you are," he said, reaching over to cover my hand with his.

"There comes a time when you have to go forward. David isn't coming back no matter how hard you hold on to those pictures. Those pictures can't hold you and comfort you. Those pictures aren't going to make love to you."

"They're all I have," I said, with fresh tears falling down my cheek.

"Simply because you won't move on. Maybe you're afraid you will fall in love again, and that love will leave you too."

I looked up into his crystal blue eyes and saw his look searching mine.

"I've been wondering that a lot myself lately. I'm so tired of being sad, Daniel. I felt that if I held on tight enough to all our memories, it would keep him from fading away. But as hard as I've tried, I can't see him clearly anymore. He just slips farther and farther away. I study our pictures every day, hoping that seeing them will keep him fresh in my mind. I try to remember how it felt to be held, but all I feel is emptiness. I try to push the memory of how he looked the last time I saw him out of my mind. That's why I look at the pictures of the good times we had. It pushes out the bad memories. But as hard as I try, they keep slipping. I get scared sometimes and feel so lonely. So that's what I spend my time doing, is trying to keep his memory alive."

"What are you afraid of, Elizabeth?" he asked, still holding my gaze. I felt like he could see all the way to my soul. "Maybe you're afraid someone will make you feel alive inside again."

"I don't know. I just get so afraid sometimes. Everything that was concrete crumbled. All my security vanished. I don't have anything solid to hold on to anymore. So I stay in the world I know. I've been dug in there for a while now."

"Go on," he said, still holding my hand in both of his.

"If it was up to me, I would still be in my home in North Carolina. If I hadn't had to come home to be with Mama, I wouldn't have come back. I wouldn't be here right now."

"And you would have robbed me of seeing you again. Why not come back here to live? Are we that bad here?" he asked, smiling.

"Have you forgotten how hard we tried to get away from this place?"

THE MOUNTAINS CALL MY NAME

"Funny you should bring that up. I used to feel just like you. I really enjoyed all the time and experience of being in the city. My medical practice was practically given to me. The perks were more than any new doctor should expect, but every time I came back to visit, the need for a doctor here would haunt me for days after I would go home."

"But why you, couldn't someone else do it?"

"That's just it; no one was coming to the aid of these people. My family, your family, they were so...."

"In need, and you gave up your dream to take care of them," I said, finishing for him again.

"We're still doing it, finishing each other's sentences. We used to do that all the time. I guess some things never change. To answer your question, yes, in the process of doing it for them, they became my dream," he said.

"What made that happen?"

"Well, not only did they have just one tired old doctor, but he was so far behind modern medicine. I kept hoping when I'd talk to Grandma she would bring me news of someone taking over his practice, but that never happened. So Grandma told me one day, 'Danny, quit complaining and do it yourself'," he said, with a smile.

"That's exactly what she told me she told you. Grandma Scott is such a tactful little woman," I said, smiling back at Daniel.

"Blunt to be exact. You know what? I didn't have an answer for her. She made me make the final decision. The doctors at the clinic where I worked couldn't believe what I was going to do. As a matter of fact, I thought maybe I needed some counseling myself, but the decision was made and here I am."

"No regrets."

"Nope, not one. I believe God had this planned since I was a little boy. He just had to put it in my heart at the right moment. He prepared me with the knowledge and education I needed and called me home. I was a little stubborn, but he kept knocking me in the head until I got it. I finally have a peace and a sense of being needed like nothing I've ever experienced before," he said.

"Being needed is a good thing I guess. I haven't been needed for a long time."

"I think if my ears haven't failed me, you just said you came because your..."

"I know, because my mom needed me, but that's a different kind of being needed," I said.

"And I ask again, what is it about this place that made you run from it?"

"I have an unexplainable fear, maybe not fear, but something....I don't know, I just can't put it in words. It feels like something is going to get me. Well not get me, but....I just can't put it into words."

"Like what, a person or thing or what?" he asked seriously.

"I wish I knew. It's haunted me all my life. I feel like there is something here that could harm me if I stay. Isn't that silly, Daniel?"

"Maybe you told yourself you hated it so much here that you can't, or won't, allow yourself to change your mind."

"Hate isn't what I feel. I love these people here. It's just this place. I've never had peace, or should I say 'contentment' here."

"Maybe it's love you have never felt here. The opposite of hate is love."

"I've never really looked at it that way."

"God, in mysterious ways, performs his greatest miracles. Ask God to reveal what you're afraid of. God's Word says He is not the author of confusion, but of peace. You seek peace. You must find it with God."

"I know, I've been trying. It felt good last night helping you with Sharon. I think it distracted me for a while. My mind was totally consumed in what to do next. I was in text-book mode. Trying to recall all I needed to know to help you. It actually felt good being needed again."

"I'll pray for you, Libby."

"Do you know you are the only one in the whole world that calls me Libby?" I said, smiling at him.

"And it never dawned on you to ask me why?"

THE MOUNTAINS CALL MY NAME

"I guess not, so I'm biting. Why do you call me, Libby?"

"It started out when we were little and I couldn't say Elizabeth. I never did tell you that it was because I couldn't pronounce Elizabeth? Anyway, Libby just seemed to fit my vast vocabulary better," he said, smiling at me.

"The people around here just called me 'Lis'beth or 'Lis'beth Anne."

The waitress came several times to fill our cups, but didn't seem to mind our taking up her space. The little café seemed like a confessional booth at the Catholic Church. We knew each other so well, even after all these years apart, our bond was still there. At last, I could open my heart a little crack to let in some fresh air and sunshine.

"Did school go well for you?" he asked.

"Yeah, it did, our hard study habits came in handy. David helped some, but he was in his own Masters study then. He didn't have a lot of time to hold my hand. The dean of the nursing school recommended me for special training in trauma medicine. I did some real intense training for that. I actually thought about going on to med school, but decided to go ahead and start in my career. I alternated stints in ICU and ER. We were the number one trauma center in the area, so we got the worst cases."

"How did you like that?"

"What, working in trauma?"

"Yeah"

THE MOUNTAINS CALL MY NAME

"Well, as you probably know, it can be very stressful, but I planned long vacations. It was going really well for David and me. He was in research for, believe it or not, cancer. He was so excited about what he was doing, but was also very proud of my career. He was my cheerleader all the way."

"I cheered you first," he said, in mock jealousy.

"If I remember correctly, you were never my cheerleader. We were always racing each other to the finish line. I don't ever remember you saying, 'go Elizabeth, go'," I said, laughing at him.

"It was silent cheering."

"A lot of good silent cheering does."

"We were good for each other, weren't we, Elizabeth?" he said, with his impish little smile.

"Weren't we?" he repeated his question.

"Yeah, you kept me on my toes. What time you weren't stepping on them."

"I was so surprised when I found out you were here. After all the promises and vows we made to never come back. Let's see, it went something like this, 'God help me, if I ever get out of here I'll never come back.'" He was repeating the words with me.

"I had a great career started at this clinic. It just so happened, the older doctor there was a mentor to me all through med school. I did my internship at Johns Hopkins University. Man, he was tough on me during my training.

He'd say, 'Daniel I'm going to make a good doctor out of you if kills both of us.' He wouldn't let anything slip by. I was surprised that he liked me so well. His pats on the back were few and far between, but when you got one, you treasured it. The long hours were killers. I could sleep standing up."

"What was your hardest rotation?"

"They were all hard and interesting at the same time. I loved working in pediatrics, and the surgical rotation was great, but I wanted to work in a lot of areas. By the way, ER was a downer. We had to be on top of our game when they rolled in with a patient. One mistake and you could end up losing them. We had great doctors right by our side. You'd better believe we were watched closely. Some doctors made you jump in quick and some made you watch awhile. The worst was when you would have to go before the board of doctors when you would lose a patient. It didn't matter if you made right choices or not. You had to know what you did and why you did it, or didn't do it. I only had to go once. It scared the crap out of me. It'll sure put the fear of God into you."

"I hated working the weekends. There was so much violent stuff, and drunks causing car wrecks," I said.

"I know what you mean. Saturdays were always bad. Lots of gang stuff. We'd sew them up, and a month or two later they'd be back again. So I identify with you. The nurses were our life savers. There was a lot of respect between us. I found out early that if you were going to make it in rotations you'd better be good to the nurses. If you got on their bad list, every time anyone wanted anything you would be the one they would call. The tiniest little thing, like a change for a patient's medication that would clearly wait until daylight, they would call you at two o'clock in the morning," he said, grimacing.

"You're talking to one," I said laughing at him.

"Did you do that too?" he said, looking shocked.

"Maybe once or twice, especially to the cocky ones that thought they were God's gift to the medical profession, and to the nurses."

"I'm truly shocked; you of all people would do that."

"Some interns learned the hard way. We could make their life a living hell, but I'll be quick to add, I wasn't one of them," I said.

"I'll bet you could be a little devil when you were pushed too far. You know how I know, because I've been at the end of your devilment before."

"I could be, if it was called for," I said, smiling at him.

"There were times when you just frustrated the dickens out of me, Daniel said, smiling at me."

"I know," I said, grinning back at him.

"Back to how I got here. Every time I would come home to visit, I would go back to my practice so frustrated. The quality of medical care here was back in the dark ages. Doc Adams was worn out, and sick himself. God bless him, he was still doing house calls in the evening, and keeping office hours during the day. The older people were afraid to go to the office, so a family member would call Old Doc to come take a look."

"Which he did," I added.

"I kept complaining to my family all the time. It really convicted me deep in my gut.

"I mean, I had it made in the shade. Dr. Sanderson, my mentor, told me he knew I wouldn't stay with him long. He really tried to make it so good I wouldn't leave him, but he knew why I had to go. He said, 'the amount of money you make is not the sign of being successful, but how you make the money.' He was *my* cheerleader. He was with me like I was with you. I never knew he was on the sidelines cheering me. When he was on me all the time, not accepting anything but my best, he was cheering me on. I always felt picked on. I got so discouraged at times. You know, feeling like you couldn't do anything right. He never let on how he really felt until one day toward the end of my rotations he called me into his office. Getting summoned to the great one's office was never without a good reason, so it was very disconcerting.

"When I entered, he told me to be seated, to relax, that I wasn't in trouble. He just sat in silence, looking at me for a long, quiet moment. Then he began to tell me what was on his heart.

"He said he had had a son my age that was killed just as he was to enter medical school. He said I reminded him so much of his son. He had wanted him to practice medicine with him one day when he graduated, but that was to never be. He watched me grow into a man and a doctor. He asked me would I come and take the place his son would have had. He told me I had a place with him in his practice as long as I wanted it. And as long as I passed my medical boards, I could join him in his practice. I told him I would be honored to join him if that was what the Lord wanted me to do. I told him I would like to pray about it and get back to him. I still can't believe those words came out of my mouth. My career was being handed to me on a silver platter and I was telling him I would think about it.

"He said, 'Daniel, I'm very proud of you son. I would have been disappointed if you had given me any other answer. I will respect your decision. When you're ready, come talk to me.'"

"How long did it take you?"

"Not long, I really felt that God wanted me with this man. He was so wise and I could learn so much more. So after graduation I went to work for him."

"But did you ever feel he wanted you there just to remind him of what he lost in his son, or because you were a good doctor?"

"You offend me, Elizabeth," he said, putting his hand to his heart. "I think there was some of that. But he would always tell me I wasn't taking Kyle's place in his heart. He just wanted to give some bright young doctor a leg up."

"Or, in this case a whole body, not just a leg," I said, laughing at him.

"I couldn't get away from the call God was putting in my heart. I really felt it was God's will for me to work with Dr. Sanderson. How could I not when everything fell into place like it did? But sometimes when you want something so badly we stamp God's will on it. It may have been God's will at the time, but after a while I just didn't have the fulfillment that I thought I would have. I couldn't get these people here off my mind. It was driving me nuts. So one day after all our patients had gone, I talked with Dr. Sanderson about the pull the mountains had on my heart. I couldn't ignore the need there any longer. So here I am. When God does the calling you can't do anything but go," he said.

"I'm proud of you too. I guess it just took me by surprise that you came back."

"I haven't always done the things I knew I should do. There are things I'll always regret not doing. Things I should have said and done, but I found out you can't go back, you can only go forward. You can't change the past, there's nothing you can do about tomorrow, but you have today. Putting my total trust in God's hands was the best thing I ever learned to do."

He still held my hand in his. He kept caressing it with his fingers.

"Maybe you can help me learn to do that," I said, looking into his tender gaze.

"If you will let me, I would be happy to. It will be kind of hard to do two hours away," he said, squeezing my hand.

"We have phones."

THE MOUNTAINS CALL MY NAME

"We need to do some praying about you being so far away. Maybe it's time you came home, Elizabeth Mason."

"Wow, look at the time! It's getting late," I said, ignoring his last statement.

He helped me on with my coat and paid the bill. We rode in tired silence toward home. Just night before last I was traveling down the same road, I thought. The same twists and turns that we were making today. I would never have dreamed that two days later I would be riding down that road beside Daniel Scott. I never even dreamed about seeing him, much less helping him deliver Sharon's babies.

Just night before last I recalled praying for God to help me get on with life. Was that just two short days ago? My mind was racing. My, I thought, It seemed like light years.

"I guess you heard me didn't you, God?" I silently asked.

But one thing I knew for certain, I wouldn't be getting on with life here. Nothing has changed about that, I reasoned. Maybe Daniel could change, but not me, not about living here. I would have to start thinking seriously about starting back to work though. I'll have to check into it when I get back to town.

I reached up to tenderly touch my sore head. I closed my eyes to shield the bright sun. My head was beginning to throb again. I was more than ready to go home. I opened my eyes ever so slightly and saw Daniel looking my way.

THE MOUNTAINS CALL MY NAME

"Are you okay, little girl?" he asked, reaching for the hand that held my head.

"My head is throbbing again. I just need to rest."

"Forgive me for keeping you out. It was selfish of me. I was enjoying catching up on things and time got away. I'm sorry," he said,

"I would have asked to go home if I wasn't enjoying it too," I said.

"We're getting pretty close to home now; remind me to give you something for the pain."

"Oh, I don't think you will have to remind me," I said, smiling at him.

I pressed my fingers to my temples to try to ease the pain. The nausea was creeping back. I could feel the sausage gravy low on the horizon, not long from making an exit.

"You need to pull over; I'm going to be sick again. I'm sorry," I said, holding my hand to my mouth.

I saw the white chapel coming into view. He pulled over in the parking lot and I quickly excited out the door. I thought my whole insides were coming up. Every heave made my head feel like it was going to fall off. Finally, with the nausea receding, I leaned on the side of the van, weak from the episode.

"I'm so sorry. I thought I could make it home. I didn't want to do this again, especially with you," I said, with tears rolling down my face.

THE MOUNTAINS CALL MY NAME

"Since I'm a doctor, I see stuff like this all the time," he said, reaching into the back of the van for some paper towels. "Here," he said, proffering me the towels.

I took the towels and wiped my face. "Thanks for being here."

"I don't like this. You shouldn't still be sick. I'm tempted to take you back to the hospital."

"Please don't, I just need to get some rest. You said so yourself."

"My instincts tell me not to let you go home, but if you promise to rest, I'll let you."

"I promise, doctor. I'll follow your orders to a tee."

"Okay, against my better judgment, I'll take you home. But I'm going to tell your mom to call me if you start getting sick again. You're a trained nurse, you know headache and nausea with a concussion is not good."

"I really think if I rest I'll be okay."

He pulled me to him and I lay my head against his chest. He patted me on the back like a little child.

"Come on, I need to get you the rest of the way home," he said, helping me back into the van.

"The last time I saw you was right here, in this little white church. I was your best man. That's the first time, and last I might add, that I have been best man for the *bride*," he said, smiling at me.

"You were my best friend. I couldn't have done it without you."

"I wish you could have," he said, looking straight ahead.

"What do you mean; you didn't want to be there for me?"

"I had a lot to do that summer with school. Plus I was trying to find a way not to say 'goodbye' to my sidekick. Then all of a sudden, the reality of it hit. We were going our separate ways. What we had worked for, for so long, had come to fruition, and now, here it was." He hesitated before going on.

"I just wasn't expecting it to feel so sad. I wasn't expecting it to be marriage that took you away either."

"You and me both. Marriage was the one thing I didn't have on my mind."

"I knew that to be a fact. That's why when you wanted this big favor done I couldn't turn you down. I just wasn't prepared to hear what it would be. I would have done anything for you, so when you asked, I jumped quickly. But when I found out what I had promised you it was too late to say 'no'."

"I didn't know you felt that way," I said, squinting at him through the bright morning sun. My head was still hurting.

"There are a lot of things that you don't know about me. Maybe I'll fill you in sometime. How you doing now?"

"Just this headache."

"Nausea?"

"Not now, that all passed, literally," I said, smiling at him.

We pulled into the driveway behind my car. He got out and came around to my side and opened my door for me. When I stood up I felt a little woozy again. He put his arms around me and pulled me close to him. I let my head rest on his shoulder.

"Should I carry you?"

"No way. I remember just last night being in the snow bank with you. See, the evidence is still there. See those two big snow angels?" I said, pointing to them. "Seriously though, I'm okay."

"I can hold you in my arms for a while and see if your headache goes away," he said, grinning at me.

"I thank you for your acts of kindness, Dr. Scott. No wonder my mom thinks you're wonderful. You have all the women charmed, I'm sure."

He walked me to the house with his arm still supporting me. Mama met us at the door. The strain of the night was evident on her face.

"I'm really glad to see you two. I've been so worried, even though you called. I just couldn't feel better until I could see ya' fer myself. It's the mama bear in me."

THE MOUNTAINS CALL MY NAME

"She's fine, she just needs some rest. I had to give her a few stitches, but she alright," he said, as he sat me down at the table to look at the stitches again.

"You're looking good. I'm going to go get my bag and get you something for pain and the nausea. If you will go hop into bed, I'll be back in just a minute to tuck you in," he said.

Mama walked me back to my bedroom and helped me get into my pajamas. It wasn't long until I heard a light knock on the door.

"May I come in?" he said.

"Yes," I answered him.

Mama left as Daniel came in. He sat down on the side of my bed, shined his light in my eyes, and rechecked the stitches he had put in.

"Does everything look okay, Doc?"

"You look great," he said, continuing to look in my eyes. "And your stitches do, too. Let me check your back. Is it sore?"

"Only when you push on it, doctor. No, really, there isn't any ache. I'm just sore. That was a pretty big load that fell on me."

"I think with a lot of rest today, if you don't have any more nausea, you can go to the funeral with me tomorrow, but you have to rest. That's why I'm going to give you a shot instead of a pill. I don't want you throwing up again. I want to keep your stomach as settled as possible."

He reached into his doctor bag and filled a syringe with some clear liquid.

"Are you sure I can't have a pill?"

"Shhh," he said, shaking his head. "Let me doctor."

"Turn over, little girl."

"Not the hip shot!"

"Yep, it's the hip shot."

"I think you just want to see my hip," I said.

"Don't make me laugh while I have this needle in my hand."

I pulled down the top of my underwear for him to shoot me.

"Hmm... I think I've seen this before somewhere."

"In your dreams," I retorted.

He was quick, and it really wasn't too bad. He rubbed the spot with a gauze pad to distribute the medicine.

"All done, my pet. I only gave you a small amount. It should wear off by this afternoon. I really want you to get all the rest you can. You will have a full day tomorrow, and I'm still not comfortable with your symptoms," he said,

I pulled up my pajama bottoms and snuggled down under the cover while he was putting everything back in his bag.

"I get tucked into bed, too? No wonder house calls are so popular."

"I'm going to sit right here in this rocking chair and watch you fall asleep." He reached over and took my hand in his as he slid his trained fingers up to my wrist to check my pulse."

"I haven't had such care in a long time. It sure feels good," I said. "How's the pulse doing?"

"A little fast , but not bad," he returned.

"Perhaps it's the closeness of my doctor."

"I rather doubt that, but I would like to believe my closeness could make your heart race," he said, smiling down at me.

"Let me check yours," I said.

"I'm the doctor and you're the patient at the moment," he said, smiling at me.

"Some things never change, do they? The next time we play doctor, I get to give you a shot and put stitches in," I said.

"Should I trust you?"

"Absolutely not. I can give one mean shot," I said.

"Is that mean, as in good, or mean as in bad?"

"That's for me to find out? No! Wait that's backwards," I said, with a slur in my speech.

"You need to quit talking and rest. Close your little eyes. Do you want Dr. Daniel to sing to you or read you a story?"

"As I remember, singing wasn't one of the things you do well. Just hold my hand. Did I tell you I had a great evening?"

"No"

"Well, I did. It's so good to see you again. Pray for me, Daniel...pray for..." I felt myself drifting far from him. Peaceful wonderful sleep.

When I awoke it was already getting dark. I climbed out of bed and made my way into the living room.

"Hi, Mama, how are you doing?"

"Well, how are you doin'?" she asked.

"I actually feel pretty good. Whatever Daniel gave me helped me sleep. My head doesn't hurt at all now. I'm just sore."

THE MOUNTAINS CALL MY NAME

"I'm doin' good now that yer home safe. Daniel called me and kept me updated. He is such a wonderful boy, or man."

"You're right about that," I said, smiling at her.

"He stayed there by yer side until you went to sleep, which wasn't very long."

"He held my hand until I was asleep?" I questioned her.

"That's what he said," she said, smiling at me.

He's the same Daniel that I knew and loved growing up. Just in a big size, and a real doctor, not a play one."

"And yer still the nurse," she said with a chuckle in her voice.

"Did he stay long?" I inquired.

"I made him some coffee and gave him a piece of pie."

"I can't believe he ate. We ate a huge breakfast and drank a gallon of coffee."

"He's a man, honey, they always hungry," she said with a grin. "I loved cookin' fer yer daddy. He said I was the best cook in the country."

"And he didn't lie. You are a very good cook."

129

THE MOUNTAINS CALL MY NAME

The phone rang, and I picked it up from the side table.

"Hello, Edwards' residence."

"Hi, you're awake," Daniel said.

"Just."

"How do you feel?

"Right now I feel great. My headache is totally gone, and I don't have any nausea."

"Don't do too much. When you eat be sure you eat something light. Soup would be good."

"Yes, doctor."

"I know you've slept a lot today, but try to get into bed as early as possible. The more you rest with this concussion, the quicker you'll heal."

"I'll try." I said, responding to his orders.

"I left a couple of pills with your mom. I told her to give them to you if your headache started up again, or if you became nauseated."

"Okay, but I don't think I will be needing anything else. She said you ate again after I fell asleep."

"I purposely waited until you fell asleep so you wouldn't know. Your mom wasn't going to tell you."

"Did you rest any today?"

"A little, I went back to the hospital and checked on some patients. Then I went home and just chilled."

"I hope I can sleep after having slept all day."

"If you can't, I can come over and hold you and sing to you."

"I suddenly feel very tired," I said, faking a yawn.

"Okay, I get the point. I'll pick you up in the morning about 11:00. The funeral is at 12:00. I thought we could talk to Sharon and the family before the funeral. If that's okay."

"That's perfect. I'll be ready and waiting. Our second date is a funeral, and the first was an emergency delivery. We sure know how to party."

"I wonder what we can do for number three, he said.

"Thanksgiving is next week; you can come for dinner if you want. I'm sure Mama won't care. That is if you aren't already having lunch with family."

"We're having dinner, so unless something drastic happens I could handle lunch. I know this might surprise you, but I have a hearty appetite. I think I could handle lunch and dinner. Baring anything popping up unexpectedly, I accept. You know how doctors' lives are."

"No, I really don't, but I can tell you a lot about a nurse's life."

"I'll tell you all about the doctor's side sometime. Let's put it this way, if no one has a baby, or a sore toe, or God knows what else, I'll be there. Sometimes I wonder why I went into family practice."

"Because God put you there."

"Hey, by the way, I did what you asked me to before you fell asleep?"

"What was that?"

"You really don't remember?"

"No, I don't, and that makes me kind of nervous. What did I ask?"

"You asked me to hold your hand."

"I remember that. Thanks for being there Daniel. It felt good to have someone care again."

"You asked something else too."

"And..."

"You asked me to pray for you, and I did."

"Thank you so much. How precious to have the prayers of a friend."

"It's not like I'm a super Christian, but if someone asks me to intercede on their behalf, I consider it an honor."

"Thanks for checking on me. I'll see you tomorrow."

"Goodnight, Libby."

"Goodnight, Daniel."

"I assume that was Dr. Daniel," Mama said.

"Yes, you assume right."

"Did I hear you say yer goin' to the funeral at 11:00."

"Yes, Daniel is picking me up."

"Give 'em my love. Daniel told me ever'thing that happened. Poor Sharon, she must feel awful."

"She's doing well physically. Emotionally, she's grieving, but that's a good thing. The little boy was so cute. She named him John Daniel, and the little girl, Elizabeth Rose. John Daniel for her dad and Daniel and Elizabeth Rose after me and her mom."

"I didn't know Bessie's name was Bessie Rose."

"There were a few harrowing moments up there last night, but Sharon is doing well. Ralph made it to the hospital and spent the night with Sharon. The twins stayed with Daddy John, and Bessie, of course. There were some men from the church that came to stay with them. I still think it's weird bringing a body into the house."

We talked for quite awhile that night. Mama got out her photo album, which is one of her favorite things to do with me. I loved looking at the old pictures, too. After several hours of reminiscing we closed the albums and decided to call it a night.

"I'm kinda' tired from all the excitement," she said, starting down the hall to her bedroom.

We prayed together again by her bedside. I was tired, but not very sleepy, and went back into the living room to look at some more of the pictures. It was good to see Daddy's face again. I missed him so much. I don't know if it was the residue from the shot or God beginning to work, but I felt a peace I hadn't experienced for a long time. I sat by the old potbellied stove and soaked up the last of its warmth, then headed to bed. Hopefully it would be a good night.

I arose early the next morning. The sunlight was already pouring into my bedroom. I was surprised that I felt so good. My headache was completely gone. I had some soreness, but no ache. I found some of Mama's bubble bath, and poured some into the steaming water. Soon I had a tub full of inviting bubbles. I eased myself into the beckoning water. I let my body slide slowly down the curve of the old fashioned bath tub into a blanket of bliss. I didn't stop until the water circled my neck.

I lay there and prayed for the day and all the people that I knew needed to be interceded for. The peace I felt inside was so new and wonderful. I wasn't sure what had brought such a sudden change. Maybe getting knocked on the head was a good thing. Perhaps it was just a change of focus.

It was great being with Daniel. Our bond of friendship was just like it had been so many years before. I felt so at ease with him. To think, I was concerned about what we would talk about after all those years. I found I could still open up my heart to him. I knew he wouldn't always tell me what I wanted to hear, but what I needed to hear. He could be brutally honest at times. He was right about moving on. David definitely wasn't coming back. I had tried so hard not to lose the vivid image I had of him, but every day that passed it faded a little more.

The past three years had been a quagmire of feelings that had sucked the life from me. The pit was dark and suffocating. I thought it was about time I grabbed the lifeline that was being thrown to me.

What will I do when I go back home? I thought. Work was sounding better to me. It was interesting how the nurse in me took over when the crisis hit. My thoughts were interrupted by a knock on the door.

"'Lis'beth, breakfast is about ready, honey."

"I'm almost finished. I'll be there in just a minute."

I washed the part of my hair that I could, trying hard not to wet my stitches. Which was no easy task, by the way.

I entered the kitchen to the wonderful aroma of breakfast.

"Everything looks and smells so good," I told her. "You shouldn't go to so much trouble."

"Oh, honey, yer no trouble. It's a joy just to have ya' here. It gets awful lonely eatin' by yerself all the time.

THE MOUNTAINS CALL MY NAME

That's when I miss yer daddy the most. We always took our meals together."

I heard the phone ring and went into the living room to get it.

"Hello," I said.

"Hi, how you doing?" Daniel asked.

"Surprisingly well," I told him.

"Headache gone?" he inquired further.

"Completely, thanks to all the rest I got."

"Is 11:00 still a good time to pick you up?"

"Yeah, that's good. By the way, have you eaten breakfast yet?" I asked him.

"Why, do you want to go out again?" he returned.

"No, I was going to invite you over here."

"Actually I was calling from the office. I've got to do some things here before I leave to go to the funeral, but thanks for asking. I'll take a rain check."

"Your chariot will be there soon," he said.

"See you later."

I hung up the phone and went back to my breakfast.

THE MOUNTAINS CALL MY NAME

"Was that Daniel?" Mama asked.

"Yes, he was confirming what time to pick me up for the funeral."

"I saw the hearse go down while I was cookin'. I just couldn't help but cry."

I went to her and put my arms around her. I held her close to me and comforted her. We sat around the table and talked about Bessie and the sweet memories we had of her.

"I think I might go in and lay down fer a little bit. I'm still trying to catch up from the other night when you were at the hospital."

By the time I cleaned up the kitchen it was time to get ready to meet Daniel.

I took my time finding just the right thing to wear. It had been a long time since I cared that much about what I wore. Unfortunately, it had to be a funeral I was going to. I pulled my long hair back and tied it with a scarf. At least it covered my stitches.

I heard the knock at the front door and hurried down the hallway to open it.

"Come in," I said, holding the door open for him.

"You look a lot better than when I left you yesterday."

"I would have to die to look worse. I was a real mess. I can't believe I went inside a restaurant looking like that. I hope they don't remember me." I said with a chuckle.

I took his coat and laid it across the back of a kitchen chair.

"I would like for you to check Mama for me. I just want to make sure she's okay," I said, talking low so she wouldn't hear me.

"Why, is her dizziness worse?" he asked with a look of concern crossing his face.

"No, not worse, but still I can tell she's not feeling well. I don't think she's sleeping very well. She still tries to do way too much. I try to discourage her, but she can be stubborn."

"Like her daughter?"

"Okay, that's enough."

"You can let her do pretty much what she wants to do. I really don't want her to stop doing all she feels like doing. She needs to push a little, but I *will* check her. Where is she?"

"She said she was going to lie down for a little. Her room is the first one on the right. I'll go tell her you're here."

"Mama, are you awake? Daniel is here and wants to say 'hi'."

"Come in. I wasn't sleepin', just restin' my eyes."

"Hi, sweet lady. How are you doing this morning?" he asked, going over to the side of her bed.

"If you will excuse us, honey, Daniel and I have things to talk about," she said, smiling up at me.

"Sure don't let me spoil your party", I teased as I pulled her door shut.

Since Daniel was in with her for quite a while, I was beginning to get a little concerned. Then the door finally opened.

"She's doing fine. I don't feel like her condition is worsening, she's just tired. She's going to rest while we are at the funeral. I think her grieving and all the excitement last night has taken a lot out of her," he said.

"Are you sure you're not keeping anything from me?"

"I claim doctor-patient privilege.

"So you *aren't* telling me everything?"

"I didn't say that."

"It's what you're not saying that's bothering me."

"Leave that poor boy alone. I'm just fine. I need some rest, just like he told you," Mama said, entering the room.

It was fast approaching the time we had to go to the church. Daniel helped me into my coat and we headed toward his van. We could see a few cars parked in the church lot. We pulled into a spot near the back of the sanctuary. As we entered the vestibule of the old, sweet church, it seemed the same as it did the day I was married there. I saw the coffin setup at the front with flowers placed neatly around it. More flowers than she had seen in a lifetime, I'm sure. I felt Daniel slip his arm around my waist as we made our way to the coffin. I was taken aback just a little to see the tiny bundle in her arms. Baby John Daniel was sweetly resting in the nook of her arm.

What a time they must be having in heaven, I thought.

I let all the pent-up emotion from the last few hours, or perhaps years, flow freely from me as I looked upon the serene scene. I couldn't stop the flow of tears. Bessie's sweet, dark face was shining with a heavenly glow. She always had a small frame which belied her strength. She could work harder than anyone I ever knew. She expected no less from her children, and husband, much to their dismay, I thought, smiling to myself.

I saw Daniel lift the cover from the baby. I'm sure he was taking in the same thing as I. The little face of the baby was perfect. A head full of black curls framed his pale, angelic face. It seemed to shine in the same glow of glory as his grandma's. He was the image of perfection. Why, oh why, didn't God spare him? I wondered.

We stood transfixed with the tableau before us. I felt Daniel gently pull me just a little closer to him as we stood there. He wiped his eyes several times as we stood beside the coffin. Daniel worked so hard to save this little guy, trying to breathe life into his little body, but it wasn't to be. He gently placed the snow white blanket back over the little frame of John Daniel Wiggins. What a wonderful name, I thought. Daddy John was bound to be so proud that Sharon wanted him to carry his name.

We turned and walked back down the aisle to select a seat. Daniel excused himself to go to speak to the family. I thought I would wait until I was a little more in control of my emotions. The time by myself was just what I needed at the moment. By the time Daniel came back and took his seat, I had my face cleaned up some and the snot blown away. I figured that wouldn't be a very pretty sight. Daniel took his handkerchief from his pocket, wiped the tears from his eyes, and proceeded to do what *I* had just finished doing.

"Sorry," he mouthed, silently looking my way.

"No problem," I said back.

The preacher took his place back behind the coffin and started the service.

"We are gathered here today to honor one of the old saints of the Lawd and a new little angel. Our Sister in Christ, Bessie Rose Johnson, and our little brother, John Daniel Wiggins, has left earth, and entered into their heavenly home. They both went home to be with Jesus just a few hours apart. I guess she had to get there just a little ahead to make things ready for the little fella. Alls I know is they be doin' mighty fine 'bout now," he said, smiling at the Johnson family.

I heard a hearty "amen" coming from Daddy John.

"They's where we *all* be hoping to be some fine day, at home with Jesus. Jesus *love* the little children, I know so, cause God's word says so. He needed little John

Daniel to come on home. We don't know the why for of our Savior, we just know he allus be right. And Mrs. Bessie, she was one fine lady. Alus doin' fer those what be needin' sumpthin'. We's all her family. Many a fine supper's been cooked fer those hungry, or hurtin'. She was allus there. She raised a fine upright family. No better chil'en anywhere. We want to thank God fer Sharon bein' able to be here. She went through one tough time up there in the holler last night. Dr. Daniel and Ms. 'Lis'beth took mighty good care of 'em. They weren't able to save Little Daniel, but little 'Lis'beth Rose is doin' fine. She right there in her mama's arms restin'. God gives and God takes, Sharon," he said, looking at her. "He don't ask us what we think, but he allus knows best. I'm gonna a'ks brother Hank if he'll come and play one of Bessie's favorite songs. Come on, Bro. Hank, share with us what God done laid on yer heart."

The little man, stooped from years of hard work, made his way to the front of the church. He picked up his guitar, which seemed too large for his small frame, and strummed a few times to see if it was tuned to suit him.

"If ya'll would turn to hymn 36, we'll sing 'How Great Thou Art'. I remember Sister Bessie sayin' that was her favorite."

The booming vocals of this little bent man failed to agree with his small stature. The voices resonated from the rafters, making the little chapel vibrate with its joyful strain.

"And while yer at it, lest just sing 'Amazin' Grace,'" he said.

THE MOUNTAINS CALL MY NAME

The pastor finished the service, eulogizing the wonderful life of Bessie Rose Johnson, and dismissed us to follow the little procession up the hollow.

The sunny day had given way to a cold, icy rain. How quickly things could change. That's all we needed today, I thought to myself.

We slowly made our way up the snow-and-ice-laden lane to the base of the mountainside. Darrell and David's cabin was situated in a grove of pine trees almost out of sight. We parked our vehicles in a row up and down the narrow space.

The procession of mourners proceeded past their house and up the hillside to the cemetery. The usual view was a dirt path, worn free from grass. The many visits from the people who had loved ones there had left it so. Today there was no path, just a chilling blanket of snow with fresh tracks from the people who dug the grave.

The twins kept the cemetery free of weeds and brambles and the picket fence painted as white as the snow which abounded about us. The men carrying the casket struggled through the deep icy covering, up the hillside to the gravesite. It somberly lay open awaiting its offering. I don't know how they managed to penetrate the earth in such weather. I guess the ground hadn't had time to fully freeze, not very deep anyway. They carried the casket through the open gate that led them to their place of rest. At last they lay their heavy burden on the straps that would lower the casket into its eternal place of repose.

Some men from the church helped the family up the hill to the wooden chairs that sat beside the grave. People from the church carried the arrangements of flowers from a van and placed them around the gravesite. It looked like springtime in winter. The flowers made a stark contrast to the white snow.

I saw the huge weeping willow with its canopy spreading out over the cemetery. Its branches hung heavy with the cold, icy rain. Under that tree was the place my brother and daddy were laid to rest. Daniel held my hand as we trudged up the hill to take our position behind the family. Ralph, Sharon's husband, stood behind her and put his hands on her shoulders. I was glad to see that she had left the baby with one of the ladies in the church.

The rain had already turned to sleet. It felt like tiny little needles striking my face. The preacher took his place at the head of the casket and said the last few words of farewell.

"The Lawd gave and the Lawd done took, blessed be the name of the Lawd. He gathered our Sister Bessie and little brother John Daniel to hisself, and took them to a warm place in that celestial city of God. They not here, Brother John," he said, looking through tears at the sad little man. "They not goin' down in the cold ground today. So don't be sad they'll get cold. That's just the house they lived in. Blessed be the name of the Lawd."

"Praise the Lord that's right. Preach it." Daddy John said through his tears.

Sharon was sobbing now, letting all the sorrow and pain of the last few hours escape her. I heard the mournful strains of a song coming from Daddy John. He was singing in his wavering tenor voice "Swing low sweet chariot coming fer to carry me home."

THE MOUNTAINS CALL MY NAME

As he sang, the little group that had gathered there joined his singing until all the verses had all been sung. Some of the men gathered around and helped him from his seat and down the hill. Ralph and Sharon clung to each other as they made their way down the slippery slope to the car that awaited them. The twins had yet to shed tears, where I could see anyway, but I'm sure they understood what had happened.

I heard the tolling of the bell from the little chapel. It sent chills up and down my spine. It echoed from mountainside to mountainside and cascaded down the valley between them. It was announcing to all that could hear its mournful chime of sadness that God had called another child home. It was tolling the announcement of the home-going of Bessie and little John Daniel.

My gaze went to the willow tree again. I felt compelled to go there. I picked two roses from the gravesite, and walked to the tombstones beneath the tree. Snow and ice had already covered them. They looked like soldiers standing at attention, keeping guard over God's children. The snow had begun to fall in huge wet flakes. The wind was whipping them this way and that. It was hard to see the bottom of the hill where Daniel went to help people get to their vehicles.

I knelt beside the grave of my brother first. The little tombstone was severely worn from many years of weather. The indentation cut in the stone was barely visible. There was a little lamb perched on top of it, weathered and black from all the years of being subjected to the elements. I traced my finger over the words "Jonathan Lee Edwards - loving son of Thomas and Mary Edwards - went to be with Jesus on September 23, 1947." I placed first the rose gently beside the tombstone, then

145

arose and went to the next grave. "Precious Father, Loving Husband, Gone to be with Jesus." I read out loud as I ran my hand over the words. Where has time gone? I thought.

I let my mind wander back to happier times. Mama had said that he changed a lot after I was born. He was the happiest when I was sitting on his lap or doing little dances for him. I remember twirling and prancing to the guitar music as he played, singing out-of-key songs with him as he strummed away. He always told me how much he loved to hear me sing. When company would come he would make me sing for them. How tortured they must have been, I thought. I couldn't stop the tears from rushing down my frozen cheeks, though I tried hard to stop the flow. I lay my head over against the gravestone and let all the sorrow escape that had been bottled up in me for such a long time. I wouldn't let it stay anymore. Sorrow was an unwelcome visitor that had come and occupied my being for way too long.

"I'm sorry I haven't been there for Mama like I should have," I said to my daddy's tombstone. "I promise you that from now on I'll keep better check on her," I wailed through my sobs.

I felt Daniel's hands go onto each of my shoulders. He leaned down and whispered softly in my ear.

"The weather is getting pretty bad. I think we should try to get to your house soon. That is, if you're ready," he said, lifting me to my feet.

What a stark contrast the snow made against his black curls, I thought as I turned and looked up into his handsome face.

THE MOUNTAINS CALL MY NAME

"I'm ready," I said. "This was something I needed to do. I haven't been to the grave since we buried Daddy. Of course I know he isn't here. Isn't it silly how we talk to headstones? It's as if they were real people," I said, smiling.

He brushed the snow from my hair and the tears from my face.

"Your nose looks like Rudolph's. Come on. Let's get in the car where it's warm."

He led me past the men covering Bessie's grave with the cold chunks of dirt. They were singing, keeping time as the cadence of the shovels hit the dirt. Each throw punctuated the words they were chanting.

How beautiful, I thought as we were going down the hill. The tune was unfamiliar to me, but hauntingly beautiful.

We picked our steps carefully, watching for slick spots. Daniel held me all the way down, and we reached the car without incident. Having deposited me in the van, he proceeded to clean off the windshield. He had started the engine so it would be warm when we got in. After cleaning a spot big enough for him to see, he hopped into the car with me.

"Do I have hands?" he asked, pulling off his gloves.

"Yeah, I see some," I said, reaching over to hold them in mine.

"Yours aren't any better than mine," he said, rubbing my hands with his.

THE MOUNTAINS CALL MY NAME

"Our next date is going to be under different circumstances," he said.

"I sure am sorry our getting acquainted has been such a fiasco. First I threw up on you then I cried and got all snotty."

"And threw up again," he added.

"I feel like all I've done is whine. I hate whining!"

"Did I say you were whiney?"

"No, but I have been." I promise from now on to try to act like I'm a mature woman with a life."

"Hey, I like the idea of you with a life. That's a good thing. And I like that mature woman thing. That sounds really interesting, but I like it when you lean just a little bit. I'm a sucker for damsels in distress. Like when you cry, I like the holding and comforting part."

"So you like to see me cry?" I asked.

"No, I just like the comforting part. So maybe I could just comfort with out you crying. I used to think God gave you to me when we were little. I thought you were my Christmas present. I wanted a playmate so badly that I asked Santa for one. Then lo and behold, there you were. I guess all our life I thought you were mine. I turned my back and you ran off with a salesman. While I was away the mice played and you ended up in some other guy's arms."

"You're so funny, Daniel. I wasn't in your arms to begin with. My heart was always safe with you."

THE MOUNTAINS CALL MY NAME

"I did a good job, didn't I? I always took good care not to hurt your heart," he said, still rubbing my hands.

"We made it, didn't we, Daniel. You are a doctor, and a good one. And I plan on getting back to my career soon. We have everything we dreamed of. Everything we worked so hard for, we got. Now what are we going to do with it?"

"Keep working hard, I guess. We still have to dream, because without a dream or vision we perish. That's what the Bible says anyway."

"I think I might be ready to dream again," I said.

"Good," he said, winking at me. "Now let's get this buggy headed for home."

We made it down the snowy hollow to my house without any problems.

"I'm going to walk you to the door and then I'm going to head on home," he said, opening his door.

"Won't you come in?" I asked.

"I really have to go. I've got some patients to see at the hospital before I go home. I would like to get all this done before dark."

"Next Thursday is Thanksgiving, are you going to be able to come over?"

"Yeah, I'm sure I can work it out. I'll call you. Now, get in before you freeze," he said, giving me a hug.

"No more headache or nausea?" he said, looking at me questioningly.

"No more," I said, smiling at him. "Thanks for asking."

"Is that you, 'Lis'beth?" Mama called to me as I came into the house.

"Yes, it's just me."

"Daniel didn't come with ya'?" she asked.

"No, he had a lot to do and wanted to get home before dark."

"How did everything go?"

"As well as a funeral can go. Everyone held up really well. Sharon didn't take the baby to the cemetery, but she did take her to the funeral."

"Did ya' make it up the mountainside okay?"

"Yes, the men who carried the casket were huffing and puffing and slipping and sliding up the hill to the gravesite."

"It's mighty cold outside, come and let me fix ya' some hot chocolate," she said, putting the kettle on the stove.

"I asked Daniel over for dinner on Thanksgiving, is that okay with you?"

"Sure, it fine with me. It'll be good to have ya for the holidays. How long are ya' goin' to stay?" she asked.

"I thought I might stay for a few days. It's been so long since I've been home. I was thinking about getting you a Christmas tree before I go back."

"There used to be some real purty ones up the holler," she said.

"I'll see if Daniel wants to help me after we have dinner Thursday."

"I was thinkin' about havin' a ham instead of turkey. Does that sound okay?" she asked.

"It sounds good to me. I love the hams you get from around here."

"It's gonna' be good plannin' dinner. What do you think Daniel likes?"

"Probably anything we fix. He doesn't seem to be the picky type."

Chapter Four

Time seemed to fly by, and before we knew it Thursday was here. Mama and I both got up early that morning to start on lunch. The ham baked all morning. The aroma was heavenly. Mama helped me make several things before she had to quit. She sat down in her chair by the window to read her Bible. I knew her nap would be forthcoming. The sun beaming through the window was intensified by the blanket of snow on the ground. Everything was ready for lunch. Daniel was due about 1:30. It was now 11:30, so I slipped off to take a quick shower while Mama slept. I was running low on clothing, having just brought enough for a few days. I would have to head home soon, or buy new clothes. I picked out a light blue sweater and black pants. Blue always made my hazel eyes look bluer. I pulled my hair back in a ponytail and tied a dark blue ribbon in it. I didn't want my hair in my face while I cooked. Satisfied with the way it looked, I went back in the living room to check on Mama. She was just waking up and seemed fresh and rested.

"I was just finishing my Bible reading fer the day," she said.

The jingle of the phone startled both of us. I reached it on its second ring.

"Hello, this is the Edwards residence, Elizabeth speaking."

THE MOUNTAINS CALL MY NAME

"Did anyone from there call for a doctor?" he asked.

"Why yes. I believe there was someone here that needed a doctor. Can you mend hearts, doctor?"

"That's my specialty. I'll be right there. Does the visit include food?"

"Yes, that's how we pay our bills. When may I expect you?"

"I'm on my way. I'll see you in about ten minutes."

I placed the rolls in the oven. They had risen to a perfect height. Mama hadn't lost her touch, I thought.

I set the table with her good china. The festive tablecloth was beautiful with its matching napkins. I washed the crystal goblets, making them sparkle with the light from the candles. It had been a long, long time since I had felt like entertaining. I was hoping that before the day was over, I would know more about my mom's health, after all, that was the reason Dr. Daniel was coming for lunch.

I heard the tap, tap on the door. Mama and I reached it about the same time. He was standing there with a bouquet of baby yellow roses. How could he have remembered they were our favorites? Maybe it was just a lucky guess.

"Come in!" we said in unison, laughing as we did so.

THE MOUNTAINS CALL MY NAME

"What a pleasant surprise having two beautiful ladies to welcome me," he said, handing the roses to Mama.

"Surely these ain't fer me," she said, smiling up at him.

"You can let Elizabeth look at them too," he said, smiling at me.

"I cain't remember when I ever got flowers," she said, holding them to her nose.

"Here, let me take those and put them into a vase," I said. "They will complete our dinner table. And Daniel, let me take your coat as I go."

I took his wrap, hung it in the coat closet, and went to the pantry to get a vase. I saw one that she used to put her cut flowers in during the summer, and placed them with care on to our dinner table.

"I will have lunch on the table in a jiffy. If you want, you can talk to Mama while I do that," I said, pointing him to the living room.

I took the rolls from the oven and placed them in the warming basket. I added them to the rest of the meal placed in buffet style on the kitchen counter. I lit the candles arranged at each end of the table, now adorned with a dozen little baby roses. Everything was beautiful, if I must say so.

"Dinner is served," I said to the two of them.

He got up and offered Mama his arm, then escorted her to the place of honor at the head of the table. As he pulled her chair out for her to be seated, I saw a gleam of joy in her eyes.

"If yer tryin' to impress me, Daniel Scott, yer doin' a mighty good job," she said as he seated her.

Then he came to my side and pulled my chair out for me.

"Grandma told me that I'd better remember all my manners today," he said, seating himself at the other end of the table.

"So far you're perfect," I said, smiling at him. "Did she send a score sheet?"

"No, but she'll be asking."

"Would you lead us in thanks for our food, Daniel? It's been a long time since a man has graced our table," she said,

"I would be honored. Dear Lord, we thank you for this food you have placed before us. Bless the hands that prepared it. Bless our time of fellowship. In Jesus name we pray. Amen."

"Thank you, Daniel. It so good to have you join us for lunch," Mama said. We took our plates to my makeshift buffet line.

The time passed by quickly, and we were soon making our way to the living room to recover.

"Would you care for dessert now, or do you want to wait?" I asked.

"I think I'll have to wait. There isn't any room left. Elizabeth, you mentioned a Christmas tree the other day. Would you like to hike off some of this dinner, and see if we can find one up the hollow?"

"I mentioned it to Mama the other day; she said she would like to have one. Is it okay if we go out for a while, Mama?"

"Land yes, child," she returned. "I'm gonna rest a little. I'm plumb tuckered out from all the cookin'. You two go on and find me a purty little tree."

"If you will excuse me," I said, "I'm going to go change into some jeans and my boots. I'll be right out."

When I came back into the room, Daniel was kneeling by Mama's chair taking her pulse.

"Are your pulse-taking skills weak?" I said, "Every time I turn around you're taking pulses."

"You know me, I can't help but practice. That's why they call it 'practicing medicine'," he said with a grin.

"How's she doing?" I asked

"She's doing great. Are you ready?" he asked.

I got our coats out of the closet as we talked.

"I decided to wear a toboggan I brought with me, and my warm gloves.

THE MOUNTAINS CALL MY NAME

"I'm ready. Do you have gloves and a hat?" I asked, handing him his coat.

"In the car," he answered. "Let's do it."

"I'll get an ax off the back porch. Daddy always kept one there. I guess we will need some way to cut the tree down."

"Yeah, I don't think a scalpel will cut it, huh?" he asked.

"No, the size of tree I want needs an ax."

"Where are we going?"

"Hop in, I'll show you."

We drove three or four miles past where we turned to come into our lane. I couldn't remember being there before.

"I don't remember this road," I said.

"I don't think you've seen it. It hasn't been cut too long. My Grandfather gave me this land when he died. He knew no one loved it here as much as I did. I haven't had much time to work on it. It actually meets your family's land at the top of the mountain behind your house."

"Was this the land we used to hike to when we were little? I don't think I have ever been in more trouble than the day we hiked up there and got lost. We were gone for almost a whole day. Do you remember? That's the closest Daddy ever came to spanking me.

157

THE MOUNTAINS CALL MY NAME

"It was etched in my mind, never to be forgotten. I thought he was going to whip me, too. But I was never so glad to see anyone in my whole life. Angry or not, your father was a sight for sore eyes to me. I was scared to death."

"But you never let on. You led me to believe you knew exactly where we were at all times."

"I could make you believe anything. It wasn't cool to be scared. I had to protect you even if I didn't know how, so I pretended to know where we were."

"I've never been on this side, have I?" I asked.

"Yes, but you saw it from a different angle. I used to come here with Granddaddy and hunt. He loved it here. There is a clearing at the end of the hollow that used to have some real pretty trees on it. I thought we could look there. We can drive almost to it. There is a little hiking, but not much."

The snow hadn't melted very much back among the trees, but his van had four-wheel drive and made it through okay. The traction was actually good where the snow hadn't been packed down.

"This may have been a bad idea," he said, gripping the steering wheel with both hands."

It wasn't long before we saw the soft sunlight in the clearing beyond the forest. We bumped, chugged, and finally slid to a halt right before the little meadow opened up.

"This is the end of the road, literally, the end," he said, "This is as far as I got before I quit. I figured I could do it later."

He pointed up to the top of the ridge where the tree line was mixed with thick pines and hardwood trees.

"One day I'm going to build me a house on top of that mountain. I come up here and dream about it sometimes. I do some hunting up here, too. Granddad couldn't walk very far as his cancer progressed, so I built him a road. He liked to come here at the edge of the forest and watch for deer coming down out of the mountain."

"You did all of this just for him?"

"Well, like I said, one day I plan on building a house. There are bunches of blackberry briars up there on the ridge right before the forest line starts. The berries get as big as my thumb."

"Daniel, you have your own hollow. You have to give it a name. You can't have a hollow with no name."

"How about 'Daniel Holler'?"

"That sounds like someone yelling for help. It has to be something more original," I said.

"I haven't given it much thought. Maybe I'll let you name it."

"Okay, I'll give it some thought."

He grabbed the ax and started up the hillside toward the ridge. The snow was still deep and crusty. I trudged on up the hill, trying to put my feet in Daniel's tracks. I quickly grew tired of trying to match my steps to his.

"Do you feel like climbing up there to that clump of pines?" he turned and asked.

"Sure, I just need to stop and get my breath. Lunch is pushing on my diaphragm and I have short legs," I said.

"You didn't eat enough to feed a bird," he said,

"You just didn't notice," I said.

"Let's sit here on this old log for a minute. I need some rest too," he said.

"I never knew your Granddaddy that well, not like I did your grandmother anyway. He was always out farming or something when I was around," I said.

"He loved the outdoors. He hated it when he was driven indoors because of the weather, and later on, because of his health. When the cancer got him down to where he couldn't get out anymore he just gave up his will to live. The life was just sucked out of him. Grandma tried her best to make things better, but there wasn't anything she, or anyone else, could do. That's when I made this road up here. It helped him for a while. I could see that little sparkle in his eyes. When he saw a family of deer come down to the meadow you would have thought it was Christmas. I brought him up here as often as I could. I loved watching him watch this place."

"Does it make you sad to come here?" I asked.

"No...well, maybe a little, but I choose to remember the happiness we shared here. Sitting, with him drinking in this beauty, is what I remember. He was such a brilliant man. He only completed fourth grade, but he was so smart. The wisdom he imparted to me will never be forgotten. The things I learned from him would far surpass my book learning."

"Like...?" I asked.

"Like how to treat a woman, if I ever get one and how to make wise decisions. I could go on and on, but the wisest thing he taught me was to always put God first. In all you do, put God first."

"How do you know how to do that?" I asked.

"Always pray about things. No matter how small or how big, just pray."

"How do you know when it's Gods answer, and not your own?" I asked.

"There's a peace that is deep inside you. The Bible calls it 'a peace that passeth understanding'. You just know."

"I've wanted that peace for a long time. I just didn't have the strength to find it. I felt too weak to pray. I couldn't feel God in my life," I said.

"You have to let go of the things that make you sad. Not necessarily the thoughts of David, but the tragedy of it. I think you're afraid to move on. As long as you can keep him in your thoughts it keeps him in the present. Maybe there's a little guilt about putting him in the past."

"Why would I feel guilty?" I asked, questioning him.

"Well, perhaps, a feeling of unfaithfulness to him, or to his memory anyway. Do you feel guilty being here with me?" he asked.

"No, I feel very comfortable. You're like an old shoe."

"Well, thanks. I feel so much better now," he said, acting humiliated.

"You know what I mean," I said, hitting him on the arm.

"Yeah, I do. I feel the same with you. I don't have to put guards up."

"You put guards up?" I asked in surprise.

"Well, I guess I do. You just never know the intentions of people. I don't like opening up my heart. If I don't give it away I don't have to mend it when it gets broken."

"But, Daniel, you are keeping yourself from the most exhilarating experience of your life. Love is so wonderful."

"Look what it's done to you," he said, "is it wonderful now? You're a good example of why I don't want to go there."

"But I had ten years to love and be loved."

"And the rest of your life you'll live with regrets. I choose what I can control. My practice, for instance, I love my practice. I love the people I care for, and my friends."

"I wish you could feel the total envelopment of love. It just grabs you and takes your breath away. It swallows you up, this thing called love. I don't have any regrets about falling in love, just about losing it."

"Like the love you had with David?" he asked.

"I wouldn't want you to fall in love with a man," I said, laughing.

"I have felt love like that before, Elizabeth. A long time ago. I didn't handle it very well though and I lost her and my heart," he said, picking up the ax.

He was already heading up the hillside to the pine trees.

"Let's go, lazy bones," he said, calling to me over his shoulder.

I was going to question him about this mysterious woman, but his body language told me the subject was closed. Of course, I hadn't been around him for ten years. I was sure there was a lot I didn't know about my childhood friend.

"How about this one?' he said, standing beside a little scrubby cedar tree.

"No, it's too little. How about that one up there?" I asked, pointing up the hill.

"I don't think that one will fit in your house. Maybe if we could cut the top out it would work," he said.

In several chops of the sharp axe, the big tree fell. It landed with a swish in the white snow. We did an eyeball measurement and he cut the top out of the tall tree.

"I think I might get a little one for my office. I think it would be nice to come in to the doctor's office and see a little bit of Christmas," he said, heading for the little cedar tree.

"Daniel, not that one it's ugly. You need a pine not a cedar. Look behind you, that one's cute." I said, pointing behind him.

He turned and looked in the direction I was pointing.

"I'll get it if you will help me decorate it," he said.

"I'm going home Sunday. It will have to be before then."

"I thought you were going to stay awhile," he said,

"I have, almost two weeks now. I need to get back home. I also need to check about going back to work at the hospital after the first of the year. I'm going to do what you said about getting on with my life. I've spent my last days in the past."

"Will you be back for Christmas?" he asked.

"I plan on it. After putting up this tree for Mama I would hate to miss being here for her. I promised my daddy when I was at his grave the other day that I would watch after her closer. So I plan on being here for the holidays."

"That's good," he said, "I was hoping you wouldn't stay away."

We pulled the trees down the hill to the van. Daniel had a rope in the back to tie the trees on top. It was getting close to dark when we finally made our way back up the hollow to my house.

"Sorry I'm not going to have time to help you put it up. I'm expected at my house for dinner soon. My office is closed tomorrow, so if it's okay, I can come over and help you then."

"Sure, I'm not going anywhere until Sunday."

I hated to see the day end. It had been so good to be with Daniel. The afternoon went way too fast. When we arrived back at the house, he helped me get the tree to the back porch, and tied his back on top of his van.

"Daniel, I had a wonderful day," I said as he prepared to leave. "I forgot to talk to you about Mama, her health."

"We'll talk when you come to help me with the tree tomorrow. Happy Thanksgiving. I had a wonderful day, too," he said, calling over his shoulder as he got into the van.

I stood on the porch and watched until he rounded the curve. As I reached for the door handle, the door was already opening.

THE MOUNTAINS CALL MY NAME

"Did you find us a tree?" she asked.

I held the tree up for her to see.

"Daniel said he would come over tomorrow and put it in a stand for us."

"You'll have to go up into the attic and get the decorations down. It's gonna be a good Christmas after all," she said, reaching up to hug me.

"Yeah, I think it really is going to be a good Christmas."

I brushed the snow off my feet with the broom and followed her into the warm living room.

"Did you rest this afternoon?" I asked.

"I had a good nap. Would you like something to eat?" she asked.

"I think a snack would be good. How about you?" I asked, heading toward the kitchen.

"That sounds good to me."

We spent the rest of the afternoon and into the evening going through decorations from the attic. I don't know who enjoyed it most, Mama or me. We picked through the boxes one by one, not wanting to let any go unchecked. I even found some I had made in school. Mama had carefully wrapped each one in tissue paper, as if they had been expensive crystal.

THE MOUNTAINS CALL MY NAME

We were both exhausted and ready for bed at an early hour. We stacked the boxes of ornaments that we wanted to use in the corner of the living room. I placed the others back in the attic so I wouldn't have to face doing it in the morning.

Our backs were stiff and sore from bending over the boxes so long. I tried to do most of it by myself, but Mama insisted on helping.

The bed felt wonderful to my tired bones. The blanket was warm, and I wrapped myself cocoon-like in its softness. I let my mind wander back over the day I had spent with Daniel. How comfortable I felt with him. It was with the ease of our childhood friendship that we communed with one another. I had never, nor could I ever, forget what we meant to each other. For one long afternoon I had let myself do something I hadn't done for a long time; enjoy myself. I had actually forgotten my loneliness. I felt almost childlike being with Daniel again. Between Mama and Daniel, at long last I felt that the sun was breaking through the clouds.

Chapter Five

I slept harder and deeper than I had in a long time; wonderful, dreamless sleep.

It was 9:00 o'clock in the morning, and my room still seemed dark. I wondered if another storm front was moving in. I hadn't listened to the T.V. at all the previous day. Mama and I were so busy going through decorations that we didn't take time for anything else.

I lay in my warm bed and silently prayed for the day ahead. Daniel had promised to come by and help put up our tree. After a shower and breakfast I would call him. After all the talking we did I still hadn't questioned him about my mama. How foolish of me not to have asked sooner. He hadn't seemed overly concerned, and I guess he put my fears at ease. Today, I thought, I would have that long talk with him. Our time was so fleeting yesterday. It seemed like we had just started when it was over. I only had two full days left before going home. Mama was sitting in her chair by the window when I came into the living room. There in the corner my eyes, I beheld the most beautiful tree.

"Mama, when did Daniel come by?" I asked, surprised.

"He was here early this morning. He told me not to wake ya'. He wanted it all in place when ya' got out of bed."

"I must have been dead not to have heard him out here."

"He was quiet as a mouse. He did all the noisy stuff outside. I had more fun watchin' him."

"Did he say he would call?" I asked.

"No, he left a number beside the telephone for you to call. He said he would be at his office the rest of the morning putting up the office tree."

I couldn't wait to call. I felt like a child on Christmas morning. My hand trembled as I dialed his number.

"Hello."

"You're one slick little mouse. I didn't hear a sound. When I came into the living room I was so surprised."

"Do you like it?" he asked.

"Do I like it? Of course I like it, I picked it out, and It's even more lovely inside in its stand. The branches are so majestic."

"Your mom was so cute. She was tiptoeing around trying to help me and be quiet at the same time."

"I can just see her tiptoeing, she can barely walk. I'm sure you two were a sight to behold."

"Santa couldn't have done it better."

THE MOUNTAINS CALL MY NAME

"How does yours look?" I asked.

"Just as pretty as yours, only smaller. When are you going to help me decorate it?"

"Well, I'm going home Sunday, so it has to be today or tomorrow."

"How about tonight?" he asked.

"I think that would be okay if the weather doesn't get bad. Mama and I are going to decorate ours today. We worked the rest of the day yesterday getting out decorations."

"I spent the rest of the day eating. I could go without food for two days and not feel hungry."

"I bet you had a hearty breakfast."

"Actually, I got up so early, I didn't want to bother Mandy, so I went by the restaurant and had breakfast."

"I hope they don't remember who I am."

"They asked where the pretty doctor was."

"They called me a doctor?" I asked, surprised.

"I guess the scrubs you had on reminded them of a doctor, especially since you were with me."

"Back to tonight, I guess I can come help you. What time do you think would be good?"

"I was thinking about 6:00 o'clock. I'm not having patients today, but some of the staff is in doing some catch up work."

"That sounds good."

"Don't eat supper, I'm going to order a pizza, if that's okay?" he asked.

"Why don't you let me bring some leftover food from dinner yesterday. We had so much left. We could have a picnic as we work."

"I would like to come pick you up if you don't mind. I don't want you driving in this snow that's left on the ground."

"Sure thing, I'll have the food ready."

Mama watched while I decorated the tree. We put everything on but the star, we saved that for Daniel. We decided that he worked so hard putting up the tree we would give him the honor.

I saw his headlights shining up the driveway. I had been so excited for him to get here. The tree was all ready to turn the lights on, just in suspended animation until he could put on the star. I didn't wait for him to knock on the door. I was standing on the front porch when he pulled into the driveway.

"Are you ready?" he asked, coming up the steps.

"Not quite, you have to help do one more thing."

THE MOUNTAINS CALL MY NAME

I led him into the dark living room where Mama had been waiting.

"We decided we would let you put the final touch on the tree."

I handed him the star I had left laying out.

"The daddy always puts the star on."

"Well, I guess that rules me out," he said,

"A man then. Does that qualify you?" I asked.

"The last time I checked I was. I'm touched that you would ask," he said, taking the star from my hand. "Where do you want me to put it?"

"On top, of course," I said teasingly.

"Do you have a ladder, or a step stool?"

I went out on the back porch and brought him a stepstool.

"Here you go," I said, putting the stool beside the tree.

I steadied him as he climbed to the top.

"I'm glad you picked one with a straight top in it. Stand back and see if it's standing right," he said.

"Okay, don't fall while I do it."

"Don't worry, I'll be fine."

THE MOUNTAINS CALL MY NAME

"Perfect," I said. "Now, if you could plug it in to the strand of lights so we can turn it on, that will be great," I said.

He fumbled through the branches hunting for the outlet. Finally he found it hiding at the back of the tree.

"Okay everybody, this is it," I said.

I flipped the switch on the main cord and the tree lit with a beautiful rainbow of colors.

Mama was so excited. The twinkle in her eyes matched the blinking of the lights.

"It's been a long time since we had Christmas in this house. It sure does feel good," she said, with a broad smile on her face.

"I'm glad I could be of assistance," he said, with a smile as big as hers.

I must admit I was grinning pretty big, myself.

"Well, if you're ready, we'll head on down to my place for another tree lighting. Except I don't have anything on my tree yet."

"We'll fix that, doctor."

I grabbed the basket of food off the counter and headed to the front door.

He took the basket from me while I put on my coat. I gave Mama a kiss on the cheek goodbye.

173

THE MOUNTAINS CALL MY NAME

"Don't wait up, I might be a little late," I said, heading toward the door.

"You two take all the time you need. I don't worry about you being out with Daniel. I'm going to sit here and enjoy this tree a little bit, and then I'm heading off to bed."

Chapter Six

It hadn't snowed much that day, mostly flurries. We pulled into the parking lot and went around to the back to a private entrance. All the cars but one were gone.

"Donna is still here," he said, "she's always the last to leave. I think she's a workaholic."

He got the food basket out of the trunk and walked me to the back door. I held the basket so he could sort through his keys to find the one to the door.

"I need to mark these so I don't have to fumble for it all the time."

After trying two or three, he got the right one, and the door opened into his private office. There was a lamp on the table in the corner that had a soft light burning in it. He took the basket of food and asked me to follow him. Down the hall to the right was a lunchroom for the staff. He opened the door slowly and peeked inside.

"Perfect," he said, "close your eyes and don't look until I tell you to."

"Okay, but don't let me trip on anything."

"Don't worry, I would just have to fix it, and I don't have time."

THE MOUNTAINS CALL MY NAME

He took my hand and led me into the room. He turned my shoulders so I would be positioned right when he had me open my eyes.

"Okay, you can look now."

"And what to my wondering eyes did appear..." I said.

I stood in amazement as I gazed at the remarkable table spread before me. I walked around it admiringly. It was set with a white linen and brocade table cloth. The raised satin swirls were a beautiful accent against the background of the linen. Fine white china rimmed in a gold band was set for two. Red napkins, trimmed with golden threads were folded expertly and put into the crystal goblets set at each plate. Silverware with filigree on the handles was at each plate. A centerpiece, made from white and red roses, sat on the table among different size candles and candle holders. The reflections from the flame of the candles were caught and held in the gloss of the china.

"I do believe the lady is speechless," he said.

"Daniel, I'm breathless, this is so amazingly beautiful. Did you do this by yourself?" I asked.

"Well, to tell the truth, I brought all the stuff down here this morning and Donna, my right-hand nurse, volunteered to fix this up today. After all, I had Christmas trees I had to put up."

About that time Donna came into the room.

"Does it look okay, Dr. Scott?" she said, with her hands spread out to indicate the entire room.

"It's a keeper," he said, giving her a hug.

"Donna, I would like to introduce you to Elizabeth, better know as Libby. Libby, this is Donna, whom I can't, and don't want to do with out."

We extended our hands to each other.

"It's nice to meet you. I'm a nurse too. I don't think I ever went to this length for the doctors I worked for. But I didn't work in a clinic, either," I said, smiling at her.

"He was just so pathetic, and I felt sorry for him. Plus I wanted it to look good. If you know what I mean."

"Like a woman's touch?" I asked.

"That's right, she said, smiling at me. Well, I'm gonna run. You two have a good time. I set out the decorations in the waiting room for you. I just hope Libby does most of the decorating," she said teasingly.

"Good night, Donna, don't come back until Monday. Tell the staff I want to meet them at 7:00 o'clock sharp. It's about the Christmas tree angels. I need the names of the families we're going to help. I'll need all of you to help put names on the back of them."

"It's as good as done. I already have angels cut out, and have ribbons on them so we can hang them."

"Go on, get out. I have a date," he said, pushing her to the door.

THE MOUNTAINS CALL MY NAME

He took me by the arm and led me back to our makeshift dining area. He proceeded to pull my chair out for me to be seated, and took my napkin and laid it across my lap. He went to the refrigerator and got out a bottle of sparkling white grape juice and expertly filled first my glass, then his.

"Do you want me to help you do something?" I asked.

"This is your night. You just enjoy," he said, smiling down at me.

He got the basket and put the bowls of food one by one onto the table. I had put in several dishes from the day before which I had warmed right before he came by to pick me up, and surprisingly it had stayed fairly warm.

After everything was placed just like he wanted it, he turned out the lights, and took his place in the chair directly in front on me.

"I've never seen you look more beautiful than you do at this moment," he said, lifting my hand gingerly. "I want everything to be perfect for you tonight."

"I don't know what to say." I said in a very soft voice. "I just don't know what to say, except, thank you, my sweet friend." I reached over and laid my other hand on top of his. "I will never forget this as long as I live."

"I want to remember just how your eyes catch the flicker of the candle, and how your sweet smile lightens this room more than the candles do. I don't want you to go away again," he said, not leaving my gaze.

THE MOUNTAINS CALL MY NAME

"These last few days have been wonderful. Renewing our friendship has been so good. But this... the candles, this room, what you just said about my eyes and the candle light...its... it's... I've never seen you be so romantic. You took me by surprise."

"I did, didn't I?" he said with that impish little grin he has.

I nodded my head in agreement, my smile matching his.

"You amaze me. I thought I could read you like a book, but I've never read this page before."

"I got to thinking about you leaving on Sunday, and I wanted to do something to make you remember me and this place. It's been so much fun catching up."

"It has, hasn't it? We've gone through a birth, a death, a funeral; and now we're having a beautiful candle lit dinner. I can assure you that I won't forget this anytime soon."

"Let's eat while everything is still at least a little warm," he said, letting go of my hand.

"Okay. It sounds like a good idea to me."

He had soft music playing on the office radio. Christmas songs were already being broadcast. They were relaxing, and so peaceful. Several times throughout our meal, I caught him looking at me, as if trying to see what I was thinking. If he could have read my mind I probably would have blushed. I had never told him how incredibly handsome I thought he was. His dark curls were always a tad unkempt. There inevitably seemed to be one hanging down on his forehead. His eyes were a crystal, liquid blue, and he had long, dark lashes that a girl would die for. I'm sure many a young lady had noticed what I was taking in at this moment. Funny how we had spent our youth together and I had never let myself look at him the way I was at that moment. The love we had for each other was one of mutual respect and admiration. Daniel was safe for me when we were growing up. Our dreams were the same. He had changed along the way, now his dreams were my nightmare.

I felt butterflies in my stomach. My heart was racing. I had felt that way when David first started coming to visit me. Those stirrings were familiar yet strange. Was it possible that Daniel could affect me like that? He wasn't looking at me like he did when we were 15 years old. He was looking at me like a man looks at a woman and I liked it.

"You look a million miles away. What are you thinking?" he asked, interrupting my day dreaming.

His question caught me off guard and I almost choked on my tea.

"I was thinking what a nice dinner we were having."

"Is that all?" he asked.

"Do I have to say?"

He looked at me and nodded a slow nod, still staring into my eyes.

THE MOUNTAINS CALL MY NAME

"I was thinking about how much you've changed. You've grown into quite a handsome man."

"Does that mean I was homely before?" he asked, feigning hurt.

"Oh, of course not, it's just that I never studied your face before. We were always studying books. I've always thought you were cute. I guess I purposely didn't allow myself to think about how handsome you were."

"So, since we cleared that up, what else were you thinking?"

"What? Is this twenty questions?" I asked

"I was just curious that's all. You've been kind of quiet. I figured you were either in deep thought or I'm extremely boring."

"You're a lot of things, but boring is not one of them."

"That's good to hear."

"Okay, I was thinking about how you've been looking at me this evening."

"I'm sorry. I didn't realize I was staring."

"Its like you can see right into my soul. Might I ask you the same question, what are you thinking when you look at me like that?"

"I was thinking how beautiful you've become. I wasn't prepared to see this Elizabeth," he said, extending his hand to me. "When Grandmother Scott told me you were here, I had this mental image of you at eighteen. You grew up somewhere between then and now."

"Time does that, doesn't it? We are still the same, just in grownup bodies," I said.

"No, I beg to differ, we're not the same. Life has changed us both. I would hope for the better."

"I, for one, hope I've changed. I've been in my shell way too long. When you're in the eye of the storm you can't see the raging tempest around you. I couldn't discern how things really were. My life as I knew it had ended and I didn't know how to push past the storm wall. So I sat in the middle and let it rage around me."

"What do you want out of life, Elizabeth Mason?"

"If you had asked me that question a few days ago, I wouldn't have had an answer. But in the wake of Bessie and little Daniel dying, I realized I was in the land of the living not the dead."

"Now...?" he asked, letting his sentence drop.

"Now, I think I would like to become useful again. Maybe go back into nursing. Perhaps start a different career. I don't know, it's a clean slate. I feel as if I'm Rapunzel waking up from a long sleep."

"Pray about coming home, Libby. I want you to love this place the way I've grown to love it. I haven't seen you for years and here I'm begging you to come back. You mentioned that being back here these few days has changed your life. Having you here has changed mine."

"I will be back in a week or so. I'm definitely going to come home for Christmas. We'll have some more time then."

"I promised to talk to you about your mother," he said.

"Is it serious?" I asked with concern.

He leaned back in his chair and looked intently at me.

"She's getting older and needs you closer. Her body is naturally wearing down. I think you need to be closer to her too."

"I'm not that far away. I can be home in two hours, easily. Well, maybe two and a half."

"You're needed here. Your mom needs you close by. Won't you even pray about it?" he asked.

"No! Because, I just can't come back here. I'm scared of this place. I feel oppressed just thinking about returning. All the reasons I left this place are still here. The oppression, poverty, there's nothing here for me Daniel, nothing!"

"Have you felt oppressed being here with me?"

"No, its not you, Daniel. I've felt wonderful being with you."

"Look at me, Elizabeth," he said, taking my hand again. "What are you really afraid of? You can't be afraid of not having money. With your skills you can have any job you want. So poverty and oppression can't be it. The reason we ran away a long time ago still can't be the reason you're afraid now."

"I'm afraid to look at you, I'm afraid you'll hypnotize me if I do," I said, purposely keeping my eyes on the table.

"You're not serious?" he said, laughing at me.

"Not about hypnotizing me, but about what I'll see there."

"It is that hard to look at me?"

"No, it's just that I haven't had anyone look at me with such tenderness since David died. And...and I've never had you look at me like this."

"You just didn't notice. You were afraid to look then, too. You've always been afraid to let yourself gaze into my eyes."

"You really want to know what I'm afraid of? I'm afraid of an unknown factor. I can't tell you because I don't know. I've labeled it many things. I thought I knew all these years why I didn't want to live here, but now, I'm not so sure. Look at you, you're back here and love it. But I'm still scared to come home. I feel that if I do, things will change forever, and I'm not sure I can handle anymore life changing things. I'm still reeling from the last thing."

"I really didn't plan on this evening becoming so heavy. I just wanted to make you happy. I wanted to see your eyes light up when you walked into this room, and I did. I wanted to see you smile at me, and I did. I wanted your memory of tonight to change how you see me. I wanted to become a grown up friend not just a memory of what we used to be. I want your friendship now, Elizabeth."

"Daniel, you have all those things. I shall never forget this evening. And believe me; I do see you as a man. That's just a little bit of my problem. I don't exactly know what to do with these new feelings. I feel like a teenager on a first date. I wasn't expecting the range of feelings I'm having right now. I'm definitely not dead inside, as I once thought," I said with a little chuckle. "I'm very much alive, thanks to you. Twenty questions are now over, let's go decorate that tree of yours."

He came over to my side of the table and offered his hand to me. "This way," he said, leading me into the front office.

"Daniel! The tree is so beautiful. It looks larger than it did in the field."

"I've already put the lights on, but I'm not going to turn them on yet. I have some boxes of decorations that Grandma Scott gave to me. She said she didn't have any need for them."

We sorted through the boxes until we had just the right ones. The Christmas music still played in the background, getting us into the spirit of the season. My thoughts of the evening were weighing heavily upon my mind. These new feelings I was having for Daniel were different from anything I had ever felt for him. The butterflies were still flitting in my stomach. Everything was changing and I wasn't ready, or was I?

THE MOUNTAINS CALL MY NAME

Once we had the ornaments separated, the decorating went quickly.

Daniel turned to me and said, "Close your eyes, I have one last surprise for you."

I did as he commanded. I stood before the tree with my hands covering my face.

"Don't look until I say you can, or you will spoil it," he said.

I heard the noise of a box being opened and the rattling of paper. He surely was taking a long time. I thought to myself. I could only imagine what he was doing.

I felt him move up behind me. He placed his hands on my shoulders and said, "Okay, you can look."

The room was dark except for the lights on the tree. On top was the most striking angel I'd ever seen. Her dress was a confection of white gossamer, illumined from the light that was inside her dress. Her head was encircled with a golden halo. Her long blonde hair was a cascade across her shoulders and down her dress. She looked adoringly at the infant she held in her arms. Then, all of a sudden her wings began to flutter. It made me gasp to catch my breath, in surprise.

"Daniel, you've outdone yourself. Where did you find such a beautiful angel?"

"I got it from another beautiful angel, my Grandmother Scott. She was always searching for anything associated with angels. When salesmen would come by she was like a kid in a candy shop. Their catalogs were quickly grabbed by her. She was constantly looking for unusual things. This was one of her many treasures."

"A rare one, indeed. How did you come to have it?"

"It was in the box of decorations she gave me. I called and questioned her about it, and she assured me, it was no mistake. She wanted me to have it for the patients coming in to see me. She said it would bring joy to those in pain."

"I just had a morbid thought. What if one of your patients had a heart condition and the sudden flutter of the angel wings scared them to death." I said, not being able to contain my laughter.

"Ms. Elizabeth, I'm shocked to hear you say such a thing. But I have to admit, it is funny. Talk about ruining the new young doctor's business. I can see it now, 'While visiting Dr. Scott's office, Mrs. So and So died. It appears that she was scared to death in the waiting room by the sudden flutter of angel wings.'"

We were almost in tears we were laughing so hard.

"Listen...do you hear what is playing on the radio?" he asked, speaking softly into my ear.

I nodded, as he turned me toward him. "I'm Dreaming of a White Christmas," I answered.

"Would you dance with me, Elizabeth Mason?" he asked.

THE MOUNTAINS CALL MY NAME

Without waiting for an answer, he put his arm around my waist. I placed my hand in his extended one, and we circled the waiting room. With every turn, we moved closer together. I could feel his warm breath on my hair. I let myself relax in his arms, allowing the tension of the last few days to melt away. We swayed fluidly to the sound of the soft music, our bodies moving in sync with one another. It had been so long since I had danced. I let my head rest on his shoulder, drinking in the magic of the moment. The music stopped and he still held me close to him. Another song came on, and we continued to dance. He pulled back from me with just enough distance to look into my eyes. No words were exchanged, just the look that passed between us. Our smiles, conveying an unspoken message, that all was well.

I started to say something to him, but he placed his finger tip against my lips.

"Shhh...don't say anything,' he whispered, not now. He was pulling me back into his arms.

I obeyed like a child, resting my head upon his shoulder. He took his hand from my waist and moved it up my back holding me close to him. I could feel him run his fingers through my long hair. I was carried away to a magical place were all my problems seemed to disappear. There had been times in our younger years that he had held me, but it never affected me like this. I felt lightheaded as the adrenalin rush hit my system. When the song ended he released me from his embrace. He took my face and held it in both of his hands and kissed my forehead.

"It's getting late," he said, "I'd better get you home."

THE MOUNTAINS CALL MY NAME

"I turn into a pumpkin at midnight," I said, smiling at him.

He looked at his watch, "You're about an hour overdue. Its 1:00 o'clock."

"It's the angel," I said, pointing to the tree. "She's looking out for me."

We gathered the bowls and put them into the basket.

"I'll get this room back in order before Monday," he said, turning out the office lights. "I forgot the Christmas tree lights. Wait right here, I don't want you tripping in the dark."

Neither of us spoke about what had just transpired between us. The evening had been enchanted from beginning to almost the end. The same music was playing on the radio in his van, as was in his office. It was soft and beautiful, still holding us in its magic. His hand was warm as he held mine in his. This hand that cared for the sick, and comforted the weary, was now caring for me. I let my head lean on his shoulder, allowing the music and the warmth of the car wash over me. Once we got to my house, he walked me up the path to my door.

"Daniel, I had a wonderful evening. It was ...." I stood with my eyes closed, trying to find just the right word.

"I know... me too," he said, "I'll call you tomorrow." He leaned down and kissed me gently on my lips.

189

THE MOUNTAINS CALL MY NAME

He was gone in an instant, leaving me speechless, as he bounded off the porch, and to his van. I stood and watched as he drove away. My fingers touched my lips where his had briefly been. My heart was still beating rapidly from what had just had happened between us. I hoped Mama was sleeping; I didn't want to explain this right now.

Chapter Seven

"'Lis'beth?" Mama said as I entered the living room. "How was your dinner with Daniel?" She was playfully smiling up at me.

"It was good. We got the tree decorated. Grandma Scott gave him some nice decorations to put on it. The angel he put on top was so pretty. Every so often, her wings flutter. I wasn't expecting it and it made me jump."

"Did the food stay warm?"

"Warm enough," I said. He had his secretary, or nurse, I forget which, set the table. He had candles and fine china, flowers, the whole bit. I was really surprised."

"I think the doctor was tryin' to impress the lady," she said, still smiling that big smile.

"Of course he was. We go way back."

"I'm a thinkin' he's in the here and now, not the sweet by and by."

"Well." I said, feeling myself blush, "we talked about a lot of things."

"Are you ready for breakfast?" she asked.

"I think I just want some cereal," I answered. "Have you had breakfast?"

"We must have had the same idea. That's just what I had."

"Today's my last day here. What would you like to do today?" I asked her.

"Maybe we could spend a quiet day together, sit by the fire, just visit."

"That sounds good to me. I need to wash some clothes. I'll do yours while I do mine if you want me to."

"That's mighty sweet of you. Is Daniel comin' by?"

I felt emotion sweep over me at the mention of his name. My mind traveled back to the night before and the kiss he brushed across my lips. What was happening to me? I was acting so silly, over a mere kiss.

"I said, is Daniel..."

"I'm sorry; you were asking if Daniel was coming by? I'm not sure; he said he would call me this morning."

"Did he tell ya' about his house he built on the ridge behind his daddy's place?"

"Come to think of it, we've never talked about where he lived. I assumed he lived with his mom and dad."

"Well, if I ain't mistaken he had it built before he even moved back here. I guess bein' on his own fer so long

THE MOUNTAINS CALL MY NAME

he didn't want to move home. And of course Grandma Scott lives with them since his Grandpa died."

"What made you think about his house?" I asked.

"I was just a wonderin' if he'd taken ya to see it. I hear it's a beautiful thing. Got big glass winders in it, from ceilin' to floor. Miss Mandy takes care of him."

"Who's Miss Mandy? Do I know her?"

"Well, she 'bout raise that boy. I'm surprised you don't 'member her."

"Oh! That Mandy. I remember seeing her when I visited Daniel's. Why did she go to Daniel's house?"

"I think his daddy and mama wanted him taken care of since he was comin' back here to doctor. They didn't want him burnin' hisself out like Doc Adams did."

"And Daniel allowed that."

"I think, to tell you the truth, he was happy as a lark to get her. She was just like his mammy. Matter of fact, I think she calls herself 'Mammy' to him."

"I think you might have heard Mandy and thought they said Mammy."

I went into the kitchen and fixed a bowl of cereal. I was just about through when the phone rang. I heard Mama answer.

"I think she's through eatin'. Let me call her."

"I have it, Mama," I said, picking up the phone in the kitchen.

"Hello."

"Hi, beautiful, did you have as good a time as I did last night."

"I guess you could say that. You left me with a lot to think about."

"Yeah?"

"Yeah."

"You're still leaving tomorrow?"

"Yep, bright and early. I want to get home and get settled before dark. It gets dark so early now."

"I was thinking about asking you over to my place for dinner. I probably need to take those stitches out."

"Over dinner? That sounds real appetizing," I said.

"Well, I didn't want to send you home with stitches in. And I promise I won't do it at dinner."

"I'm glad you remembered, I actually forgot they're there."

"I haven't. So what about dinner? Mandy is chomping at the bit to cook for you."

THE MOUNTAINS CALL MY NAME

"Funny you should mention your place. Mama was just telling me about your house. I assumed you lived with your mom and dad."

"Please! That was one of my stipulations, no moving in with my parents. We would have killed each other. But they did make me take Miss Mandy."

"Isn't that like having your parents around?"

"Heavens no! She spoils me rotten. She always has. You would love her, Libby. She wants to cook dinner for us tonight. But I think she just wants to see who's been keeping me out lately."

"If it wasn't for the stitches I might object. Since it's my last day I should spend it with Mama."

"What if we made it a late dinner? Then she wouldn't know you were gone. I've got to see you before you go."

"Okay."

"You wanted to see me too, didn't you?"

"Yes." I said, letting my voice fall a whisper.

"Okay, this is the plan. I'll come over and stay with you this afternoon and then we can come here for dinner later."

"I think Mama wanted it to be just the two of us, you know, a quiet mother daughter time."

THE MOUNTAINS CALL MY NAME

"Okay, plan two. I'll come late and stay just a little. Then we can have dinner here."

"You aren't going to give up, are you?"

"No."

"Okay, plan two it is," I said.

"I'll tell Mandy it's dinner for two at Scott's diner."

"I have a lot of packing to do today anyway."

"Elizabeth, I really had a good time last night."

"I did too."

"Everything?" he asked, imploring.

"Everything."

"I'll see you later," he said.

"Okay, bye."

I heard the phone click on the other end, and went into the living room to tell Mama about my dinner plans.

"How's Daniel?"

"He's good. He wants me to come to his house for dinner tonight. He needs to take out these little stitches."

"Well, I think if the young doctor wants you to dine, you should."

THE MOUNTAINS CALL MY NAME

"It's going to be a late dinner, so you won't miss me that much."

"I don't mind at all. You two have a wonderful evening. He sure is spending a lot of time with ya'."

"We're just catching up for all the years we missed."

"It's good to see yer goin' out."

I went to the back porch and brought in some wood for the stove. The fire felt good on this chilly day. My open suitcase lay before me on the bed. I thought I would be more excited about going home. It seemed like a lonely place to go to now. I was definitely ready to get busy doing something. The ray of light that I saw through the darkness seemed pretty good. It's strange how we get accustomed to the darkness. Somehow it doesn't seem as dark as it really is. When compared with the light, we see how dark it really is. I gathered my dirty clothing and went to put them in the wash. My mind kept going back to the night before, especially the kiss. It was so light, and sudden, but explosive in my mind. I was very aware that our relationship was going a different direction. My body was telling me one thing and my mind another. Could Daniel be more to me than just a friend? I had never allowed myself to think of him in any way other than that. Could he have changed his feelings for me that quickly? My mind was spinning with questions. I guess tonight would be a further exploration of the night before. What answers could I give him when I don't even know the question? I was moved by him. His closeness made me feel alive inside. For those few short hours, David never once entered my thoughts. It was his kiss and his closeness that lingered. Just a few short days ago, David consumed my waking moments. Now they were being crowded out by another. Daniel was right, I thought; I do feel like I've been unfaithful to his memory. But this new feeling seemed right. Was it because of my familiarity with Daniel? My guard was down and he waltzed me into a place I had never allowed him to take me before. A place I had shielded him from, not consciously of course. How could I have been with him all those years and not have seen him as I did last night?

Questions...questions...

I was brought out of my daydreaming by my mama calling my name.

"'Lis'beth, what would you like for lunch?" I heard her call from the living room.

"Just a minute, I'll be right there," I answered.

I couldn't believe it was already lunch time. The day was passing by too quickly.

"What did you say?" I asked.

"What do you want for lunch, honey?"

"I think just a sandwich. How about you?" I asked.

"I'm not very hungry right now, but you go ahead. I'm still full from breakfast."

I fixed myself a sandwich and joined her in the living room while I ate. I wasn't very hungry either, but still ate a little. I knew that dinner would be late and I didn't want to be too hungry.

THE MOUNTAINS CALL MY NAME

"I washed your clothes with mine. I'll fold them and put them away for you. Are you sure you don't mind me going to Daniel's?" I asked.

"No, I want you to tell me if what his grandmother said is true about the winders. I ain't ever seen no winders that big."

"I'll remember every detail and share them all with you."

"All of them?" she asked, smiling.

"All of them."

"'Lis'beth," she said, looking more serious. "It's time for you to move on. David wouldn't want ya to be alone the rest of yer life. Yer young and beautiful and have a lot of years ahead of you."

"Mama, what about Daddy, wouldn't you feel guilty about a new relationship in your life?" I asked.

She laughed out loud at my question.

"Oh, child, can you imagine an old woman like me with a new man. I'm way too old to be ponderin' about a man."

"You know what I mean, and by the way, I've heard of older women than you getting a new man," I said teasingly.

"I wouldn't know what to do with one."

"I don't think you're so old you've forgotten."

THE MOUNTAINS CALL MY NAME

"I promised the Lord if he helped me get through the one I had I wouldn't take on another one," she said, laughing again.

"But you, 'Lis'beth Ann, you are a vibrant young woman. There is a whole nother life for you. You'll never ferget David, but you've got to have a new vision. The old one died, and ya cain't resurrect it. Ya cain't die with him, even though ya tried. All you can do is put it in a special place and move on. It's been three years. Ya been grievin' long enough, baby girl."

I went and knelt before her and lay my head in her lap. She stroked my hair like she did when I was little.

"I love you so much, Mama. I'm sorry I haven't been here more. It wasn't because I didn't love you."

"Don't ya think I know that? I'm yer mama, I knowed why. I just missed ya company."

"I'm going to change that. I'll be home more often, I promise."

"It's been so good havin' ya here."

I sat there at her feet a long time, feeling the strokes of her hand on my head. Letting myself be her little girl for a while.

"Yer wound is all but healed," she said, I can see a lot of new hair. Daniel did a good job fixin' it. It's barely noticeable."

"Don't tell him, he already has a big head."

THE MOUNTAINS CALL MY NAME

I heard the buzzer on the drier, and excused myself to empty it. I brought the basket of freshly dried clothes and dumped them on the couch.

"Let me help ya."

She took some on her lap and we worked on the pile together.

"'Lis'beth, I hope ya don't ever stop lovin' me."

"Why would I do that? There's nothing in this world you could do to make me not love you."

"Promise me ya'll always love me."

"I promise I'll always love you, you silly little woman. Why would you even have to ask?"

I worked off and on the whole afternoon packing what I could into the car. I hadn't moved it since I parked it there. I guess it still worked. By the time I finished, it was already beginning to get dark out. I turned on the Christmas tree lights for Mama and me to enjoy. I turned on the radio, trying to find the station that Daniel and I listened to the night before. It wasn't long before I found the soft familiar music.

"That's purty music," Mama said.

She closed her eyes and leaned her head against the back of her chair. It wasn't long before I saw her nodding off to sleep. I left her to nap and went in to take a long, hot bath. The water was so inviting that I about fell asleep in its comfort. I loved the scented bath oil I put in the water. I lay there until the water got too cold to stay in. I had refreshed it twice with hot water, so I figured it was time to get out. I blow-dried my hair and let it fall loose around my face. I found an outfit I hadn't worn, and put it on. It was one of my favorites, a straight black sheath dress. It had both a scooped neckline and back. I wore a simple little strand of pearls. I just hadn't found the right time to wear it before.

It was still an hour before Daniel would arrive and here I was all ready and waiting. I hated counting minutes. I went into the living room to see if Mama was awake. I found her in the kitchen talking with Anna Belle.

"Hello, Anna Belle, it's good to see you. How are you doing?"

"I'm doin' fine Miss 'Lis'beth, and you?"

"I'm doing good."

"You look awful purty. Are ya goin' somewhere?"

"She's goin' out with the doctor again," Mama said with pride in her voice.

"Dr. Daniel?"

"Yes, that's the one. I'm going to his house for dinner."

"Ya know what I heard. I heard there's big winders in his house. They all the way from the floor to the roof," she said with wonder in her voice.

"I promised Mama I would remember all the details so I could tell her."

THE MOUNTAINS CALL MY NAME

"And me too?" she asked.

"And you too, Anna Belle."

She smiled from ear to ear. Evidently, my date was almost as special to them as it was to me.

"Yer Mama said I could spend the night. I been kinda lonely. I saw the tree lights a shinin' through the winder. It looked like stars twinklin'."

"I'm glad you're going to spend the night. I'm sure Mama will enjoy your company."

I saw the lights shining up the hollow road, and my heart began to beat a little faster. I went to the back to check my makeup and hair one last time. I sprayed a little of my favorite cologne on. I heard his knock on the door. I wanted to run answer it but I would give Mama the enjoyment. I heard his voice resonate down the hallway as I made my way to meet him.

"'Lis'beth, Daniel's here," she said, raising her voice.

"I'm right here, Mama," I said. "I'm right behind you."

She turned slightly and with an embarrassed little laughed said, "I didn't see ya."

Daniel helped her to her chair, and extended his hand to Anna Belle.

"Anna Belle, it's good to see you again. It's been a long time. I've heard a lot of good things about you."

THE MOUNTAINS CALL MY NAME

She put her hand in his and blushed at the attention.

"Thank ya, Dr. Scott."

"Don't forget to come see me if you ever feel bad. I'll treat you real good."

"Oh, I don't ever get sick. When I do, they's stuff that fixes me right up, good as new. But if it happens not to work, I be comin' to see ya."

"You've been a good friend to Mrs. Edwards. I appreciate it a lot. If you ever need me she has my phone number. I gave her a little sticker to put on her phone so she doesn't have to look it up."

"We kinda look after each other. The blind leadin' the blind," she laughed.

"Are you ready Elizabeth?" he asked, looking my way.

"Yes, I'll get my coat."

When I returned, he helped me into it, and with a round of goodnights we were out to his car. He had his own car this time, a pretty little sports car.

"I brought the limo tonight. The roads are clear now so I decided not to bring the big job."

"I love the red color," I said admiringly.

He made his way to his side and we were on our way out of the hollow.

THE MOUNTAINS CALL MY NAME

"Mom and Dad bought this little toy for me when I graduated from medical school. I decided to keep it when I moved here. I had to have some little flash of the city."

"It definitely is that."

"Mandy is ready for us. She has been so excited today. She's been cleaning and cooking all day. She even made me work."

"No, not you," I said, smiling at him.

"You're going to laugh when I tell you this. Mama would kill me if she knew. She said, 'you've got to tell me about his windows, I heard they are all the way from the floor to the ceiling.' Your Grandmother told her about it one day when she was in the store."

"Grandmother... it's hard to tell what she's told those old women about me. She probably tells them all my secret things."

"If you knew what she was telling them you probably wouldn't practice medicine here."

"I don't know, it may bring in more business," he said, laughing.

"Remember, until today I didn't even know you had your own place. As I told you, I just assumed you lived with you parents."

"That's what you get for assuming something. When you assume things, they're usually wrong."

"I'm beginning to believe it."

THE MOUNTAINS CALL MY NAME

We had driven a few miles farther than we had when we went to his Grandfather's property. I remembered coming here as a little girl to his birthday parties. I could make out the white fence even in the dark. It rimmed the road all the way through the meadow to where his parents' house sat. The road extended on behind their property up the side of the mountain to the top of the ridge. It was a classy, rustic-looking two-story log cabin. Big trees surrounded it. The paved road wound up behind the house before stopping in front of an attached garage. It looked the way I had envisioned a grand hunting lodge would be.

"Wow, Dr. Scott, you have good taste in homes, too."

"Well, I figured if I was coming back, it was going to be in style. I needed a house to match my car," he said, laughing at me. "No, actually I just liked this floor plan. A friend of mine is a contractor and we worked together to make it just like I wanted it. We talked a long time about the logs. I almost did it in brick, but I thought my granddad would like it in logs."

"He did a wonderful job. Do I know him?"

"You should, his name is Drew Waggoner. He dropped out of school in the eleventh grade to work with his dad."

"No way. Drew did this?"

"So you do remember him?"

"Of course I do. I just can't imagine him doing such beautiful work."

THE MOUNTAINS CALL MY NAME

"I'll show you all the neat little things he added once we are inside."

"I guess it just goes to show you don't have to have a college education to make it in this world."

"His college education was from his father. His daddy was well known in the area for his work too."

He came around to my side of the car and opened my door.

"Right this way," he said, pointing the way to the side door.

A large black woman met us before we could get into the house. Her wide smile showed off her beautiful white teeth.

"Daniel, don't go bringin' company in the back door."

"Mandy, this is Elizabeth Ann Edwards Mason; Elizabeth, this is my sweet Mandy."

"Don't go sweet talkin' me, Master Daniel," she said, wrapping me in her large arms. "It's so good to see you again Ms. 'Lizabeth. I 'member you comin' up here when Daniel was just a little thing. You sure growed up to be awful purty.

"Thank you Mandy. I remember you too."

"Daniel, take her into the front room. I'm not quite ready."

THE MOUNTAINS CALL MY NAME

Daniel led the way through the big kitchen to the unforgettable front room. Surely enough, there were the big windows Mama was talking about. I'd seen a lot of beautiful homes in my life, but I'd never seen one like Daniel's.

"This is lovely, Daniel. Why the huge windows?"

"I wanted to be able to see the wild outdoors. I see deer all the time. I put them in for my Grandfather. I would bring him up here and he would set for hours on end looking for animals out those windows."

"Come sit by the fire. Let me take your coat and hang it up."

"This is awesome," I said, giving him my coat, "you've outdone yourself."

"And *you've* outdone *yourself*," he said, looking at me admiringly. "You look stunning."

"Thank you."

We sat down on the sofa, facing the fireplace. The flames were snapping and crackling as if they were giving me their own warm welcome.

"I'm so glad you came. I might just keep you. Then you couldn't go home tomorrow."

"I'll be leaving first thing in the morning."

"I already miss you," he said, reaching over and taking my hand in his.

THE MOUNTAINS CALL MY NAME

"And I'm not even gone," I finished.

"And you're not even gone," he repeated. "I woke up this morning and knew that I had to spend some of today with you. Last night was wonderful. It was all I had planned it to be."

"You planned the kiss too?" I asked, smiling up at him.

"Well, actually I didn't think about what would happen last night. I was hoping we would have a relaxed evening. It ended up being a little more than I had dared to hope for. The kiss was just icing on the cake."

"You didn't wait around long enough for me to respond."

"Well, I wasn't sure what you would do, so I thought I would kiss and run."

"Okay, children, it's time to eat. Daniel, bring 'Lis'beth into the dining room."

I followed him into the gorgeous room. The small mahogany table sat before another fireplace with logs roaring with fire. It matched a larger dining table in front of the gigantic windows. The table was set in an exquisite array of lovely china and crystal. Baby yellow roses graced the middle of the table.

The room was dimly lit with white candles everywhere. There were two long taper candles in the middle of our small table. Everything was picture-perfect.

THE MOUNTAINS CALL MY NAME

The aroma from the kitchen was making my empty stomach long for food. Mandy brought a salad first with little toasted rounds of bread to eat with it. The water in the crystal goblets was chilled to perfection. She proceeded to bring dish after wonderful dish, finishing with a flaming 'Cherries Jubilee'.

"Mandy, everything was great as usual," Daniel said.

"Ms. 'Lis'beth, do want anything else?" she asked.

"You might call me a doctor," I said, smiling at her.

"I leave the doctorin' to Master Daniel," she said, grinning at him.

Daniel came to my side and helped me to my feet.

"This way," he said, "I wanted to wait until you came to light the Christmas tree. Mandy has been working on it all week. "

We went back into the living room. The tree was in front of the massive windows. It must have been nine feet tall. He picked up the switch by the tree and motioned for me to come and stand beside him. He placed it in my hand and showed me how to turn it on.

"You do the honors," he said, smiling at me.

I flipped the switch and the tree came to life. It was so terribly beautiful. And there, on top, was an angel that looked like the one in his office.

I was going to ask if she fluttered, but he beat me to the question.

"She doesn't flutter," he said. "Grandma only had one like that."

Mandy's eyes were large with awe. I could tell she liked it as much as I did.

The whole house was arrayed with seasonal decorations. Live balsam was hung in swags and wreaths throughout the area I had seen. There were big red bows adorning them. Snow could be seen past the Christmas tree through the colossal windows. It looked like a gigantic Christmas card.

"Would you like a tour?" he asked, motioning with his hand to the upstairs.

"Sure"

He led me up the winding stairs to the upper level. At the top you could look over a banister to the floor below. The tree was so tall that I felt like I could touch it, if I could only reach far enough. The garland was intertwined in the banister and strung with tiny little white lights. I suddenly became aware of the music in the background. He led me down the hall to the master bedroom.

This is my room, he said, leading me inside. It was decorated in dark green and burgundy hues. His desk stood in one corner with book shelves lining either side. There was a large leather chair in front of it. Lying open on his bedside table was a Bible with a red bookmarker inside. And the windows were the same floor-to-ceiling kind.

"Daniel, did you think about cleaning these when you had them installed."

"No, I guess I didn't think about keeping them clean."

"Are they everywhere? I asked.

"Only on the backside of the house. I would show you the master bath, but Mandy would kill me. She didn't have a chance to inspect it after my shower. I know you might be surprised, but I do pick up after myself. Come; let me show you the guest room."

He walked down the length of the hall and opened the door. It was a room done in cherry wood. There was a queen-size four poster bed with a canopy overhead. The bedspread was white, with layer after layer of ruffles flowing down to meet the floor. It was so high that one would have to have a stool to get into it. In the corner was a small writing desk. There was a vase of baby pink roses sitting beside an array of writing supplies. A small fireplace was situated in the middle of the wall. The carpet was a dusty rose color, picking up the rose colored pillows on the bed and window seat. This was the only room I had seen with a window seat. The windows in this room were actually a little smaller than the others. There were lamps on the bedside tables. Their shades had just a hint of rose color in them, causing a soft glow over the room. There was a bathroom in one end of it. I looked inside to find an old fashioned, footed bath tub. How inviting it looked.

THE MOUNTAINS CALL MY NAME

"Daniel, this is the most beautiful room of all. Did you have someone in mind when you designed it?"

"Actually, it was my mother who designed it. She said if she ever came to spend the night she wanted a beautiful bedroom."

"She lives at the end of the driveway. Do you really think she would come?"

"As a matter of fact, she has, many times. Sometimes when Dad goes on trips she will come and stay with me and Mandy. Oh, and Grandmother Scott comes, too. Her room is downstairs near Mandy's. They love to play board games together."

"Do you mind when they come to stay?"

"Heavens no, I enjoy having the house full. One day it will be filled with children, I hope."

"Be sure your bride knows that," I said, teasing him.

"She will, and like it." he said cockily.

"You seem awfully sure of yourself," I said, teasing him.

"You can see how many offers I've had. You see a bride anywhere?"

"Nope, not a one. Unless I count, I was a bride at one time."

"Sorry, it has to be my bride, and don't forget the house full of babies." he said, smiling at me.

"I wanted a baby so badly. I would have given anything to have one, but it never happened. I guess it just wasn't meant to be."

"It's probably not any of my business, but why couldn't you?"

"Why, Dr. Scott, are you taking my credentials?" I said, sounding shocked.

"I'm sorry. I guess it sounded like it, but I was just curious. You really don't have to answer that question."

"I know I don't have to, but I will anyway. David was the one with the problem. There was some kind of genetic problem. He felt really bad when he found out that he was the reason."

"That would be a real bummer. I hope and pray when the day comes that I want children that God will bless me."

"Show me the rest of your mansion," I said, changing the subject.

"Right this way."

He guided me around the banister to the opposite side of the house. There was one small bedroom at the end of that hall. The design was similar to the other ones. It was done with light colored walls and lighter oak furniture. A smaller bed was in this one.

THE MOUNTAINS CALL MY NAME

"This is the baby's room." he said, smiling. "People do want the baby on the same floor don't they?"

"I would, if it were my baby." I answered him.

"I told you I was building for the future."

"Is this why you built such a big house?"

"Well, I was thinking about resale value too. You remember I told you that I was going to build a house on Grandfather's land?

"Yeah, I do."

"I knew that land would be mine some day, so I built this home knowing I would be putting it on the market. I have a design in mind for my home someday."

"Can you tell me about it? I asked.

"Not yet, it's still up here," he said, pointing to his head. "It's in a secret place only for me to view."

"It sounds so mysterious."

"Not really, let's just say it's a work in progress. I haven't even told Drew what I want."

"If it's better than this one, I want to be the first in line to see it."

"So you like this one?"

"What's not to like?"

THE MOUNTAINS CALL MY NAME

"What do you like most?"

"The windows, it's got to be the windows. It's like you're outside when you're in."

"Like I said before, it was for my Grandfather, but everyone fell in love with them."

"Make sure the house on the blackberry ridge has big windows."

"You've just named my place; it will be 'Blackberry Ridge.'"

"Really...you would name it that?"

"Yeah, I like it, don't you?"

"It sounds pretty good."

We stood at the top of the steps and looked down on the floor below. It was such an inviting scene to look upon. The reflection in the window mirrored the fireplace and the lights twinkling on the tree.

"Come, let's go down and sit awhile."

He ushered me down the winding stairs to the overstuffed sofa before the fire. I took off my shoes and stuck my bare feet out toward the warming flames.

"Are you cold?" he asked.

"Just my feet. Pantyhose are not conducive to warm feet, especially in the winter."

"Why do girls do that? Why don't they just wear socks and boots?"

"I don't think that even deserves an answer, but I will give you one anyway. It's a feminine thing. We want our legs to look good, so we sacrifice warmth for fashion. Boots wouldn't go very well with this dress."

"I knew that," he said, smiling at me. "I'm glad you do the senseless things you do. We may wonder, but we like it."

I heard the phone ring in the background. It was only a minute until Mandy appeared behind the sofa.

"Master Daniel, it's the hospital calling."

"Excuse me, I have to take that."

"Ms. 'Lis'beth, could I get you something to drink? I have some coffee and some hot chocolate."

"Hot chocolate sounds really good."

"I'll be right back," she said, leaving the room.

I pulled my feet up beside me and lay my head down on the sofa arm to watch the flames of the burning logs. The sparks were shooting up the chimney with each crackle of the logs. This room was cozy, and with the warmth of the fire made me feel sleepy. All I needed to do was to fall asleep. How embarrassing, I thought.

Daniel entered the room and came to take his seat beside me. I straightened up and put my feet back on the floor. As he sat down, he put his arm around my shoulders and pulled me close to him.

"Sorry about that, I had to take care of that. I have a cancer patient with a lot of pain. The nurse said the pain medication was wearing off and needed permission to administer more."

"It was always hard for me to see patients suffer. We would get some sad cases in the intensive care. I wanted to just help some die. They were so close to going on. I don't mean killing someone, but when they are right at the threshold of death, you want to take away all the pain."

"I know how you feel. Speaking of taking the pain away, we need to get those stitches out," he said. "I'll be right back." He left the room, and returned in an instant with his medical bag.

"Are you going to do it right here?"

"No, come follow me into the bathroom."

I traced his steps down the hall to the bathroom. He motioned for me to sit on the commode, and turn my back to him. He took a little suture kit from his bag and in no time at all had the six stitches out. I think that's how many he said there were.

"It looks great," he said. "The master has come through again. You're a great healer."

"You can put that on my bill."

He cleaned up our mess and we went back into the living room to set before the fire.

I let my head rest on his shoulder, relaxing my body against his. Mandy came in with the steaming cups of hot chocolate.

"Excuse me, Ms. 'Lis'beth wanted some chocolate. I knows how you like it so good, Master Daniel. I brought you some, too."

She sat the cups on a side table and came back with a tray with legs and set it down in front of us.

"That's perfect Mandy. Thank you so much."

"Will you be needin' me any more tonight?" she asked.

"No, we'll be fine, and if we do need anything, we can get it."

"I'll be sayin' goodnight. Ms. 'Lis'beth, do come again."

"It was nice meeting you, Mandy. I hope to see you again sometime."

"Goodnight," she called to us again as she left the room.

"Goodnight," we returned in unison.

"I probably should be going soon. It's getting late."

"Don't go yet, its still early."

"Okay, I'll stay awhile longer just because you asked so nicely."

"Earlier in the evening you asked me about the goodnight kiss. I've wanted to do that since we were little, but felt you would laugh at me. I used to practice on the mirror in the bathroom. Real lips are so much better, and warmer."

"I wouldn't have laughed. I might have run away from you, but I wouldn't have laughed. I didn't want to give my heart to anyone."

"You did a fine job of that, Libby. I wanted to tear down the wall that was there, but I didn't have the courage to. I was afraid to let you know how I really felt."

I slowly turned to face him and saw that he wasn't joking. "Tell me now, Daniel, how did you feel?"

"Are you sure you want to know? Will you promise not to run away?"

"I'm leaving tomorrow, does that count?"

"As long as I'm not the reason you're leaving."

"You're not, that's my home remember?"

"Okay, here goes. I thought you were the most beautiful girl in the whole world. You were smart, funny and cute. You don't know the times I've wanted to take you in my arms and hold you. To kiss those cute little lips, and the tip of that turned up little nose. I used to dream of that. You told me so often that you wouldn't let any boy into your heart, I was afraid to tell you. I didn't want to lose you completely. So I took what I knew I had and didn't rock the boat. You must have suspected something, when you were the only girl I was ever with. When your attention was drawn to some new boy, or you started to pay attention to some of the flirts we had at school, I would get so jealous."

"Daniel, I think deep down I knew, but I wasn't going to allow myself to check and see. I was in my comfort zone with you. I could always count on you being there. We had the same dreams, or so I thought."

"Didn't you ever want to just lose it with some guy. I don't mean your virginity, just to be kissed until you couldn't breathe?"

"I wasn't dead, Daniel. But when I would think how nice it would be, I would get this mental image of factory work, babies, and a dead-end life. Ice water wouldn't have been as effective. It made me wake up really quick."

"What would you have done if I had done this?"

He slowly lifted my face to his. He lowered his head toward me, placing his lips to mine. For the first time in a long time I knew I was ready to move on. I couldn't keep from responding to his warm lips. They sought mine and I hungrily accepted. He kissed my face and neck and returned to my lips. I wanted more of this and he knew it. After a long while, I pulled back from him, visibly shaken.

"If this is what would have happened it's probably good we didn't," I said breathlessly.

He pulled me into his arms again and held me close to him.

"I've wanted to do that for such a long time. It was even better than my dreams were," he whispered into my ear.

"It's getting late, Daniel, I should be going."

"Not yet," he said, "his voice husky with emotion.

He turned ever so slightly and pulled me back to him. I closed my eyes and waited for him to kiss me again. The emotion that his kisses generated surged through me, and I knew where we could easily go if one of us didn't stop this train.

"Elizabeth." He said, holding me close to him. "I can say this without reservation. I love you, I have never loved anyone the way I love you. I've waited for you a lifetime and I'll be darned if I loose you again."

"Daniel, my life isn't here. My life is two hours down the road."

"What did you feel when I kissed you just now?" he whispered into my ear.

"I think you know I can't fake that. You definitely woke up all my nerve endings. It's been a long time since I've been kissed like that. I wasn't quite ready for what it was going to do to me."

"I can't believe you opened the door for me, Libby. You've never opened the door of your heart before, except to David. When I heard you wanted me to be in your wedding, I was so shocked; I often thought, how could you do that to me? Then I would remind myself that you didn't know how I felt. I wish I had tried to kiss you. Maybe things would have been different."

"Daniel, I had no idea, or I would never have asked you to stand up with me. I would never have hurt you that way," I said with a tear escaping my eye and running down my cheek.

"He held my face in both of his hands and kissed the tears away. "I know that, he said, gently kissing my lips again."

"I'm so sorry," I said between his kisses. "Things happened the way they were intended to. I fell in love with David because I was supposed to. I'm here in your arms tonight because I'm supposed to be here. I quit trying to figure life out a long time ago. From now on I'm just going to let it happen.

"All I ask is that you give me a chance to show you how much I love you. Don't lock me out or run away."

"And all I ask of you is that you give me a chance to absorb all the information I've received in the last few minutes. My head is still spinning with the passion of your kiss. I'm on this roller coaster, and I just hit the first dip and I'm headed back up the hill again. I need to catch my breath, before I start down the other side."

"I'll give you all the time you need. Just don't go marry anyone else while you're thinking about it. I want you to know this love thing didn't just happen today when I kissed you. I've loved you for such a long time. I gave up hope of it ever being reciprocated the day I saw you marry

David. Then all of a sudden, God threw you into my arms, and I'm not letting go."

"I really do have to go home tomorrow. I'll be back in two weeks. In the meantime, I do have a telephone."

The fire in the fireplace was crackling and sparkling, and the heat radiated over my body. Maybe it was the kisses that made me so warm. Whichever, it was so cozy being there in Daniel's arms. It felt so right. How quickly our lives change, I thought, the good and the bad. I was half sitting, half lying, in Daniel's arms. He was still holding me as close as he could. I laid my hand over his heart and could feel the pounding under it. His roller coaster had taken the dip too. I wasn't sure when I fell asleep; I was just aware of Daniel waking me.

"Libby, it's time to wake up. I probably need to get you home."

"I'm so embarrassed, I was afraid I was going to do that."

"Don't be, you felt so good in my arms. I didn't want it to end."

"I'll be back, Daniel, don't worry."

He got to his feet and pulled me up, straight into his arms. I raised my face to receive the kiss I knew was waiting. The passion of it electrified me. It had been a long time since I felt such desire for a man. Much to my surprise, and to Daniels, I'm sure, was my response to him.

"My dreams were never this good. I don't know what I expected this evening, but this far outweighed anything I had imagined. Your kisses were fabulous. I don't think I could have managed kisses like this at eighteen. God is so wise to have held you back from me," he said, smiling down at me." I need to go get your coat while I still can breathe."

When Daniel returned with our coats, he helped me into mine and then put his on. The car was so cold. Any heat I had managed to muster was now gone. We made the trek down the hollow to the main road. The trip to my house was over too quickly. I knew our last goodbye would be soon. He pulled into the driveway and leaned over to give me more kisses. He came around to my side and opened the door pulling me into his arms. Once again he covered my face, and neck with stimulating kisses.

"Be careful with my neck. I wouldn't want to have to explain passion marks."

"I always wanted to give a girl a passion mark to wear to school. It's like a badge of honor to go to school with hickeys."

"It's like everyone knows what you were doing. I wouldn't want to do that."

"Boys are different. They like to show off their work. Let me give you one," he said, pulling me into his arms and kissing my neck. "Let me check. No, not enough passion I guess."

"Or maybe I'm too frigid."

"Frigid is one thing you're not. You're actually pretty hot. Those little kisses sure warmed me up."

THE MOUNTAINS CALL MY NAME

It was like we were kids and just discovered the art of kissing. He led me to my front porch. Mama had left the front porch light off and all that illumined us was the glow of the full moon.

"You look so beautiful in the moonlight." He took my face in his hands and lightly kissed me again.

"One of us is going to have to say it, Daniel."

"It's going to be way too long before I can kiss you again. I always knew one kiss would never be enough. I know all of this is so new to you, but I mean it with all my heart when I say 'I love you'."

"I know you do, and I've always loved you too. It's just never been the way you love me. I'm not saying it could never be. I'm just saying you have to give me some time. But I know I really like what transpired between us tonight."

"I know you did," he said, pulling me to him and kissing me breathless again."

"I'll give you all the time you need. Just don't shut me out."

"Never again, Daniel, never again."

We kissed again long and deep. I knew this would be the last one, and we made it count.

"I can't say goodbye." He kissed me on my nose and bounded off the steps to his car.

THE MOUNTAINS CALL MY NAME

My heart was full. A song of joy was back in it. I didn't know God was going to answer so quickly. Talk about moving on. I guess I got a jump start tonight. I let my mind think back over the events of the evening. Daniel was a terrific kisser, or maybe it's just that I hadn't been kissed in such a long time. I forgot how good it could be. His timing was impeccable. It was going to be hard to leave him, now that we had ventured into this area. Two weeks wasn't that long. I can't believe I was already looking forward to coming back. I didn't think my mind would ever entertain those words. Never say never!

I opened the door as quietly as I could so I wouldn't wake Anna Belle and Mama. Anna always slept in the guest room down the hall from mine when she slept over. I tiptoed down the hallway into my bedroom. It had been such a long time since my heart was so full and my spirit so light. I turned on the dial to the electric blanket and slipped into my nightgown. I remembered that I needed to add some wood to the old stove. I slipped quietly back down the hall and filled the stove. I pulled the rocker up close to the stove and put a knitted throw around my shoulders. I heard the big clock ding out three soulful chimes. I couldn't believe the night had passed so quickly, but of course I had slept some of that time. I still felt warm and exhilarated from Daniel's kisses. When God decides to move you, you better hold on. I didn't dream that Daniel would be God's answer for my loneliness. Now what was I going to do?

Okay, God, you brought me to this point. I trust you to take me on, I silently prayed. I moved the rocker back away from the stove and made my way down the hall to my warm bed. I saw the light coming from under Mama's door. I knocked lightly and heard her, quiet frail voice respond.

THE MOUNTAINS CALL MY NAME

"Come in."

"Are you okay, I saw your light on as I was heading to bed."

"What time is it anyway?" she asked.

"It's a little past three."

"Are you just getting in from you date?"

"Yeah."

"It's good I don't have you on a curfew, young lady." she said, smiling at me.

"Come, get in bed with me. I want to know everything that happened."

"Everything?"

"All of it."

"Let me turn out the light."

"You just don't want me to see the glow on your face. Start with the winders. Was it true what I heard?"

"Yes, the windows were from floor to ceiling. Actually there were two levels of windows. One for the lower floor and one for the top level. He had a Christmas tree at least nine feet tall placed in front of it decorated with the most beautiful ornaments. He let me be the first one to light it. Mandy was as excited as I was."

"So Mandy is with him."

THE MOUNTAINS CALL MY NAME

"I believe she was the daughter of the Scotts' maid. She worked along side her mom. When Daniel returned and built his home, his mother insisted she go be Daniel's caretaker, as if he needed one. So that's how she ended up there."

"I remember her and her mama was like family to 'em. They been with 'em ferever. It just seems right that Mandy'd end up at Daniel's. She adored that boy."

"He showed me the whole house. It's his own design, you know. He even had a room for a nursery, and had an intercom system put in so he could hear the baby in the master bedroom."

"It looks like he was plannin' fer the future."

"Anyway, Mandy prepared a wonderful dinner. We ate by the fireplace in the dining room. She had this small dining table set right by the fire. It's hard to relay just how unique it was."

"It took you until 3:00 to eat. She musta had a lot of courses," she said with a little chuckle.

"We sat by the fire for a long time. Mandy brought in some hot chocolate. I got so cozy and warm I fell asleep, and Daniel didn't want to wake me up."

"So ya'll just sat by the fire and slept?"

"We talked a lot. And there's something I need to tell you."

"I bet I can guess, but I want you to tell me."

THE MOUNTAINS CALL MY NAME

"He kissed me, and I kissed him back."

"I would have been surprised if you hadn't. Don't you think it's about time you thought about another man?"

"I just couldn't get past David's love. To even entertain the thought seemed like adultery."

"Daniel changed that, did he?"

"All of a sudden he was kissing me and it seemed so right. I didn't even stop to think about David. For the first time in three years I didn't think about David. All I could think about was Daniel."

"That's not a bad thing, child."

"Something else happened tonight."

"Is this somethin' you can share with yer mama?"

"Mama! Mama...not that! My goodness! What happened was, he told me he loved me, and that he has loved me his whole life. Even when we were hanging out together when we were in high school, he loved me then. He just couldn't tell me because he knew I wasn't going to go for the forever thing. I wanted to go away to school so bad, and wasn't going to let anyone or anything stop me."

"And David fit right in because he was already where you wanted to be, so you were safe with him. It didn't matter if you let your heart go to him 'cause he would take you away from here. Right?"

THE MOUNTAINS CALL MY NAME

"I figured he must have been the will of God for my life, and I still believe he was. But I didn't know how Daniel felt. He even stood up with me. How could he have done that?"

"Love makes you do things ya don't want to. You asked him, and he loved you enough to let you go. What good would it have done him to tell you then? It would have just ruined yer weddin' day. Yeah, he loved ya enough to let you go, and you returned to him. You know the old sayin' if ya love somethin' let it go, and if it's meant to be yers, it'll come back."

"I think, deep down, I wondered about Daniel when we were teenagers, but was afraid to venture down that road. I was afraid of loosing my dream. I don't really know what I feel for Daniel."

"What did ya tell him?"

"The truth, that I had loved him all my life, but not the way he loved me. After tonight I have to rethink all this. All I know is, right now I have joy in my heart. I prayed just a few nights ago and asked God to restore my joy, and help me move on. I guess He knew I was ready. When he wants you to move, you'd better hold on tight."

"I saw it in yer face when you first come into the room. If ya hadn't said a word I would a knowed. They's a glow about ya."

"Mama...?"

"What, sweetie?"

"Everything is going to be okay."

THE MOUNTAINS CALL MY NAME

"I think yer right. Stay with me till I fall asleep. We ain't done that fer a long time. I'm really gonna' miss ya. It makes me sad in my soul to think about ya goin'."

I could hear her sniffing, and knew she was crying.

"Shhh...go to sleep now. I'll be back before you know it."

It didn't take long for her to drift into sleep. I felt her body relax beside me, and her breathing was soft and deep. I slipped out from under the covers and tiptoed down to my room. The bed was oh so warm as I crawled beneath the covers. Sleep wasn't long from finding me.

I was awakened by the noises from Anna Belle's room. I heard her moving around. I glanced at the clock. Bleary eyed, I finally focused on the bedside clock. It said 6:00 o'clock. No wonder it seemed like I had just gone to sleep, I *had* just gone to sleep. I thought of how much I had to do to get ready to go, so I pulled myself out of my comfortable cocoon and proceeded down the cold hall to the shower. I was sure that would wake me up. When I finished and was dressed, I heard Anna Belle and Mama in the kitchen talking. I had just about everything packed, so it wouldn't take me long to get it done. I worked on that while Mama cooked breakfast. Anna Belle excused herself and went home early. There were things she needed to get home and do. As she was leaving, she gave me a hug and thanked me for coming.

"Don't forget to call me anytime you need me. You can call collect. I don't mind at all."

"I sho' will Ms. 'Lis'beth. I watch yer mama real close. Be careful now."

THE MOUNTAINS CALL MY NAME

"I will, I love you, Anna Belle," I said, giving her another hug.

I was all finished packing and went into the kitchen to have breakfast with her. She had full fare. Biscuits, ham, gravy and a panfull of scrambled eggs.

"My goodness, it looks like you're cooking for an army."

"I thought Anna Belle would be stayin', but she had to go on home."

We had just set down at the table when there was a knock at the front door.

"Anna Belle must have forgotten something," I said, rising to go answer it.

I opened the front door to find Daniel standing there.

"Well, hello," I mumbled.

"May I come in?"

"Sure, pardon my manners. I'm still half asleep. My date kept me out late last night."

"As a matter of fact," Mama said, "it was about 3:00 o'clock."

"Sorry, did we wake you?" I asked

"No, it was just one of my frequent wakeup times. I don't sleep so well," Mama responded.

THE MOUNTAINS CALL MY NAME

"Aren't those sleeping pills working I gave you?" Daniel asked.

"I ran out and didn't want to bother you."

"I'll make sure you have some before another night is here," Daniel answered. "How has your pain level been lately?"

"A little worse, I think."

"You might need to come in and let me give you a good checkup. I know it's time for some more blood work. It's been about a month since we did the last. As a matter of fact, I think you better come in today. You think Anna Belle could drive you."

"I'm sure she could. I'll ask her."

"Call me when I get to the office and let me know. If she can't, I know a lady that lives right near here that could get you."

"I don't want to be no bother."

"Remember, we've had some long talks about this. You need to listen to me."

"Okay, I promise I will."

"Excuse me for interrupting you two," I said, frowning," but can you tell me what's going on here. Is she sick, Daniel?"

"Don't worry, we have everything under control, don't we, Mrs. Edwards?"

THE MOUNTAINS CALL MY NAME

"Do I need to stay and bring her to you?"

"No, you need to get on the road. We can handle it," he said.

"You would tell me, wouldn't you, Daniel?"

"If you needed to stay I would be the first to tell you. But you do need to come back really soon."

"Two weeks, just two weeks and I'll be back."

"Daniel, would you like to stay for breakfast?"

"Sure, if you have enough."

"They's plenty."

"Then I would be more than happy to."

"I have everything packed and am ready to ride right after breakfast.

We had a pleasant time lingering over our meal. Daniel and I volunteered to do the dishes. Mama went into her chair beside the window to rest. We washed, wiped and swept everything we could find to delay my leaving. Daniel pointed in the living room to where Mama was dozing.

"Shhh...he said, putting his finger to his lips. "I've wanted to do this from the moment I saw you this morning," he said, pulling me into his arms.

THE MOUNTAINS CALL MY NAME

I willingly went. His kisses where sweet and inviting. We both were soon lost in the passion that flowed between us.

Pulling breathlessly away, I looked up into his crystal-blue eyes.

"Daniel, I don't know if I'm ready for all of this."

"Trust me, you're ready. I would know if you weren't."

"You really surprised me last night."

"And you really surprised me. I had no idea you would respond to me the way you have. I want you to know I don't do this with all the girls I meet."

"I don't even have to tell you that I haven't been kissed like this in a long time."

"I know that, and I respect that. I didn't want to rush you, but things sort of just happened."

"You don't have to explain anything. You don't see me running away, do you?"

"No, thank God. I hate to see you leave today, but I know you have to. I'll try not to make it more difficult than it is."

"Like coming over for breakfast?"

"I had to see you this morning. I couldn't let you go without seeing you again. Forgive me?"

THE MOUNTAINS CALL MY NAME

"You were so handsome standing there in the door this morning. I was secretly hoping you would come."

He pulled me close to him and held me tightly to his chest. I drank in the scent of his cologne as he held me. I would remember this as I made my way home that day.

"Your hair smells so good, and you feel so wonderful in my arms," he said, barely above a whisper.

"I'm going to have to go, Daniel. The longer I stay, the harder it's going to be to leave."

"I know," he said, still holding me close.

He was the first to pull away this time. I still had my eyes closed, not wanting to break the moment. The tears were so close to falling. I knew if I opened them they would escape. He kissed my forehead, my eyes and then, one last time, planted a long, sweet kiss on my lips that neither of us wanted to end.

When at last we had to part, he said he would go start my car so it would be warm when I left.

I went in to wake Mama to tell her I was leaving. I gently shook her arm.

"I'm sorry I must have dozed off," she said, giving me a sly little wink. "Help me up and I'll walk you to the door."

"You're a sly little fox," I said, smiling at her.

THE MOUNTAINS CALL MY NAME

She got slowly to her feet and we walked arm in arm to the door. Daniel was waiting on the porch to walk me to the car.

"Bye, Mama, I'll see you real soon. I love you, and listen to Daniel."

"I will, sweetie."

She waved to me as I made my way to the car. Daniel opened the door for me to get in.

"I'm not going to say goodbye," he said, gazing into my eyes.

"I remember coming up here, how I hated it. I hated every mile of it. I was already counting the days when I could go home. Now, I hate to leave. I've gotten so turned around. My head is spinning with all these new emotions."

The tears I had been holding back escaped down my cheek. Daniel took his finger and wiped them away. I saw his eyes misting, too.

"You'll be back soon. We can pick up where we left off. When I first realized that God was bringing me back here, I was going through the same emotion. The things I ran from my whole life were pulling me back with a vengeance. When I finally let myself surrender to the will of God, that's when the peace came. I tried to pass this doctor job on to someone else, but God wouldn't let me. Being here was God's plan for me all the time. But he first had to take me away to get me ready to come back. Does that make sense?"

"Yeah, perfect sense," I said. "I can't believe I'm getting ready to ask you this, but... would you kiss me one last time?"

"No! He said, smiling at me, all the while leaning toward me.

With each kiss he gave me, I could feel myself being pulled back to the mountains I tried so desperately to leave. I couldn't understand how things could change so drastically and so quickly. I still wasn't ready to accept what my heart was telling me.

"Scoot. That will have to last until you come back."

I got into the car, closed the door and rolled down the window.

"Daniel, pray for me. Okay? There are a lot of things I have to do when I get back home. Things I have to put away that I needed to do a long time ago. I can do it now. But it will still be hard. Do you understand what I'm trying to say?"

"I'm trying to, but I've never lost a mate before, so it would be hard for me to say what time frame is right or wrong. Everyone does the things they have to, or think they have to do, anyway. I'm doing better with the David thing because of where we are now. I actually hadn't thought about you and me because there never was a 'you and me', only a me. That sounds confusing, doesn't it? I guess I made peace with all that the day I stood by you at the altar. The man of honor, I guess I would be called, since a woman would be called the maid of honor. I wanted to be David so badly that day. I wanted to be the one you pledged your heart and life to. I felt you slip away. I saw how you looked at him and wanted you to look at me that way. I actually imagined for a brief moment it was me you were saying those words to, not him. You didn't have a clue, and I couldn't tell you. I waited too long and lost you. I had to get past you to be able to move on. I knew you had David, so I kissed it all goodbye, just regretting that I never did tell you how I felt. Work covers a multitude of feelings. I didn't have time to think about lost things. I put them all away in a neat little bundle, never again to be remembered. When Grandma told me you were here in town, I felt a rush of emotion. It resurrected itself from the place I had buried it. I knew, God willing, I would never let you go again without telling you what you meant to me. And look, God gave me another chance. And forgive me, Libby, for even thinking this, but I knew David was gone, and I might have a chance."

"There's nothing to forgive. You spoke from your heart. I hope I will be able to speak from my heart from now on."

I kissed my finger tips and gently pressed them to his. I saw the silent movement of his lips telling me again that he loved me.

Chapter Eight

Daniel followed me all the way to the entrance of the interstate. He blinked his light at me as my car turned away from his. I couldn't believe how fast the trip home was. I hardly remember driving. My mind was filled with thoughts of Daniel and how my whole life had changed in a few short hours. It's hard to believe it hadn't even been twenty-four hours since our first kiss. I could still feel him close to me, his warm breath in my hair. Our bodies so close I could feel his muscles taught against me as he held me. God had really opened my eyes to this handsome doctor, my childhood friend. I couldn't help but think that God kept him for me until now. Could it be possible that he kept this love for me all these years, ready to bud anew when he caused our paths to cross again? I was kind of embarrassed to think how passionate our kisses had become so quickly. It all seemed so natural. I saw the exit to Durham, the one that would take me home. A whole lifetime of hating that place and now wanting to go back because of the passionate affection of a childhood friend.

I decided to go by the store and pick up some flowers to take to David's grave. I hadn't visited there for a long time. I figured now would be a good time to do that. I knew he wasn't there in the truest sense, but I wanted to go to the last place I visited him. I picked up a few groceries and selected some roses to take with me. I knew there would be no food in the house and that I would need a few things. It wasn't far to the gravesite from the grocery. I parked on the street at the gate to the cemetery. I soon spotted the big willow tree where he was laid to rest. The thought just occurred to me about the tree. By some coincidence, Daddy and Jonathan were both buried beneath a willow tree, too.

The sky had become overcast and the wind had picked up considerably. I got out of the car and started up the hill. The air had a sharp chill since the wind had picked up. I pulled my coat close about me as I walked. I had had a little bench placed by his tombstone so when I visited I wouldn't have to sit on the ground. I placed his flowers in the urn at the base of his tombstone. On top was an angel. This angel was in the image of a man instead of a woman. I liked the way he stood as if keeping watch over David.

"David?" I said aloud, "I had to come by. I came to release you, or perhaps to release me. I found out that I can move on now. I found someone that God sent to help me. I think you would approve of him. His name is Daniel Scott. You remember my 'man of honor' at our wedding. You gave me such a hard time over him instead of a girl," I said, laughing to myself. "I think you might have been a little jealous of the bond between us. Well...he wants to be a part of my life now. He said he's loved me his whole life. Maybe you perceived something I didn't. Could you see that he was in love with me? I've cried a million tears sitting on this bench, and none of them brought you back to me. I need a life, David. Knowing you the way I do, I think you would be pleased that I've been healing. God is helping me to move forward. I just wanted you to know I will never stop loving you. You were my first real love, the one who taught me to open up my heart. Thank you for being patient with me when you were here. I did a lot of crazy things while we were together. I was a little girl who thought she was so grown up. You taught me so much about life and how to live it. I can make it now because of you.

"Goodbye, sweet love. I'll come back some if I need to talk. I'm going home now to put away your things. At last, I can do that, but not without tears. The darkness has finally lifted. I've been rescued from the deep despair."

Everything became quiet and still. The wind ceased, and the air seemed to warm. The only sound I heard was a robin chirping on the fence beside me. Maybe I wanted the earth to move or an apparition of David to appear. Perhaps his voice to sound audibly to tell me to go love Daniel. But all that came was a soothing peace.

I turned and ran down the hill to the car, my spirit lighter than I can remember it ever being. I pointed the car toward my house, happy to be home again. At last it would no longer be a sanctuary for the dead, but an abode for the living. Maybe I would put on a new coat of paint and some new wallpaper.

The key turned easily in the lock. I opened the door and walked into the dark, musty house. I would give it a good scrubbing and cleaning, just like what had happened to my soul. I had been scrubbed and cleaned and felt fresh and alive.

After I put the groceries away, I went next door and got my cat, Sammy. I hadn't had him long, but he seemed to remember me well enough, and was rubbing all around my legs as soon as I got him in the door. I had a ton of mail to sort through. I fixed a sandwich and settled into the recliner to start the arduous task of mail sorting. I had been at my task for about and hour when the phone rang.

"Hello," I heard a male voice say.

THE MOUNTAINS CALL MY NAME

"Daniel, how good to hear your voice."

"Did you make it home okay?"

"Yeah, the trip passed by quickly. I was home before I knew it."

"I hope you were thinking about me?"

"Yeah, all the way home. For some reason I couldn't get you out of my mind."

"It was hard today trying to take care of patients and think about you at the same time. I hope I didn't prescribe some medications I shouldn't have," he said, laughing.

"I can see Mr. Jones going home with hormone replacement treatment."

"His wife would probably have some questions," he returned.

"I don't even remember driving. I went into auto pilot. Now that could really be dangerous."

"Don't go kill yourself. God just brought you back into my life."

"And I just got mine back. If anyone had told me what would have transpired on this trip I would have told them how crazy that was."

"And if anyone had told me what was to transpire I would have done the same."

"In our wildest dreams, Daniel, we couldn't have planned this."

"I wanted so badly to tell Grandma. She would do wheelies in her wheelchair."

"Did she ask if you saw me?"

"She knew I was having you up to dinner, but I didn't fill her in. I know as soon as she sees me she is going to want a full report."

"My Mom wasn't asleep this morning while we were cleaning the kitchen. She pretended so we could be alone for a while. When I went to wake her she just looked up at me and winked."

"That little devil. I bet she peeked through those little eyelids. She didn't say a word when she came in today."

"I forgot to ask about her. Is she doing okay?"

"I took some blood work. Her blood pressure seems to be on the low side. And I gave her some samples of sleeping pills. I think these will work well for her. I just have to make her feel free to call when she needs something. That is a major problem with my patients, not asking questions. I have to make sure that I tell them everything I want them to know because they won't ask me anything."

"What do you suspect with Mama?"

"I suspect the low blood pressure is affecting her equilibrium. I didn't detect any inner ear infection. She has been having frequent headaches. I'm waiting for some tests to come back and make sure, and then I will see her again. I do see her declining somewhat."

"You did say '*declining*'?"

"She seems to be. She didn't seem to have the energy that she did when I first started checking her."

"It could be, Dr. Scott, that she's been waiting up for me. You have kept me out late."

"I'm guilty, but I think it's more. I'll let you know when I get the tests back. Our lab only does the most minor testing. I usually send the major ones to Roanoke or Richmond. They both have pretty quick turn around for results."

"Promise me, Daniel, you won't keep secrets from me about her."

There was a long pause on the other end.

"I promise to tell you all I can. I have to go, Ms. Elizabeth, I have a ton of paper work to do, and the day is almost gone."

"It's been good to hear your voice," I said softly into the receiver.

"I wish I could hold you right now and kiss your sweet lips. Has it only been since morning when I last held you? It seems so much longer."

THE MOUNTAINS CALL MY NAME

"I was thinking the same thing. You've made me so happy, Daniel. I'm afraid when I wake up in the morning it will all have been a dream."

"Believe me, you're not dreaming. I think it's the reverse. I think you just woke up. This is reality."

"My heart is filled to overflowing right now. I can't explain it. I just traveled from the darkness into the sunlight, and it has warmed my soul."

"What are we going to do now, Libby? We can't continue to stay apart. It will kill both of us."

"I don't know what to do. I have to think. I'll be home in two weeks. Maybe I'll have some answers by then."

"We, Libby, it will be we who find the answers together. It involves both of us now."

"But I fought so long to be out of the mountains. How can I just come back? How can I make an about face after all this time?"

"You're asking the right person. Remember, I'm the one you dreamed that dream with."

"And you're the one that was a traitor."

"Did I look unhappy to you?"

"No, you seem very happy."

"My dream of leaving this place was as fierce as yours. It was God, Libby; he was the one that changed my

THE MOUNTAINS CALL MY NAME

heart. When he speaks to you, you have to listen. I resisted for the longest time, and then I just said 'God I give up. I'll go back, just give me back my peace'. And instantly, I had it."

"I can't believe how our paths crossed. It was an immediate connection."

"God didn't show me you, I didn't have a clue I would be holding you and kissing you last night. In my wildest dreams I would not have expected you in my life. But God already knew. If I hadn't listened to his calling, I would have missed you, the love of my life. I would have totally missed it."

"Everything is happening so fast. I went from being bound in this web of grief to being carried away in the passion of your kisses. How can you do that, Daniel? It just doesn't add up. I feel so crazy inside. I went by David's grave today."

A long pause, then he responded, "You did?"

"I took flowers. I haven't been there in a long time. This is the first time I didn't cry. I released myself from any more grieving. I gave myself permission to go forward. I told him about you and that…"

I couldn't speak anymore because of the tears that were falling now.

"And that…" He repeated to me.

I collected myself and finished.

THE MOUNTAINS CALL MY NAME

"And that I thought you would take really good care of me."

Silence followed.

"Are you still there, Daniel?"

"Yeah, just give me a minute."

After a brief pause he continued. "I can't believe my ears have just heard what they heard. You talk about it being fast for you, we've just hit the same hurricane. I haven't allowed you to be in my thoughts for years, except in passing, when your name would come up in the family. Like when David died, they told me, and other things in passing. But when I saw you the night we went to Bessie's house, everything came rushing back to my memory. You've grown into such a beautiful woman. Remember, the last time we saw each other we were eighteen years old. Time and space has treated you well."

"When I saw you I thought how incredibly handsome you were, and wondered why I didn't see this when we were younger."

"I guess God told me to shut up and he blinded your eyes. It wasn't God's time when we were eighteen. I think everything has happened so fast because God has opened up our eyes and our hearts."

"Daniel?"

"Yes."

"I want you to know, just in case you've wondered, when I've been with you and when we've shared some passionate moments, I've never pretended that you were David. I've been totally aware of you. How strong your arms felt around me, the scent of your cologne, are now memories of you, not David. The times I had with David are now a fading memory. You have awakened the woman within me. Need I say more?"

"No, I think that about covers everything. But just so you know, I knew it was me you responded to, not David. Well, it seems we're right back where we were this morning, neither of us wants to say goodbye."

"We can't stay on the phone for two weeks."

"And I can't stay away from you for two weeks, so one of us is going to make a three hour or so trip this weekend. Will it be me or you?"

"I guess you'll have to come here."

"There is a doctor I graduated from school with. He lives in Durham and works at Duke. He keeps asking me to come down and check out the hospital and the pool of doctors that are looking to transfer to other areas. I'll give him a call tomorrow and see what I can work out."

"I can't wait to see you. I'm going to try to quit analyzing things and just let them happen."

"One of us has to say it so I'll be the one, or I won't get home from the office until midnight. I have to recheck my work I did today to see if I made any horrible mistakes."

"Okay, I have to go pay bills and throw away all the junk mail I've received."

"I love you, Elizabeth Anne Mason, and I have no doubt that one day you will love me the way I love you. Goodnight, my love."

"Goodnight, Daniel"

No sooner had I hung up the phone than the door bell rang. I emptied all the mail in my lap and went to answer it. I wondered who could be here so late. I opened the door to see a man holding a box of flowers.

"Are you Mrs. Elizabeth Mason?" he asked.

"Yes"

"These are for you," he said, extending the box to me.

"Wait just a minute," I said, leaving to go get a tip for him.

"Thank you," he said, turning to leave.

I took the box back to my chair and untied the ribbon that was on it. I picked up the note that was inside and slowly read it. "To my darling Elizabeth, may our dreams become one again. All my love, Daniel".

He remembered, I thought as I looked at the flowers. There were a dozen red roses and a small bouquet of baby roses. My tears fell on the flowers as I held them close to me.

"Oh, Daniel, you're not letting up are you," I said aloud.

THE MOUNTAINS CALL MY NAME

I went into the kitchen to get a vase to put them in. As I went to place them on the mantel of the fireplace my gaze went to the wedding picture of me and David. My tears became fresh again. I picked up the picture and held it close to my heart.

"Oh, God! Help me to move past this. Daniel loves me, and these feelings I'm having for him have been so welcome in my heart. But when I look at this picture, I feel so guilty for having felt the passion I have for Daniel. It seemed so right just a little while ago, and now, when I see the love from Daniel and the wedding day with David I feel so ripped apart inside. Help me..." I sobbed, "help me ..."

I took the picture upstairs to my bedroom and lay on my bed holding it to my heart. I'm not sure when I fell asleep, but it wasn't long before I drifted into this weird dream of David and myself. He was sitting by me on the bed. His hand was stroking my hair. I heard him calling my name. "Elizabeth, Elizabeth, wake up I need to talk to you."

"David it's you! You've come back to me!"

"No, little one, I came to tell you, it's time for you to let me go."

"No! I can't, I can't do that," I said, throwing my arms around him.

"You, have to let me go. Don't you think it's time? Where I'm going, you can't come, and I can't come back here."

"No! No! No!" I yelled at him.

"Shhh..." he said as he held me close to him. "Be happy, sweetheart. Just remember, I want you to be happy."

As he held me his voice changed and he became Daniel that was holding me and telling me he loved me and would always take care of me. "David is gone, I'm the only one here. Rest now, my love."

I woke to the phone ringing beside the bed. I couldn't believe I slept the whole night without changing clothes.

"Hello," I heard Daniel's voice say.

"I was sleeping."

"I'm sorry. I didn't realize you don't keep doctors' hours."

"I just had this really weird dream."

"I was going to say I hoped you were dreaming about me, but if it was weird, I don't know."

"It *was* about you *and* David. Just really confusing."

"You want to share?"

"David came to see me last night. It was so real, just like he was sitting by me. He came to tell me ..."

"Are you crying, Libby?"

"Maybe, just a little."

THE MOUNTAINS CALL MY NAME

"You don't have to tell me, you know."

"No, I think I should. It was just so real. I would swear he sat here by me. I could feel him when he held me."

"Are you really sure you want to tell me this?"

"Yeah..." I took a deep breath, and proceeded. "I need to tell you this. He kept asking me to release him. He said he had to go where I couldn't follow. He called me 'little one'; he always called me 'little one'." I sniffled and continued. He told me to be happy."

"That..." He started to reply.

"Let me finish. As he held me...," I hesitated because it was so hard to get the word out.

"And, as he held you..."

"He became you, Daniel. Right before I woke up it was you telling me how much you loved me. I was in your arms. David left and you came to me."

"I'm sorry. I know this must be an awfully hard time for you. I'm really trying to be sensitive. If ever I'm not sensitive to you about David, would you please tell me?"

"This is new for me, too. This transition has hit me hard since I came home. I knew it would. When I was there I didn't have all these reminders of David in my face. Everywhere I look, Daniel, I see David. That's why I said I would need some time here, before I came back. I've got to put all his things away. I've put this off three years, it's about time."

"Can I come help you?"

"Now, that's one thing I know won't work. You helping me put David's things away. It's something I have to do by myself."

"I can pray for you. I'll be lifting you up every time I can. Only God can help you through this, sweetie."

"No one better, I assure you."

"I'll be there Friday night. We'll go to dinner. I plan to make it a day at Duke Medical Center. I'm going to meet a Doctor Thomas. He's the one I told you about being with me at medical school."

"Daniel, I thank you for those beautiful flowers. I'm sure what brought on my dream was the flowers."

"I didn't mean for them to make you feel bad."

"When I took the flowers and placed them on the mantel and my gaze went to mine and David's wedding picture, there sat your beautiful roses beside that picture, and all of sudden I felt guilty for having shared those moments with you. Silly, huh?

"Well, we have shared some moments in the last two days that have made some sparks fly. That's not a bad thing. At least I think we both enjoyed it."

"That's the problem, I forgot David when ...during our times together I didn't even think about him. And when I saw our picture I felt I had betrayed him in some way."

"Listen to me, sweetie, he's gone, and he isn't going to come back. I'm here, and I'm not going to leave you. He can never hold you again. His lips will never kiss yours again. Maybe your dream was a message from him. I know part of your dream was true, I do love you."

"Are you sure that's what you feel for me, Daniel, and not just lust."

"Wow, you go straight for the juggler. Lust, that's a big word for just four little letters. But I assure you there is another four letter word that is more appropriate. That is L-O-V-E. I don't think I would substitute passion for lust. However, when does it change from passion to lust, or from love to passion to lust? What is love without passion? I'll have to think about that one."

"I actually didn't mean to say lust. I kind of embarrassed myself."

"Elizabeth, I have no doubt that I know I love you. It just makes the passion so much more beautiful. How can you love and not be passionate. I'm passionate about my medical career, and I love what I'm doing in that field. You can be passionate about many things."

"Daniel I would not exchange any moment I've had with you. You make me alive inside. You've made me excited about tomorrow, and the next day, and the next. I can't wait until Friday when you will hold me and kiss me again. You've moved into my heart. I wouldn't have dreamed this possible a few short days ago. God placed us together. I think that's why things seem to be moving so fast. When God decides to put things together there is no time limit."

"My heart is so full of you, my sweet Elizabeth. I can't eat, or sleep without thinking of you. My day is consumed with thoughts of you. I'm sure I feel the way I would have felt at eighteen. I have never, ever loved anyone the way I love you. I think God took all my feelings for you and kept them for me until now. I'm walking with my head in the clouds. You remember meeting the nurse here the night I had her fix up our dinner? She knows I've been smitten. The other day she said, 'Dr. Scott, you've finally fallen in love.'"

"What did you tell her?"

"Guilty, as charged."

"Thanks for everything, Daniel. Today will be especially hard. I plan to box everything up and do something with it. I'm sure his suits and the rest of his clothing will be of good use to someone."

"I will bathe you in prayer today. I've got to go to work. We've talked for almost an hour and I'm still at home. I've really got to run. Nothing like starting your office visits an hour late. People just love that."

"Daniel?"

"Yes, what is it?"

"I really care for you."

"I love you, too."

THE MOUNTAINS CALL MY NAME

Buzzing on the phone line told me that he was gone. I rolled over and laid the picture I had taken to bed down on the night stand beside me. I had that peace wash over me again. How thankful I was that Daniel had called when he did. The dream was so moving. I think God gave me a moment with David. I think He does speak in dreams sometimes. I climbed into the shower and let the hot water run down over my body. I lingered there until the heat was almost gone. After drying my hair I went downstairs and put Sammy out for his morning outing. I had some cereal, and read some of the paper, dreading the job that lay before me.

I got some boxes from the storage room and started to work. I wanted to do the hardest first, which was David's closet. I boxed all his clothing and shoes except a shirt that was his favorite. I slipped it on over my own and put my arms into the sleeves. I wrapped my arms around myself hoping to feel his arms once again. I brought the sleeve to my face trying to catch a scent of him. All was gone except the smell of the musty fabric. I slipped it off and carefully folded it and put it in the box.

I heard the door bell ring and ran down the stairs and opened the door to the same flower delivery person, carrying another box.

"Mrs. Mason, I believe I have some more flowers for you."

I gave him a tip and took the box. I opened it and gazed at an array of tulips. A dozen, and none of them the same color. How in the world did he find these in the dead of winter? I thought, as I took out the note. *My sweet Libby, I'm bathing you in prayer. All my love, Daniel.*

THE MOUNTAINS CALL MY NAME

His timing was, as usual, impeccable. It was lunch time by then, a good stopping place, I thought. I put the bouquet on the mantel beside the others, but not with tears this time. After lunch I went into David's bath and gathered his toiletries, placing them in a shoe box. I wasn't quite sure what to do with them. His toothbrush and razor, these things had touched his skin. I stood for a moment and closed my eyes and imagined him standing there, using these items. I took the lid off his cologne and sniffed it. It was getting harder to see him in my mind's eye. Each day he faded a little more. I finished and cleaned everything, scrubbing every scent and sight that reminded me of him. I should have done this a long, long time ago. Next would have to be the hardest of all, our pictures. I knew I was going to have to put them all away if I were to move on. It was getting late in the day. The sun was already going down. I heard the door bell ring again. I knew without opening the door who it was, and I was right.

"Mrs. Mason, more flowers," he said, smiling.

I gave him his usual tip and anxiously opened the box. A dozen daffodils, all with double blossoms. An array of pastel spring colors. I tore open the card and read, "My sweetheart, a breath of spring for you on this dark day. I'm bathing you in prayer. All My Love, Daniel". I brought it to my lips and kissed it.

"Thank you, Daniel," I whispered aloud. "Thank you for loving me."

But my thoughts carried forward. He's as close as he can be, I guess. He has brought the sun to me today.

THE MOUNTAINS CALL MY NAME

I placed them beside the others on the mantel. I could see them plainly as I started to sort through the albums of memories.

I went through page after page of pictures and remembered the times we had together. There were stories behind each one. I saved the wedding album for last. I just felt a need to go through it one more time. There was my sweet daddy, standing so proud beside me. I think it was the only time I saw him in a suit. And my mother, she looked so beautiful that day. And Daniel, I caught my breath as I looked at him, the sadness on his face was never so evident as it was to me now. I could see behind his smile the sadness in his eyes. I guess because now I know what happened. David was so handsome that day, and the joy we shared was so apparent in our smiles. Who would have known how the story would have evolved. I slowly closed the album and placed it in a box with all the other things that reminded me of David. I taped it up and placed it in the storage room with all the other boxes. I sat down in the recliner where I could look at the flowers Daniel had sent. It was about eight o'clock and I had realized I hadn't eaten dinner. I guess I would fix a sandwich. I had just gotten the fixings from the fridge when I heard the door bell ring again. I thought to myself I was going to have to get more cash if he sent many more flowers. I opened the door to see Daniel standing in there.

"I thought I would bring you some flowers."

"What... How... what are you doing here?"

"I would like to come in. It's been a long drive."

I took the flowers and asked him to come in.

THE MOUNTAINS CALL MY NAME

"How did you know where I lived?"

"I have ways, come here," he said, pulling me into his arms. "I couldn't let you be by yourself today. So I decided to come to see you. Oh, and I brought food. I picked up some Chinese out off the beltway. I was hoping you hadn't eaten."

"Daniel, I'm speechless. I don't know what to say."

"Don't say a word, just come kiss me."

I was in his arms and once again was reminded that he really did love me.

"I love you so much," he whispered as he pulled away from me.

"Let me go get the food out of the car."

When he returned I had set the table with dinnerware.

"What would you like to drink, my prince?"

"Do you have tea?"

"Yes, I made some today.

I put ice into his glass as he opened up the boxes of Chinese food.

"Do you like Chinese food?" he asked.

THE MOUNTAINS CALL MY NAME

"Yes, David and I..." I stopped in mid sentence, realizing what I was about to say. He reached over and put his hand over mine as I mouthed to him, "I'm so sorry."

"Don't be sorry. It's going to happen and I don't want you to ever be sorry about things you say. If you want me to hear something about you and David it want hurt me. I promise."

"Anyway, yes, I like Chinese food. David and I used to eat take out a lot. When we would both work late I wouldn't want to cook, so we would get take out."

"How did you do today? I don't think I have gone to the throne of God more than I have today. I just felt I needed to come to you."

"I won't lie, it's been a hard day," I said with a tear escaping down my cheek.

He reached over and wiped it away with his finger.

"It will be better. I promise you. If I can help it, you will never experience such pain again."

"No one could help this, Daniel. I guess there is someone going through this every hour of every day somewhere in the world."

"Before I prayed for you, I first prayed for myself, that I would be for you what God wanted me to be. Then I prayed for our relationship. I want us to please the Lord in all we do, Libby. I know God has given you to me. As sure as I have just driven over two hours to see you, I know that you're going to be mine."

THE MOUNTAINS CALL MY NAME

"Wow, you say that with such surety," I said, smiling at him.

"Can't you feel it between us, Libby?"

"Yeah, I'm not exactly sure what it is but there is definitely something there."

"You're just afraid to say it, but you know you're falling in love with me."

"Is it possible to fall in love so quickly?"

"Love at first sight it does happen. I loved you when I first saw you when we were little things. Remember, I thought you were my Christmas present. When I was twelve years old and my testosterone was raging, you were the first girl I felt love for. It was then that I saw you as a girl, not just a playmate. When you have a playmate you don't see them as boys or girls they are just your friends. I had a crush on you as big as the world. I asked you to be my valentine that year."

"But you asked me every year. We've gone through all our first stages together."

"Except one. I wanted to be the first one to make love to you."

"That's true." I said blushing. "But we know that didn't happen. When you kissed me and told me how you felt about me, I began to think back on our school days. You never forced me to look at what we felt for each other. You were always there for me. I felt so secure with you. I guess it was unfair of me to keep you so close to me then marry someone else. I never had to wonder who I would go to a dance with, or spend Saturday nights with. You were always, always there. If you had..."

"Would things have been different? I guess we'll never know, will we."

"I loved being with you. I would have been very sad if you had ever been involved with another girl. But, what did I know about love. You made me feel protected. I was secure with what we had. Didn't we have a lot of fun?"

"That we did," he said, smiling at me.

"We always wanted the same things. We took the same classes, went to the same parties." I hesitated for a moment before finishing. "Then we went our separate ways."

"That was the killer. We went our separate ways. The stranger wins your heart and the friend goes to college. That was a bummer."

"But look what you've become. We went after our dreams, Daniel. Did we succeed?"

"Well, you had success in running away and I became a doctor. I guess we did.

"I'm back where I started, living in the Virginia mountains, a driveway from my mom and dad and still in love with the same girl. I have fulfilled some dreams and I'm still dreaming."

"Look what I've become. A widow and a 'has been' nurse."

"You've become a beautiful woman, a widow, and a very good nurse, that just happens not to be practicing."

"Widow, that sounds so matronly."

"Matronly you're not. Well, as nice as this is, I have to get back to the big city. I have office hours in the morning, and have two patients in the hospital. As a matter of fact, Karen is watching out for me. If I get any calls she is supposed to call here. I'll check the hospital before I leave and see how my patients are doing."

"You didn't have to come."

"Au contraire, I couldn't let you go through today and not come. Did you finish everything you wanted to do?"

"Yes, just before you got here. I just finished packing away all the pictures. I needed to get things out of sight for a while. I'll have to put up some new ones."

"I was thinking on the way down that if you had David's stuff packed I could take it to up the mission. There are a lot of men there that need clothing."

"There will be some well dressed men in the mission. I have everything out in the storage room. I'll show you when you get ready to leave. Can you sit for a little while?"

"Sure, that didn't take much persuasion did it? By the way, you have a beautiful home."

"Compared to yours, it's very modest."

THE MOUNTAINS CALL MY NAME

"It has your touch, and it's beautiful, just like you are."

"I must be a mess. I don't even have makeup on."

"Would you like a tour of my abode?"

"Sure."

As we entered the living room, I saw the box of unopened flowers.

"My flowers, I'm so sorry, I got so excited about you standing there that I didn't open them."

I pulled the red ribbon from the box and lifted the lid to a dozen long stem roses. I picked up the card and opened it. It read, "I won't stop until you're mine. All my love, Daniel".

I went into his arms once again and this time it was I who initiated the kiss.

"It's been a long time since I've been courted, be patient with me."

"I must tell you that you're doing quite well so far. It's been a long time since I've courted a girl, so we're even. If we make blunders we'll just correct them."

"You've already seen the downstairs, let's go upstairs. We ascended the stairs hand in hand. "This is the master bedroom," I said, taking him into my room. "It's still a mess from where I've been cleaning out. At the end of the hall is a study. David would spend hours in there when he was doing research. It's full of books and things.

THE MOUNTAINS CALL MY NAME

I don't know what to do with it all. Perhaps it would be something you would like to have."

"Perhaps"

"And this is the guest bedroom. We didn't have many visitors. David wasn't very close to his family. They just weren't the visiting type. We would go to Kentucky to visit them sometimes. We got along okay, but his mother and father divorced, and it was always so uncomfortable for him to visit either of them. He never did bond with his stepmother and stepfather. He was an only child and devoted to both his parents. The divorce was horrific on him. He loved his grandparents dearly, but they both died about a month apart not too long after we were married. It was just David and me. We carved out a little nest here in Durham, and cut ourselves off from the world. You pay a price when you do that."

"An island unto yourself?"

"Something like that. It makes it easy to hibernate."

"No more hibernation for you, young lady. From now on you're going to have lots of people to love you."

"And who would that be?"

"The whole Scott family. They've always loved you."

"You talk like I'm already part of your family."

"You just don't know it yet, but you are. Would you mind if I used your bathroom."

THE MOUNTAINS CALL MY NAME

"No, not at all. You can either use mine in the master bedroom or the one in the hallway."

"It doesn't matter, as long as I use one," he said, smiling at me.

He went into the one in the hallway. The one I had just taken all of David's stuff out of. At least it was scrubbed clean. I realized I had missed packing the picture of our wedding day. The one I had slept with the night before. I picked it up about the time Daniel came into the room.

"I missed one," I said, laying it on the dresser.

He picked it up and looked at it. "It's a nice picture. Is this the one that was on the mantel by my flowers?"

"Yeah, it is. I forgot it was up here. I need to put it in the box with the rest of the pictures."

I took the picture from his hand and laid it face down on my dresser. I would put it away later, I thought to myself. We made our way back down to the living room.

"Have a seat," I said, pointing to the sofa. "It's pretty comfortable, I guess. I never really sat on it much."

He sat down and pulled me down beside him. He put his arm around me and snuggled me close to him.

"Are those the flowers your admirer sent you today?"

"Spring flowers. Where in the world did you find a florist that had spring flowers?"

"You just have to know who to call. Do you like them?"

"Every time I hit a rough spot today, flowers came. God must have directed you."

"I just told the florist to spread them out over the day."

"Your love has filled my heart today."

"That's why I came tonight, I felt like you needed me."

"How perceptive of you."

"I'll always be here for you, Elizabeth. I'll make it so you can't live without me."

I took his hand and raised it to my lips. I kissed it and held it to my face.

"I'm so glad you came. I did need you today, and you knew it."

"When you told me about your dream, I knew I had to come. God has given you to me to love and take care of. I know you think this is all so sudden, and it is, but I know as surely as I'm holding you right now, I'll be holding you for a lifetime."

"I'll settle for this moment, right here, right now."

He put his finger under my chin and lifted my face to his and kissed me. It felt so right, being held and kissed by him. At this point in time I had no reservations about anything. All I knew was the passion I felt as he continued to kiss me. I felt his hand on my flesh as it moved underneath my blouse. His touch was electrifying. It had been so long since I had been held and kissed like this. I'm not sure who was first to pull back, but nevertheless, we did. We didn't speak for a long time. He just held me and caressed me. My heart was racing wildly within my chest. I was glad he couldn't tell.

I let my head rest on his shoulder. I closed my eyes, hoping not to break the spell of what was transpiring between us. After a long time he spoke, so softly that I could barely hear what he was saying.

"Ever since you came back into my life I've prayed for you, and for me. That only if it was his will, did I want this to continue. I promised him I would always treat you with the highest respect and honor, and that I would never make you compromise anything for me. Just now…"

"Just now," I said finishing his sentence, "I wanted you to kiss me. I wanted you as much as you wanted me."

"Libby, what I'm about to ask you will probably sound strange. What I would like for you to do with me, is to kneel down here and pray with me for relationship."

"Oh, Daniel! I've never had a request like this before. David and I never prayed together. We prayed, of course, but never together."

We knelt there before our Lord and poured our hearts out to him. We prayed for guidance and strength, and for God to keep our relationship pure before him. Our hands, hearts and tears mingled as we united before him in prayer. My heart was overflowing with the love I felt at that moment. It had been such a long time since I had felt this close to the Lord. We rose from our kneeling position and Daniel took his big handkerchief from his pocket and wiped his eyes.

"I would share this with you," he said, holding up his handkerchief, "but I don't think you want to," he said, smiling at me.

I excused myself, got a tissue and blew my nose. I returned to the sofa where so much had just occurred. My heart was full and tender. I sat beside this sweet man and held his hand to my lips again.

"That's what started all this before, remember?" he said, looking at me.

"Daniel, my heart is so full right now that I don't even have words to express what I feel. I can't believe what I'm about to say to you," I said with new tears starting to fall.

I wiped my eyes and nose and tried to tell him what was in my heart.

"Something is happening between us."

"I know," he said, smiling at me again.

"I feel so moved right now, Daniel. I don't know what else could make my heart so full, except…"

"Except…"

"Except I'm falling in love with you."

He looked at me so tenderly. "If only it can be so, Elizabeth. I've waited a lifetime to hear you say that. I just want you to be sure. I don't think I could take losing you again. So much has happened that I don't want you to mistake what you're feeling right now for love if it isn't. I really will be patient with you."

He lowered his head to mine and gently kissed me, and I eagerly responded. He slowly pulled away from me.

"I need to hit the road. It's getting late. Show me where the boxes are and I'll put them in the car. If I don't leave now, I won't."

I led him to the storage room and together we carried the boxes to his van.

"I don't think I'll come back in. It'll take me another hour to get out the door.

"Daniel, I didn't want you to stop kissing me awhile ago."

"Don't you think I know that, I didn't want to either, but silly me, I would have prayed that prayer just today. If I go back in, I'm not sure God will make a way two times in one night for us to escape temptation. It would be so easy to waltz you back in that door, but I want it to be right. Do you realize how foreign this conversation would be to most of the world? The world would say, 'If you're two consenting adults it's fine to have sex.' I have waited a lifetime for this and I can wait until we say 'I do'. This is not the time or the place that I will make love to you, Elizabeth Mason, but there will be a day not too far into the future. I hope anyway."

"Daniel, I think you do need to come back in for just a minute."

"After that long dissertation you are asking me to come back in. Have pity on me."

"I was just reminding you that you need to call the hospital."

"Right, he said, hitting his forehead with the palm of his hand. "I forgot, fine doctor I am. For some reason that wasn't where my mind was."

I showed him the phone and left him to make his call. I lifted the box of roses up to smell them. I felt like a school girl getting her first flowers.

"Everything is fine," he said, hanging up the phone. "I do need to hit the road though. I'll have a long day tomorrow."

"I hope it was worth the trip."

He took my face into his hands and leaned down and placed a kiss on the tip of my nose.

"It was the most important trip of my life. I came to declare my love, and I did. What you gave to me tonight was more than I could dream for. I promise I will take very good care of the love you have placed in my hands."

"I have no doubt about that," I said, smiling at him.

THE MOUNTAINS CALL MY NAME

"The hardest thing I've ever had to do is to leave you when I know how badly you need me to stay. There's too much distance between us. We're going to have to fix that. But until we do, I have to go home."

I walked him to the door and put my arms around him.

"This has to be a quick goodbye," he said.

He kissed me lightly on the lips.

"See ya Friday."

"Bye, see ya Friday, drive carefully, please. Call me when you get home. I'll be worried about you."

He waved and was off.

Chapter Nine

The week went fast and before I knew it, it was Friday. Daniel called and I was to meet him at a steak place he had found downtown. I was ready way before time to meet him and decided to leave early and go by the mall. It had been a long time since I had gone to the mall to window shop. I couldn't wait to see Daniel. He called every morning and every night. I waited anxiously to hear his voice. I felt that my cup was running over with joy. I praised God daily for what he was doing in my life. And yes, I thanked him for sending me Daniel. I knew for sure that I was falling in love with him. I couldn't believe things had changed so quickly. I did a lot of house cleaning and heart cleaning. I knew my heart was ready to receive whatever it was that Daniel had for me.

I bought one red rose and had it wrapped and a ribbon put on it. I found a card at the mall that had one red rose imprinted on the front. The inside of it was blank and I wrote these simple words 'I know that I know'."

I met him in the parking lot, and to my surprise he had a man with him that I knew from the hospital. He and David had become good friends there. He was a marvelous surgeon. We were so surprised to see each other.

"Libby, I would like for you to meet…"

"Chris, I can't believe it's you!" I exclaimed.

"Elizabeth, where in the world did you disappear to? After David died I lost contact with you. Are you still in the area?"

"Actually, I didn't go anywhere. I just didn't go back to work."

"Damn shame, you were one of the best nurses I've ever had the privilege to work with."

"You're too kind."

"It's the truth."

"I guess you two don't need an introduction." Daniel said, looking at first one, then the other.

"No, Elizabeth and I go way back. When she worked the I.C.U. she took care of a lot of my cases. I was always glad when it was she that took care of my patients."

"Was he hard to work for?" Daniel asked.

"No harder than any other doctor. Once I got him trained he was okay," I said laughing.

"That wasn't funny," he said to me.

Dr. Thomas had called and got reservations so we didn't have to wait. Once seated, we continued our conversation.

"David Mason was one of the best researchers we ever had. It's a shame he died so young. Did you know him, Daniel?"

"Well, actually Elizabeth and I were best friends. So when she and David were to marry I was asked to be her maid of honor. Okay, don't look at me like that."

"Oh, really? Maid of honor, huh?" he said, grinning at Daniel.

"He was my best friend. We grew up together. I couldn't think of anyone I was closer to. I didn't have any close girl friends."

"So…do we need to change the subject?" he said, winking at me.

"No, when David and Elizabeth were married I went to medical school and she came here. We just happened to meet over the holidays and got together after all these years. I haven't seen her since her wedding day."

"Did you know he's trying to get me to move to Virginia?" he said, looking at me.

"I didn't know it was you he was entertaining. I knew it was a doctor, but not the great Dr. Chris Thomas."

"Flatter me some more. And did you bring her to fatten the pot? Is she part of the deal? I am single now, you know."

"I'm trying to get her to move there, but for me, not you." he said, winking at me.

"You just about had me. I thought if you were going to throw Elizabeth in to sweeten the deal, like maybe give her to me as a private nurse, I would have to say 'yes'."

THE MOUNTAINS CALL MY NAME

"You've been a great friend, Chris, but I get the girl this time," Daniel said.

"If he's as persuasive with you as he's been with me today, you don't stand a snow balls chance in hell," he said, smiling at me. Looking at Daniel he said, "When I found out you gave up that job with the professor, I thought I would have to check you into the mental hospital."

"I felt so guilty every time I would visit my family. I finally admitted to myself it was me that was going to be the new doctor. We just need some more good doctors up there. The load is so heavy. I don't know how Old Doc Adams made it as long as he did. We also need to upgrade our surgical staff and you were the first one that popped into my mind."

"If you two will excuse me, I have to visit the little boys' room," he said, leaving the table.

Daniel looked at me apologetically. "I'm sorry, it just kind of snowballed and he ended up coming to dinner with us."

"Don't be sorry. It's really good seeing him again. I'm here to tell you Daniel, if you get him to move to Virginia, you will have the coup of the year. He's absolutely fabulous. He doesn't accept anything but the best from himself and everyone else. When he wants something hell nor high water will not prevent him from getting it."

"That's the way he was in med school. He drove us all nuts at times. He was cocky from day one. We all disliked him to begin with, but he kinda grows on you."

THE MOUNTAINS CALL MY NAME

Our dinner was delicious. I enjoyed watching these two brilliant doctors jostle for position. I could see that Daniel had scored points with him. I just wasn't sure if it was enough to get him pried away from the money and position he had here. It would have to be more than that to him. Maybe this was enough of a challenge to him that he wouldn't turn it down. It didn't hurt that his roots were in Virginia also.

It was around 9:00 o'clock when he said he got a call from the hospital. It was an emergency and he had to run. That left Daniel and me by ourselves for the rest of the evening.

"Let's go sit in the car for a little while. I got a room here in town, so I won't be going back to your place."

"Let's drive around a little," he said.

"I have to get something out of my car first."

I got the rose and card from my car before getting in with him. When we were settled into our seats, I gave him the rose first, then the card.

"What is this for? I'm the one that's supposed to bring the flowers."

He tore open the card and read the five little words I had written inside. I saw his eyes mist from the emotion the words brought to him.

"I don't know what to say. You caught me off balance."

He put his finger to his eyes to clear the tears.

THE MOUNTAINS CALL MY NAME

"Daniel, look at me. I know for sure I'm falling in love with you. God sent you to me. That's the only reason I can tell you it happened so fast. I've really sought the Lord this week, and I know that I know."

He took me into his arms as best he could in the little sports car. He kissed me long and tenderly.

"I can only say I will never make you sorry you love me. I promise you with all that is in me I will protect you and will never purposely hurt you."

"I can't think of anyone that I would want God to give me other than you. I promise you I won't run from you ever again."

"Does that mean you'll come back to Virginia or do I have to move here?" he said, looking deep into my eyes.

"You're not serious are you?" I asked. "You have to move here, of course."

"I will if that is the only way I can have you."

"Daniel, I would never ask you to give up what God has called you to do. I'll come home."

"Elizabeth..." He whispered to me as he held me close to him. "How can I be so blessed? Is there someplace we can go so I don't have to kill myself over the console?"

"Well, our options aren't very good. It's either my house or your hotel room."

"Your house," he said. "I'll follow you."

THE MOUNTAINS CALL MY NAME

"I will be strong, Lord, I promise you, I will be strong. Or should I say, 'help me be strong'. I know I shouldn't open myself up for this kind of temptation, but I need some more time with him before he leaves me."

It didn't take long for us to reach my house. I waited for Daniel to park, and we walked arm in arm to the front porch. He took my key from me and opened the door.

Right before he let me pass him he stopped me and said, "Remember what I told you when I left you last time? It won't be here that I make you mine, not in the home you shared with David."

"Yeah, I remember."

"And I meant it, with all that is in me I meant it. I won't have our life start out where the last one ended."

I went about the living room turning on lights. I asked him for his coat to hang up.

"I meant to tell you how handsome you looked tonight. You always looked good in a navy suit and white shirt. I like the tie, too."

"Are you flirting with me?" he said, smiling at me.

"I was just noticing how handsome you look."

"And you look beautiful, as usual. I thought for a moment that Chris thought I brought you for him. The way you two went into each other's arms had me worried for a moment. I thought, Daniel, what in the world have you done?"

THE MOUNTAINS CALL MY NAME

"You're funny. I was so shocked to see him with you. If I had had false teeth they would have fallen out. I think we were all doing a double take. He'll probably tell you about it when he calls you."

"So, you know him really well?"

"Oh Yeah, Chris and I go way back. He always told me if I were ever free he would make me his."

"He said that?" he asked, looking so serious.

"He told David that all the time. I think that's why he decided to come and hang out with Chris," I said, chuckling.

"And I ask you again. Did you know him well?"

"As much as I can know a doctor. We pulled some all-nighters together when I worked in ICU. Sometimes there where nights his patients were so sick he wouldn't leave their side. So, when I was on duty we talked a lot. He really got on with David. They were forever picking each others brains. They met one night when David came to have lunch with me, and the two talked all night. They were a mutual admiration society."

"He told me he wasn't married, and didn't have any children."

"Well, that's not exactly true. He was married once, but I think he was married to the hospital instead of her. She got really lonely, I guess, and had an affair on him. So they parted ways. He couldn't, or wouldn't, budge on being at the hospital so much. He made his choice and she made hers."

"Did he play around?"

"Chris? No, well, I say no, but I never saw any evidence of it. He always seemed straight as an arrow. He would pick with us nurses but we knew he didn't mean it. If anyone would know it would be the nurses, because they're the ones that he would have hit on if he was going to."

"Did you get hit on by doctors?"

"Sure, but I was never tempted. Doctors usually know the ones that will give it to them."

"Did I miss something? It sounds like a Peyton place," he said.

"It happens everywhere, Daniel. I bet you hit on some cute little nurses."

"I admit I dated some cute little nurses and some cute little doctors too. But I realized if I was going to make it as a doctor I would have to put my social life on hold. I didn't want to end up divorced while I was still in medical school. The hours were horrendous. But I had some fun along the way."

"You're just too cute not to have driven the nurses wild."

"Me?" Daniel said.

"Yes, you. When a woman wants something bad enough, she goes after it."

"What about David, did he work a lot?"

"Since he was in research, it wasn't like having a practice. When he left work there was no phone ringing, which was nice. There were times when he would be on to something that he would be absent a long time, physically and mentally. That's when he would lock himself away in his study."

"What about me, I have a practice? Would long hours bother you?"

"I'm sure if that day ever arrived I would work through it.

"Would you like something to drink?" I asked him.

"No, I have to be going. I need to start home early in the morning. I should be going back to the hotel. It's been a long day.

"We've done so well, Elizabeth. We've carried on a conversation just like two people that weren't in love with each other."

"Don't make me start thinking. It all starts in the mind you know. For what the mind conceives the body will do eventually. That's paraphrased Bible. The secret is, don't dwell on things too much. That's where it all starts, right in here," I said, pointing to my head.

"You're a wise little girl. I'm going to have to keep an eye on you. I just caught you off guard the other night."

"Maybe, but I enjoyed every uncontrollable moment of it."

"You little vixen!"

"You can call me anything you want to. Just call me," I said on the way to get his coat from the closet.

"I'm elated that you love me. You have no idea what your card meant to me. I want to hold you forever. There will be a day when I can. I hope it won't be a long time away."

He put his arms around me and pulled me close to him. I raised my face to him for the kiss I knew was forthcoming. It was no disappointment. I knew it was going to be so hard to let him go.

"Daniel..."

He looked deep and tenderly into my eyes.

"I love you, I know that now. I'm falling head over hills in love with you. It isn't just the passion that you stir in me. I really love you. I think I loved you a long time ago, but was so afraid I would loose my dreams if I admitted it. Now you've become my dream. Even the idea of coming home sounds good."

He held me close to him and reiterated how very much he loved me, too. After several more long kisses, I knew he had to leave. We had been standing in the doorway for almost an hour.

"I guess the couch is off limits. You can't get too carried away standing in freezing weather with an overcoat on. I'll see you when you come home. I won't be back this way unless you need me for something."

"I'll be home next weekend."

THE MOUNTAINS CALL MY NAME

"How long are you going to stay?"

"I don't have anything to bring me back here. Unless Chris decides to call me and ask me out. You know, since he knows I still live here he just might do that," I said coyly.

"And what would you say? He seems to really like you."

"If I'm in town I might accept just to see if I can persuade him to go to the mountains with me."

"You wouldn't."

"Do you think I would?"

"Well, I kind of hoped not. But, when you decide to move on, girl, you move on."

"Not to worry, my prince. You're the only one that my heart will pine for. I only want you."

"Just don't forget me. If I had a class ring I would ask you to go steady with me. Would you anyway, even though I don't have a ring to give you?"

"Would I what?"

"Go steady with me?"

"Yeah, but I was really looking forward to that doggone class ring. I don't have anything to show off to anyone."

"I'll fix that, Christmas is coming."

"I'm going now. No more kisses. I'm going to my car right now," he said, kissing me again. "I can't get enough of you." He was groaning at this point.

"The last words I want you to hear me say are, 'I love you, Elizabeth Mason'."

"And I love you, too, Dr. Scott."

Again, I stood and watched him leave me. I was going to have to go to Virginia so I wouldn't have so many goodbyes.

Chapter Ten

Daniel woke me every morning with a phone call. I talked to him every night before I went to sleep and every morning before my day began. He told me the last thing he did at night after he talked to me was to thank God for me, and to ask for wisdom for our relationship.

I was so lonely for him. I counted the minutes between times for him to call. We would talk for hours at night. Letting him go on the phone was as bad as leaving him in person. It was as hard for him as for me. We would tell each other bye a dozen times before we would finally say goodnight.

I just couldn't believe all this was happening to me. I wanted to tell my mother, but I wanted it to be in person. I had talked to her on the phone twice since I'd been home. She still sounded weak, and so tired. Daniel said he would go over her testing with me when I came home. He was going to do some x-rays that week at the hospital.

The phone call that would change my life forever came in midmorning. It was Daniel, he said my mother had been admitted to the hospital and I needed to come home right away. He said he would explain when I got there. I had already started to get things ready for my trip, so it didn't take me long to load the car. My poor cat! He probably thought I was deserting him again. My neighbor was so sweet to take my mail like before.

THE MOUNTAINS CALL MY NAME

I was on the road by 1:00 o'clock. I tried not to speed. Daniel warned me to not kill myself getting there. He said she was stable, but needed me. I knew for Daniel to call me home wasn't a good sign. I just had to think positive.

Christmas was fast approaching. I guess I was going to get home earlier than I thought. I could have gone even earlier, but I had things to settle before I could leave. I got to the hospital at 3:00. Daniel told me I was to go to the lobby and have them page him as soon as I got there.

"Hi," I said to the phone operator. "I'm supposed to have you page Dr. Scott."

"Just a minute," she said.

I heard the call going out over the intercom. It seemed like I waited forever before he came down.

"Hey, sweetie," he said.

"How is she?" I asked. My voice trembled with the fear I felt.

"She's stable, but I need to talk to you before you see her."

"It sounds serious, Daniel."

"It is, but I don't want to tell you in the hallway. We'll go to the doctors' lounge. It's more private there."

We rode the elevator to the fourth floor into an area marked *no admittance*. He took me into a small lounge with

THE MOUNTAINS CALL MY NAME

soft looking furniture. He sat me in a chair, pulled another up in front of me and took my hands in his.

"I got the results back from the test I took week before last. I told you I was going to do some x-rays. I'm so sorry, Libby, it was cancer."

"No! No! No! Don't tell me that, Daniel! Tell me anything but that. Could you be wrong?"

He shook his head and looked at me with such sadness in his eyes. "No, the mass is rather large and it's in her liver. Which told me there was probably something somewhere else. The liver is usually the last place it assimilates. Because of the bleeding in the bowel I had Dr. Ramsey do a colonoscopy which confirmed what I was afraid of.

"Colon cancer?"

He nodded his head and he looked at me. "She's been bleeding from her bowels. That's why she has been so weak."

"She never mentioned it to me. I guess I've been wrapped up in self pity so long she didn't want to upset me. Why didn't I question her more when I was home? I just assumed you were on top of everything. Why didn't you catch it?" I asked accusingly.

"I guess one reason is, I'm not is a mind reader. The last blood test came back and showed that her platelets were low. I've only been here since September, so I really haven't had a chance to get to know how these people tick. Don't you think I second guessed everything I've done with her?"

"I'm sorry. I don't blame you, Daniel. It just all seems so senseless. Colon cancer is so curable."

"I'm sorry, I did all the tests I knew to do. She didn't tell me until last week that she has been bleeding for quiet awhile. She was too embarrassed to tell me. I don't know what else I could have done."

"Can you operate?"

He shook his head. "It's gone too far, she's in stage four already."

I was sobbing so much I could hardly breathe.

"Daniel, tell me it isn't true. She's all I have." I pushed him away from me, and started to pace the little room.

"Can we get another doctor?"

He came to my side and put his arms around me.

"Libby, look at me, would I lie to you. I love you. I wouldn't do anything to hurt you. I told you that there is nothing, absolutely nothing that anyone can do! You have to accept this. I'm sorry; I wish I wasn't her doctor. Then I wouldn't have to be the one to tell you all this. I had another doctor here check behind me. He concurred with what I thought it was.

"That's why I came back, Libby. Someone has got to start educating these people. They are so scared and embarrassed at testing."

THE MOUNTAINS CALL MY NAME

"Did you know this, Daniel? When you were down last week, did you know it then?"

"I suspected something, but I didn't want to alarm you. I wanted to be sure."

I couldn't stop my tears, as hard as I tried I couldn't quit crying. I heard them paging Daniel.

"I'll be right back; I have to answer this page. Will you be okay for a minute?"

There was a bathroom to our left, so I went in and splashed cold water on my face. I had to get myself together before I went to her. Daniel took a while coming back, and by then I had pulled myself together somewhat.

He immediately came to me and held me close to him.

"Can I see her now? Does she know?" I asked questioningly.

He nodded and led me down the hall to her room. The doors were shut that lead to the hall she was on. The sign overhead read *Intensive Care Authorized Personal Only*.

"Intensive care, she's in intensive care?"

"It's the best place for her now. We are keeping her comfortable. I gave her a unit of blood this morning and she seems to be a little stronger."

He led me to the cubicle that was hers. There were doors going into each room, so we could have some privacy.

THE MOUNTAINS CALL MY NAME

"Mama. Hey, are you awake?"

She was hooked up to so many tubes and monitors. Daniel knew I would know what each beep and monitor reading meant. He was right and it wasn't good.

"'Lis'beth, I'm so glad yer here. I hope I didn't sceer ya. Dr. Daniel, he's been so good to me. I'm just a little weak now, but I'll be home fer Christmas. Won't I, Dr. Daniel?"

"We'll see how you're doing in a few days."

"In a few days she'll be gone. I cain't let her be by herself at Christmas. She's been alone too much," she said, squeezing my hand.

"I'm fine, Mama, you just relax and get well. If I have to, I'll spend Christmas with you here."

"No, little girl, I'll be home by Christmas. I know it in my heart. I'm goin' home." She closed her eyes and I thought she had drifted off to sleep. I started to take my hand from hers and she held it tight.

"Don't go, sweet girl."

Daniel was on one side of the bed and I was on the other. He slightly nodded for me to leave the room.

"Mrs. Edwards, Elizabeth has had a long trip. I'm going to take her to get a Coke. You rest and we'll be back soon."

"Okay, don't go far. I think I'll sleep a little while yer gone."

"We'll be back soon," I said, reaching over to kiss her forehead.

We went back to the little lounge. I let myself drop onto the sofa. My tears came freely again.

"She's bad, Daniel, she's real bad."

"I know, I wish I could tell you something different, but we can't ignore the truth."

"Don't ever, ever lie to me Daniel! Don't ever keep things from me. If she is going to die, I need to know."

He cleared his throat. I could tell he was near tears also.

"She's going to die, Libby. It's not going to be long."

He just held me and let me cry. It seemed for hours we just sat there. Darkness came and he turned on the lamps that were on the side table.

"We have to think about what we're going to do. You really need to get some rest. She will sleep for the night.

"I can't leave her. I need to be close in case she needs me."

"I have a private room where the nurses stay when the weather is too bad for them to leave the hospital. I've made sure no one will bother us. I'm going to go check her again. I told the nurses to call me if there were any changes. They know where I am. But I think I need to go for your sake."

"Can I go?"

"Sure."

We saw the nurse come from her room as we entered the hallway.

"Hey, Bekka, how's the patient?"

"No change, doctor. She's been sleeping for a while. Her blood pressure is still pretty low. I haven't seen any change for better or worse."

He gave the nurse some new orders, and joined me in her room. She was still asleep. I read all the monitors, taking mental note of their readings. Sometimes I think ignorance is bliss. I knew too much, and I knew she was in a lot of trouble.

I walked slowly back down the hall to the private room Daniel had arranged for me. It was a regular hospital room with a bed, recliner and TV. He wanted to make sure that I had everything I needed.

"I won't leave you, sweetie. I'll be right here by your side."

He called for two dinner trays to be sent up to us.

"I'm not hungry, Daniel."

"Try to eat something. You can't get down. You have to be strong for your mom."

I managed to eat a little. It was getting quite late and Daniel pulled the covers down on the bed and told me to get in.

"No, I need to stay awake in case she needs me."

"If there are any changes I'll let you know immediately."

"Okay, but promise."

"I promise."

I raised the head of the bed so we could watch some TV. Daniel lay down beside me and took the remote to see if he could find a movie.

"What will the nurses say if they find us in bed together?"

"I'll be the talk of the hospital," he said, grinning at me.

"We'll be the talk of the hospital."

"They'll say that Dr. Scott finally got a woman. I think they were concerned that I was going to end up a bachelor."

"A waste of such a hunk of man."

"You think I'm a hunk?"

"Absolutely, and you're mine. Remember we're going steady."

THE MOUNTAINS CALL MY NAME

"Oh yeah, I forgot for a moment.

He was wearing teal colored hospital scrubs, which made him look so sexy. Every nurse there probably wished he were hers. His black curls always seemed to have their own mind as to how they would lie. I especially liked it when that one curl hung on his forehead.

"What are you thinking about? he asked."

"I'm trying to watch this mystery movie if you will let me."

I reached up and tugged at the little black curl that fell down on his forehead.

He took my hand in his and kissed all my fingers. Then he just held them close to his heart. I lay down with my head cradled in his arms. We snuggled close together. He turned on his side to face me. We lay face to face; our lips were almost touching. I wanted him to kiss me, but he just lay there with his eyes closed as if he were asleep. I moved a little closer and kissed him. His response was a welcome relief to my emotion filled day. He had truly been my rock. I reached my arm over his side and pulled him closer to me as we lay there in the bed. I needed to be close to him. My world was rocking and holding on to him made it a little more stable.

"I love you, Daniel," I said, relaxing in his arms.

"I love you, too, my little princess," he said, bending to kiss me again.

I had shifted to my back and Daniel followed my kiss. He raised himself on one elbow and was slightly over me when the nurse came in.

"Oh! Dr. Scott, I'm sorry I can come back."

"No, everything's fine. What is it?" he said, getting hastily to his feet.

"You're being paged. I wasn't sure if you heard it or not. You asked me to keep you informed."

"Thanks, Bekka, I'll get it."

"Sorry, I have to check this, he said to me."

He picked up the phone beside the bed and dialed the extension the nurse had given to him, then ran his fingers through his dark curls.

"I have to go change some orders. I'll be back soon. Try to get some rest," he said, kissing my forehead.

I don't know when I drifted off to sleep, but I didn't remember Daniel coming back into the room. I woke up at 5:00 o'clock with the room still empty. Where was Daniel, I thought? Had he been gone all night? Then my eyes wandered to the recliner beside the bed and I saw a blanket crumpled up in the seat. He must have slept there. I guess he didn't want to venture back to bed. I went to the bathroom and freshened up some. I brushed my hair and decided to let it stay loose. I needed to get a haircut soon, I thought as I studied my unkempt self in the mirror. My clothing was wrinkled from having slept in them. I was just coming out of the bathroom when Daniel entered the room. His eyes were red-rimmed, I was hoping from lack of sleep, but it looked as if he had been crying.

"Is everything okay?" I asked with a concerned look.

"It will be. I have been with your mom for quite awhile. She wanted to talk, so I obliged her."

"Why didn't you come get me?"

"She wanted to talk to me, no offense. She wanted to know what my intentions were where you were concerned. She told me many stories about her life and raising you. She can be a very entertaining lady. I gave her an extra unit of blood and she finally drifted off to sleep just a little while ago."

"Can I see her?"

"Yeah, but try not to wake her up. She's very tired."

"How much time does she have, Daniel?"

"Only our Father in heaven knows that answer."

"But you're a doctor, you should have some idea. I've heard doctors hedge before to spare the family. Is that what you're doing?"

He pulled me into his arms, and held me close to him.

"Maybe a few days. Surgery is out of the question and we're too late for chemo."

THE MOUNTAINS CALL MY NAME

I drew a deep breath, determined not to cry this time.

"Okay, let's go see her."

We made the same trek down to ICU. I quietly opened her door. She was resting so peacefully. She looked so tiny under the covers and tubes were in so many places. I kissed my finger tips and lay them lightly on her forehead. I made it from the room before the tears began to flow. A familiar arm went around my shoulder as we walked down the hallway.

"I'll be okay," I said, wiping my eyes.

"I've called Mandy and she's preparing breakfast for us. I think we need to get away from here for a while."

"Do you think it will be okay if we leave?"

"I'll be in close contact with everyone here. They all know how important this is."

"Okay, if you say so."

Daniel got my luggage from my car and transferred it to his. "You're going to be staying at my house. The guest room is all ready. I'm not going to take no for an answer."

I was too sad too object. I was ready to let someone else take charge of my life for a while. I couldn't believe I was about to loose my mother. We rode in silence to Daniel's house. I rested my head against the headrest and kept my eyes closed. Daniel reached over and took my hand in his as he drove. The same beautiful music played on his car stereo, but it didn't soothe me the way it did before. Everything was changing and I couldn't stop any of it. I felt like I was on a runaway train and helpless to stop the collision that was sure to come.

I hated death. It seemed to come calling too often lately. Had it been just a few short days ago that I heard the plaintive song of Daddy John singing on that cold, dark hilltop? "Swing Low Sweet Chariot" still rang in my ears. It seemed the chariot would be swinging down again.

I let the tears fall silently down my face, too tired to wipe them away. Daniel found some tissues in the console of his car and handed them over to me without speaking. When we arrived at the house Mandy met us at the car. As soon as I got out, her sweet arms went around me. I let my tears flow on her large, soft shoulder. She held me and rocked me as if I were her child.

"There, there sweet chil'. Mandy's got you now, I'll take care of you."

"Thank you," I managed to get out between snubs.

She took a big old hanky and wiped my tears.

"Let's go get some breakfast. I made somethin' real special just fo' you. Food allus make the pain better."

Daniel took my suitcase to the bedroom and came back to the living room. Mandy had left me there to go fix the dining table. I was sitting on the sofa waiting for him. He came and sat down beside me.

"We'll see this through together," he said, taking my hand in his.

Mandy had a large breakfast prepared with everything I could possibly want. I forced myself to eat so I wouldn't disappoint her. After we had finished, Daniel and I went into the living room to rest. Daniel got down on one knee before me and reached in his pocket and brought out a small black box.

"Elizabeth, I know you might think this is terrible timing, but ..." He opened up the box to show me a beautiful diamond ring. I had never seen one so beautiful.

"... I know, that I know, that I know, I will love you for the rest of my life. Would you do me the honor of becoming my wife?"

He took the ring and placed it on my finger.

"Daniel! Oh Daniel! Yes, I know, that I know, that I know, I will love you the rest of my life. I would be honored to be your wife."

He took me into his arms and kissed me, through snot and tears. Tears were streaming down his cheeks too. I reached out my hand to wipe them away. He took my hand in his and kissed the finger that held the diamond ring.

"I will never fail you, Elizabeth. I vow to you, I will never fail you. Would you pray with me? I've prayed so hard for this moment. I know God gave you to me. This moment in time God kept for me and you. I've often wondered why there was never anyone I really fell for. All these years, my heart has never belonged to another. I wasn't against loving someone else. There just was never anyone I fell in love with. I rarely thought of you over the years. Occasionally I would remember something we had done together.

"That day at the altar when you married David, I gave you up. I knew I had lost all hope of your loving me. From that day on you were gone from me. But when Grandmother told me you were in town, I was anxious to see you. Then the night we worked over Sharon together, it was as if I was transported back in time and everything came rushing vividly back to me. All the feelings I had buried since I was eighteen washed over me. The more I was with you the more I wanted to be with you.

"I'm not sure when it dawned on me that I could hope again. I think it was the night that you responded to my kiss. I think it was then that I knew you were going to be mine. I knew God brought you back to me. You're the only one I've ever loved, Elizabeth. I set you free, and God brought you back."

I knelt there in the floor in front of the sofa and listened to him pray.

"Dear Heavenly Father, this is a time for joy and sadness. There are some tough times ahead. Give me wisdom and grace to handle what I have to handle. Give Libby grace to hear what has to be said. For this I will be eternally grateful. Thank you for giving this gift of love to me. I will treasure it with my life. You've guarded my heart all these years for this moment. You know I've never loved another. Help us to stay pure and holy before you. Guard us against temptations that weaken us. It's in your precious and holy name we pray. Amen"

"Dear Lord." I continued. "I'm so weak now. I hardly know what to say. Thank you for this precious man you have given to me. This sudden movement in my heart must have come from you. I thank you for this treasure. Help me to be what I need to be for him. First you gave him to me as a best friend, now you are giving him to me as a husband. It all still sounds so strange coming from my lips. I know the healing is from you. It was only a few days ago I begged for you to send me joy, and you sent it abundantly. Now, my mother is dying. I guess you knew when to send an angel to stand by me. Help me in my weakness. I don't think I'm handling all this too well. But you tell us that in our weaknesses, then we are strong. I'm asking for an extra measure of grace. I love you, my Savior. Amen"

We got up from our kneeling position and sat back down on the sofa. He was unusually quite and seemed to be pale in color. I could tell something was troubling him. Every time he started to speak he cleared his throat, as if it were too difficult to speak. He excused himself and said he would be right back. He took a few minutes before coming back to the room. He came and sat down beside me again. He took both my hands in his, still finding it difficult to tell me what he wanted to tell me.

"I gave you your ring earlier than I intended because I wanted you to know that you have me to support you no matter what happens. Remember, I told you that your mom wanted to talk last night?"

"Yes."

"She had quite a story to tell. It's a story you've never heard before. She asked me to tell it to you for her. After I tell you, she said she would talk with you, but she couldn't be the first to tell you what I'm about to tell you."

"Daniel, what are you talking about?"

"This is probably the hardest thing I've ever had to do in my life, including saying goodbye to you at the altar."

I felt the blood drain from me. I tried to brace myself but didn't know how.

He stopped for another long moment.

"Daniel, just tell me," I said with a trembling voice.

"I wish I could keep this to myself and shield you from the pain it's going to cause. Here goes. A long time ago, after Jonathan died, your father was very distraught. He drank a lot and left about that time to go work in West Virginia."

"I know all about that. Mama spoke often about feeling so lonely. It was about that time when I was born. He worked locally after that."

He took a deep quivery breath, and slowly let it escape.

"As you said, it was about the time you were born. It seems that while he was working there he got a young waitress pregnant. Probably because he was suffering, she comforted him, and comfort and compassion can do strange things to your thinking. Especially if you're drinking."

"No way, is this what she wanted you to tell me? That just means I have a sister or brother somewhere. She thought I wouldn't understand that. Oh, Daniel, she's afraid I won't understand that? I would be unhappy that he would do such a thing, but I would have forgiven him."

"There's more," He took another long pause and pressed his fingers to his eyes, as if to stop a flow of tears. "The child that was born to the waitress was you."

"Then...then...let me get this straight!" Panic was rising in my throat and I was beginning to yell at Daniel.

"You're telling me that Mary Margaret Edwards is not my mother?"

"Yeah, that's what I'm saying."

I felt numb and speechless. Nothing had ever shocked me like this, not even David dying in front of me in the hospital. I got to my feet and ran out the door. All I knew was that I had to run. Daniel tried to stop me, but I was too quick for him. I ran as far as I could before he caught me. We fell onto the icy ground in my struggle to get away from him. He held me in a vise-like grip. There was no way I could free myself from him. We sat coatless in the frigid snow. I just remember screaming over and over that he was lying to me.

"See this ring, Elizabeth?" he said, holding my ringed hand up before my face. "That's why I gave it to you before I told you this. I promised I would never fail you. I've had to deliver some devastating news to you. I would never lie to you."

"Oh God, Daniel, please tell me it's not true. That's all you have to do is just say, 'Elizabeth, I'm not telling you the truth'."

THE MOUNTAINS CALL MY NAME

"I can't," he said, rocking me in his arm. His salty tears were mingling with mine. "You can't run from this, sweetie. You can't run this time; I won't let you run this time."

He stood and lifted me to my feet.

"We've got to get back inside. You're going to freeze out here."

"I don't care. The numbness I feel is far greater than freezing. Maybe you could just leave me here for a while. The cold might numb my soul."

"Come, you know I'm not going to leave you here. If I have to I can carry you, but I would rather you walk. I'm not leaving you here."

He led me back into the house.

"Get me a blanket, Mandy," Daniel said as we came into the house.

He wrapped me in the warm blanket, and I lay on the sofa with my head in his lap. The fireplace was going. Mandy must have started it. She looked at Daniel with her big, loving brown eyes filled with compassion for me.

"Mandy go to my bedroom and turn down my covers, and get that electric blanket in the closet and put it on the bed."

I didn't ask anymore questions. I was afraid of the answers. Mandy came back to Daniel and told him it was ready.

THE MOUNTAINS CALL MY NAME

"Now, I want you to go run a toasty warm tub of water and make it like girls like it. You know, with bubbles or whatever mom left here."

"Yes, Master Daniel."

"I'm going to give you a light sedative and I want you to take a warm bath and rest for a while."

"I don't need a sedative, Daniel, I just need you."

"You have me, but trust me; I want you to have a sedative. You're going to have to go to the hospital and face your mother. You need to rest before we go."

"She's not my mother. You just told me that. Who am I visiting, Daniel? Who is this woman, the one I called 'Mama' my whole life?"

He led me up to his bedroom, took a pill out of his medical bag and made me take it.

"Master Daniel, Ms. Elizabeth's bath's ready."

"Okay, Mandy."

"You scoot; we got girl things to do. You go take a shower or something. I'll take care of this chil'."

Mandy so tenderly helped me out of my clothing and into the bath.

"You just leave it to me and Master Daniel. We take care of ya. Whatever da problem, it'll be okay. Our Heavenly Father know what's comin' 'fore it get here. Just let him have it, baby."

THE MOUNTAINS CALL MY NAME

"Mandy..."

"What, chil'?"

"Did Daniel show you this?" She was the first to see the diamond on my hand.

"He did. Master Daniel is jest like my baby. He came to me when he got back from Norf Ca'lina the fust thing he did was drag out dat box. His eyes was a beamin'. He loves you, chil'. I didn't know it was gonna be today, but I knowed it was a comin'. He'll be good to you, and you'll become my chil' too. Fer what belongs to Master Daniel's mine. I feel jest like I'm his mammy. I love him wit' my whole heart."

She sat with me the whole time I was in my bath.

"Master Daniel tol' me not to leave ya."

When I was thoroughly washed, soaked and scrubbed, she helped me out of the tub into a big bath towel. I felt like a little girl. By the time the bath was over the sedative was well on its way to working.

"Mandy?"

"What, baby?"

"What would you do if you found out that something you thought to be the truth your whole life, ended up being a lie?"

"Well, I thinks I would find out why. Then I would pray to my Lawd fer strenf to understand."

THE MOUNTAINS CALL MY NAME

There was a knock on the door.

"Mandy, can I come in?"

"Yes, we all ready."

She had helped me into my pajamas and I was already in Daniel's big bed.

"Thank you," he said, hugging her. "We'll be okay now."

He pulled the cover up around me. I had warmed from the bath and the blankets, and was drowsy from the pill Daniel had given me.

He lay down beside me on the bed. He took me into his arms and held me.

"It's going to be okay. I promise you, baby, it will be okay."

"How can it ever be okay, Daniel? I don't even know who I am. Who was my mother if this woman wasn't? Did she bother to fill you in on that? It would be good to know."

"She said she would tell you the whole story later. She just said she needed to let you know the truth before she died. She was the last link to the truth."

"Why did she feel the need to come clean? Why couldn't she just take the truth to the grave? She did awfully well up till now? What is the purpose of all this? Why couldn't she just let it be?"

THE MOUNTAINS CALL MY NAME

"Maybe she needed to be set free from the burden. Think about what a wonderful woman it would be to take another woman's child and raise it as her own.

"Why did she have to tell me?" Why couldn't she just not tell me?"

"You'll have to ask her that question. I don't have the answer."

I could hardly keep my eyes open. Daniel's closeness and the warmth were overcoming to me. I remember trying to ask him another question but couldn't get it out."

"Shhh... just rest now. I will stay until you fall asleep."

He took my hand again and pressed it to his lips. My last thoughts were of the warmth of him near me. I don't know if it was because of the sedative or not, but the nightmare that came when I did sleep was a tormented one. I kept seeing these faceless women coming to me asking if I was their child. When I woke, I was running in these woods hiding from them behind trees so I wouldn't be found. I must have been calling out in my sleep, because Daniel was shaking me awake, telling me it was all a dream. I was trembling when I finally woke up.

"It was just a dream. You're awake now."

I relayed my dream to him. And when I was finally calm, he told me that the hospital called and said Mama was asking for me.

311

THE MOUNTAINS CALL MY NAME

"What am I going to do, Daniel? I don't think I can go. I can't see her. What am I going to say? What will I feel?"

"Libby, look at me."

He took my face in his hand and made me look at him. We need to go. Do you understand what I'm trying to tell you? We have to go now. The last report wasn't good. You don't have much time, Honey, I'm sorry."

A new wave of tears came for this woman I called "Mama".

"Oh God, Daniel! I can't do this! I can't do this! I'm not strong enough."

"I'll be right beside you. Draw your strength from me. You can lean pretty heavily on me. I'm going to go change. I'll be right back."

As if on cue, Mandy was immediately at my side. She picked out an outfit for me to wear, and helped me into it. She got a brush from the dresser and brushed my hair.

"The Lawd know, sweet girl, the Lawd know. He won't let you go alone. He's been down where ya hurtin'. He say he won't let you go alone. I be prayin' fer ya."

Daniel's light knock came and he entered.

"I called the hospital. They say she is getting quite agitated. She isn't going to rest until you get there. She knows now that you know. I promised her I would tell you today. Her vitals aren't doing so hot. Are you ready?"

THE MOUNTAINS CALL MY NAME

"I guess, ready as I'll ever be. Please pray for me, Daniel?"

He held me close and prayed. Mandy stood beside me with her arms around the both of us. Together they both lifted me up to the throne of God.

# Chapter Eleven

The hospital was quiet when we got there. Visitation hours were already over. It had been barely twenty-four hours since I started this odyssey. What would I say when I saw her? Should I just listen or should I talk first? I was shaking with emotion. A wave of nausea hit as the uncertainty visited me anew. We went in through the physicians' entrance in the back of the building. Daniel led me into a vacant room. He lifted my face and kissed me.

"Remember, whatever she has done, it was out of love for you. I have to remember she's my patient. She's very weak. If you can't handle this right now and stay relatively calm with her, I'm going to ask that we go another time."

"Oh God! What am I going to do? I can't promise you, Daniel. You're asking something that is going against everything I'm feeling. I don't know if I can hold up or not. I'm just not sure. Don't forget, I just found out she isn't my mother. How can I not be emotional?"

He put his arms around me and held me so tightly to him. I could tell he was fighting two battles. One for me, and one for my mother.

"This is what we'll do. I'll let it go as far as I think she can stand it. Reason being, she doesn't have much time. If we wait, you might not ever hear her story, but if she gets too emotional she might not make it. It's all in God's hands."

He pulled me to him and whispered a prayer in my ear for grace. For all of us. We entered the back elevator and got off at the fourth floor.

"I need to stop by the nurses' station and give Sarah some orders for your mom."

He went behind the desk, took my mother's chart and looked intently at it. He wrote something on it and handed it to a nurse. I assumed it was Sarah.

We need to wait here just a minute. I'm getting a sedative for her. I want her to have it just a little before I let you in. Sarah handed him a syringe and he headed for my mom's room. About ten minutes later he came back and handed the empty syringe to the nurse.

"What did she say?"

"She asked if you were here, and I said you were. She asked if I had told you everything, and I assured her I had. She asked if you were okay and I said as well as could be expected."

"I guess that's about as true as it gets. I'm so sorry you are in the middle of this horrendous situation."

"I wouldn't be any other place. I love you, and I love her, and God loves us all. This afternoon when you were sleeping, I sat in my chair before the fire and read some of the Psalms. They are most comforting in times like this. In Psalm 27:14, God says: 'Wait on the Lord and be of good courage and He shall strengthen your heart.' Be courageous, Libby."

He took my hand and we went down the hall together. We stopped in front of her door. He turned me to face him. He lowered his head to mine and lightly kissed me. A lonely little tear escaped my eyes. I quickly brushed it away.

"Let's do it."

I slowly opened the door. She lay there, very quiet and still. The figure of my mother, so helpless and near death. I'd loved her my whole life. I wanted to touch her, but couldn't bring myself to cross the invisible barrier that lay between us. The barrier of truth and lies. On one side was the lie that she was my mother. On the other side was the truth about who I was. Could I just walk out and pretend that I never heard what Daniel told me today? When I crossed over, there would be no return. I would become a bastard. A child born out of wedlock. A child born to a whore. A child with a mother I didn't know. A cast-off from an illicit affair. I was good at pushing things away. I did it for three years, and was quite successful. I could go back to my home and close all the doors and windows and hibernate.

I knew the mountains would bring disaster. I told Daniel that bad things would happen if I came back. My heart told me so. I had run from these mountains all my life, maybe now I finally knew why. Maybe all my life I sensed the secret. Perhaps if I had run far enough I wouldn't be here right now. I would forever believe this lady was my mother.

How could she have lived with this? And my father... it made me nauseated to think of him lying with a waitress just to fulfill lust within him. My precious father, the one that would lay down his life for me. I would never look at him the same. Everything was ruined. My life would forever be different. Who would think a few short hours, or moments, could deal so much grief, and such joy. I raised my hand to study the diamond that now rested on my hand, and couldn't help but smile.

My gaze was fixated on my mother. I raised my eyes to meet Daniel's staring at me. I quickly turned toward the monitors and saw that the readings were dangerously low. Her heart was erratic, and her blood pressure had dropped drastically. She seemed to be sleeping peacefully. How I wished that I could.

I turned and started to walk out of the room. I couldn't wake her. I couldn't cross the barrier. Daniel quickly made it to the door before I did and blocked my way. He put both hands on my shoulders and pulled me into his arms again.

"Hey, you two, I think you need to come closer," my mother's faint voice said.

I could feel the color drain from me. I turned slowly and went to the side of her bed. She reached her little hand up toward me. The IV needle had turned the area purple where they had poked for her tiny little veins. I took her hand in mine and raised it to my lips.

"You must hate me, little girl," she said, her eyes glistening with unshed tears.

THE MOUNTAINS CALL MY NAME

"I could never hate you. You have given me too much love for me to hate you. I just don't understand how…" My voice trailed off with the unasked questions.

"I think it would be easier if I just told the whole…" she struggled for breath.

Daniel took his stethoscope and listened to her lungs. He reached for the oxygen valve above her bed and turned it up. I looked at the reading on her monitor, and her oxygen saturation level was dangerously low. She lay still, gathering strength to begin again.

"The day yer daddy came home and found Jonathan had died, I saw the light go out in his soul."

Her voice was coming in breathless little gasps. She was so weak that I had to set close to her whispered words.

"It just about kilt him. He stayed drunk all the time. He rarely drew a sober breath. It wasn't long 'fore Jonny died that he got laid off at the saw mill. Him and a bunch down the next holler 'cided to go up to West Virgini' and get work in the mines. They were to work all week and come home on weekends. Sometimes it would be two weeks 'fore he'd get to come home. Well, they all got jobs. Mr. Harmon had a big truck with a thing over the back and he hauled ever'body.

"Come Friday he'd lay in the back of that truck and drink all the way home. By the time he'd get here he'd be drunk as a skunk and smell as bad." She smiled at her description of him.

THE MOUNTAINS CALL MY NAME

"I hated yer daddy then. Ever' Friday was a dark day fer me, even when the sun was a shinin'. I'da rather been lonely then put up with a drunk.

"My heart hurt so bad I thought I would die myself. If I'da had the courage I would a kilt myself. I had those thoughts some time. But I didn't know how to do it. I was afraid of guns and didn't have any pills. If it hadn't been fer Bessie, and Anna Belle, I think I'da purely died.

"Bessie, dear sweet Bessie, she never let me down. She'd spend hours with me. She was my rock in the time of storm. After she'd get her work done and the kids in bed, she'd come down and be with me. Sometime we'd talk, sometimes we'd cry, sometime we'd laugh, and sometime just sit and be quiet. God says in His word He'd send His angels to camp 'round us, and watch over us. I think she was my angel.

"She was here to help me lay out Jonathan when he died. She washed his cold little body. Her tears dropped on him as she cleaned him. When the undertaker came he was all ready. He looked like a little doll. I wished God woulda tooken me, but He had a job fer me to do and no one else could do it. I didn't know it at the time. He only revealed it to me later. Times were bad then. They was dark, dark days, black as midnight, they was. I wanted yer daddy to hold me, and tell me it was gonna be okay, but he were off somewhere in his mind. A place he didn't let nobody go but him. Maybe the pain went away there, I don't know. They's times I wished I was a drinker, but I weren't. I knowed how ya felt when David died.

"Yer a lot like yer daddy 'Lis'beth. Ya'll just digged this deep hole, crawled in it and shut out the world. You did that when David died. I saw your soul light flicker out just like yer daddy's. When you shut me out after David died, my mind went back to that time when yer daddy did that. I wanted to hold ya, and take care of yer pain. But ya went where yer daddy did and shut the door. I pained so fer ya, 'Lis'beth Ann. I just wished I coulda made it all better fer ya. I knowed only a new love would put that light back again.

"He coulda at least talked to me. I deserved better than that. But my God gave me strength and I made it. I waited and waited fer him to love me and he never would. So my God loved me. If'n he coulda' just put his arms around me, just oncet it woulda' helped me. He never did, not then anyway. But God held me in those lonely nights when I waited fer Jonny to cry, and he never did. When the bed was cold wher yer daddy once warmed it, God held me close to his bosom. It was in the cold lonely nights I learned what God's love was about."

She took several deep breaths. I could tell it was painful to relive all this. She continued, never once looking at me. I don't think she could have gone on if she had.

Daniel took a cool cloth and laid it on her forehead.

"I think deep down he musta thought I kilt that little boy. God in heaven knowed I couldn't he'p it. He jest went to sleep and woke up with Jesus. Oh, the times I wished God woulda tooken me instead of Jonny. He was such a beautiful baby. Did I tell ya how beautiful he was, 'Lizabeth?"

She waited just a moment as if looking at the image she carried of him in her mind.

"The death angel came a callin' and got the wrong one. I don't think yer daddy woulda minded half as bad if he tooken me instead of his little boy. I don't think I ever hurt that bad before, or since 'cept now."

The tears were stealing down her cheeks. Only God in heaven was holding us both together. If I had to speak one word right now I would break into a million pieces.

"I wished they was a place I coulda run," she continued. "But wher would I go? The holler was the onlyest place I knowed. So I stayed wher God put me and made the best of it."

She was quiet for a few minutes. I thought she was asleep. I started to speak her name and she began again. I saw Daniel was anxiously watching her monitor, and me.

"It was along about the first of July when my life changed ferever. Mornin' was about to break, my child. The dark night was about to turn to day. You know that old sayin', 'joy comes in the mornin'? Change comes fast, 'Lis'beth Anne. When it comes time fer God's hand to move it ain't nothin' gonna stand in its way. Mark that down and don't ever ferget it."

Her eyes opened and she looked up into Daniel eyes and I saw a sweet communion pass between them. A look of understanding and compassion.

Suddenly she took in a sharp breath and winced with the pain that came. A moan escaped her drawn lips.

Daniel took his hand and gently turned her face to his.

"You can quit now if you want to," he said tenderly to her.

She shook her head and continued.

"I 'member it all jest as if it were yesterd'y. He'd been a workin' up there about a year, and things stayed about the same, him a drinkin' and everthing. I was sittin' in the swing tryin' to catch a breeze. I looked and saw yer daddy comin' up the holler. I hated it when he'd come home. But it seemed this time they were somethin' differ'nt. He wasn't staggerin' and fallin' down. I hadn't seen him sober since yer brother died.

"It was awful hot that day. I'd stay on the porch till time fer bed, 'cause our little house got so hot. I was just sittin' there, swingin'. He came up on the porch and set down in the swing beside me. I cain't 'member when was the last time he had done that. Just come and sit with me. He didn't speak fer the longest time. Jest set there and rocked. I'll never ferget the look on his face as long as I live. I knowed somethin' had happened. I thought maybe he lost his job or sumpthin'. He set there holdin' his hat in his hand just starin' at the floor. He just kept a twistin' the brim of that old hat over and over. The sweat was pourin' off his face. He'd take his big ole handkerchief and wipe it off.

"Then he spoke up. I could tell he was havin' a hard time. He said 'woman I got to tell ya somethin'. If I could change things, I would, but what I done cain't be undone. I wished to God it could, but it cain't. I got into some trouble up at the mine.'

"He jest kept settin' there and finally I told him to 'jest spit it out, old man'.

"He never oncet looked my way. Jest set starin' at the floorboards of the porch. Then he told me a story that shook me to my very bein'. He started to tell me about him and the men he worked with. He said they'd go out to this tavern and drink until the wee hours of the mornin'. They'd shoot pool, play cards and drink 'til time to go back to camp. One night he said the tavern keeper's daughter was there. First one and then the other was a dancin' with her, but she kinda took to yer daddy. They got to drinkin' and dancin' and playin' around together."

She stopped then and seemed to have trouble breathing. Tears were streaming down her drawn little face. I didn't think she would be able to continue.

"Mama, you don't have to..."

She held up her hand to stop me, and just nodded her head.

"One thing led to another and they sneaked off to the back wher she lived and, well, you was conceived then."

My hands were clinched into a tight fist; I could feel my nails cut into my palm. I silently prayed to God for strength to sit quietly and listen to the horrible story of my creation.

"He said it was only one time, and he was so drunk he didn't remember it happenin'. He said, 'I swear to you it was jest one time.'

"It didn't matter to me; one time was as bad as a hunderd. I was sick to my stomach. Here I was, him not even talkin' to me and layin' with another woman. God says 'be sure yer sins will find you out'. I was too angry to cry. I hated him fer even tellin' me. He violated our marriage bed and that was unforgivable. Who did he think he was? You woulda thought he was the only one that had his heart ripped out. Was he the only one that lost a son? He buried his pain in a bottle; mine was raw with nothin' to numb it. It felt like he took a hot poker and run it through what was left of my soul."

The monitors where getting even more erratic as Daniel and I watched.

"Mrs. Edwards, I think you should stop now and rest a bit," Daniel said.

Sarah came into the room and stood beside Daniel.

"Dr. Scott?" she whispered to him.

He nodded toward the door, motioning for her to step outside the room. He was only out there a second before he came back into the room.

She was back quickly with a syringe. She handed it to Daniel and he put the medicine into the IV catheter. Whatever it was he gave her made her rally slightly. I could tell the pain had once again eased by the look of relief that crossed her face. Daniel looked at me and shook his head. We both knew we were racing for time.

"Let me finish," she said with pleading eyes. "She's got to know."

I reached over and took her hand in mine once again. It was as cold as ice.

THE MOUNTAINS CALL MY NAME

"I'm almost through," she said softly.

"It's okay, Mama," I said, kissing her hand.

"He told me him layin' with her wasn't the worst part.

"What little bit of life that was left in me drained away, fer I knowed what was a comin'.

"He said he got her pregnant. She gave birth to two little girls about two weeks before, and died given' birth to 'em. One of them died and one lived. He told me, 'she ain't got nobody. He said, 'I'm askin' fer this baby, do you think we could take her and raise her?' He never quit starin' at the floorboards of the porch. 'The girl's mother said she'll give her away to the first person that comes through the door and asks fer her. She said she cain't bother with her. She has the tavern to run and it ain't no place fer a baby to be. She ain't got no family. She said if I don't come get her she'll be gone in two weeks. She said the first person to claim her gets her.'

"He promised me the moon that day. He said if I would help him raise her he wouldn't go back to the mines, he'd never drink another day and would start goin' to church and doin' right. I told him I would have to pray about it fer a while. He said there weren't time to pray. she's gonna give her away tomarry.

"I didn't have much time, so God gave me a quick answer. I figgered this little girl didn't ask to be born'd to a whore and a drunk, but I shore could make this little girl feel like a little princess. I didn't do it fer him but fer that little girl that nobody wanted.

THE MOUNTAINS CALL MY NAME

"Mr. Harmon knowed about everthing, and he took us up there. We traveled fer several hours to the town he'd been a livin' in. I thought we lived in a shabby place, but that place back up there in the mountains was an awful place.

"We pulled up in front of this honky-tonk place and he went in to get his baby. I was hopin' she hadn't already given it away.

"He went in by hisself, 'cause I jest couldn't go in that sin hole. He came out a-carryin' this little bundle wrapped in rags. He opened the door and placed her in my arms. I pulled back the old rag blanket that kivered her to see the most beautiful little doll baby. I can see it just like it was yesterd'y. Her little head was kivered with brunette fuzz. She looked straight into my face and smiled. My heart was hers from the moment she smiled at me.

"She was so dirty, and smelled bad, but it didn't matter to me. I held her real close and told her I would love her till the day I died. She wrapped herself around my heart that day and didn't let go.

"Yer Daddy said you didn't have a name. No one even bothered to give you a name. I knew the thing I should do but it was real hard. 'What's her mama's name?' I asked him. He kinda sputtered out 'Rose Anne'. I felt we should give you part of yer mama's name. I don't know why I felt so strong that I should do that but I did, 'cept God made me do it. So I said her name will be Elizabeth Anne. Anne after her mama and Elizabeth because it means 'oath of God'. She will serve the Lord God and he will be her savior.

THE MOUNTAINS CALL MY NAME

"I just couldn't find no love in my heart fer ya daddy at first. But I shore loved that little girl. I figgered he'd be back a drinkin', but it never happened. We all went to church that first Sunday you was with us, 'Lis'beth. He was at the altar repentin' and cryin'. I figgered if God could fergive, was I better'n him? I asked God that day to restore some kinda love between us again, and he did far above all I asked. Yer daddy spent the last of his days makin' up fer all my sad times."

She turned to me for the first time and looked directly into my eyes and soul. I will never forget the words she told me, if I live to be a thousand.

"I kept this secret all these years because I didn't want anyone callin' my little angel a bastard child. Not this little angel God placed in my care. You had a mama and a daddy that loved you and that was all anyone needed to know. People never did really know how you came to live with us. I never mentioned yer daddy's sin, I figgered he paid the price. It was never spoke of again between us.

"Don't hate him, 'Lis'beth. Because of his pain from losin' his baby, the devil got into his life. We can all slip there.

"I did it all because I loved you," she said, barely above a whisper. "Forgive me, but I kept the secret, not from you, but *fer* you. I didn't want ya to feel bad, like ya weren't wanted, or ya was a mistake. Don't ya see?"

"You're my mother. I have nothing to forgive you for."

THE MOUNTAINS CALL MY NAME

She held out her other hand toward me. She had been holding it in a tight little ball. She slowly opened her fingers to reveal a small key with a red ribbon on it.

She smiled a sweet smile at me and said, "There's some things waitin' fer ya... It's time ya saw. I'm so tired, sweet girl..." Her voice trailed off to nothing. There were no more words.

I took the small gold key from her lifeless fingers and stared at it as if it could talk to me.

Daniel came to my side and pulled me up into his arms. He drew me close and whispered in my ear only for me to hear.

"You need to release her, Elizabeth, there's nothing more that can be done."

"But she didn't say what the key was to. I need to know what this goes to."

"It's too late, sweetheart. She can't hear you anymore."

"Maybe another shot or something like you gave her before. I've got to tell her goodbye, and I need to know what this key is to."

Daniel pulled back from me enough to look me in the eyes and shook his head.

"She's beyond coming back to us, sweetheart."

"Take the machines off her, Daniel. Let her have her rest," I managed to get out through my sobs.

THE MOUNTAINS CALL MY NAME

One by one he stopped the beeping of the monitors and the hissing of the oxygen. He slowly and lovingly proceeded to take out all her tubes and wires. The room became totally silent as the last monitor was unplugged. Her eyes were already set, staring blankly into another world. If I could be still enough I think I could feel the rush of angel wings as they came to carry her home. If only I could see from behind those eyes to what glory she was beholding.

I lowered the rails of her bed and lay my head on the pillow beside hers.

"Mama, its okay, you can go now. Do you see Daddy and Jonathan? You've been a good mother to me, and a loving wife. Thanks for protecting me with your secret. Give Daddy a kiss for me, and tell him I love him," I said, sobbing into her pillow.

I heard the familiar death rattle that I had heard a thousand times in the ICU, but now it was painfully new. I held her hand in mine, wanting to feel the warmth in her body for as long as I could.

There were just the three of us in her room.

"Take as long as you need. There's no hurry," Daniel said softly to me.

"Daniel, there are angels in the room! Do you sense their presence? They've come to take home a child of God," I said, trying to control my tears.

"I have to go sign some papers and make some phone calls."

"Don't leave me here by myself," I said anxiously.

He came to me and helped me to my feet. "I'll stay with you until you're ready to go?"

I leaned down and gave her one last kiss on the cheek.

"I love you, sweet lady."

I pulled the covers up around her shoulders. I wanted to tuck her in one last time. The tears I thought were gone came flooding back. Daniel held me and gently rocked me in his arms.

"Come, let's go home."

As I walked out the door I turned and looked one last time at this tiny little body that was once my mother. I looked at the key that I held in my hand, not having a clue what it went to or what secrets it would reveal.

Chapter Twelve

We left the hospital through the same back door which we had come in. Numbness flooded over me. It was snowing again as we made our way to his car. No words were spoken between us. He opened my door and helped me in. Once we were on the road, it dawned on me; I needed to make arrangements for someone to get her body.

"Daniel, what am I supposed to do about the funeral home?"

"It's all taken care of. I told you that at the hospital, but you must not have heard me. When I was with your mom the other morning while you slept, she told me exactly what to do for her. She didn't want you to have to do anything."

"Everything?"

"Clothing, songs, preacher, pallbearers, everything that was to be done, she had planned. All I had to do was to take notes."

"She didn't know about our engagement. She would have been so happy."

"Well, I guess I'm a little old fashioned and I knew she wasn't long for this world, so I asked her permission to marry you. She was as elated as she could get as sick as she was."

"You two did have a long night, didn't you?"

"She was afraid to be by herself that night. She told me if she didn't get the things said she had to that night it may be too late. So when I went in to check on her, she was awake and waiting for me."

"What about her clothing, Daniel? How did you get that?"

"I called Anna Belle and talked to her. She knew what your mother wanted and told me she would get it to the funeral home when she was ready for it."

The snow was coming down thick and wet. The slapping sound of the wipers swishing back and forth kept time with the throb of my headache. I took my fingers and pressed them to my temple.

"Are you okay?" he said, reaching up and taking my hand in his.

"I have a terrible headache. Probably from crying too much. I'll be okay after I rest some."

The clock on the dash said 4:00 o'clock.

"When is everything going to happen?"

"You mean the funeral?"

"Yeah, everything."

THE MOUNTAINS CALL MY NAME

"Don't worry, sweetie, just put your head on my shoulder."

I did as he commanded, and welcomed the softness I found there.

"Tomorrow we'll have to go to the funeral home and tell them what to do, right?" I asked groggily.

"Tomorrow morning sometime we'll go tell them how to do the service. I'll go over everything with you in case there's something you want done that she didn't think of. She wanted it as trouble-free as possible for you."

"She was always thinking of me. I don't think she put herself before anyone her entire life. How wonderful it must be for her to be in heaven. For once she will be first."

"She told me to make sure you were happy. I told her I would die trying," he said, smiling a sad smile at me.

The pain seemed to lessen some as we drove. I suddenly remembered that I didn't ask her who my mother was.

"Daniel, I still don't know who I am. Why didn't I ask her? Now I'll never know. Did you remember her mentioning any last names or the name of the tavern or...." Then I remembered the key I had placed in my pocket.

"No, she didn't."

"Maybe this will help me find out," I said, holding the ribbon and letting the key dangle from my hand.

333

THE MOUNTAINS CALL MY NAME

"Let me tell you who you are. You're Elizabeth Anne Edwards Mason, soon to be Elizabeth Anne Edwards Mason Scott. You're my best friend. I've known you your whole life. I know exactly who you are."

"I mean the real me. I mean..."

"I know what you mean," he said, squeezing my hand.

He took the key from me and held it in his hand.

"We'll search together to see what this key goes to," he said, letting it dangle from the ribbon that held it.

"I won't rest until I find the one who gave me away. Would you have asked me to marry you if you had known my mother was a whore? Not to mention the fact that I was from a one night stand, an illicit affair. I think I would be referred to as a bastard."

"Don't ever refer to yourself as a bastard in my presence again!" he interjected. "You're just about to make me mad, Elizabeth!"

"I'm sorry," I whispered.

"Do you realize how hard your mother worked to make sure no one, including yourself, would ever call you that name? Your mother was Mary Margaret Edwards. She was a godly woman who loved you. Your father was John Thomas Edwards. He made a mistake that he spent a lifetime trying to correct, and I might add, he did a darn good job. You're the product of a wonderful home. The woman that gave birth to you is dead. Maybe someday God will allow you to know the grandmother that forsook you, but if you never know her, be happy with what, and who, you are."

I could tell he was upset by the tone of his voice. Maybe he would regret asking me to marry him when the truth really hit him. Maybe it was good I didn't have children, maybe I have bad blood or something, maybe, maybe, maybe, echoed through my aching head.

"I would like to say something else," he said.

Not waiting for my response he continued.

"You don't have a clue what type of woman your birth mother was. You assume she was a whore, but maybe she was just a kid that wanted some love. Grant it, it was in the wrong place, but maybe she wanted to be held and loved. Evidently your father was looking for something to soothe his pain. Maybe their needs were met for a brief moment."

"I'm living proof that their needs were met."

"Libby, sex is a strong thing to combat when your head is clear, but when you're already out of control with booze and you're needy, anything could happen. She was just a kid, Libby, just a teenager. The Bible tells us before you judge a matter you must first know what the facts are. That's paraphrasing a little."

I noticed the small white chapel as we turned the corner in the road. A sob caught in my throat as we drove by.

THE MOUNTAINS CALL MY NAME

"The bells are going to be ringing again." Tears rolled down my cheeks again. "Will they ever toll for joy again, Daniel?"

"The day we say 'I do' they will toll long, and hard, *Daniel loves Elizabeth,* ringing to all that hear them." He reached over and held my hand again.

"Will it all ever end, Daniel? When does death stop?"

"When time is no more, that's when death will stop. From the time we're born we start to die."

"David, Bessie, baby Daniel, Mama, who will be next? Will God take you from me, too?"

"If I had a crystal ball I could try to answer that, but I don't. I will live until the day God takes me home to Glory, and I might add, that goes for you, too. I could ask the same question. Will God take you away from me? I would rather think on all the times we have to love each other. I like to think about getting married, having children, growing old together. Not how little time we'll have together, but how long."

We pulled into the garage behind his house. The automatic garage door closed behind us as we pulled in. Warm, dark silence filled the car when he cut the engine off. He turned to me and pulled me into his arms. He began kissing my face, my eyes, my tears and my lips. The closeness of him was so welcome to me. The sadness seemed less when he held me and kissed me the way he was now. All there was room for at the present was his love. All of a sudden, he pulled away from me and started to say something, but I didn't want any more words just then.

"Libby…"

I placed my fingertips over his lips to silence his words.

"Not now, Daniel, I don't need words now, I need for you to kiss me. Take me some place away from the pain." He passionately found my lips and I responded in kind. We kissed our way into an ocean of love carried on waves of consuming passion.

We sat for quiet a while in the darkness loving each other. The calming affect of his kisses far outweighed any sedative he could have given me.

"It's getting cold, lets go inside," he said, reaching for his door handle.

"I didn't notice," I said, smiling at him in through the blackness.

We entered the dark house, trying not to wake Mandy. He turned the light on in the kitchen. The sudden brightness made me shield my eyes. He went to the cabinet to get something to drink.

"Can I get you anything?"

"You could kiss me again."

"I meant something to cool you down," he said, laughing at me.

THE MOUNTAINS CALL MY NAME

He poured himself some orange juice and offered me a drink from his glass. I took it and gulped down several swallows.

"That was good; I didn't realize I was thirsty."

"And hot," he added.

I looked at the kitchen clock. It said 6:00 o'clock.

"I didn't realize we were in the car so long," I said, yawning.

He sat the empty glass into the sink, stretched his arms over his head and seemed to catch my contagious yawn.

"I'm so tired. It's been some kind of day. We probably need to get to bed. You've had a long emotional day, and need to get some rest, too. How are you doing?" he said, looking intently into my eyes.

"My head hurts. It's been hurting a lot lately. Stress will do it every time."

"I'm sorry, sweetheart. If I could have made today disappear, I would have. Life throws us some real curves sometimes."

"That's not good when you're not a good catcher."

He pulled me back into his arms and held me close. I could hear the beat of his heart from where my head lay.

"I promise you I will be your shield. I'll keep all the hurt I can from you. I love you so much. How can a few short days do such wonderful things to a person's heart? You've swept in and turned my uncomplicated life upside down." he said, pulling back from me and looking into my eyes.

"I could say the same. You've swept me off my feet. You've captured my heart and put some kind of spell on me. I can't seem to get enough of your kisses. This is coming from a girl who, up until a few days ago, was floundering in the darkness. You brought me sunshine, Daniel."

He drew me to him again and kissed me. His kisses electrified my tired, aching body. When he was holding me like this, everything else was forgotten. I melted into his arms. He waltzed me backward to where he had turned on the light. With me still in his arms he reached behind me and turned the lights off. We stood in the lightlessness of the kitchen, soothing our tired souls on each other's love. I felt his hands on my skin underneath my sweater. His hands were warm as they caressed my back. I needed him at that moment more than I had ever needed anyone. He pulled me ever closer to him as he kissed my neck. We were being carried on a wave of passion to a place I would never run from.

"Don't stop." I whispered as he held me.

"I love you so much, Elizabeth, one day I won't be able to stop," he said, covering my lips with his again.

Suddenly the lights were bright in the kitchen again, taking us both by surprise. I wonder how much of this she just heard, I thought to myself.

We stood, barely able to breathe, trying to act normal. It was actually kind of funny.

"Master Daniel, what are you doin' here in the dark? I heard noise in here and it sceert the life outta me. You lucky I didn't shoot you."

"And I you, Mandy" he said, smiling.

"How are you, Ms. 'Lis'beth?"

"Well," I said, clearing my throat, and running my fingers through my disheveled hair, "I'm doing okay. I think I want to lie down for a while. Daniel, which bedroom do you want me to take?"

"Mine, you can take mine."

"Not while you're in it, Master Daniel." Mandy said, pointing a finger at him.

Mandy winked at me as she led the way to Daniel's room. She knew as well as we, what she had interrupted in the darkness of the kitchen.

"I only have honorable intentions. I can at least walk her to my room, can't I?" he said, putting his arm around my waist.

We walked up the stairs, arm in arm, to his bedroom. Mandy was two steps ahead of us with her nightgown flapping in the breeze. I excused myself to the bathroom in Daniel's room. I heard him and Mandy talking as I washed my face. Sleep was going to be a welcome respite from the memories of the night. Most of the memories, anyway. The memories from a moment ago,

THE MOUNTAINS CALL MY NAME

I wouldn't forget any time soon. It seemed the more we kissed, the harder it was to leave him. It had been a long time since I'd had these feelings for anyone. I had forgotten how overpowering the emotion of love could be. I suddenly felt a little embarrassed about having asked him not to stop. My face was still flushed from his kisses. I joined the two of them as Mandy plumped the pillows.

"You're gonna be alright, little girl. Miss Mandy gonna take care of ya. Master Daniel, scoot, so 'Lis'beth can get to bed."

He took my face between his big hands and kissed me.

"I'll look in on you in just a little bit," he said, looking down into my eyes.

"Thanks for everything," I said. "Get some rest, you've been going nonstop."

"I still can go on intern hours. It hasn't been that long ago since I pulled some long, long shifts."

"We both know you need rest," I replied.

"I will. Goodnight, sweetie, or should I say good morning?"

My luggage was already in his room from the day before. Mandy helped me get into my pajamas again. She tucked me in and turned off all the lights except a little night light on Daniel's desk. I still felt flushed from the touch of Daniel's hands. I could see how easily my mother could have lost herself to my father. I could have done the same with Daniel. I guess I could label myself the same

341

thing I called my mother. How could something that seemed so right go so wrong? I already knew the answer to that question. I knew what God would have me do. I know Daniel's vow to God for me, that our relationship would be pure and holy before him. How can I be lying here thinking about my purity with Daniel when my mother had just died? I was running the gamut of emotions tonight. I went from deep sorrow to overwhelming passion. There's got to be middle ground somewhere. I thought about the key that Mama gave me. I would have to go soon to find the box that held my future. I felt the welcomed sleep flowing over me.

When I awoke, I saw Daniel asleep in his recliner beside my bed. His Bible lay open on his lap. My head was hurting again. It was in the same area that it had throbbed previously. The pain would come sharp, and then recede to almost nothing. I lay there with my eyes closed taking slow, deep breaths. Maybe if I stayed really calm, I thought, it would go away. I felt a hand brush my hair from my face.

"Good morning, angel." he said, kissing my cheek.

"Good morning," I said, smiling up at him. "What time is it?"

He squinted and looked at his watch. "If I can see correctly it's 9:00."

I stretched my arms above my head and yawned.

"What do we have to do today, Daniel?" I said in a hoarse whisper.

THE MOUNTAINS CALL MY NAME

He lay down beside me. I rose up and positioned myself so I could lie in his arms. He stroked my hair with his free hand.

"Sometime this morning we have to go to the funeral home and finish making the final arrangements. Then we can just come back here and rest until the funeral tomorrow."

"I'm so tired of funerals. I don't want to ever go to another one, unless it's mine. I don't even think I'll go to mine."

"Lets make a deal, we'll both just wait and go up in the rapture."

"Deal," he replied to my statement.

"Well, as nice as this is, lying here in bed with my bride-to-be, I'm going to get up and go take a shower."

As he grasped my hand, I turned his face to mine.

"I love you, Daniel. I couldn't have made it without you. Thanks for being there for my mother."

"I wouldn't have had it any other way. I'm just sorry it's all happening to you. If I could take away your pain, I would."

"You did a pretty good job in the kitchen last night, or was that this morning? I was feeling no pain," I said, smiling at him.

"I vaguely remember you asking me not to stop, or was it to stop? It all just seems to run together," he said, returning my smile.

"I'm sorry about that. I was kind of embarrassed about that later when I thought back on it. I guess it was just the heat of the moment," I said, covering my face with my hands.

"I was just thinking about us and what's transpiring between us. Do you realize that this is new to both of us? I mean I... it's... what I'm trying to say is, you haven't been like this since David died, or at least I don't think so."

I hit him on the arm as he continued.

"And here I am. I've never been in love before. I've kissed girls before and naturally been... well you know."

"No I don't. Would you like to tell me?" I said, looking seriously at him.

"What I'm trying to say and not doing such a good job is, when love is a factor it makes it a whole new ball game. I just don't want to let you go, and the more I hold you and kiss you the more I want of you and..."

"Daniel, we're going to be okay. Right now I'm devastated by the news you gave me, I'm mourning the loss of the lady I knew as my mother, and I've never been happier in my life. How can you put so much in such a short period?"

"God's grace is going to sort all of it out. God took your mother and then gave you me. Not that one cancels out the other, it's just he gave you to me to help you through all of this. What I had to do yesterday, telling you about your mother, was the hardest thing I've had to do in my life. I knew it was going to totally change your life as you have known it, and I couldn't escape it. I just didn't want you to hate the messenger," he said, retaining his matchless smile.

"I could never hate you. This new awakening of love is just blowing me away. I must have stars in my eyes, or be seeing stars anyway."

"I love you so much. When I'm near you all I want to do is hold you and touch you. With you so responsive to me, it's getting more difficult all the time. I think, because I'm enjoying you so much. Someday, and soon, we won't have to find a stopping place."

"I don't know who was more shocked this morning, Mandy or us," I said, stifling a laugh.

"Well, ice water would not have been more effective. I think it embarrassed her a little," he said, joining my laughter.

"Master Daniel, what are you doin' in the dark?" he said, repeating Mandy's words.

"If someone had told either one of us two months ago that we would be here lying in bed together we wouldn't have believed it," I said, raising my hand to stroke his face.

He took my hand in his again, kissing my finger with the diamond.

"Only God could have done all this so quickly. We haven't set a date. We need to do that."

"Oh my, I hadn't thought about a date."

"You thought we would just have an eternal engagement?"

"No, things have just moved so quickly."

"How about New Years Eve?"

"I don't think that would be a good idea." I said, slowly shaking my head.

"Oh man, I just remembered, sorry," he said, rubbing his hand through his hair.

"I don't think I want to get married on the day David died."

"How about next week?" he asked. "It will be in between Christmas and New Year's."

"I don't even have a wedding gown, Daniel. I have to have time to at least get a proper dress."

"How much time does it take to buy a wedding gown?"

"What about invitations?" I said.

"There's the telephone," he said, nodding toward it.

"Daniel, think about your mom and dad, there are things they are going to want to do. You're their only child. I'm sure your mom has looked forward to this day since you were a baby."

"My mom can throw together something real quick. If she says its okay, can we do it next week?"

"Daniel! Daniel! Daniel! Yes, if everyone can do it, I'll marry you next week"

"Elizabeth, we're talking about Scott Corner, how many people do we know?"

"I'll bet Grandmother Scott can get the word out," I said, laughing.

"None of my family knows about our engagement yet. Mandy does, but I swore her to secrecy."

"If we're going to get married next week, I think we probably need to tell them, don't you think?"

"My mother's gonna kill me for cutting it so short," he said, laughing.

"Maybe we need to rethink the date. Maybe move it to January," I threw out to him.

"No, I don't want to wait. I've waited a lifetime. Maybe we could elope and get married in the church later. You know, we could do it real big with a reception and the works," he said, looking at me questioningly.

"Your family would never forgive us."

THE MOUNTAINS CALL MY NAME

"Of course they would, it's not like I'm eighteen."

"But like I said, you're their only son. They won't get another chance to do this. At least I hope not," I said, gently stroking the side of his face with my fingers.

"Think elope, Libby, think elope," he said, slowing turning to me.

He kissed me on the cheek.

"Your beard is prickly," I said, pushing him away.

"You're already getting testy and we haven't even slept together yet. Is this a preview of things to come?" he said in mock shock.

"This would be a good way to keep each other at bay. I don't brush my teeth and you don't shave or shower," I said, laughing at him.

"Elizabeth darling, I have a feeling that isn't going to make any difference," he said, pulling me into his arms.

His kiss was warm and sweet, prickly beard and all. He pulled away, and smiled down at me.

"See, it was a good thought but it ain't gonna work," he said, looking dreamily at me.

"In that case, I think you'd better get out of my bed, Master Daniel," I said, whispering into his ear as he kissed me on the neck.

There was a light knock on the bedroom door.

THE MOUNTAINS CALL MY NAME

"Are you in there, Master Daniel?"

"Yeah, come in Mandy," he said, not moving from his place on the bed beside me.

"There's a phone call fo' you. They say it's the funeral home."

"I'll be back in just a minute," he said, bounding off the bed. "I'll take the call in the other bedroom."

He had turned off the ringer on the phone in his bedroom, and we didn't hear it ring.

"Ms. 'Lis'beth do you want I should run a bath fer ya?"

"That would be nice, Mandy."

I crawled out of the warm bed, and gathered the clothing to wear to the funeral home. I felt an unusual peace that day. Mama was finally at rest. I was happy she was with daddy but I would miss her.

"Your bath is ready, sweetie."

"Mandy I know I don't have to explain anything to you, but I want you to know, Daniel has been a perfect gentleman with me."

"Ms. Lisbeth, I loves Master Daniel. He just like my own. I knows him like a book. He ain't ever been nothin' but a gentleman. When I was a cleanin' this mawnin' I eased open the do', and Master Daniel was down 'side yer bed prayin'. I don't worry much about my baby."

THE MOUNTAINS CALL MY NAME

"He loves you too, Mandy. I don't think anyone has to tell you that. When we get married, I want you to know you will always have a home with Daniel and me. As far as I'm concerned, anyway."

"Go on, baby girl, get in the water while it warm. While you soak, I'll make the bed."

I heard Daniel and Mandy while I was finishing dressing. My head continued to ache, but not as bad as it had been. I opened the door to find Mandy alone.

"Master Daniel said when you through to come on downstairs and join him fer breakfast."

I really didn't feel like eating, but I would join him there.

"You look beautiful," he said, standing as I entered the room.

He pulled out the seat beside him and beckoned me to sit down. Mandy had steaming food on the table. *How could that woman's timing be so perfect?* I thought to myself.

"The funeral home said we could come anytime we wanted to. They asked how they should fix her hair. If you have a picture it would be good."

"I think I have one in my purse. What about the grave. Are they gonna be able to dig it in the snow?"

"Yeah, you'd be surprised what they can do around here. You're not eating, are you feeling okay?"

"My head still hurts. The ache kinda comes and goes."

"I'll get Mandy to get you some aspirin. Mandy," Daniel called out to her."

"Yes, Master Daniel."

"Would you bring me the aspirin bottle out of the bathroom cabinet, please?"

It wasn't long until she appeared with the bottle. Daniel opened it and handed me two. I took them and tried to eat a little breakfast.

After we finished Daniel said we should be going. He got my coat from the coat closet and helped me into it. The road was scraped and not difficult to maneuver. It was a winter wonderland outside. Everything was in a thick cover of white. All pure and spotless. I thought about how warm heaven must be. My mother would never be cold again. The ground she was going into would not hold her spirit, just her shell. I would have to keep reminding myself of that.

The funeral home was dressed in white siding with dark green shutters. It sat on a little knoll right outside of town. The lot was empty except for two or three cars. We trudged up the unswept sidewalk to the front door. There was a small man dressed in a black suit that met us at the door. He asked us to follow him to the back to his office. It was there where Daniel explained what my mother wanted done for her funeral. It was a simple process really, with everything paid for a long time ago. My father took care of it all before he died. Anna Belle was coming later with her clothing. They would have her at the church at

THE MOUNTAINS CALL MY NAME

12:00 tomorrow. Her coffin would be open for one hour before the funeral so friends could view the body. He said the family could come by later today for a private time to make sure she looked the way we wanted her to.

"What time will that be?" I asked.

"She should be ready about 4:00 o'clock."

"We'll be here," Daniel said, standing to shake the man's hand.

We made our way back to the van, tracing our steps from before.

"Let's stop by and see Mom and Dad. I think it's time they knew they're about to have a baby girl named Elizabeth."

"You're so sweet. I forget some times that I'm getting a new family."

All the Scott vehicles were in the driveway as we pulled in.

"It looks like everyone is at home; they must have Uncle Joe running the store," Daniel said as we got out.

We walked into the house unannounced. Everyone was in the living room by the fireplace.

"Hey everybody, how's it going?"

"Daniel," came the voices in unison.

His mother was the first to reach us.

THE MOUNTAINS CALL MY NAME

"You brought Elizabeth. Hello, my dear, we were wonderin' when this boy of ours was gonna bring you to see us. I'm so sorry about your mother, dear," she said, reaching to embrace me.

"Thank you."

Daniel's father was next in line. He extended his hand and gave me a firm handshake.

"'Lis'beth, come give this little old woman a hug," Grandmother Scott said, wheeling her way to me.

I stooped to give her a kiss on the cheek, and as I did, the old familiar throbbing was starting in my head again.

We joined them by the warm fire. Daniel and his dad talked for a little while. I could tell he was popping to tell them.

"Well," he said, Elizabeth and I have something to tell you. Last night she agreed to become my wife. So, I guess you'll finally get that little girl in the family."

His mother's mouth dropped.

"Mom, I've never seen you speechless. Are you happy?" he said, smiling at her.

"I couldn't 'ave picked anyone I would rather have for a daughter. It was kinda quick, is all. Of course you're welcome to our family," she said, coming to hug me again.

THE MOUNTAINS CALL MY NAME

"Daniel, we were worried we'd never get any grandchildren, now maybe that'll happen. I've wanted to be a granddaddy fer a long time."

"Dad, I didn't say we were going to have a baby, I said we were going to get married," he said, getting a big hug from his dad.

"Grandmother you've not said a word."

"Danny boy, you did good. I told ya to go see her, didn't I?"

We knelt beside her and hugged her from both sides.

"You two done me proud. You're gonna make beautiful babies. Don't make me wait too long to see 'em." Her eyes were misty with unshed tears."

"When is this to take place?" Mrs. Scott asked.

Daniel cleared his throat; "Well," he said, looking at me. We're thinking next week."

Her mouth dropped again. Having slightly recovered, she finally spoke.

"Daniel, that's impossible son, there's so much that would have to be done. We could use the community center fer the reception. All our family's right around here so we could spread the word purty quick through the store. I guess we *could* pull it off. But what about you, my dear, can you be ready?" she said, looking wonderingly at me.

THE MOUNTAINS CALL MY NAME

"I don't have a dress, but Daniel said not to worry, I could find one easily."

"We're real excited about you two gettin' married, Daniel, but don't you think this is just a little sudden?" his father questioned.

"Well, Dad, I know it seems that way, but Elizabeth and I go way back. We were best friends all the way through school. So we aren't strangers."

"Elizabeth, do you still live away from here?"

"Yes, at this moment I do, but I plan on moving back here."

"We sure wouldn't want to loose Daniel as a doctor," he said with a concerned look.

"I would never ask him to leave here. I respect his work too much."

"You were married to a doctor, weren't you Elizabeth?" his mother inquired.

"Mom!" Daniel said, looking at her.

"I was just askin'," she said apologetically.

"I don't mind answering. Yes, yes I was, he was killed in a car wreck three years ago."

"What do you do, Elizabeth?" his father asked.

"Well right now, nothing, but I'm considering going back into my nursing career."

THE MOUNTAINS CALL MY NAME

"We just want ya'll to make sure before ya jump. Daniel, you've waited a long time fer this. We just want you to be happy. If you two love each other, who are we to say if it's too quick?"

"I want you to know that we love each other very much. I've actually loved her all my life. It didn't just happen in the last few days. It's just that God didn't bring her to me until now," he said, smiling down at me.

"Elizabeth, we want you to make our Daniel happy, and of course we want you to be happy, too."

"I will spend the rest of my life trying to achieve that," I said, smiling at Daniel.

He leaned over and kissed me, not caring if we were the center of attention. When he looked back at his family they were smiling too.

"Ya'll are just glowin' with love. I can't wait to get to the store and tell everybody," Grandma Scott said.

"Grandma, you're a hopeless romantic. And I love you for it," Daniel said with a chuckle.

"Mom, do you think we can pull off a wedding?" he said, going to her and giving her a hug.

"Do you know how long I've waited for a daughter? I can't wait to add this precious girl to our family. But, Daniel, are you thinkin' about *her*? It's an awful lot to ask this young lady to bury her mother and get married so quick. She might not be able to handle so much."

I went to her and put my arms around her.

"I can't wait to be a part of this lovely family. Daniel is taking good care of me. He's very attentive."

"If you'll let me, I'd love to help you find a gown. Since I don't have a daughter, I would consider it an honor. Daniel doesn't know much about things like that. We'll make ya the most beautiful bride that ever was. And anyway, we don't want him to see what you're gonna look like. Maybe in a couple of days we can talk about it."

"I think that would be great. I would be honored to have you help me."

"I'm so sorry about yer mama. What time is the funeral tomorrow?"

"It's at 1:00 o'clock. Daniel and I have to go back down at 4:00 to see if everything is okay with how she looks, you know, her hair and dress and everything. I guess I'm the only one that can do that."

"Mom, I think I'm going to take Libby home now. We were up all night, and I want her to get some rest before we go back to the funeral home."

Mr. and Mrs. Scott walked us to the door, telling us to be very careful out on the snowy roads.

"A week from tomorrow you'll be my bride. I still have to pinch myself. I feel like I'm going to wake up and it will all be a dream. Tell me I'm not dreaming, and that you love me."

THE MOUNTAINS CALL MY NAME

"You're not dreaming and I love you. I can't believe all the changes that have taken place in my life. Just a few short weeks ago I didn't have a clue I would fall in love with another man. I didn't want to fall in love with another man, and you came in and stole my heart away. I guess it happens, it's just never happened to me. I've no doubt about my love for you. When you kiss me I melt inside."

"If I remember correctly, it happened pretty quick with you and David."

"Oh yeah, I guess it did, but when you know, you know," I said, smiling at him.

"One week and you'll be mine. One week, can you believe it?"

"Daniel, what about your office hours? Don't you have patients to see today?"

"The office is closed because of the snow, and I have no one in the hospital. So I'm yours all day, unless someone calls."

"I think my aspirin is wearing off. My headache is coming back with a vengeance."

"Where's it hurting?" he asked, as concern spread over his face.

"Just all over the back and top. It comes in sharp and then after a while it recedes. It's probably just stress. Not that I've had any lately," I said, smiling at him.

"Maybe Mom is right, am I rushing you?"

THE MOUNTAINS CALL MY NAME

"Yes, you are, but I'm not objecting," I said, patting his hand.

When we got back to the house Mandy had a light lunch ready for us. I told Daniel I thought I would take a couple more aspirins and lie down for a while. Sleep came easily to me as I lay on the couch with my head in Daniel's lap. He had the fireplace going and it was so peaceful. His hand gently stroked my head. Mandy got a small blanket and spread over my legs. It seemed as if I had just closed my eyes when Daniel was waking me up.

"Elizabeth...Elizabeth... time to wake up," he said, kissing me on the forehead.

"My prince, so nice to be kissed awake."

"How's the headache?" he said, kissing me again.

"It still hurts, but I think it's going away. The sleep was good. I dread going to the funeral home. I don't really want to see her in a coffin, but sometimes I guess we need to do things we don't want to."

"You know, if you don't want to, you don't have to go."

"Daniel, I'm the only family she has. If I don't go, no one will."

"She's not there really."

"I know, but I really need to do this. I wouldn't forgive myself if I didn't."

THE MOUNTAINS CALL MY NAME

"Okay then, I'll leave you to freshen up a bit, and then we'll go."

We pulled into the Wilson's Funeral Home parking lot once again. Everything was the same as it was in the morning. The same three cars were parked there. Our tracks were the only ones that had been made in the snow. The heat of the foyer was a stark contrast to the bone-chilling weather outside. The funeral director was very gracious to us as we entered. He showed us to the small room where her body lay. He said he would speak to us before we left.

I took a deep breath and walked slowly to her coffin, conscious of the pounding of my head. Nausea was creeping up my esophagus. *Please, God, just keep it down, I don't want to be sick in here.* The heat and the scent of the flowers came rushing over me. It reminded me of the night at Bessie's house.

She was lovely in her sky blue dress. It was one that I had given her for her birthday. How quickly I had made the decision to buy it. I had no idea then that it would be her burial dress. Her white hair was fixed just like the picture I left with them. The pink of her cheeks belied the way I saw her last, so pale and drawn. She looked very peaceful. There even seemed to be a little smile on her lips. For the life of me I couldn't cry. I knew her burdens had been lifted and her pain was gone. She was in a place where there were no more tears or pain, only joy and happiness. How could I wish her back? My emptiness and sadness was covered with a cloak of numbness. All of this would probably hit full-force later. Daniel stood silently behind me with his hands on my shoulders. I sensed someone moving up beside me. I turned to see Daniel's parents. His mother put her arms around me and held me close to her.

"Do you think I would let ya do this by yerself, child? You're our girl now. Parents don't let their kids go through things all by themselves."

I was moved by her compassion. The tears that seemed to be dry came freely now. She held me to her bosom and let me cry.

"You still have a mother, 'Lizabeth. God gave you another one when he gave you Daniel. Whatever you need, I'll be there fer ya."

"You're too kind."

She handed me a handful of tissues and I wiped my tears away.

"Can I give you a hug?" Daniel's father asked, reaching for me.

I went into his arms as a little girl would go to her father. An instant bond of love formed between us as we stood beside my mother's coffin. I could sense her smiling down on the little scene from heaven. I looked at Daniel and he seemed to be trying hard not to cry. I saw so much of his father in him. I could tell he had the same gentleness as his son.

"I can't believe you all came," he said, hugging his mother.

THE MOUNTAINS CALL MY NAME

"Do you think we would let you and 'Lizabeth go through this all by yerselves? Family just don't do that to each other. We'll always be here fer ya."

"You will never know how much it meant to me to have you come here for me today."

"We can go anytime you want to. I've already talked to Mr. Wilson, and everything is all set for tomorrow."

"I'm through here," I said.

"Daniel, how did you know what to do?" his mom asked.

"Mrs. Edwards gave me all the instructions the other night when I was sitting up with her. She wanted to spare Libby."

"I'm so proud of you, son. You've grown into quite a man. I'm real proud of ya."

"Well, I guess we're through here. We're just going to go back home. Thanks for coming. Mr. Wilson has done a great job with everything. Libby hasn't been feeling well, so I think I'll take her home to rest."

"Are you sick, 'Lizabeth?" Mrs. Scott asked with concern showing on her face.

"Just can't get rid of this darned headache. It comes and goes. It's probably just stress."

"Daniel, you're the doctor, son, fix her up," his dad said.

THE MOUNTAINS CALL MY NAME

"Don't worry; I've waited too long for her to let anything happen to her."

The snow was frozen and hard, cutting at our legs as we walked back to the car. All of this was made a lot easier because of the support of the Scott family. My head was pounding and unfortunately the nausea was not abating.

"Daniel, I'm not feeling very well. Be ready to stop, because I'm feeling very nauseated."

"Do I need to stop now?"

"No, just drive. I'll try to make it home."

"As soon as we get home I'll give you something for the nausea. I'm getting concerned about those headaches. It's been going on for quiet a while now. I think maybe you need something a little bit stronger than aspirin. Have you had migraines before?"

"A long time ago. I can't remember how long ago, but it's been a long time."

"That may be what it is. Just put your head back and rest. We're almost home."

"I can't do that. If I shut my eyes everything spins."

We just made it to the house when I lost it. I was able to get to the side of the driveway before I threw up. At least I didn't regurgitate in his car. My prince was very gentle with me. He took his handkerchief out of his pocket and wiped my face. As chilled as it was I broke out with a cold sweat. The pain in my head worsened with the strain of throwing up. I held my head in my hands to try to stop the throbbing.

"Let's get inside. It's freezing out here," he said, leading me into the warm house.

I barely made it inside to the hall bathroom and was sick again. Daniel didn't desert me though; he held a cold, wet cloth to my head. We made it up to his bedroom with Mandy close in tow.

I sat on the side of the bathtub not wanting to get very far away from the commode. The nausea was somewhat better. He was back in just a little bit with something to calm my stomach.

"Here, take this," he said, holding the pills and a glass of water in his hand.

"I don't think that's going to stay down, but I'll try." I took the pill and swallowed it with just a tiny gulp of water.

I felt weak and dizzy as Daniel helped me to his bed. I had never felt worse in my life. The headache was persistent; I could say that for it.

"Libby, did you ever have headaches like this when you were stressed out over David dying? I know that's a strange question, but I need to know the answer."

"No, I've never had a headache as bad as this one is getting, I said, pressing my hands to my head."

Is it still mainly in the back of your head, or is it all over?" he said, trying to look into my eyes.

"I can't talk anymore; it hurts too bad. I think I need to throw up again." I grabbed the pan from his hand and opened my mouth again. The pain was horrible. With each heave it felt like my head was coming off. There was nothing coming up, just dry heaves.

"I need something for pain? The pain is blinding," I said, squeezing his hand with mine.

"You just threw up your medicine. I think I'm going to give you a shot, because you're not going to keep down a pill long enough for it to work. It's either going to be a shot or a suppository.

"I can't see that happening right now. As sick as I am, you will *not* give me a suppository. Shoot me if you must, but that's all."

"You're a bad patient. Don't you think I could give you a suppository?"

"Oh, I don't doubt you could, but you're not. The dry heaves would feel better than that."

All the time he was talking he was looking through his black bag getting the injection ready for the nausea.

"I'm going to have to give this to you in your hip."

Through the pain I couldn't undo the button on my pants so he could get to my hip. He laid the syringe on the night stand.

"Elizabeth, help me with your pants," he said, reaching to undo my button and zipper. He pulled my pants down and expertly rolled me onto my side.

"Do you realize how many times I've done this in the short time since you first came back?"

"Too many," I answered.

"It's good I'm a doctor or we would have had several trips to the emergency room."

He finished the injection and pulled my pants back up. I think we'll just leave them unbuttoned. Mandy, got a blanket and put it over me.

The nausea was quieting some, but my headache was not.

"I want to take your blood pressure and pulse. Just humor me if you would."

I was beginning to get sleepy from the shot he gave me. I thought if I could close my eyes the pain might go away. I was beginning to feel irritated that Daniel wouldn't leave me alone to sleep.

"Stop! Just quit checking things," I said, expressing my frustration. "If you would just let me rest I think my head would quit hurting. What are you looking for?"

He pushed my sleeve up and took my blood pressure again, and then my pulse. He got his little flashlight out and shined it in my eyes.'

"Open your eyes and look at me, sweetie."

"I can't focus, everything is whirling. I think I'm going to be sick again. Where's the..." I was trying to fumble for the pan.

THE MOUNTAINS CALL MY NAME

"It's right here, go ahead."

The heaves came again, only not as bad this time. Daniel held me in his arms as I cried out with pain.

"I can't see very well. I think it must be the shot you gave me." Everything seemed to come out all jumbled.

"Oh God, Daniel the pain is so bad."

"Something just isn't right here," I heard Daniel say as much to himself as to me.

He took my blood pressure again, then my pulse rate.

"Have you had headaches since you fell at Bessie's?"

"Yeah, I moaned."

"Elizabeth, it's important that you listen to me. I'm going to have to get you to the hospital. I can't take you in my car because you're too sick. You're speech is getting slurry. I think you might have something going on with from the fall."

"No, no, no, head hurts." I grabbed the blanket as my head swirled. "Falling…"

"You're not falling, I'm holding you."

"Sick…sick again…" I murmured, but couldn't raise myself up to vomit. He turned me on to my side so I could hit the pan, but there was nothing to come up. The heaving was making my head explode.

THE MOUNTAINS CALL MY NAME

"Pain, Daniel...pain..."

"I know, sweetheart, I'm trying, just hang with me. I can't give you anything now. I don't know exactly what the problem is."

"I'm calling the rescue squad. I don't want to take a chance on driving you. You just have to trust me."

"No hospital, Daniel, just hold me."

"I'm telling you, you need to go..."

I felt myself slipping and drifting farther and farther away from the sound of his voice...

Chapter Thirteen

I felt myself coming out of the swirling sensation into a sunlit meadow. I've never seen the sun so bright, but it didn't hurt my eyes. The grass was perfectly manicured. The flowers were every color of the rainbow.

"Elizabeth, we've been waiting fer ya."

I turned to see my mother and father standing hand in hand.

"Mama! Daddy! How did you get here?"

I ran into their waiting arms.

"Mama, you look so young and beautiful, and Daddy, look how handsome you are. I've missed you so much," I said, embracing them both.

"Where are we?" I asked, looking around me.

"Why, we're in heaven, child."

"How did I get here? I was at Daniel's house.

"God brought you here."

"Mama! Everything is so beautiful," I said, twirling around with my arms spread wide. I just don't understand why I'm I here."

THE MOUNTAINS CALL MY NAME

There was a crystal river running down the middle of the broad meadow. The bright grass went right to the rivers edge. There were people walking hand in hand through out the gorgeous field. Children were laughing and playing among the flowers. Everyone was dressed in the same long white robes. No one seemed in a hurry.

"'Lizabeth? Daddy and I have someone we want you to meet."

There was a little boy with brown hair looking out from behind Mama.

"This here is Jonathan, yer brother."

"Jonathan, little Jonathan... My brother?"

"I've waited a long time for you to come to me." He was in my arms hugging me tight.

"Jonathan, how I've longed to meet you. Our family is all together. Daddy, I've missed you terribly since you left us."

"I know, little girl. I've followed you closely since we've been apart, but you didn't know, of course."

"I just placed roses on yours and Jonathan's graves. I was so lonely for you."

"I held you as you cried, but ya didn't know, of course."

"I felt your presence that day. I wanted so much to let you know I would watch after Mama closer than I had."

"You were sick yerself and it was hard fer ya to look after yer ma. But she was looked after by the angels, and you was too. Ever' tear ya cried was caught by an angel. You were never alone, 'Lis'beth Anne."

"I felt so alone, Daddy. I wanted to die at times. But God wouldn't let me. Then he sent me someone named Daniel. You would really like him."

All of a sudden, I wanted to see David. If I was truly in heaven, then David must be here.

"Mama, where's David."

"He's comin' real soon. He wanted to give us time with you before he come. In heaven when yer heart wants somethin' that's when God gives it."

I sensed his presence before I actually saw him. I turned and there he stood, strong and well before my eyes. His arms encircled me and drew me to him.

"I've missed you so. My heart has ached so long to hold you," I said, looking into the tenderness of his brown eyes.

"I was there with you as you mourned for me. I saw your tears and couldn't hold you. I kept telling you I was okay, but you couldn't hear me."

"I saw you in my dreams the other night. You came to me and asked me to release you," I said as he held me.

"That's true; I was there with you that night. God allowed me to come to you in your dream."

THE MOUNTAINS CALL MY NAME

"Then you must know about Daniel?"

He just smiled as he looked at me. "It's time for you to move on with your life. I can't be there to meet your needs. You've been lonely far too long. Daniel is a good man. There are things God still has for you to do. That's why I came."

"I feel so guilty."

"There is no guilt in heaven."

"Then why do I stand here before you and feel the guilt of loving another man?"

"Because you haven't crossed over yet. There's still a silver cord that has yet to be broken. It connects your body and soul. As long as you have that cord you will have earthly emotions."

"Then why am I here?"

"Because God has allowed it."

"Am I dead?"

"No, not yet. The cord is still not broken."

"Where is it? I don't see any cord," I said, picking up my long white robe as I looked for the connection.

"Because you don't have spiritual eyes yet."

"So I'm somewhere between heaven and earth?" I asked earnestly.

THE MOUNTAINS CALL MY NAME

He nodded his head and smiled patiently at me.

I felt like a child asking questions, and not understanding the answers.

"How will I know when I've crossed?"

"You'll know."

"Am I going to cross over?" I asked, imploring him to answer me.

"Only God knows that, Elizabeth."

"David, the night you crossed…"

"Yes."

"Did you see me right before you di…crossed?"

"Oh yes! I saw you. I wanted to reach out and tell you I wasn't in pain, but I couldn't. I felt *no* pain, Elizabeth. I'm glad God has given me the chance to tell you. I looked awful, I know, but God had already taken my spirit out."

"Thank God."

"Yes, I did thank God."

"Were you scared?"

"No, there's no fear in death. Jesus was with me all the way."

THE MOUNTAINS CALL MY NAME

"It was on your birthday. I couldn't get over it being on you birthday."

"What better day to come to glory than on your birthday? What a birthday present!"

"I don't feel like I'm dreaming right now. I can touch you and feel you. You're not a ghost."

"No," he said, pulling me close to him again. "I'm not a ghost."

"I'm really seeing you," I said, smiling at him.

"You're really seeing me," he replied, trying to make me understand.

"What's happening to me, David?"

"Don't worry, sweet pea, you're safe here."

"Sweet pea, I haven't heard that since you... died." The word was so hard to say. "I still don't like saying that word."

"Death is a part of life. To get here you must die."

"But I'm not here yet. Right?" I asked quizzically.

"Right," he said, laughing at me.

"I'm just checking to see if that cord has broken yet."

"Not yet. It's still there."

THE MOUNTAINS CALL MY NAME

"You can see it?"

He just nodded and smiled at me. I looked around me and saw that Jonathan, Mama, and Daddy had left us.

"They'll be back. They haven't gone far," he said, answering my question before I asked it.

"Let's walk," he said, taking my hand in his.

We walked to the edge of the water and sat on bank.

"Do you want to get in the water?" he said, motioning to the crystal clear river.

"Is it cold?" I asked.

"Come," he said, rising.

He took my hand and helped me stand up. He gently led me into the water. It wasn't cold at all. We waded for a long time in the edge of the current. The brightly colored pebbles were smooth under my bare feet. Hand in hand we went deeper into the river. We got to a point were I couldn't keep my head above the water line.

"Let's go under," he said, smiling at me.

"But I won't be able to breathe."

"Sure you will. You don't need to breathe in heaven."

He ducked himself beneath the surface, and I did the same. To my chagrin, I really *didn't* need to breathe.

Still holding hands, we floated under the exhilarating water. We could talk just as if we were on the shore. When we emerged, I was surprised once more to see that our robes were instantly dry.

"Everything is perfect in heaven. You won't stay wet."

I could see that he was so happy showing me these new wonders.

"Do I get to stay with you, David?"

"Only God knows that answer."

"Why am I here, David? If I can't stay, why did God allow me to come? I know... God knows the answer," I said, smiling at him.

I saw my mother coming to me with another woman and a little girl about Jonathan's size.

"Your mother needs you now. I'll be back."

"But..."

"I'll be back," he said assuringly.

The distance between us was covered in an instant.

"'Lis'beth, come, let's go sit in the grove of trees there in the meadow."

We walked arm in arm. The lady that walked with us was silently smiling at me. Her eyes looked at me with such tenderness. She was dressed in the same white robes as everyone else. When we arrived at their chosen place, all four of us sat down on the grass in a circle. The lady kept smiling at me as if she knew me.

"'Lis'beth, I want ya to meet yer mother. This is Rose, the one that gave you life, and this is yer twin sister.

A gasp came from within me. "My mother! *You're* my mother! And…and you're my twin sister?" I kept repeating things people said to me. But I was astonished at the news.

They nodded in unison. I was looking at the image of myself when I was her size. She came to me and put her arms around me.

"Elizabeth, my precious Elizabeth Anne. I wanted so bad to tell ya how much I loved ya. I wanted you to be loved so badly. God sent this precious lady who gave you all that I wished I could've. I prayed so hard fer ya as I carried ya in my womb. I loved ya with my whole heart. God sent Abby on with me, but he had somethin' special fer you to do. So he left ya in the care of Mary.

"I don't know what to say. I…"

"Words ain't necessary." She said looking at me with that same tender visage.

I embraced her and was filled with the glory of her love for me. When she released me I noticed that we were by ourselves.

"Where's Mama and Abby?" I asked, looking around me.

THE MOUNTAINS CALL MY NAME

"They'll be back. We're all given our special time with you."

"I still haven't crossed, have I?"

"No," She said, shaking her head and smiling at me. "You still ain't crossed. There is somethin' you have to do, Elizabeth. Your grandmother, my mother Ruth, doesn't know our Savior yet. You're goin' to have to go find her and tell her who you are. Tell her who Jesus is and that he loves her. You see, she ain't felt a lot of love through her life. She was raised without much love; she was a harsh, bitter woman. I think she was hurt real bad by something when she was growin' up. She's had a rough life, so it's hard fer her to know what Jesus' love is all about."

"What if I stay here, then who will go will go find her?"

"Then God will send another."

"How do I find her? I don't know where to look."

"God will show you the way. He gave me this time with you to tell you how much I love you. I got saved while I was waiting fer you to be born. Without God I woulda died of loneliness. One day you'll know all about it, and I pray you'll understand."

"Mother Rose," I said, haltingly, "I said some awful things about you. I..."

"It 'as just because you were hurtin' child. I've watched over you yer whole life. I've watched you grow into a beautiful lady. I loved you and tried to send you feelin's of love yer whole life. And now I get to tell you."

THE MOUNTAINS CALL MY NAME

"I..." I stammered with my words. "I love you, too." I said, holding her in my arms. "You're so beautiful."

I turned and David was standing behind me.

"It's time, Elizabeth," he said, looking tenderly at me.

"Time for what?" I asked.

"Time for you to come with me."

"Where are we going?" I implored.

"For a walk."

We walked hand in hand through the meadow and on along a scenic winding path that led through a forest. The shafts of light came filtering down between the branches and made patterns like lace on the forest floor. We continued walking together without a word being spoken between us. The beauty was so overwhelming there that it rendered me to total silence. We came to a clearing in the woods and before me stood a stately white marble bridge crossing over the crystal river. On the other side I saw my family standing arm in arm, smiling at me.

"They allowed me to be the last one to be with you. My darling... sweet Elizabeth... I want you to be happy."

A tear escaped down my cheek. He took his finger and wiped it tenderly away. He leaned down and kissed my cheek.

"Are you getting ready to leave me?" I said, barely above whisper.

"Our time is short now, but there will come a time when we will not be parted again."

"You can't leave me, David. I just found you again." I threw my arms around him and held him close to me.

"It's time for me to go, but I'll see you again soon."

"Can I come with you? Is my cord still there?" I said, turning, trying to see if I could see the cord myself.

"The cord isn't broken yet. If you choose to do so, you can come with me, and that is when the earthly cord will be broken."

"You mean I can just walk across that bridge and the cord will break?" I said with unmistakable joy in my voice.

"Yes, it's your choice, but there's no going back. Once you walk across the bridge you can't return to earth."

"Then I choose to go with you," I said with happiness spreading over my entire being.

I took his hand and we started across the bridge.

"Elizabeth, turn around and look at me." The voice seemed to resound through out the heavens. It was Daniel, standing at the end of the bridge from which I had just walked.

"Daniel! I exclaimed in surprise." What are you doing here?"

THE MOUNTAINS CALL MY NAME

"I've come to take you home," he said, pleadingly.

"I'm sorry, Daniel, I can't. I have to go with David."

"No! You don't," he yelled back at me. It isn't time for you to go. Please, Elizabeth, don't go."

"What am I going to do?" I said, looking at David.

"It's your choice, Elizabeth. Just be happy," he said, holding my hands in his.

"Elizabeth, don't forget yer grandmother." I heard my mother, Rose, calling from across the bridge.

"You have to decide now," David said, looking down at me with such tenderness. "It's your decision."

"Elizabeth! Turn around! He demanded. Turn around and look at me! You can't cross that bridge yet. Don't leave me, Elizabeth. Please don't leave me. I just found you, don't leave me!"

His voice sounded so sad, and touched me deeply. Not like the peaceful voice of my loved ones there. My heart was pulled to him. I needed to go comfort him, but the call of this beautiful place was so strong.

"I don't know what to do, I'm so confused."

"When you make that decision, you'll have perfect peace," David said in such a soothing, calm voice.

I looked across the bridge to where my family had gathered. They stood there with smiles, one and all, no persuasion whatsoever. I looked at David, and he, too, wouldn't help me decide.

"Daniel, help me, I don't know what to do?"

"Keep your eyes on me, and walk toward me. Don't look back," he said, holding his arms wide to receive me when I reached him.

His eyes held my gaze and I saw a love I couldn't leave. I also had a vision of the lost grandmother I needed to find. I let go of David's hand and started running toward Daniel. His arms were suddenly around me and holding me tightly to him. I turned and looked back across the bridge and they had all disappeared.

The bright light began to dim and the darkness covered me. A jolt of heaviness and pain gripped my body. Voices were filtering into me through this haze. Whose voices were they? I thought, as I struggled to open my eyes. My eyelids felt heavy to lift. My body felt weighted down and I couldn't move.

"Open your eyes, sweetie? Come on, try real hard." Was that Daniel's voice I heard?

"Come on, open those pretty blue eyes. There's no reason you can't."

"Pain..." I mumbled.

"I know you are hurting, but open your eyes for me."

I tried so hard to pry my eyelids up. I barely got one open a small slit.

THE MOUNTAINS CALL MY NAME

"Good girl, good girl." I heard another voice say.

"Chris? What was Chris doing at Daniel's house?" I thought.

"I told Daniel you would open your eyes for me."

"Where am I?" I asked weakly.

"You're at Duke, surrounded by people who love you."

"Daniel, where are you?" I said. I was trying hard to focus, but couldn't.

"Right here, baby… I just needed to step aside so your doctor could check you."

Chris was standing over me, lifting my eyelids and looking into each pupil.

"Follow this light, sweetheart." Chris said, moving it from side to side. "Stick out your tongue for me. Now move it from side to side. Can you raise your arms for me?"

"Too heavy," I murmured.

"That's okay; we'll work on that latter. Can you wiggle your fingers?"

I tried to follow the instructions he had given me.

"Now, one last thing, can you wiggle your toes?"

"No, I don't have toes."

THE MOUNTAINS CALL MY NAME

"Try to see if you can wiggle those toes you don't have." Chris commanded again.

I tried to shake my head "no", but it hurt.

"Oooo...pain... hurt... stop!" I mumbled through the fog.

"I'll stop when you wiggle your toes," Chris commanded again.

I wiggled my toes slightly.

"Go!" I said.

"You're a stubborn little thing," Chris answered me. "Everything looks good," he said to Daniel.

"Tired...head hurts," I said to Chris.

"We've been sawing and hammering in there. You're gonna' be hurtin' some. The nurse will be in with something."

It took all the strength I could manage, but I raised my hand to feel my head wrapped with bandages.

Daniel took my hand and held it to his lips.

"What happened?" I whispered hoarsely.

"Blood clot, from the fall you had at Bessie's."

"Am I at your house?" I asked confused.

"Duke Hospital."

"How?"

"It's a long story. I'll fill you in later."

"But how?"

"Chris had you flown here. The blood clot wasn't in a very good position, and I knew I couldn't get it. So I called Chris. He said he would send life flight for you and here you are. Chris arranged it. We didn't have the tools or the specialist to do the brain surgery where you were. So, I got you as stable as I could, and Chris had life flight pick you up. And here you are."

"I don't even remember. I missed it," I said with a weak smile.

"I never left your side. I flew with you. I almost lost you," He said, with tears misting his eyes.

"Shhh… Don't do that," I whispered to him.

"You've hung in a balance for days. There were several times Chris said he didn't think you were going to make it. And to be honest, I didn't think so either. But you kept fighting, and I kept troubling God."

"How long have I been here?"

"Two weeks and three days."

"No way."

"Don't ever scare me like that again."

THE MOUNTAINS CALL MY NAME

"You'll never guess where I've been?" I said, rubbing my fingers along Daniel's tear stained face.

"Where have you been?"

"I've been with David." I was about to tell him and the pain medication took over and I couldn't talk.

"Don't talk now, sweetie, you can tell me later."

I seemed to drift in and out of sleep. Every time I awoke, I found Daniel sitting by my bedside. I was lulled into blissful sleep by the beeping of the IV machine and the humming of the monitors they had on me.

"You need to start waking up, little girl." I heard Chris say. "I've been nice long enough. How are you feeling today? Headache better?" he asked.

"No pain. Was it just last night I woke up?"

"Try two nights. We've kept you pretty quiet. I didn't want any undue stress going on. If you sleep, you don't talk."

"Chris? Thanks…"

"You about scared the crap out of Daniel. You remember how I used to set up with David?"

"Yeah."

"Well, I got to baby-sit Daniel a lot over the last couple weeks. He hasn't left your side."

"That bad, huh?"

"Yeah, I won't lie. There were a few days I didn't see how you could have pulled through. But you're one tough little cookie. I kept telling Daniel that you were a fighter."

"I don't remember..."

"You'd been carrying that little blood clot since you fell in Virginia. I guess it just decided to get a little bigger. When Daniel got you here he had you on life support. You evidently stopped breathing at some point in time. If you hadn't had Daniel with you when this happened you would have died."

"Life support? So that's why my throat is sore?"

"Yeah, I had the surgical team ready when he got you here. He already had the clot pinpointed; he just didn't have the things he needed to fix it."

"Poor Daniel, I bet he's been a basket case." I said, smiling at Chris.

"Well, what I did was, I took him into surgery with me every time I scrubbed, that took his mind off of you for a few minutes. You're going to marry another brilliant doctor. How do you manage to do that? If I had known you were available, I would have been over to visit you myself."

"Chris.... you're crazy."

"I'm serious as I can be. I would have asked you out in a heartbeat. Would you have gone?" he asked.

"Chris, you're crazy."

"You just said that. Answer my question. Would you have dated me?"

"Okay, if I hadn't already met Daniel, maybe I would have."

"Damn, I'm always late. If he ever backs out or dies, I'm next, right?

"Yes, you will definitely be next."

About that time Daniel walked into the room holding a Coke in his hand.

"I go to lunch and you try to take my girl," he said as he came to the bedside and kissed me on the lips.

"Hey, beautiful."

"I think she's waking up a little more. She seems to be doing great." he said to Daniel.

"Thanks, Chris."

"No problem, we just need to kick her out of here and get her home where she belongs."

"I couldn't agree more," he said, shaking Chris' hand.

Daniel put down the rails on the side of my bed. He took my hand in his and kissed each of my fingers. I looked down and saw that my diamond was gone.

"Where's my ring?"

He pulled it out of his pocket and placed it on my finger.

"Right here," he said, "They took it off when you were in surgery."

"Daniel? Chris said you had me on life support when I got here."

He just nodded his head and closed his eyes. He started to talk and couldn't for a few minutes.

"I thought you were gone. We had the right people at the hospital when I got you there. You quit breathing just as the paramedics got into the house. I put a tube in so you could breathe and we ran with you. I don't think I've ever gotten to the hospital that fast."

"Who's been working your office hours?"

"Funny you should ask. Chris has been rotating fourth year interns up there. They've loved it and the people have too."

"Did we get married while I was sleeping?" I asked, smiling at him.

"I don't think so. I was worried I wasn't going to have a bride."

"I came back to you. I was given the choice to stay, but I came back to you."

"You told me two days ago that you had been with David. Were you dreaming?"

"No, well actually I don't know exactly where I was, but he was there with me. He told me a lot of things while I was there. Right before I woke up I was going across this bridge with him and I heard you call my name. You kept yelling for me to turn around and look at you. You said 'Elizabeth, look me in the eyes.' I turned and looked at you and knew I couldn't leave you. I turned back around and David was gone. I could have gone with him, Daniel, but you wouldn't let me go."

"Because we couldn't get the swelling to go down we didn't know if you would pull through. I went down to the chapel two or three times a day and begged God to send you back to me. I didn't care if you were crippled or what condition you were in, just to please send you back to me."

"Your love brought me back. I was running to you when I woke up."

"We could tell by your brain waves that you had been trying to wake up. So Chris told me to start calling your name. When you woke up, I was telling you to open you eyes and look at me."

"That was when I was on the bridge."

"I'm so glad you came back, and that you are whole. At this point we don't think there will be any residual effects from the blood clot."

"I bet I look awful." I said, putting my hand up the feel the bandage again.

"He didn't cut a tremendous amount of your hair off, and anyway you're still beautiful."

THE MOUNTAINS CALL MY NAME

"When can I go home?"

"I'm not your doctor, but if you continue to do well, maybe next week."

"I think since your house is as close as it is, we should go there first."

"We? Are you going home with me?"

"Yeah, I'm not letting you go by yourself. I've been here for two weeks; I'm not going back to Virginia without you."

"Do you think that's wise, Dr. Scott?" Being at my house with no chaperone? What will the neighbors think?"

"I don't think I care what they think."

"Daniel, let's get married here at the hospital? I don't want to wait any longer to be your wife."

"What, you don't trust me to be alone with you?" he said teasingly.

"I just want to be your wife. We would have been married last week if I hadn't been in here."

"The sooner the better as far as I'm concerned. I'll talk to Chris. If he thinks it's okay, then we'll be married tomorrow."

"Tomorrow? Do you think we really could?"

"I think we really could. Remember, I'm a mover and a shaker."

THE MOUNTAINS CALL MY NAME

"We could still be married at the chapel. Your mom and dad would be able to see us married."

"My mother would have a fit if that didn't happen. She wants to share this with you so bad."

"I'm glad she's going to be my mother-in-law. Oh, Daniel! The funeral, what about the funeral?"

"From what I hear, it was a beautiful celebration of her life. Mom and Dad took over for me, and carried out your mother's wishes. Dad called and said it went off with out a hitch."

"I was with her in heaven when I was in a coma. There is so much I have to tell you about where I went, but I'm kind of tired now. I've talked so much."

"You've already told me you were with David. I actually felt a little jealous that you were dreaming of him and not me."

"It wasn't a dream Daniel. At least I don't think it was a dream. Everything was too real to be a dream. And you're jealous of a dead man?"

"I have been very jealous of this dead man, because you loved him the way I wanted you to love me," he said seriously.

"And I will always love him. But it has nothing to do with the love I have for you. I could have gone with him, you know, but I chose to come back to you. The bond of your love was too strong and pulled me to you."

"I begged God not to take you away, and he didn't. I wasn't so sure he heard me. You teetered on the cusp of heaven and earth too long."

"It's that cord thing, Daniel. It didn't break."

"What cord thing are you talking about?"

"I can't explain it now, but I will."

"I was so scared," he said, closing his eyes. "I have always been so sure of everything, but this one threw me for a loop. Your life was in these hands." He said holding them up before him and looking at them. "Just one wrong move and I could have lost you. For the first time since I've been a doctor I began to question what I knew to do, or not to do. I also knew I couldn't hesitate for one second, because you didn't have many seconds left."

"But you didn't, and here I am."

"The frustrating thing was, I knew what to do and didn't have the resources I needed to save you. God help me, Elizabeth, if I have to go to Congress itself, I'm going to get funds to upgrade that hospital. We need better equipment and specialists to operate them. We need a lot of new doctors."

"But you got me here to Chris."

"Only by God's grace. There is absolutely no logical reason you should be living right now. God kept you alive. I might have tried Roanoke, or another city, but Chris wanted you brought here, to him. Life flight was already in the air returning from a training run in West Virginia. Can you believe it, they weren't thirty minutes away when Chris contacted them. Everything just fell into line."

"I've worked with him so much. A lot of people didn't like his cockiness. It's just that he knows what he can do and isn't afraid to do it. He just takes command of everything. I've never seen him waver. Not in front of anybody anyway."

"I'd be willing to bet if it was someone he really loved on that table, you'd see a different Chris Thomas."

"Oh, so you're telling me he doesn't really love me? That's not what he told me earlier," I said, smiling at him teasingly.

"At least he better not love you like I love you."

"I'll ask him later."

"Anyway, he had his trauma unit meet me at the helicopter pad when we landed. They told me he was waiting in the surgical suite for me, and wanted me to scrub for the surgery."

"He let you scrub with him?"

"Yeah, he did. I've never been intimidated by surgery. It's always been so fascinating to me, but I felt physically sick about going in to watch him cut you open. I never let him know that though. He wouldn't have let me in if he had known my hesitation. I had to be in there. I didn't actually assist him. They just let me in the room to observe. I was the prayer warrior."

"Sorry I caused such a stir."

THE MOUNTAINS CALL MY NAME

"I know now how you must have felt watching the monitors when your mother was dying. To know what everything means, all the readouts, the beeps, the lingo, it was all so unnerving. Every word that was spoken between Chris and his staff was sifted through my brain trying to glean some hope. I knew nothing looked promising at that point. All any of us knew was, you were still alive. Even after the clot was removed your vitals still weren't good."

I reached over and ran my fingers down his cheek.

"I love you," I whispered to him. "You've been through some rough days."

"*We've* been through some rough days."

"When did you know that I was going to be okay?"

"A day or two before you opened your eyes. For some reason Chris couldn't get you to wake up. It must have been pleasant where you were. You sure didn't want to come home."

"God brought me home." I said, smiling at him.

"I've met a lot of your friends. Everyone kept coming by to check on you. Chris kept telling me there wasn't any reason you couldn't wake up. He had taken you off the ventilator not too long after surgery. You could breathe on your on, you were moving your arms and legs, you just wouldn't wake up, he said. Your brain waves were very active. You just were hiding in there and wouldn't come out."

THE MOUNTAINS CALL MY NAME

"You need to go get some rest. You've been here such a long time. The keys to my house are..." I said, looking around me. "I guess I don't have my keys with me. The next door neighbor will give you her key, I'll have to call and tell her."

"That sounds like a good idea. I've got some plans to make first."

"Daniel? There is a nurse here named Donna Light, she went to the church that David and I went to. Ask her to call my preacher to come see me. I'm sure he would perform the ceremony."

"I've already met him. He's been by several times, but you were sleeping."

"He's a nice man," I said, remembering the kindnesses he had shown me during the loss of David.

"I gathered that much about him. Wouldn't you feel strange about his performing the ceremony since he was yours and David's pastor?"

"It doesn't matter who it is as long as I become your wife."

"I would like to tell you something I've never told another soul." He hesitated before going on. It seemed difficult for him to begin.

"I've never had sex with a girl before. I come to you as a virgin. The Lord impressed on my heart a long time ago when I was just a young man that if I expected my bride to come to me pure and holy before him, then she should expect the same from me. It's a vow that I've never broken. Little did I know it was you God had saved me for."

"I don't know what to say. It... I...I really don't know what to say. Would 'thank you' be appropriate?" I stammered around trying to find the right words to express my feelings.

He just smiled at me.

"You're right. No one in today's world would believe what you just told me, or why you would even consider it in the first place. I'm sure it has been difficult at times to stay true to that vow. As handsome as you are, I'm sure you've met many young ladies that didn't share the same ideals as you. I'm honored that I will be the first one you make love to."

"That's it, Libby love, to make love to, not have sex with. It makes a world of difference. I've been tempted at different times in my life, but God has been good to me. He has always made a way of escape for me, and thanks be to Him, I've taken it."

"I want you to know I do believe you. I just didn't stop to think about any of that."

"Isn't it funny how people expect a girl to come to her husband a virgin, but there's a whole different set of standards for a boy, or man? I've heard it expressed before, that it's okay for a man to sow his wild oats, but not for a girl. What about the girl he used to satisfy his raging testosterone? Is she then cast aside for the next one? Then, this same young man gets ready to head to the altar he wants to find a virgin, someone that no other man has

THE MOUNTAINS CALL MY NAME

touched. I choose to see it as God sees it. Does that make me strange or something?"

"No, not strange, just different. It makes me very proud to have a husband with such high standards. You're one in a million, Dr. Scott, one in a million."

"I'm gonna' go try to find Chris and see about some wedding plans. You get some rest and I'll be back in just a little bit."

He leaned over and gently kissed me on the lips.

"I love you," he said, as he left the room.

Chapter Fourteen

It was dark in my room when I awoke. I had slept a long time. The cafeteria lady was coming into the room with my supper tray. I hadn't been hungry for a long time, but for some reason I was starved today. Chris came in about the time the tray did.

"Hi, how are you doing?" he said, smiling at me.

"I guess I need to ask you that question."

"You're looking good. I wasn't sure I would be able to say that again when I first saw you in the operating room."

"If what Daniel said is true, you asked him to bring me here?"

"Well, life flight was in the area, if you can believe that, and I thought by the time Daniel could get you somewhere else, it would have been too late. Plus, I didn't want you in anyone else's hands."

"You're that good?" I asked, smiling at him.

"I'm damn good and you know it," he said, smiling back at me. "Ask anyone."

"I'm very blessed that you are as good as you are."

"I'll share a little secret with you. The other night when you came in I..."

"Dr. Thomas, don't go shatter my image of you. Don't tell me you don't have a license to practice or something like that."

"As I was going to say, I had to push really hard to pretend you were just one of my regulars. It's not often that I would volunteer to operate on a friend. I just prayed to God that you wouldn't die on the table. But we got that little sucker out of there, and here you are."

"Did Daniel find you today?"

"No, I've been in surgery all day. Is something wrong?"

"We want to get married tomorrow. Do you think we could?"

"Married?"

"Yeah, we want to get married."

"Why the hurry. Can't you wait a couple of weeks, or months, for that matter? You're not going anywhere."

"We just want to. Do you think I could handle it?"

"Well, Elizabeth, I don't think you're quiet up to a honeymoon night."

"Chris, you know better."

"You're right. I do know better, and you're not up to it. Just the emotion of it is a little too much. Maybe in a couple of days. After you're eating, walking, standing, you know doing simple body functions, I'll reconsider. Speaking of eating, your dinner is getting cold." He pulled the lid off the dinner tray, and opened the containers.

"Is this what I ordered for you? If you eat this and don't get sick you're gonna' be doing real good."

He took the spoon and handed it to me, and watched while I ate my soup.

"Don't you have anything important to do?"

"I'm hiding while we talk. No one knows I'm here. I'm all yours."

"This soup is really quiet good."

"If you keep that down, I'll see about a different diet tomorrow. I don't want you heaving from being sick. How do you feel?

"No nausea, no headache. I haven't had anything for pain for several hours."

"I'm going to take that bandage off in just a minute, after you finish your supper."

"It's been itching today, I think it's ready. I don't want Daniel to see me when you take it off."

"Are you going to hide?"

Tears started rolling down my cheeks unexpectedly.

"I'm afraid to see it. I know I'll be so ugly." I put both hands over my face so he wouldn't see me cry.

He pushed the food tray away and sat down on my bedside. He put his arms around me and told me not to cry.

"You are so beautiful, Elizabeth; a shaved head is not going to change that. You've got your life; your hair will grow back. I've done pretty good work back there. The stitching is perfect, if I must say so."

"Why am I crying, I know that. I just feel so weepy."

"That's why I don't want you thinking about getting married tomorrow. He'll be here when you're stronger."

"What's the hurry with this wedding?"

"It just seemed like a good idea."

"Who's idea, yours or Daniel's?"

"Does it matter?"

"I just wondered."

"It was mine. Last Saturday was supposed to be my wedding day, and I was in here."

THE MOUNTAINS CALL MY NAME

"And if I'm not mistaken, you're still in here. You're still hooked up to all kinds of things. I think we'll put the wedding off until you at least have your catheter out. That doesn't make for a pretty bride."

I couldn't help but laugh at his last description.

"The boy isn't going anywhere. He's been parked right here at the hospital since he brought you in. Don't push yourself. I think you ought to wait until you can walk down the aisle to him. What difference would a few weeks make?"

"Can I travel all the way to Virginia?"

"You drive a hard bargain. We'll see how you feel when I release you. Don't forget, you have a doctor for a fiancé. He's not gonna let you get by with anything."

He called for a nurse to bring some scissors in so he could take the bandage off and check the incision. Daniel came in about the time the nurse arrived with them.

"Hey guys it looks like I'm just in time."

Chris took the scissors and cut the thick bandage from my head. It came off fairly easily, only sticking in a few spots. He and Daniel were looking intently at it. Chris was tenderly touching different spots.

"Would you like to assist me, Dr. Scott?"

"Yes, I believe I can handle that."

The staples were gently removed and handed to Daniel.

THE MOUNTAINS CALL MY NAME

"All done, everything looks great. How's the patient?" Chris asked.

"Not bad, just a little weak. I guess it's from sitting up."

"You'll feel better after you rest a little bit."

"I think I might need a little something for pain."

"Sure. You need to get some rest. Remember what we talked about? Don't rush things. It'll be waiting for you."

Daniel walked him into the hallway. I could hear them talking. The nurse came in and brought me a couple of pills for pain. It took the edge off the weepiness I was feeling. Sleep began to creep back in. I tried to stay awake and wait for Daniel, but to no avail. When I woke up it seemed as if it had been hours. Daniel was sleeping in the chair beside me. He looked so peaceful in the dim light of the room. I wanted to touch the curl that had fallen down on his forehead. I lay in the silence of the room, thanking God for all he had given to me. The nurse had removed all the tubing but my IV. This was the most peaceful I had been in a long time. The pain pills had taken away any discomfort I might have had. Daniel stirred in the recliner beside me. He opened his eyes to find me watching him.

"You caught me sleeping," he said, smiling at me. "How ya doing?" he asked.

"I couldn't be finer."

THE MOUNTAINS CALL MY NAME

He moved the chair up close by me and looked me in my eyes. He lowered his lips to mine and kissed me long and tenderly.

"I've wanted to do that for several days," he said, kissing me again and again.

"That was nice," I said, smiling. I kept my eyes closed; relishing the feeling his kisses brought me.

"Do you know how much I love you?" he asked, pressing my fingers to his lips.

"I do, and speaking of I do..."

"I know, I had a long talk with Chris. He's right, you know."

I shook my head 'no'. "I want to marry you now," I whispered.

"I want to marry you, too, but I really do think we need to wait. I think you need to get through this trauma you've been through first. You've been so sick. I just don't think you're up to it yet. We'll have a lifetime to be together. Chris said he would see what he could do about getting you a flight back to Virginia. That way I can take you home with me. Mandy and I will nurse you back to health, and then we can get married. I won't leave you; I'll stay right by your side. Did you think I would leave you if you weren't my wife?"

"No," I said with tears trickling down my face. "It's just that time is passing by so fast and I want you to be mine as quickly as possible. I don't have any family left, and if I married you, I would have one."

THE MOUNTAINS CALL MY NAME

"Oh, sweetheart," he said, taking me into his arms. "Don't you know you're already in my family? I'm going to take care of you the best I know how. I just happen to agree with Chris that we should wait a few days until you're back on your feet."

"Okay, I guess you're right. I just got carried away with the idea."

"I love you more than life itself. I would have traded places with you when you were so sick. I love you that much."

"When can I go home, Daniel?" I said, barely audibly.

"Well, first we have to try to get you up and out of bed. Would you like to try to sit up a little bit?"

"Yeah, that would be a good idea. It wasn't too long ago that I had those pain pills. I think now would be a good time, before the effect wears off."

Daniel helped me into the side chair. I was able to sit up for about thirty minutes before going back to bed. I was just getting settled back under the covers when Chris came in to visit me.

"Hey you two, I've got some good news. How would you like to go home tomorrow?"

"To my home?" I required.

"To the hospital in Virginia, not exactly home, home. You're stable enough to fly, and I know Daniel would like to get back to his practice. I've arranged for a medical flight to take you home first thing in the morning."

"I owe you one," Daniel said, standing up to shake Chris's hand.

"You owe me two, but who's counting. Elizabeth, tomorrow I'm going to transfer your care back to him, do you trust him?" he said, pointing at Daniel with his thumb.

"With my life," I said, smiling at Daniel.

"He's not as good as I am but he'll do in a pinch. What about the wedding?"

"We're going to wait until I'm better."

He winked at me and said, "You can't have sex anyway until I say it's okay."

"Chris, I can't believe you said that," I said, putting my hand over my face.

"I can still make you blush. Haven't lost my touch, have I? Speaking of weddings, and since you two are determined to get married, I have a present for you."

"You've already given us two presents. First, you saved my life, and tomorrow you are flying me home with Daniel."

"I was just trying to show off by saving your life, and the air flight was no biggie, but I hope this last thing is. Daniel, I accept your offer to move to Virginia."

THE MOUNTAINS CALL MY NAME

Our jaws dropped with surprise. We were both speechless. Daniel was the first to recover enough to speak.

"You're not joking? You're really going to join my practice?"

"If you'll have me, and about three others."

"Three... what are you saying, Chris?"

"You know the three senior residents that have been rotating in and out of your practice?"

"Yeah, I know them well."

"They graduate in about three weeks, so upon finishing their boards they want to join us, if you'll have them."

"What is you opinion about them." he asked inquiringly.

"You know I've worked very closely with them, and I think they will do great. They're a sharp bunch of young men."

"What will that give us?" Daniel asked excitedly.

"Me - a surgeon, a gynecologist, an ear, nose and throat guy and last but not least, an internist. What do you say, Dr. Scott, do you have room for four new doctors?"

"What if I don't marry Elizabeth, do you still come?" he said, smiling at me.

"Of course, because if you don't, I am."

"Seriously Chris, Are you sure about this?" Daniel questioned.

"Dead serious. I'll get there just as soon as I can tie things up here. I'll probably get there just in time for the wedding."

"We don't have the facilities like you have here."

"You don't now, but you will. I happen to have some good connections. I know where we can get the money and the equipment. It will take a little time but we'll make it."

"I can't believe my ears. Do these doctors realize that it won't be lucrative to come there?"

"Yeah, they know. They've met your people there and have fallen in love with them."

"It's an answer to my prayers," Daniel said, grinning from ear to ear.

"Well, I've had a long day, and I'm going home. I'll be here in the morning to check you over before I release you to this kind doctor here. I heard you sat up for a while, and that's good. Each time will help you get your strength back a little more. You two have a good evening. I'm outta here."

"I can't believe we're going to get some new doctors. I've had a chance to talk to the doctors he was talking about. They are all real nice. I'm sure their youth will be a stumbling block, but we're breaking new ground."

THE MOUNTAINS CALL MY NAME

"I'm so happy for you, and for the people of Scott's Corner. They will trust you more and more."

"I get to take you home tomorrow. I'm as excited about that as I am about getting new doctors. I think Chris is getting everything lined up."

He sat down on the side of my bed and looked tenderly in my eyes.

"You're so lovely," he said softly. "I can't wait to make you my bride." He leaned down and kissed me tenderly on the lips.

"Look at me," I said, lifting my hands toward my head. "How can you say I'm lovely?"

"Because you are. Don't you know it doesn't matter if your hair is cut, or you don't have on makeup? I love you no matter how you look; that's what true love is all about. It's called 'unconditional love'."

"I love you that way, too. I know why I came back across that bridge. It was because your love was too strong for me to resist."

"I think I'll take you up on the offer to stay at your house tonight. I need a good night's rest."

"You can even sleep in my bed. Since I've slept in yours, you can sleep in mine."

"We're going to get this together one day and sleep in the same bed at the same time."

THE MOUNTAINS CALL MY NAME

I called my neighbor to let her know that Daniel would be picking up the key. I would never get tired of his sweet lips against mine, I thought, as he kissed me goodnight.

Maybe tonight I would be able to rest. The pain had begun to diminish somewhat. I lay there with my eyes closed and let my mind wander back to the trip I took to heaven. I thought about my real mother. I wasn't ready to tell Daniel yet. I wondered if he would think I was crazy.

How would I find my grandmother? Where could I start? I wasn't afraid now to find out who I was, because I had already met the one who gave me life. One day soon I would tell the whole story to Daniel, but for now, I'm going to sleep.

I woke up early the next morning to the clanging of the breakfast trays in the hallway. I was able to get up by myself and set in the side chair to eat breakfast. I was weak, but felt more strength than I did the day before. I was just about finished with my breakfast when Daniel walked in with Chris.

"Good morning, princess," Daniel said, leaning over to kiss me.

"Huh, maybe I'll try that. Good morning, princess," Chris said, also leaning down to kiss me.

I pointed to my cheek.

"I think I'll follow you around, Dr. Scott, your technique works pretty well."

"Hey, she's spoken for. I don't know if I trust you. It was okay while she was unconscious, but I don't know about now."

"I'm as innocent as a baby," he said, winking at me.

"Chris, thank you for all you've done for me. It would take a lifetime for me to repay you."

"Just go make some beautiful babies, so I can be called 'Uncle Chris'."

"I'll try to do that."

"Well, your chariot will be ready in about forty-five minutes. We need to get you ready for transport. Daniel, you need to come with me so I can transfer her over. There are some papers we both need to sign. I'll be back to see you in just a few minutes.

"I came to help get you ready for transport," the nurse said, coming into the room.

"I don't have much to transport. I just came here in what I've got on, a hospital gown."

"The only thing you're going to be hooked up to is this IV. The flight crew should be here in just a minute. You shouldn't have any worries. Dr. Scott is going to be crew chief on this flight. It's been nice being your nurse, but I'm glad you're going home."

"I'm very glad to be going home."

"We felt so bad for you when David died. It was such a tragic thing."

THE MOUNTAINS CALL MY NAME

Daniel walked into the room about that time. I was glad the conversation stopped there. I didn't want to rehash everything with her. The flight crew was right behind him with their stretcher.

"We're ready, sweetie. I've signed all the papers and we're ready to fly."

Chris came in right behind them.

"Am I about to miss the party? I want to talk to her a minute by herself. Everybody out."

He came over to my bedside and leaned down and kissed my forehead.

"You are very special to me, Elizabeth Mason. I didn't want to say goodbye in front of everybody. You are a very lucky young lady. I wouldn't have given a nickel for your life when you got here. I always bragged about my being the greatest surgeon in this hospital. I have to believe that every time I operate on someone. But I know I'm only as good as the one who guides my hands. The only greatness in me is God who gives me the knowledge and grace to do what I do."

"Dr. Thomas, I don't believe I've ever heard you speak of God before. You always sound so..."

"Cocky?"

"Yeah, something like that."

"Cocky, overbearing, a jerk, I've been called them all and some more."

"I've probably called you some of them," I said laughing.

"God's working on me. He's teaching me to be humble," he said seriously.

"Don't ever ask for God to humble you. He has the neatest ways to accomplish that task. Trust me, when he is through, you will wallow in humility."

"You humbled me when you came in here so sick. Everything changes when it's someone you care for. If I hadn't been cocky the night Daniel brought you too me, he would have lost his last little bit of hope. I made him believe I could do anything. In reality, only God could have saved you that night, and he did. I was only an instrument used by him. That's what started me thinking about coming to Virginia to work. I want to make the rest of my career count."

"You've always counted, Chris. You've saved so many lives, and have taught so many others to be good surgeons. I'm thrilled that you're coming to Virginia, and Daniel is one happy doctor."

"I'm sorry about your wedding postponement, but I really didn't think you were ready to handle all the stress of a wedding right now. Take your time, sweetie, Daniel isn't going anywhere."

"I knew what you were saying was true, I just kind of got carried away with the thought of going home with him as his wife."

"I guess I better let them back in, they get kind of antsy when they're ready to fly. If it doesn't work out with Daniel I'm waiting in the shadows."

"Why, Doctor Thomas, if I didn't know better I would think you were coming on to me."

He raised my hand to his lips and kissed it, and winked at me.

"Stay sweet," he said, heading out the door. "Come on in guys and take this woman home."

"I was beginning to wonder what you were checking," Daniel said, entering the room.

We headed down the hall to the elevators. Daniel walked by my side holding on to the stretcher. He chatted with Chris as we headed up to the roof to board the helicopter.

When we were on the rooftop, Chris bid us all a final farewell. He leaned down and kissed my cheek and gave me a thumbs up.

"Take good care of her, Daniel," he said, shaking his hand.

Chapter Fifteen

I lost sight of Daniel while they were loading me, but he reached in and squeezed my hand, then proceeded to buckle himself in beside me.

The ride to Daniel's hospital seemed to take forever. I tried to sleep but everything was too noisy. Daniel tried to talk to me but I couldn't hear what he was saying. So, he finally gave up. I finally made out that he was saying he loved me.

I smiled and, remembering Chris' signal to me, gave him thumbs up to let him know I got the message. Daniel took my blood pressure again. He asked if the flight was causing any pain. I nodded affirmatively. He then took a syringe and put something into the tubing of the IV. It wasn't long before I drifted off to sleep. I woke up when they were getting ready to unload me at the hospital. I guess I was doing okay; there wasn't anyone running to the helicopter pad. They took me straight to the room Daniel had prepared for me. I was more than ready to get back into bed.

"How are you doing? Daniel said, leaning down to kiss me as he settled me into the bed.

"I'm very tired right now. It was a rough trip."

"Each day you'll get a little stronger. And before you know it, I'll take you home."

THE MOUNTAINS CALL MY NAME

"When will that be?"

"Maybe two or three more days. Your incision is healed, and your vitals are stable. I don't see any reason to keep you here. I just want you to be a little stronger."

"I'm ready to go home, and I'm so tired of hospitals. I just want all this to be over and get back to normal."

"And you will; you already are getting back to normal."

I picked up my hands and touched the stringy hair hanging down beside my face.

"I've got to do something with this. Do you have any ideas?"

"Whatever you want to do, I'll do it for you, or arrange to have it done."

"Do you think I need to cut it all off? I said with tears escaping down my cheek.

He came to me and took me in his arms and held me close to him.

"You don't have to do anything with it."

"Yes, I do. I look terrible."

"To whom?"

"I just know I do," I said, sobbing into his chest.

THE MOUNTAINS CALL MY NAME

"You're just tired from having gone through so much. You're body's been through such trauma that it's normal to feel a little down. And you've had a long flight home. You're just really tired."

"I'll be right back. Don't go away," he said, heading out of the room.

I slowly got out of the bed and stood holding the IV pole. The bathroom was just a short distance from my bed, and I was heading that direction when Daniel walked back into the room.

"Where are you going?" he said, shocked that I was out of bed.

"Just to the bathroom. I thought I could make it. I got up by myself this morning." I said defensively.

"You make me nervous. You could fall and re-injure your head," he said, scolding me.

"I can do some things for myself," I said, irritated.

"I can see this is not going to be an easy road for us. I'm overprotective and you're headstrong. We're going to drive each other insane before you get better!" he said with a deep sigh.

"I'm sorry. I just want to feel stronger and I need to go to the bathroom."

He helped me into the bathroom, and stood at the door while I was relieving myself. I stood at the sink to wash my hands and saw for the first time what I looked like. Tears started to flow again. The image I saw before me was horrific. My hair hung in greasy dirty strands down the side of my face. I couldn't stop crying. As hard as I tried to quit, the more the tears fell. Daniel came into the bathroom where I was and held me close.

"It's all going to be okay. Trust me; it's all going to be okay. You'll feel better tomorrow." He led me back to the bed and tucked me in. The nurse brought in a syringe and gave me an injection in my hip.

Daniel lay down on the bed beside me and again pulled me to him.

"Listen to me, in just a short time all this is going to be behind us. We'll be married, and our life will be beautiful. We'll have the most wonderful wedding Scott's Corner has ever seen. We'll have perfectly gorgeous babies, because they'll look just like their mother. I'll hold you every night and be beside you every day. Just lie here and rest in my arms and think positive thoughts."

"Okay," I said, snubbing like a little child. "I just feel so weepy today."

"You'll start feeling better in just a little bit. The injection will take the edge off of everything. I'm not going to leave you. Just cuddle up to me and let me love you."

I snuggled in his arms. He was right, I was beginning to feel better. I could live forever right here in his arms. I would settle for this for now. I could feel his heart beat beneath my hand. I closed my eyes and let the medicine roll over me. I was aware of the warmth of his body close to mine. The faint scent of his cologne wafted through my nostrils.

His finger traced the outline of my lips. He gently tilted my face to him, and then his lips were on mine, sweet and gentle. I felt like I was in a dream floating aimlessly in the ocean of his love. I could tell by his kiss that he needed to feel my closeness as much as I needed his. The combination of the shot and his kisses left me like putty in his hands.

"Do you feel better?" he whispered to me, still holding close to his body.

"You're better medicine to me than the injection. Take me home, Daniel, please take me home."

"Soon, I promise it will be soon. I know you're really tired of hospitals. Just as soon as you can possibly go home, I'll take you."

"Why did all this have to happen to me? I could have already been your wife."

"I can't answer that question with anything except 'it just did'. Unfortunately we can't choose what happens to us. I do know whatever happens to us is first sifted through the hands of God. If we can make it through this, then we can make it through anything."

I lay in his arms and drank in the sweetness of his love and affection. I soon felt myself drifting off to sleep, and I welcomed this peaceful river that swept me away in its current. My emotions had been on a roller coaster. Chris was right; I wasn't ready for marriage right now.

When I woke up awhile later, I was still in Daniel's arms. I shifted slightly and realized that he had gone to sleep also. My movement awoke him. He smiled down at me, his eyes still dreamy from sleep.

"This is where I want you to be the rest of my life. I want to make you feel loved and safe, and take all your sadness away," he said, snuggling up to me.

"You've done an excellent job so far. What would really make me happy is for you to let me go home tomorrow."

"Tomorrow? Don't you ever give up?" he said, smiling at me. "I don't know about tomorrow." Daniel stretched and yawned.

"But you'll be there with me, and Mandy will be as good as any nurse. And you, yourself, said my vitals have remained stable, and my incision has healed. I would feel so much better at your house."

"Are you sure you're not a lawyer instead of a nurse? You argue so convincingly."

"I just want to go home!"

"Maybe. I won't promise, but I'll think about it. I want to be sure you're completely out of the woods. You've been very sick you, know. You've just started eating, and yesterday was the first time you've been up. I'll think about it. Right now I've got to get up from here and go to my office for the afternoon. All you have to do is rest and get better. I'll be back before you know it," he said, getting his lab coat off the back of the chair where it lay.

"You look so handsome in your doctor uniform."

THE MOUNTAINS CALL MY NAME

"My doctor uniform?" he said, laughing at me. "I haven't had it expressed quite that way before."

"How in the world someone hasn't snagged your heart amazes me. I'm sure it's not for their lack of trying," I said, looking at him admiringly.

"You're just trying to make me not go to work, and it's not going to happen," he said, giving me a kiss on my forehead. "See ya later baby."

"See ya."

I took the opportunity to take a shower. The nurse brought everything I needed for my adventure. She helped me into the warm spray of water. She said since my incision had healed it wouldn't hurt to wash my hair.

The rivulets of water felt good running down my body. It had been so long since I had a real bath. As good as it felt, I knew I wouldn't be able to linger because of the weakness I still felt in my body. I gently shampooed all the oil and grease from my hair.

When I had finished, the nurse helped me dry off and get into a fresh gown. She had unhooked the IV earlier so it was a lot easier to get in and out of the shower. By the time I got out, I felt as if I had done a day's work.

I sat in the chair by the bed and the nurse brushed my hair for me. She pulled it back and tied a ribbon in it which she had found in the nurses' station. Chris said he shaved as little as possible in order to still do the job. Most of it was at the lower back of my skull, so I could pull it over it and cover up the bare spot.

THE MOUNTAINS CALL MY NAME

I thanked her for helping me. I felt like a new person, and it couldn't help but make me look a little better, I thought.

Daniel came in right behind the dinner trays.

"Hey, princess, feeling better?" he said, planting a kiss on my cheek. You look great. Did you take a shower?"

"Yeah, not too long ago, and I'm so tired."

"Are you hungry?" he asked me as he took off his lab coat.

"I'm starved," I replied.

The nurse followed him in with another tray.

"I thought I would have supper with you. Let's see what we have."

He raised the lid to steak with all the trimmings.

"Did you do that?" I asked him.

"I made a little visit to the kitchen on my way to the office. They love me down there. Anyway, I convinced them to bring us something special."

He unloaded our trays on to a little table in my room. We ate as he conveyed what he had done at his office. He was clearly excited about the new doctors coming.

"The staff is excited about Chris coming. I worked on his office space in between seeing some patients. The staff had the highest of praise for the doctors that have filled in for me. I'm trying to work out something about their office space. It's amazing how God brings things together. We needed new doctors so badly. You asked earlier why things happen. Just look at what your illness has brought to Scott's Corner."

"Maybe all this happened to bring doctors here. I wish he had chosen another way," I said, smiling.

"Me too," he said, reaching over and squeezing my hand.

"I'm so happy he's coming. I can't believe it was Chris that you were entertaining to come here. We were really good friends when I worked there."

We talked at great length about what he had done all afternoon. Dinner had indeed been a treat.

"Did you like dinner?"

"Yes, it was very good."

"I can't promise that every time. There's only so much a doctor can do," he said, smiling at me.

He cleared the little table our food was on and placed the dishes back on the serving tray.

"It's time for you to go back to bed, my little princess. You've been up way to long."

"Yeah, I have to agree with you for once. But before I do, I think I'll use the little girls' room."

THE MOUNTAINS CALL MY NAME

As usual, he waited by the bathroom door to escort me back to bed. He turned out the overhead light and put the night light on overhead.

"Daniel, do me a favor."

"And what might that be?"

"I want you to go home and get some rest. I'm feeling good, and it's been a long time since you've been home."

"I can't agree more," his mother said, walking into my room.

"Mom! Dad! I'm surprised to see you guys."

"Well, when you called and said you were bringin' our little girl home we had to come see her. We figgered you'd be wher' she was and we'd get to see the both of ya."

She handed me a beautiful bouquet of flowers.

"How are you doin', sweetie?" she said, bending to give me a hug and kiss.

"I'm doing fine. I just look terrible. I've got to do something with the hair I have left."

"You look lovely, don't she, Daniel." she said, beaming down at me.

"That's what I keep telling her, but she doesn't believe me."

"These eyes aren't deceiving," I answered.

"We've been prayin' fer you, Elizabeth. You had us so sceert. We thought we done lost ya."

"I want to let you all know how much I appreciate you taking over at my mother's funeral. I would have rather been there than where I was."

"We did all we knew to do, to honor your wishes. You woulda been proud of all the people that came. The important thing is you're gettin' well. Daniel tells us you're comin' home in a day or two."

"I want to go home tomorrow. I asked Daniel to let me."

"I'm thinking about it," he said, smiling at me.

We talked on and on about first one thing and another. Even though I enjoyed their visit I was hoping it would end soon.

"Are you having any pain now?" he asked, picking up the cuff to take my blood pressure.

"Is everything still good?" I asked him.

"Perfect, now answer my question; are you having any pain now?"

"No, not since this morning when we arrived here."

"Any depression or nervousness"?

"I feel much better than I did this morning. That man you sent in to sleep with me fixed everything. I woke up feeling like a new woman."

"I think he enjoyed it too," he said, winking at me.

"Who, Daniel?" his mother asked.

"It was me, Mom, I was just teasing her," he said, shaking his head. Do you actually think I would send someone to sleep with her?"

"You had me fooled fer a minute," she said, laughing.

"Honey I think we need to let 'Lis'beth rest. Why don't we get outta here?" she said, looking at her husband.

"You're right, I'm kind of tired too," he answered her.

"We gonna be goin' on. Daniel, are you comin' with us?"

"I'll be on in a little bit. I need to tuck her in."

His mom gave me a kiss on the cheek, followed quickly by one from his dad.

"Take care, sweetie, we'll be back," she said, waving as she left the room.

Daniel followed them to the door, escorting them to the hallway. When he came back in, he closed the door behind him.

THE MOUNTAINS CALL MY NAME

"You need to go, too," I said.

"I will, but not quite yet. I can't bring myself to leave you."

"Come lie down with me," I said, patting the bed with my hand.

"Do you always invite men into your bed?" he asked, taking his shoes off and lying down beside me.

"Only the ones that are incredibly handsome or the one I'm engaged to," I said, smiling at him.

He took my hand with the diamond on it and held it up so it would catch a ray of light to make it dazzle.

"I still can't believe you're actually going to be my wife. Dr. and Mrs. Daniel Scott or Elizabeth Scott, I like how they sound." He kissed my hand and then placed it on his chest above his heart.

"This heart will only beat for you," he said, looking tenderly into my eyes.

He shifted so I could lay my head on his shoulder. I was nestled securely in his arms.

"You are so precious to me. During those long, dark hours sitting and waiting for you to wake up, I tried to remember what it was like not having you near me. It seemed as if you've always been a part of my life. The years we were separated seemed more like weeks, and not ten years. You swept in on angel wings and took my breath away."

THE MOUNTAINS CALL MY NAME

"It was you that swept in on angel wings, and rescued me from the dark pit I was in."

"I think God had our lives collide at exactly the time he wanted them to. I think 'collide' would be a good term for it, don't you?"

"I couldn't have described it better myself," I said, smiling at the thought.

He shifted toward me and drew me closer to him.

"Have I told you in the last five minutes how deeply I love you?" he said, kissing me again.

His hand felt warm and gentle against my skin where my gown had separated in the back. Sickness did not deter my response to his touch. The sensation was electrifying as his hand caressed my bare back. He held me for a long time, slowly and gently caressing me as we lay in the quietness of the dimly-lit room.

"I can't get enough of your closeness." He whispered as his lips kissed the curve of my neck.

"Daniel," I whispered, with barely enough breath to say his name. I was helpless to stop him as his hand slid down my waist to my hip and down my thigh. He pulled me ever closer to him.

"I love you so much," he whispered to me.

I looked up into his eyes and saw a new depth of his love.

"Kiss me, Daniel," I said softly, "kiss me again." I closed my eyes waiting for the rapture the kiss would bring.

He kissed my face, my lips and my neck. I whispered his name over and over as he caressed and held me. The excitement of his closeness made everything around me fade into nothingness. This hospital bed became our island of paradise. I wish this moment wouldn't have to end. My inhibitions were slowly slipping away with each kiss and caress.

"It's getting late and I need to go," he said, still holding me close. "I'll be back before you miss me," he said, slowly separating himself from me.

"I already miss you," I said. "Do you really have to go?"

He kissed me again and again, neither of us wanting it to end. I felt his muscles tighten as my hand slipped under his hospital scrub to caress his broad back.

We were jarred back to reality with the echoing of a voice from the intercom above my head.

"Dr. Scott? Are you in there?" The faceless voice asked.

"Yeah, I'm here," he said, straightening himself in the bed. He reached over and helped pull the gown back up on my shoulder from where it had fallen.

"You had a long distance call come in. The hospital operator wants you to call her for the information."

"I didn't get a page. Did she page me?" he asked, looking around for his pager.

"I assume so. She called our station asking if I had seen you."

"Okay," he said, swinging himself around to a sitting position.

He got his lab coat and looked in the pocket for the elusive pager.

"There it is," he said, looking at the number. "I guess I just didn't hear it. That doesn't happen often." He was looking sheepishly at me.

He called the operator and got the message.

"It was Chris; he wants me to call him."

He moved to the chair beside the bed, and let his head rest on the back of the seat. He sat there with his eyes closed, visibly shaken from his recent visit to my bed.

"Are you okay, Daniel?" I asked softly.

"I will be," he said, pulling his chair up close to the side of my bed.

"Are you?" he asked in return.

"It's been a long time since I've felt this way toward a man. Maybe it's because I never did have to hold myself back from David. I have forgotten how all consuming passion can be. I don't remember ever being moved with passion the way you move me. It was wrong of me to invite you into situations we have difficulty controlling. I just need your closeness."

"You're just saying that to make me feel good."

"Oh, no, I wouldn't lie to you. It's not just the passion you arouse in me, but it's the love I feel that makes it all overwhelming. I feel your love through every word and touch."

"I told you, I've never had sex, well, I didn't say I hadn't been tempted. The difference is this, before I was tempted to have sex because it was there. Now, it's the depth of love I have for you that makes it complete. It's hard finding a stopping place. The more I hold you and kiss you, the more I want to hold you and kiss you.

"I've only had sex with one person, my husband. I didn't have any lessons on what to do."

"I can vouch for that. You never were with anyone but me, and I sure didn't give you any."

With you it's going to be totally different."

"How do you figure that? Am I made different than David?"

"I sure hope not," I said, smiling at him. "It's just that you've already shown me you're going to be different."

"How am I different? I would be interested to know the answer to that question."

"You absolutely drive me crazy with your kisses, and your touch. I've never been moved like you move me."

"Perhaps it's just been a long time since you've been moved," he said, smiling at me.

I closed my eyes and tried to say just the right thing.

"When your hand caressed my back, the senses throughout my whole body heightened. My stomach did flip flops and you took my breath away. I wanted you to make love to me."

"I'm sure you've wanted David to make love to you too. How is it different with me?"

"It's what you do to me. It never was so spontaneous before."

"I wanted to make love to you, too. You know how very close we came?"

I nodded with my eyes closed.

I've never touched a woman like I did you tonight. Touching patients in the examining room doesn't count; trust me I've never been turned on in the exam room."

"Would we have stopped if the intercom hadn't gone off?"

"We'll never know, will we? he said, picking my hand up and kissing my fingers. I've never been this close before."

THE MOUNTAINS CALL MY NAME

"So it moved you, too?"

"That's putting it mildly. If you'll notice I'm in the chair and not in your bed."

There's safety in distance," I said, smiling at him.

"So, we can't touch bare skin again until we are married, except to hold hands. No more getting in bed with each other either, right?"

"Right, no more touching bare skin or getting in bed together."

"I know when the time comes it will be one of the most beautiful things that's ever happened to me."

"To us," he said, smiling at me.

"Do you think we'll be able to make it to our wedding day?"

"I don't think you even have to ask that question. God always gives us a way out of temptation."

"That's his promise to us. Isn't it? I guess we can't keep tempting fate," I said, looking intently into his eyes.

"So, if you can keep your hands off me, I'll keep mine off you, and then we'll be safe," he said, laughing at me.

"It was fabulous and spine tingling. And other adjectives I could add," I said softly to him.

"I think talking about what it does to us is off limits too," he said, grinning at me.

"I'm too close to your bed, and everything is still very vivid in the sensual part of my brain. I was a little too close for you not to have had on anymore clothes than you did."

I took his hand, held it to my lips and kissed it.

"I'm sorry Daniel, I knew better," I said, looking into his dreamy eyes.

"No, please don't be sorry. Don't ever be sorry for having shared love with me. It was the most wonderful moment of my life. I've never been this close to anyone before, physically or emotionally."

He lowered himself to me and gently kissed me.

"I'm not sorry for loving you, just sorry for temping you."

"Now, since I can breathe again I'll call Chris," he said, grinning at me.

He dialed the number the operator gave him and Chris readily answered the call.

"Hey, this is Daniel."

"She's doing great; she just had some residual pain earlier but nothing more."

"Sure, here she is," he handed me the phone.

"How ya doin'?" he asked.

"A little tired but other than that I'm doing good. I sat up for quite a while today, I took a shower and washed my hair."

"Be careful you could get dizzy and fall. I'd hate for you to mess up my pretty incision."

"Daniel said the same thing."

"You'd better listen to him. It's for your own good. I'm glad you're doing well. Let me speak to Daniel again."

"I worked on your office space today. I'll have you a secretary by the time you get here."

"Sure I'll call you. Oh! She wants to go home tomorrow; do you think I should let her?"

He sure was taking a long time to answer.

"Okay, I'll tell her. Oh, and by the way, your timing is impeccable. Bye"

"Well what did he say?"

"He said he thought since you made the trip so well he didn't see why not, especially since I was taking you home with me."

"So that's a yes?"

"That's a yes. Now let me go. I've got to go tell Mandy."

THE MOUNTAINS CALL MY NAME

He kissed me lightly on the lips. "I'll see ya in the morning. Sleep well, sweetheart."

"You'll be in my thoughts and dreams," he said as he headed out the door.

Tomorrow I would be going home, I thought, and soon Daniel would be my husband. I couldn't wait.

I slept soundly throughout the night. For the first time in a long time I had no need for pain medication. I was awake early anticipating the arrival of Daniel. I hoped that he had remembered clothing. I didn't want to go home in a hospital gown. I was sitting up in the side chair when he came in. He carried a small overnight bag.

"Your clothing," he said, holding up the bag.

"Thank you. I'm so ready to go home."

"Mandy helped me pack for you. I think she's more capable than I am. She is so excited about my bringing you home."

"Do you need any help getting dressed?"

"No, I don't think so, if you will excuse me, I'll get ready to go home."

"I can help you?" he said, leaning down to kiss me.

"I don't think either one of us could handle that right now," I said, taking a deep breath and smiling at him.

THE MOUNTAINS CALL MY NAME

"You're probably right. I'm afraid I would take more off than I put on."

"I don't have very much on as it is," I said, laughing at him.

"How well I know," he said with a deep sigh.

He reached the buzzer on the bed rail to call for a nurse.

"May I help you?" the voice said.

"Yeah, this is Dr. Scott; could you send someone in to help Mrs. Mason get ready to go home?"

"Sure thing, someone will be right there."

It wasn't long before the nurse came in.

"You're going home so soon?" she asked.

"I'm going home with the kind doctor here. I'm sure I'll get extra special care."

"Would you help her get dressed while I get papers for her release?" Daniel asked, leaving the room.

She took the things out of the small overnight case. Mandy had selected a pair of slacks and a blouse that buttoned up the front. I was glad I wouldn't have to pull anything over my head. The nurse balanced me while I put my feet into my pants. They were almost loose enough to fall off my hips.

THE MOUNTAINS CALL MY NAME

I wonder how much weight I have lost, I thought as I finished dressing.

I was ready by the time Daniel came back to the room. He was pushing a wheelchair. I would have no complaints about riding one this time.

"Let's go home, sweetheart," he said, locking the foot rest in place while I got in.

The nurse tagged along with a cart that held my flowers. Daniel had the van waiting right outside the door with the engine running. He had gone out while I was dressing and started it. The cold air struck my face as we rolled out the door. It actually felt good to be in the crisp air. It had been such a long time. I noticed there were patches of snow still on the ground.

Daniel opened the door and helped me inside. He carefully buckled my seatbelt over me, and went around to his side and got in.

"Let's go home, baby," he said, reaching for my hand.

"Let's go home," I repeated back to him.

I felt weak and shaky from having been up so long. Daniel had slightly tilted the seat so I wasn't sitting straight up. He had placed a small pillow behind my head so my incision wouldn't be directly against the headrest.

"Are you doing okay?" he asked, looking at me with concern.

"I'm fine. I'll just be glad to get home. I'm weaker than I thought I was."

"Mandy fixed up the downstairs bedroom so you wouldn't have to climb the stairs. She's all ready for you."

"And I'm ready for her. It's been a long journey."

"Just a few weeks ago you weren't even in my life and now look what we've been through. I wouldn't have dreamed anything like this would be happening to me."

"I was shut up in my little world in North Carolina, destined to be a lonely widow, and then my world changed forever."

"For the better I hope?"

"Yes, definitely for the better. If someone would have told me I would be head over heals in love with Daniel Scott I would have told them they were crazy."

"Is that such a crazy idea?"

"No, it's just that I was so wrapped up in my misery I couldn't imagine loving anyone again. And now I can't imagine not having you in my life."

"Holding you last night and everything was..."

"Almost too much..."

"Yeah, almost too much. There is so much waiting for us," he said, squeezing my hand.

THE MOUNTAINS CALL MY NAME

I closed my eyes and lay my head against the small pillow he brought for me. I smiled to myself remembering the night before. Remembering the feel of his hand as he caressed my bare skin sent shivers of joy within me. Our vow of purity before marriage was getting harder to abide by. Soon, very soon, I had to become his bride."

It wasn't long before we arrived at his house. Mandy was waiting for us in the drive way. She must have been watching for us from the window.

"Welcome home, youngun, welcome home," she said, taking me into her arms.

Daniel got what little belongings I had and followed us into the house. Mandy led me to my room and helped me into bed. Once she was satisfied with how I was arranged, she left Daniel and me to ourselves.

"You need to get some sleep."

"I will. I'm so tired. But I'm so glad you let me come home. I needed to be here so badly."

"I needed for you to be here. It seems so strange being home. But I wouldn't have come back and left you in Durham. I just couldn't do it without you."

He placed his hand on my forehead to check for fever.

"Am I hot?"

"Not now, but you sure were last night."

"You make me blush," I said, smiling up at him.

THE MOUNTAINS CALL MY NAME

"You must have gone through such a bad time when I was unconscious," I said, rubbing my fingers along his cheek.

He took my hand and held it to his lips. He sat that way for a few minutes with his eyes closed, as if trying to collect what he was going to say.

"It was the hardest thing I've ever had to go through. I've never loved anyone that could do to me what you have. You've intertwined yourself tightly around my heart. The enormity of all that has happened just suffocates me some times. There were many times over the last few days that I thought I was going to lose you. But you kept fighting to stay alive, and I kept fighting to save you. Just when I thought you couldn't get worse you did. Your vitals would go crazy. Then Chris and I would do some adjustment with your medicine and the machines, and you would stabilize. God didn't take you away from me, but there were several days I wasn't sure which way it would go.

"Ever since we've been reunited it's been one crazy ride. It seems like I've spent more time in a hospital bed than any other place."

"It's been interesting. Actually I've never been in a hospital bed until you came into my life. I wonder sometimes what they're saying at the hospital. I get a lot of smiles," he said, reaching for my hand.

"Daniel," I said, looking into his eyes. I love you with my whole heart. I promise you I will give to you everything I can. I can't give you much right now, but when I'm well I'll be there one hundred percent. I want to be the wife you deserve."

"Just being you is all that I want. You're my dreams come true. You don't have to change anything. I loved you when you were a little girl, and I really love you as a woman."

I was fighting to keep my eyes open.

"I'm so tired, Daniel. I think I need a little nap."

"I think you need a long nap. While you sleep this afternoon I'm going to have to go into the office. I have some patients that I have to see, but I'll be back before you wake up."

"Okay, just kiss me before I fall asleep."

He kissed me gently on the lips and pulled the cover up over me.

"Sweet dreams, princess."

I slept the whole afternoon, waking just in time for Daniel to arrive from work. Mandy came in to see if I needed anything. I told her I needed to go to the bathroom, but thought I could make it by myself. Nothing would do but for her to follow me.

"I have strict orders from Master Daniel not to let you up without being by your side."

"Thank you, Mandy, you're so good to me."

"I just thank Jesus he done spared your life. I was so sceert' when you got so sick. I weren't sure you'd be comin' home to us. When Master Daniel tol' me you was okay, I just praised the good Lawd."

"Mandy, we're going to get married soon. I can't wait to be his bride. I just want it to be real soon."

"And he cain't wait to be you' husband. You two just look so cute together," she said, chuckling.

"Do you want to go sit in the livin' room some?"

"Yeah, I think I would like to do just that."

Mandy gently brushed my hair and tied it back with a ribbon.

I was sitting on the couch when Daniel came in. He came and squatted down on the floor in front of me, feeling my pulse as he held my hand.

"Are you doing okay?" he asked with that familiar look of concern on his face.

I nodded my head and smiled at him.

"I feel great, just a little weak. I slept all afternoon, without medication I might add."

"Good girl. Are you comfortable?"

I nodded again.

"I'm going to go change out of these scrubs and get into something more comfortable. I'll be right back."

444

THE MOUNTAINS CALL MY NAME

"You look so handsome in your scrubs. There's just something about a doctor that turns me on."

"Maybe I should just leave them on, if it makes you feel so good."

He winked at me and left to go change. He was back in no time and came to sit by me on the couch. I lay back in his arms and looked up into his beautiful blue eyes. Mandy had the fireplace going as usual. The one thing I wouldn't like about warm weather is the fact that I couldn't enjoy the fireplace. She knew how we both loved to sit in front of it and watch the flames.

"This is just how paradise is supposed to be; a man and his woman relaxing after a hard day at the office," he said, smiling at me.

"Daniel, I need to ask you a question."

"Shoot."

"What am I going to do with my hair?"

"You sound so serious. I thought you might be leaving me or something. In response to your question, what do you want to do, sweetheart? I think you're beautiful just like you are, but I don't think you're happy with the way it is."

"It's not all going to grow out the same. What if I shaved it off, or cut the sides short?"

"What if I get my aunt to come by? She's a beautician and does Mom's hair all the time. I could ask her to come to the house and give you some suggestions?"

THE MOUNTAINS CALL MY NAME

"Would you? You would really do that for me?"

"Sure. I'll call her tonight and see what we can set up."

He pulled me close and held me. I relaxed in his arms. The closeness of him was soothing to my spirit. All my problems rolled away when he was near me. Mandy brought our dinner to us and served us on a little table that was in the living room. The food was delicious as usual. I surprised myself by having such a hardy appetite. Mandy came and took all the dishes away and moved the table to the side.

I saw Daniel look over toward the big windows.

"Come with me. I want to show you something," he said, taking me by the hand and pulling me up beside him.

We walked over before the full length windows, and there before me was the most beautiful full moon, rising up over the tree line. It was stunning.

"Oh Daniel, I've never seen it more beautiful."

He stood behind me and pulled me close again.

"I have so many wonderful things to share with you. I'm so glad God gave me the chance."

"I feel so much stronger today. My head hasn't hurt all day. I've been pain-free for the first time since I don't know when."

THE MOUNTAINS CALL MY NAME

"I'm glad I brought you home with me. This is your home now, Elizabeth. You're never going to leave," he said, turning me around to face him.

He pulled me to him and kissed me long and tenderly. We both seemed to be cautious about how far to allow ourselves to go. The night before was all too fresh in our minds. How could we keep going to the edge and not step over that line. We had been so close that last night; we both knew that.

We held each other a long time standing there before the full moon. Finally Daniel broke the silence.

"Elizabeth, we've got to have a plan. Holding you next to me last night and touching you was wonderful. At one point I didn't care about anything but that moment. And your response to me told me you felt the same way I did. Each time we're together it seems we become bolder and bolder, going further than the time before. If it hadn't been for the phone call, would we have made love?"

"How should I answer that question?"

"Honestly," he said.

"This is kind of embarrassing." I hesitated before going on, trying to search for the right words. "Okay, I'll try. I was swept away in the same ocean as you. Your caresses took my breath away," I said, closing my eyes and remembering the exhilaration. "Anyway, would we have? I don't think so, because it wasn't the right time."

"What if we were here and there were no phone call, and no one to interrupt us. What would happen then, would we give in or would we wait?" he asked me.

"You told me about a vow you made to God. I know that a vow made to God is not to be taken lightly. We're just going to have to be very careful and not allow ourselves to go that far again. This is so new to both of us. It's so exciting to be loved. The feelings we have are just waiting to explode."

"It's going to be very difficult you know? That's why I was thinking about a plan today."

"A plan? That already sounds interesting."

"I have a close friend that is a judge. I think if I brought him to the house he could marry us."

"But could we still have the wedding at the chapel later?" I asked him.

"Of course, no one would have to know but us. What do you say? We could keep it a secret from everyone but Mandy. I would want her to know. After all, we would be sleeping together. I wouldn't want her to misunderstand."

"I say yes."

"Tomorrow wouldn't be too soon?" he said, smiling at me.

"I could be your wife tomorrow," I said as I threw my arms around him and held him close to me.

"Tomorrow, if I can arrange it," he said as he held me.

"I think I need to sit down. I feel awfully tired all of a sudden."

After we were seated on the sofa, he pulled me to him.

"I can't believe that tomorrow I could be your wife. It's incredible, just incredible."

"It's incredibly wonderful," he said, kissing me lightly on the forehead.

"I can't believe where I am right now. Is it too quick, Daniel? How could I have moved so far so fast? It hasn't been all that long since I couldn't live without David, and now I can't live without you. I long for things with you that I used to have with David."

"Don't fret, sweetie. When God brings people together like he has me and you, it's not uncommon for things to move fast. Are you concerned about what you feel or what other people might say?"

"I don't have any doubts about what I feel for you. I've leaned on you so much lately. I don't want to marry you just because you take care of me."

"But that's just the thing I want to do."

"I need to be as strong as you. I've got to be able to give back to you as much as I receive from you."

"Don't you think you already have? You've given me more happiness since I've known you than I've had in a lifetime. You complete me. You were talking just now about this being so fast, but you forget how much we know each other. It's not like meeting as strangers. And look at you and David; you didn't even know him and you married quickly."

"Do you think it's a good reason for a couple to marry because they can't keep their hands off each other?"

"Haven't we just gone through all of this?" he said, looking directly into my eyes.

"I'm sorry; I just want everything to be right."

"Do you feel things aren't right?" he asked with concern crossing his face.

"I feel that I've invited you to my bed one too many times. It's my fault that things have escalated. If I had resisted wanting to be so close to you, we wouldn't have gone so far so quickly."

"I could have resisted getting into bed with you. There were clothing and covers between us. Most of the time anyway. Maybe I should have been the one to have resisted you, but I wanted to hold you. Our need was mutual. Neither of us was thinking where it would lead."

"Isn't that the way Satan is Daniel? He doesn't show people where they can end up. Your vow not to have sex until you get married would be a frivolous thing to some. Something to throw away the first time you were close to a girl. But it's been important to you all your life. I assure you it's not frivolous to God, and it's not to me. I'm so honored that you will be coming to me pure before God. We're being tested now. I don't want to be the one to make you break that vow. Even if we were to marry afterwards, we would have still broken the vow."

THE MOUNTAINS CALL MY NAME

"You still want to be my wife?" he asked.

"With all that's in me. Like I said before, I'm so honored that you have chosen me."

"Tomorrow you will be my bride. We've gone too far in this relationship to be together like we are. We know how it feels to hold and caress one another. It's on our mind even when we try to not think of it. I can't have you any other place but here. You love me with the same intensity that I love you. Sure, sex enters into it because we are sexual beings. We just don't all of a sudden, on our honeymoon, develop passion and desire for one another. We're just supposed to control them. The more we're together the harder it will be to control. I think that's why God says it's better to marry than to lust for each other. That's paraphrasing some."

"Daniel, it's three and a half weeks until Valentine's. I think we can wait until then. I need a little time to prepare. I need to feel a little better and little stronger."

"So I guess the judge thing is off and the waiting is still on?" he asked.

"I know it seems like we're going in circles, but I think it's probably best. What do you think?"

"I'm sorry, Libby; I guess I was thinking of myself. How thoughtless of me. Of course I can wait until Valentine's. We're going to have to set some limits."

"I have an idea that will take care of everything. Let's just not kiss again until we meet at the altar on our wedding day."

"Okay, but we'll start tomorrow not today. Let me kiss you one last time. Just once?" he asked pleadingly.

"Oh, Daniel, Daniel, Daniel... what am I going to do with you?"

"Kiss me goodnight." he said, with that dreamy look that made me melt inside.

"Once on the cheek," I said, smiling at him.

"No, not on the cheek you've got to remember it has to last for three and a half weeks." He shifted himself so he could face me better, put his finger under my chin and lifted my face to him. He looked longingly into my eyes.

"I love you with all my heart. I promise to keep this vow not to kiss you. I won't make you compromise anything, or myself for that matter. It will be the hardest thing I've ever had to do, but I can do it. Can you?"

"I love you, Daniel Scott, and I promise to help you keep your vow to God. I can, by God's grace, not kiss you until we meet at the altar. I will never make you regret this," I said chuckling.

"Goodnight sweetheart," he said, rising from the couch. "It's way past your bedtime."

"But I thought you were going to kiss me before we totally quit," I said, rising to meet him.

"You sure?" he asked, smiling at me.

THE MOUNTAINS CALL MY NAME

"You're right, we shouldn't. Goodnight Daniel," I said, hugging him. I started to head to my bedroom when he pulled me back into his arms.

"I love you so much right now. You are my life, my joy, and my sunshine. You're the smile that's in my soul. You take my breath away with your beauty. Your spirit and your sweetness overwhelm me," he whispered hoarsely into my ear. He pulled back from me and looked deep into my soul.

"My life would be pointless without you. I almost lost you a few days ago. The emotion of it is still fresh in my mind. Waiting for a ray of hope seemed so long in coming. I realized then how deeply I had fallen in love with you. To answer a question you had a moment ago, it's not just about making love to you, but it's about being in love with you. All that comes with it is just icing on the cake. I'll have you the rest of my life. That is what I'll think on for three and a half weeks."

I saw tears escape his eyes, unbidden I could tell, but unable to hold back. I raised my hand to wipe them away, and he mine. My heart was so full of love for him it overflowed.

He lowered his lips to mine and for one last time we traveled to familiar places that reminded us why this would be the last time we could visit there. Neither of us wanted it to end. We kissed until we were both shaken by its intensity. Afterwards he held me tightly and rocked me gently in his arms. My tears fell as he held me. I needed him to hold me, but I knew this would have to be the last time we could be this close until our wedding day. Neither of us was strong enough to pull away from these intense feelings many more times.

THE MOUNTAINS CALL MY NAME

"Are you okay? he said to me as I cried.

All I could do was nod. He reached on the table behind me and got a tissue, and wiped my tears.

"I'm just tired."

"Are you having any pain?" he asked, showing genuine concern.

"Just my heart, not my head. It's going to be so difficult not having you hold me. I need your arms around me so bad right now. When you're with me I need to feel you. I need to touch you even if it's just to hold your hand. You're all I have right now. You're my anchor. I'm afraid to let go," I said, sobbing as he held me.

"Oh baby... Shhh...I won't quit holding you, I promise. You'll feel better when you're stronger. You've been up way to long. Come let's go to bed. Or should I say, 'let me put you to bed'."

He took me into my room. Mandy had already freshened my bed linens. The nightlight was turned on in my room and cast a warm glow over everything. He sat me down on the side of the bed and removed my slippers. He took my housecoat from me and laid it on the foot of the bed. Then he lifted my legs and swiveled me around under the cover. He put his hand to my brow to see if I was feverish. I had stopped crying but felt so drained.

"I'll be right back; I'm going to get you something to help you sleep. It's something mild, but it will help you rest."

THE MOUNTAINS CALL MY NAME

He came back and handed me a small white pill and a glass of water. I took the pill and handed him the glass. He pulled a rocker up beside my bed and held my hand in his.

"You'll feel better tomorrow, I promise," he whispered softly to me.

"We've come full circle, haven't we?"

"Yeah, I guess we have."

"I wasn't rejecting you, Daniel. I just want our wedding to be at the altar in our little white church. The time will pass quickly."

"I didn't feel like you were rejecting me. I know you need to feel better and stronger. Valentine's will be a perfect time to make you my wife."

"I felt really strong until we had our last kiss, and I realized I'm really going to miss the intimacy. I know neither one of us is strong enough to last through many more."

"We aren't strong, Libby, but God is strong in us. It's in our weakness that God makes us strong. I'm going to pray for us and then I'm going to sit by your bed until you fall asleep. I need to go get my Bible and read awhile.

"Dear heavenly Father, keep us from ourselves. Keep our relationship strong and pure before you. Help us keep the vows we've made to one another. Bless Libby, the precious gift you've given me. Help me be strong for her. Guide me and give me wisdom for her. Help me not to ever fail her. I love you, Lord. Forgive me for my shortcomings. Help Libby to heal quickly and give her strength day by day. For it's in Your precious and holy name I pray. Amen."

"Amen," I said.

The pill Daniel had given me helped me to relax; I knew that sleep wouldn't be far away. Daniel came back into the room with his Bible and sat in the rocker by my bed.

"Will the light bother you?" he asked.

"No, would you read to me, Daniel?"

"Sure, what would you like to hear?"

"Something from the Psalms."

The sound of his voice, so soft and deep, lulled me into dreamless sleep.

Chapter Sixteen

Two weeks had passed quickly. Now there was only one week left before I would become Daniel's wife. Mrs. Scott's sister came to help me style my hair so it all didn't have to be shaved off. I was surprised to see how good it looked when she finished with it.

My strength had come back almost to its pre-surgery state. Daniel had been working long hours at the office helping to get Chris settled into his new suite. He had to hire a secretary for him. So God had taken care of our being together for long extended times. We hadn't broken our "no kiss" rule. Even though at times it had been very hard. We worked puzzles, played board games and did many other things to keep our "alone time" busy with other things.

Mrs. Scott wanted me to come to her house the next week to spend some time with her. She told me she thought I needed the time away from Daniel to make our nuptial day more special.

My wedding gown problem still had not been solved. She promised we would have no difficulty finding one. So the next day I would be packing my bags to go to her house. Daniel protested just a little, but agreed it would probably be a good idea. His mother eased his pain by asking him to dinner in the evenings.

THE MOUNTAINS CALL MY NAME

I couldn't imagine being in Durham during this time. It would have been horrific for both of us. I was so used to seeing Daniel every day that I was going to miss him as badly as he did me.

Mrs. Scott and Daniel had covered everything there was to cover about the wedding. They consulted me but took it upon themselves to do all the phone calling and errand running. They both seemed especially busy the last few days.

My days with Mrs. Scott were to be ones I was sure I would live to treasure. Days too that she would never have been able to give to a daughter of her own. I missed my own mother dearly, but Daniel had filled my lonely nights, and Mandy, the balance of my days. I can't imagine what it would have been like being all alone during that time. How I made it through David's death all by myself, I don't know, but I know now how it is to let people who love you ease the pain.

I had just finished packing when Daniel came home. He knocked lightly on my bedroom door.

"Anyone home?" he asked.

"Come in." I returned.

"I see you're getting ready to leave me," he said, giving me a tight hug.

"It's just a few short days, and then I'll never leave you again."

"Is it too late to say no?" he said, rocking me in his arms.

"Your mother would kill us. She's looking forward to this so much. I couldn't rob her of a moment of it."

"But you would rob me of seeing you every evening?"

"Do you realize that one week from tomorrow I will be you wife?"

"No, I've totally forgotten. What's your name again?" he said with mock confusion.

"You better not forget me," I said, tapping him on the arm.

"Why do you have to go this weekend? Why can't you go on Monday?"

"Because your mother wants to do some special things with me this weekend. One thing we need to do is get me a wedding gown. That is an important matter that has to be taken care of. You two haven't let me lift my finger until now. The gown is one thing I have to be involved in. Your mother says she has a surprise for me for the wedding."

"Oh, no, only God in heaven knows what that can be. But my mom has wonderful taste, and I'm sure whatever it is, it will be good."

"Is Chris getting settled in?"

"Well, he's still in the process. He's going back to Durham today to get some more stuff."

THE MOUNTAINS CALL MY NAME

"You're sure he didn't have a problem being your best man?"

"Oh, was I supposed to ask him?"

"You told me you did," I said scolding him.

"Yes, he's elated. He wants to see you, by the way. I'm thinking about asking Mom if I can bring him to dinner."

"I'm sure she wouldn't mind. And it would keep us entertained. No chance of kissing with company around," I said, smiling at him.

"Right now I would kiss you in front of anyone, and not be ashamed."

"Not the way I want to kiss you," he said, smiling at me.

"Right now..." he said, looking longingly into my eyes. "I want to kiss you more than anything I can possibly think of."

I closed my eyes as he pulled me close to him. For a moment I thought our vow had been broken. I was like putty in his hands. He kissed my cheek, my forehead, and finally my neck.

"I love you so much," he whispered into my eager ear.

I held him tightly to me, enjoying our not kissing. But I knew even this was going to be too much.

THE MOUNTAINS CALL MY NAME

"Daniel," I said breathlessly, you've got to let me go."

"I can't' right now, just give a little bit longer. You smell so good. I love that cologne you have on. You know it drives me crazy," he said, kissing my neck again.

"Kids, its time to get washed up fer supper," Mandy called from the kitchen.

"I think it's a good idea that I'm going away for the rest of our imposed prison term."

"I don't want to let you go. Not even for a short time. I've gotten used to coming home to you."

"And I, you. I love you so much. When the new wears off, will it still be this exciting?"

"The excitement of being with you will never diminish."

"You say that now, but when I'm old and gray and overweight, will you still love me?"

"I ask you the same question, will you love me when I'm old and gray and cantankerous?"

"I can take care of you any way I find you."

"Dinner's gonna get cold, you two," Mandy commanded from the kitchen.

"Are you ready?" I mumbled into his chest as he held me.

"No, not yet," he said, shutting the door with his foot and pulling me closer to him.

"Yes we are. We've come this far and we can make it one more week without kissing."

"I bet we could make love without kissing, don't you?"

"Daniel! That's enough! Let's go eat supper before Mandy kills both of us."

"I would die a happy man," he said, smiling at me.

"What's gotten into you today?" I said, wiping my lipstick off his face.

"Pent up energy maybe?" he said.

"One week, Daniel, just one week, and I'll never leave you again."

"Promise?" he said, reaching behind me to open the closed door.

"I promise you, God as my witness, and helper, I will never leave you."

"You asked me what got into me tonight. It's knowing you're going away tomorrow and I won't see you for several days. I just got carried away. Did you like it?"

"No. I hated it, couldn't you tell?"

"We didn't kiss, aren't you proud of us?"

THE MOUNTAINS CALL MY NAME

"You kissed everything but my lips."

"Just think of the fun we're going to have when we can kiss."

"At the altar, Dr. Scott, I'll meet you at the altar."

"That's where I'll be waiting for you, my princess, at the altar. There, I will declare to God and everyone that you are mine and I am yours."

"Let's go eat supper," I said, pulling him to the kitchen.

Mrs. Scott was to pick me up at nine for our shopping trip. Daniel had to meet Chris at the office to help him get set up for Monday. He was to take all of Daniel's patients while we had a short honeymoon. That word still sounded funny to my ears. Honeymoon with Daniel. He told me he had made all the arrangements, but wouldn't give me a clue where we were going. Only that I would love it. I was getting so excited about the wedding. I'm so glad that we didn't marry early. Next week couldn't come soon enough. I had just moved my luggage into the kitchen when Mrs. Scott came in.

"Hi, sweetie, are you ready for some fun?"

"I'm ready to get out of this house. I've been cooped up so long; it's nice to finally be going somewhere."

THE MOUNTAINS CALL MY NAME

"There is a store about forty-five minutes from here that has the most beautiful weddin' stuff. If yer up to it, I thought we could drive there."

"I feel great, let's hit the road," I said, helping her carry my luggage to the car.

We talked all the way to the store. It seemed as if I had been close to her all my life. Our conversation flowed easily. She told me tales of weddings in the Scott family. Some funny and some sad. She told me of the hopes and dreams they had for Daniel, and how pleased they were that he had come home to doctor. She reiterated how thrilled the family had been that Daniel had chosen me to be his bride.

It seemed like no time till we were at the store. She was true to her word; the store was full of the most wonderful wedding gowns I'd ever seen. Row after row of gowns.

"Elizabeth, I love this one," Mrs. Scott said, holding up a beautiful confection with layers of lace and ribbon.

"It kinda reminds me of an old-fashioned gown."

"I like it too, I wonder if they have it in my size," I said, holding it up to me. I don't even know what size I am now that I lost so much weight. I picked up one that I thought was right and took it to the fitting room.

"I can help ya if ya like?" she asked as we entered the area where the fitting area was.

THE MOUNTAINS CALL MY NAME

"I would love for you to," I said, entering one of the big rooms.

"I always wondered what it would be like helpin' a daughter pick her weddin' gown, now I know. Thanks fer lettin' me be part of this."

"I wouldn't be able to do this without you," I said, hugging her.

We undid the many buttons on the back and finally had it ready to step into. I held it up to me as she tackled the row of buttons again.

"Mr. Scott and I would like to buy yer weddin' gown."

"No, I couldn't possibly let you do that. You've done so much already. I can afford to buy it."

"I know ya can, but it would make us feel so good to do it. Let us have this little bit of joy. Just be my little girl fer a while and let me do what I'd a done for my girl."

"You've been so special to me. You've really been there for me during my illness. You are the only mother I have now, and you're a really good one," I said, hugging her again.

"Let's get this dress buttoned up, or whatever it is we have to do," she said, wiping a tear from her eye.

The dress had tiny satin buttons all the way up the back, which was scooped low, almost down to my bra line. Three strands of pearls connected the back from side to side up above where the buttons stopped. They connected with a small hook and eye. The front bodice was completely covered with tiny seed pearls forming a pattern of hearts intertwined with bows and ribbons. The delicate pattern was repeated over and over. The skirt was satin, covered with more seed pearls forming larger hearts. It looked like diamonds were scattered here and there over the entire skirt. The sleeves stopped right at my elbow. The cap of each sleeve was a bit puffy, but not too much, and tapered to a close fit at the bottom. The train was chapel length.

The room attendant told Mrs. Scott to go set in the chairs in the outer fitting room so she would see me after I had everything on. I picked out a veil when I selected the dress. The pearls on it came to a small V shape on my forehead. It all connected to my head with a comb that would go into my hair. I was careful to pick one that wouldn't touch my scar on the lower part of the back of my head.

When every button was buttoned and the veil was in place, the attendant took me to a raised platform to model the gown before Mrs. Scott. Behind the platform was a mirror that covered the whole back wall. The attendant spread the fullness of the dress and train. I was awed as I saw myself in the array of mirrors around me. I could just see Daniel eyeing me for the first time in this. This dress made me feel like a true princess. The veil covered my hair exactly like I had hoped it would. I was caught up in the process so much that I forgot for a moment that Mrs. Scott was looking at me as I turned before the mirror. When I finally noticed her, she was holding her hands to her mouth and tears were rolling down her cheeks.

THE MOUNTAINS CALL MY NAME

"Daniel won't be able to make it without cryin'," she said as she gazed at me.

"This is the dress, Elizabeth, this is the dress. Do you like it as much as I do?"

"I love it. It was made just for me. The size is perfect and the lady says I can buy it off the rack. It won't have to be ordered."

The attendant helped me off with the dress and bagged it for me. By the time I was ready to get out of the changing room, Mrs. Scott was already at the register. I hadn't even looked at the price. I hoped it wasn't extremely expensive. She asked if there was anything else we needed to get.

The attendant mentioned the slip and garter. I hadn't thought of that either. "And shoes," she continued, "Mrs. Scott said we've got to get you shoes and hose." We went on and on through the store.

"If you would let me I wantta buy these things fer ya. Remember it makes me happy doin' this."

"Mrs. Scott, I can afford these things."

"I know that, but just pacify this old gray-haired woman."

"Okay, if it means that much to you, then go for it."

"I'm starved, how about you?" she asked as we made our way out the door with our load of packages.

THE MOUNTAINS CALL MY NAME

"I'm hungry too. It sure makes you hungry trying on clothes."

We put the packages in the car and made our way down the street to the restaurant.

We both ordered a vegetable plate and talked while it was coming.

"I never mentioned it, but Daniel had a baby sister. She died at birth. I think the cord had been around her neck. Anyway, it really didn't matter how, what mattered was, she was gone. She was a beautiful little angel."

"Funny, all the time Daniel and I have known each other he never mentioned it."

"I guess he just put it out of his mind. She was dead three years before Daniel was born. I guess he never had no connection to her."

"I'm sorry, my mom lost a little boy. He died in his sleep when he was just a few months old. I never did know him either. His name was Jonathan."

"So you see why I want to do this for you? It's like I had little April back again. It's been such a wonderful time helpin' you with all this stuff. Thank you for lettin' me be such a big part of your plannin'."

"I don't have my mother, so we meet a need for each other," I said, reaching across the table to take her hand in mine.

THE MOUNTAINS CALL MY NAME

"Mrs. Scott, there is one last thing I have to do today. I have to buy Daniel's wedding ring. That's one thing I must buy myself."

"Okay, but just *one* thing."

We went to the jeweler that was just a few doors down and I bought Daniel's wedding band. It had a row of diamonds across the top in a little channel. It sparkled in the light as I turned it in my hand.

"I'm ready now if you are? I said as we left the store.

"I'm ready too. I think we got a lot done today," she said, smiling at me.

I was exhausted by the time we reached home. After we got all the packages in and put away I was ready for a nap. It was kind of late for one, but I felt I couldn't go on without resting some.

"Mrs. Scott, I'm going to go lie down for a bit. I'm so tired."

"Of course, darlin', I'm sorry I didn't suggest it. Daniel will shoot me if I get you sick. I'll have Charlotte turn your bed down."

"I can do that."

"No, I insist on getting Charlotte."

While I was changing into something more comfortable, Charlotte fixed my bed. I snuggled down under the cover and was quickly sound asleep. It seemed I had just closed my eyes when I felt a gentle tug at my arm.

"'Lizabeth, I think you need to wake up it's gettin' late and you might not sleep tonight."

"What time is it?" I asked.

"It's almost 6:00."

"Wow, I really must have zonked out." I said, stretching.

"And Daniel is concerned because you've been sleeping so long. He calls every few minutes."

"He's overprotective. But I like it."

I went into the living room where the family had gathered, and sat down on the couch. I had no sooner set down than the phone rang.

"You may as well get that, It's probably Daniel again." Mr. Scott said, smiling.

"Hello."

"Finally, you're awake. Are you okay?"

"Yes, I'm fine, just tired from shopping."

"Did you find a dress?"

"Oh, did I ever find a dress. You're just not going to be ready for this."

"I'm ready for everything. Saturday can't get here fast enough."

"Can I come over?" he asked.

"Do you want to?"

"I'm so lonely for you. I don't know what I did before you came along."

"I would love to see you, too. What did you do today?"

"I helped Chris finish getting settled. Then we went and picked up our tuxedos. There were several things I did that I can't tell you about."

"That sounds mysterious."

"I've got so many surprises for you. I had so much fun planning this thing."

"I can't wait to find out."

"Where are you now?"

"I'm sitting in the living room with your parents and grandmother."

"Are they listening to you now?"

"I can't tell, but things are pretty quiet."

"Trust me, they're listening. Tell me how much you love me."

THE MOUNTAINS CALL MY NAME

"Now?"

"Yeah, just do it."

"Daniel, I love you with all my heart and can't wait to be your wife. You're my joy, and my sunshine. How's that?

"Now tell me how much you enjoy kissing me and what it does to you."

"Daniel Scott, you're teasing me."

"It sounded good though. Do you want me to tell you what your kisses do to me?"

"No! I said, laughing into the phone.

"Are you blushing?"

"I'm sure I must be. We need to change the subject."

"I'm actually going to let you go eat, and I'm going to do the same."

"I miss you, and I love you." I said softly into the receiver.

"And I miss you and love you, too."

"I bought your wedding ring today."

"You did?"

"Yeah, it made it all very real."

THE MOUNTAINS CALL MY NAME

"I have yours, too. I got it when I bought your diamond."

"I guess I'm a little late. Better late than never, I guess."

"I can't wait to see the dress, and see you in it."

"I hate to hang up. I don't want to stop hearing your voice."

"Can I come over?" he asked.

"No, you need to go eat dinner."

"One last thing. I have something for you I've had a very long time. I've just been waiting for the perfect moment to give it to you."

"You haven't been around me for a long time. I wonder what it could possibly be?"

"All I know is that it will be a tremendous surprise," he volunteered.

"May I speak with Mom? There's something I need to talk to her about."

"Sure, I love you. It will be Saturday before you know it."

"I love you too. Bye, sweetie."

I left the two of them to their planning and went into the kitchen. There was some food set out on the stove for me. I fixed me a plate and sat down at the table to eat dinner. It wasn't long before Grandma Scott came rolling into the kitchen. She had a small box in her lap. When she got to the end of the table where I was, she took the box from her lap and extended it to me.

"I've waited a long time to give this to someone. I promised Daniel a long time ago, when he married I would give this to his bride. It was given to me by my mother on my wedding day."

I opened the box to find a beautiful string of pearls. They looked as if she had had them restrung.

"Grandmother Scott, they're too beautiful to give away. Are you sure?"

"Oh, yes. They will look so pretty with that new weddin' gown. June and I talked a long time today while you was asleepin'. She showed me yer gown. I hope you didn't mind me seein' it."

"No, not at all. You'll be the first to see me when I put it on," I said, rising to kiss her on the cheek. "I don't know what to say except I'm so honored to wear these. One day I'll pass them on to our little girl, if God gives us one. David and I couldn't have children because of some problems he had. I hope God will bless Daniel and me with children." I couldn't help the tears forming.

"You mark Grandmother's words. God is gonna' give you and my little Danny some beautiful children. I hope this old woman will live to see them. So don't wait too long to try."

"I've loved you all these years and now you're going to be my grandmother. How blessed I am."

THE MOUNTAINS CALL MY NAME

"When you came home fer Bessie's funeral, I knew I'd better get Daniel the message to see ya. And look what happened. If it weren't fer me it wouldn't a happened."

"So you just gave me two presents, these pearls and your grandson. That makes two of your precious possessions you've given to me."

"I'm so glad it's you my Danny fell in love with."

"Me, too."

"I've bought me a new dress fer the weddin'. June got it fer me. I'll show it to you tomarra."

Mrs. Scott came into the kitchen as I was holding the pearls up again to admire them.

"They gonna look beautiful with that gown."

"You all have done so much for me. I won't ever be able to repay you."

"Just always make Danny happy, and love him. That's all I ask. I've never seen him in love before. He's just like a kid at Christmas."

"I promise you I'll do the best I can."

"That's all I can ask."

"Well, if you'll excuse me, I think I'll go take a long, hot bath. I still feel a little weary from our trip today."

"Danny just gave me strict instruction fer ya. He said to make sure you get yer rest and not to run you

475

around anymore," she said, smiling. "That boy is gonna spoil ya rotten"

I gave them both hugs before retiring to my room. I stopped on the way down the hall and told Mr. Scott goodnight.

The week had passed quickly. Daniel and his mother had been running around and arranging things all week. Mandy was making our wedding cake, and Daniel was having my wedding bouquet made. He wanted to do it all. He said if I would allow him to, he wanted to make sure I didn't have anything to do except marry him. Chris had already picked up on the protocol of the office and staff. He had been a godsend to Daniel this week. It seemed that the old folk had taken a shine to Chris, which didn't surprise me. Ever since I worked with him at Duke he was so good with his patients. Mrs. Scott's sister worked wonders with my hair. She said the way Chris made the incision left me with enough hair to cover the shaved area. The style was a little shorter than it had been, but looked good. It was almost time for Daniel to come pick me up for the wedding rehearsal. I checked my hair and make up one last time. I heard him come in the kitchen door. His voice sounded so good to my ears. I was just starting out the bedroom door when he came in.

He was getting ready to say something and stopped with his mouth agape.

"What have you done to yourself?"

"Why, is something wrong?"

THE MOUNTAINS CALL MY NAME

"No, you look so...so wonderful. I love your hair, and...everything."

I threw my arms around his neck and gave him a kiss on the cheek. He responded by drawing me close to him.

"I've missed you so much. It's been all I can do to drive by here each night and not come in."

"This is the beginning of our festivities and I'm so ready. I've rested so much I don't ever want to slow down again. I don't have any pain at all now, and my strength is almost returned to normal. We'd better hurry; we're going to be late."

"Daniel...'Lis'beth... we better hurry; we're gonna be late."

We looked at each other and started laughing. She had my coat ready for Daniel to help me into. When we pulled into the church lot, emotions swept over me. I looked longingly up the hollow road that I had traveled up and down so much in my life, and now there was no reason to go. There was an empty feeling that swept over me. Unbidden tears fell down my cheeks.

"What's wrong, sweetie? Why are you crying?"

"It's seeing the road to home, and knowing no one's there," I said, dabbing at my tears.

"I'm sorry, I had forgotten in all my excitement that this was home to you, or close to home, I should say."

He took his handkerchief out of his pocket and gave it to me to dry my tears.

"Thank you," I said, smiling at him. "I think I will be shedding quite a few of these in the next few hours. It's a woman thing," I said, smiling at him.

I took the handkerchief from him and wiped my tears. While placing it in my purse, I saw the little gold key with the ribbon on it. One day soon I would have to go find the box the key went with. I felt a foreboding feeling of what I might find there.

"Let's not keep our guests waiting," Daniel said, proffering me his arm.

We entered into the little chapel with everyone already gathered at the front. When they saw us enter, a little round of applause arose from them.

I stood in silence taking in what my eyes beheld. Daniel had transformed the little white chapel into a wonderland.

A large heart candelabrum stood on each side of the kneeling bench. They were intertwined with ivy, ribbons and satin bows with long streamers. The taper candles were already in place, but unlit. Tulle was draped from pew to pew with large satin bows adorning each section. An archway was at the end of the isle decorated with ivy, ribbon and tulle for us to walk under. And of course, the white prayer bench was centered at the altar. Candles were everywhere.

"Oh, Daniel! What have you done?"

THE MOUNTAINS CALL MY NAME

"I've made this place ready for my princess. Actually, it was the florist, but I told her what I wanted. She's bringing the flowers in the morning so they will be fresh. Do you like it?"

"I love it."

"You two come on down here, we're ready to get started," Pastor Simon said.

Chris was standing there, tall and smiling, ready to take his place beside Daniel. Mr. Scott was going to be his best man, but he wanted Chris there also. I guess he was going to have two best men. At least he didn't have a woman as his best man.

I had asked Sharon to be my matron of honor, for without her I probably wouldn't have met Daniel. She and Ralph had to come in and check on Daddy John and the twins, so it was no problem for her to be here. I told her just to pick out a dress she felt good in, and it would be perfect. She was so excited about my asking her to be my attendant.

So our little wedding party proceeded to walk through our parts. Preacher Simon told us what he would be asking us to say. We had written our own vows, but would not be saying them until the next day.

We had asked Chris to sing the wedding prayer. I had learned that he was talented when I worked with him. He had pretended to protest, but later confessed that he would be honored to be there and serve in any way he could.

THE MOUNTAINS CALL MY NAME

"Everyone, listen up," Daniel said. "We're going to go to the Woodland Inn. I think you all know where that is, but if you don't we could just follow each other; we should arrive there about the same time. Chris, you can ride with Mom and Dad, if you would like. I brought my sports car so there's just room for Libby and me."

"That wouldn't have been on purpose would it?" Chris asked, smiling at Daniel.

"Chris, yer more than welcome to keep us company," Mr. Scott said, patting him on the back.

We all got into our respective vehicles and headed for the restaurant.

"I'm going to give you your special present tonight, but not until after dinner when we're alone. You're not going to believe what I have."

"You have me so intrigued. I can't imagine what it could be."

The lodge we were going to was a beautiful place nestled by a lake at the edge of a forest. Tiny lights outlined the massive reservoir. The reflection of their light shimmered in the ripples of the dark water. A walkway was built all the way into the middle of the lake. A gazebo at the end of the walkway was outlined with the same kind of little lights.

"Daniel, everything's so gorgeous. If you don't do anything else, it's been perfect," I said. He went around to open my door. As I arose from the car seat I lifted my face to his, wanting so badly for him to kiss me. He drew me to him, and his lips lightly brushed my cheek. He whispered, "Our guests are waiting, we should go on in."

I threw my head back and looked into his eyes as best I could in the darkness.

"Daniel, are you going to make me wait until tomorrow to get my kiss?"

"Yeah, but it's going to be so-o-o-o good."

"There's something I need to ask you about tomorrow night," Daniel said in all seriousness.

"I'm not sure if I can answer your question but I'll try. Maybe you should ask your father, not me," I said, smiling at him.

"You make me laugh, little girl. No, there's a specific reason I asked, and it's the doctor in me. It's personal, so if I overstep my bounds, just say so, but it's really important. Did you get your physical?"

"Well, actually I haven't been to the doctor for that purpose. But I think everything works okay, at least it used to."

"I don't doubt it works, but do we want to have birth control, or not? he asked.

"I haven't started taking the pill."

"Well," he said clearing his throat, I can get something, but if you want to take a chance on getting pregnant…well, we need to discuss that, too."

"I guess, because I was never able to get pregnant, birth control didn't enter my mind. The thought of having a child with you makes me very happy," I said, putting my arms around him and holding him close to me.

"We can go au natural, and let God decide, he said, pulling away from me and looking into my eyes. Whatever you want, I'm thrilled with. But, I think because of your recent surgery maybe we should wait."

"Why doesn't one of us talk to Chris? I wouldn't mind if you wanted to talk to him," I said.

"If I had been thinking, I would have seen Chris this week and had him give me a physical."

"And do a pelvic exam?" he asked, suddenly aware of my dilemma.

"I don't think it would have been a good idea. I mean, it's not like I've never had one done. I've had hundreds over the years, but it would have been between you or Chris."

"I know this sounds strange but I would hate for Chris to have been intimate with you before me," he said, laughing.

"We've got to get inside. Hopefully they won't ask what was keeping us from dinner," I said, joining his laughter.

"We've got to talk after dinner."

"Okay."

THE MOUNTAINS CALL MY NAME

Everyone was seated, waiting for us. The tables were round and overlaid with a white brocade tablecloth. There were arrangements of roses on each table, with a hurricane candle flickering in the middle.

At the main table were Mr. and Mrs. Scott. We had enough people for four tables. Our room was small and cozy and we had it all to ourselves. Soft music flowed throughout the room. There was a roaring fireplace in the corner. A dim glow was cast over the entire room from the chandelier that hung in the center. Daniel and I made our way to the table. I couldn't remember having been this happy in a long time. As soon as I was seated the waiter came in with a huge arrangement of red roses and presented them to me.

"For you, Miss," he said, setting the charming arrangement of flowers in the center of our table. He offered me a small silver tray with a card lying on it. I took it and opened it. *This is only the beginning of what I have planned for you. Happy pre-Valentine's Day. My heart belongs to you. All my love, Daniel.*

"A gift from my husband to be," I told those looking on.

"Do you like them?" he implored.

"I like you and them," I answered. "I don't think that's very good English, is it?"

Mr. Scott stood and asked for everyone's attention.

"Let's thank God for our food, so when it comes we can go ahead and eat. God bless my son and his little bride to be 'Lis'beth. May yer light always abide on 'em. And God bless this food we are about to receive. Amen."

Amens were echoed in the room. The waiters were close behind with our delicious meal. I ate until I was stuffed. At the end of the meal Daniel and I gave Chris and Sharon a small token of our appreciation for them standing up for us. He gave Chris an engraved pocket watch because he was always loosing his wristwatch. We all watched as he opened the small box.

"You shouldn't have," he said. When he saw what it was, he couldn't help but smile.

"Read the engraving," Daniel encouraged.

He opened it up and stood quietly as he read what Daniel had put there. "Thank you for giving us this day."

"Elizabeth..." he paused to compose himself. "The night Daniel brought you to me I honestly had little hope that you would make it. And even after surgery, I couldn't promise Daniel what he would have, even if you did wake up. It's God that brought you back to us." He paused again, gathering himself. "I'm mister tough guy, so this is kind of hard for me. I could only give God the glory. And your recovery since you've been home has been way beyond my expectations. He guided these hands and gave me wisdom, but it wasn't me. You are God's gift to us all, Elizabeth. If someone had told me in September that I would be here in these beautiful Virginia Mountains, practicing medicine, I would have denied it. But along came my long-lost friend from med school, and my intensive care nurse, and wooed me away with their siren call. So I lift my glass to the both of you, live long and have many children."

THE MOUNTAINS CALL MY NAME

"Thank you, Chris," I said, lifting my glass toward him. He came to where Daniel and I were, and hugged the both of us.

"And the watch," he said, looking at it, "I'll use to keep Daniel on time when he gets back from his honeymoon," he said, smiling at Daniel.

"That is if you don't loose it," Daniel said, smiling back at him.

"I have a gift for Sharon," I said, taking the gift to her.

She gave me a big hug as she accepted my gift.

"I just want to say how much I love 'Lis'beth. It's so special she wants me to be with her on her weddin' day. Her and Dr. Daniel save my life and the life of my little Rose," she said with tears rolling down her cheeks.

She opened the box where I had placed a silver heart engraved on the back. She turned it over to read the inscription, "friends forever".

"I love you, Sharon. You are like a sister to me." Daniel and I both hugged her.

"I have something I would like to say," Mr. Scott said, standing beside his chair.

"Daniel, it's about time you gave us a girl. We are so proud of ya, son. We have loved you as much as we could love anything, and 'Lis'beth, we already love you. Mom and I got a little gift fer the two of ya." He took an envelope out of his pocket and handed it to Daniel. "God has blessed us with so much. We gave ya to the Lord when you were born to use as he saw fit. He took ya away from us and made you a doctor, and then he brought you back to us to be our doctor. You gave up a lot to come here. Then, lo and behold, he brought your bride here. We always thought you'd marry one of them city girls, which would have been okay, but God gave you one of your playmates to be your life mate. So we wanted to start you two off with a special get away."

"Hey, does that mean I can come, too?" Chris said, grinning.

"Not on *my* honeymoon," Daniel said, opening the envelope. He took my hand, had me stand beside him, and we looked on together as he opened the card. It read, *To our son and new daughter: may you get to know each other in the islands of Hawaii. From Mom, Dad and Grandma.*

I couldn't speak for a moment.

"Is this for real, Dad, you're not joking?" Daniel managed to get out.

"This is beyond anything I could have imagined, thanks Mom, Dad," he said, hugging them.

He went into his mom's and dad's arms, and they in turn pulled me into the circle of their love.

"We thought we would give you time to pack and all that, so we left the departure date up to you two."

"That's why I killed myself to get up here so fast," Chris said, smiling at the two of us. "I knew I would have to learn the ropes before I could let Daniel leave."

"Well I think I'm gonna call it a night. Tomorrow is going to be a long day," Mrs. Scott said.

"If that's all, I think we'll head out and see all of you tomorrow.

I went to the two of them and hugged them.

"And be sure to tell Grandmother Scott 'thank you'."

"She wanted to come so bad, but couldn't make both tonight and the wedding tomorrow," Mrs. Scott said.

"Are you sure you want to do this Hawaii thing for us? Why don't you two go, you've been married a long time, surely you must want to go?" I said to Mrs. Scott.

"We're too old to enjoy it. And anyway, we don't like to get too far away from home," Mrs. Scott said, picking up the vase of roses off the table.

"I'll take these home fer ya. We have more room than you do. We need to get on home to mother. She's waiting fer details."

"Give her a hug and kiss for me."

"You can give her one yerself when you get home."

"She might be asleep by the time Daniel and I get home."

"Daniel, ya better get this girl in early, she has a long day tomorrow, and she needs her rest."

THE MOUNTAINS CALL MY NAME

"Yeah, Dr. Scott this girl needs her rest," Chris interjected.

I excused myself to go to the ladies room. Daniel said he would wait for me outside in the lobby. When I came out of the door I saw Chris and Daniel huddling together near the outside door.

I cleared my throat as I came up behind them. "Am I interrupting anything serious?" I asked.

"No, we were finished, weren't we, Daniel?" he asked, turning to me.

"How are you feeling?" he asked me.

"I'm doing well. No pain and I'm still regaining my strength. I've had a real good week.

"I told Daniel to take it easy on you."

"Chris, you're making me blush," I said, putting my hands over my face.

"I only intended to. I've got to go; Mr. and Mrs. Scott are waiting on me." He gave me a hug and whispered into my ear. "Have a wonderful honeymoon."

"I'm sure I will."

He bounded arm in arm down the sidewalk to join the Scotts. Everyone had left but Daniel and I.

"Come, let's walk down to the gazebo. It's such a beautiful night. Look at that moon," he said, leading me toward the water. The lights magically illuminated our pathway.

The music from the dining room was piped to the gazebo area. He took me to the middle of the little round room.

"Are you ready for your gift?"

"You have it with you?"

He nodded. "It's in my pocket." He reached in and produced a small, wrapped container that looked like it could be a jewelry box.

"Here," he said, offering it to me.

I carefully took the ribbon and paper off, then opened the lid and removed the layer of cotton. I found what appeared to be a charm bracelet. I held it up to the light and saw one heart hanging delicately from the sliver links.

"Daniel, you remembered. How could you have remembered? It's been so long ago. I'd even forgotten about it. The one I had like this, I lost on my wedding day. Remember, you gave it to me for my sixteenth birthday?"

"It's one in the same," he said, smiling at me.

"How did you get it? I lost it."

"And I found it. I've kept it all these years. I gave it to my mother to keep. I had every intention of giving it back, but I never saw you again. Then, the other day Mom

489

asked me if I remembered the bracelet she had that was yours."

"I was so sad that I lost it. I loved this bracelet. When I realized I lost it, I had no idea where to look."

"I was kinda surprised you wore it on your wedding day. When I found it on the ground outside the church, I had every intention of giving it back. It was something we shared. I knew it didn't have the same meaning to you as it did me. I put it in my pocket to give to you later and forgot, until it was too late to give it to you."

"I might cry. When I thought you couldn't do more than you already had, you surprised me once again."

"You can't cry. Your tears will freeze."

"I'm afraid I might wake up and find all this is a dream. Hold me Daniel."

He pulled me close to him and we danced to the music that was swirling around us.

"Do you remember the first time we danced?"

"You mean since we've grown up?"

"Yeah, at the clinic?"

"That was the night I felt something change inside my heart. Your closeness took my breath away. I knew something was happening between us that night. I was so unready for it then. You swept me away on angel wings."

THE MOUNTAINS CALL MY NAME

"Grandmother's angel, the one with the fluttering wings?"

"Yeah."

"My love for you cracked the ice that had encased your heart. You know how ice will crack when it begins to thaw? That's what you felt that night. It was the thawing of your heart."

"It was cold and dark in there until you slowly melted the ice."

"My heart was racing wildly as I held you that first time. I had waited so long to hold you that way. I was afraid you would run away if you knew how I cared for you. I wanted to kiss you that night the way I want to kiss you right now," he said, smiling.

We held each other for a long time there under the stars, swaying to the music. The magic of the evening enveloped us and swept us up in its power.

"I need to get you home. The sooner we go to sleep, the sooner tomorrow will come, and the sooner you will be my bride," he said, reluctantly leading me up the walk to our car.

THE MOUNTAINS CALL MY NAME

Chapter Seventeen

I woke up early that morning and sat in the chair in my bedroom, trying to read my Bible and pray. It was so hard to concentrate. I thought I heard noises in other parts of the house, but wasn't ready to share my day with its occupants.

Today, I thought, I would become Elizabeth Scott. How I wished I had my mother here to share this joy with me. As it was, I didn't have any family. That in itself was a lonely feeling, knowing I didn't have another living soul to call family. Then, my mind went back to my visit to a place that seemed like heaven. I thought of seeing all my family there. I remembered my Mother Rose telling me about a grandmother that I had somewhere in West Virginia. The gold key was lying on my open Bible. Soon I would have to go find that box. Maybe there will be a clue about this grandmother in the mysterious box. I guess there was someone I had on this side after all. When Daniel and I were settled, I would have to tell him about the grandmother I needed to find. But where would we start? I thought, holding the key in my hand. I was lost in a mist of wonder when I heard a gentle knock on my door.

"'Lizabeth, are you awake?"

"Yes, come in."

"I thought I saw your light on. I hope I'm not intrudin'."

THE MOUNTAINS CALL MY NAME

"No, I was just reading my Bible, and I was thinking about my mom."

"I thought ya might be needin' her today. I'm not much of a substitute, but I'm here if you need anything. I ain't been with a daughter on her weddin' day, so if I don't do it right, ya have to tell me."

The tears that I had been holding back came freely now.

"Did I make ya cry?" she said, putting her arms around me.

I shook my head, no. "I was just missing my mom. God sent you at the right time. It just dawned on me that I don't have any family here to stand with me on this special day in my life. The last time I was married, my dad walked me down the isle and I wore my mother's wedding dress. It's kind of sad, but then God made me realize what a wonderful family he's giving to me today. You've been great about everything. Helping me, or rather doing everything, and taking the pressure off me. Today is going to be a *very* special day. I'm so excited. I can't wait to see Daniel.

"I told Charlotte to bring us a breakfast tray. I thought the two of us could have some quiet time together."

Charlotte brought the tray in and set the food on a table that was in the room. Everything smelled so good; like the breakfasts Mama used to make for me. We sat and talked about the things we had to do. I had the bracelet on my arm and she happened to notice it.

THE MOUNTAINS CALL MY NAME

"I see Danny gave you your bracelet."

I held up my arm to look at it again. On the back of the heart was engraved, *friends forever*.

"I was shocked to see it. I didn't think I would ever see it again. I thought maybe he had gotten me one just like it."

"I've kept it in my jewelry box all these years. I thought I would see ya sometime when you were in and give it to ya. But over the years Danny and I both fergot it was there. I guess I was just savin' it fer yer weddin' to Danny."

"It's like a sign from God that everything is okay," I said, gazing at the little heart.

"Well, I've got to get movin'. I've got a lot of things to check on. Danny is sendin' yer bouquet later this mornin' from the florist."

I worked on packing my luggage for our honeymoon. I had gotten exquisite, dainty lingerie when we had gone on our shopping spree. That was one thing I didn't let Mrs. Scott help me with. It just didn't seem right. I found one that was very sexy, but yet feminine. This would be a surprise for Daniel. Charlotte set out all kinds of bath stuff, so I could choose what I wanted to use. By the time I had done my packing it was time to take my bath to get ready for the wedding. I couldn't wait to put on my wedding gown. I lingered a long time in the hot water.

When I finished my bath I found my bouquet lying on the bed for me to see. Alongside was a wrapped box with a ribbon on it, sitting on top of a card. My bouquet was made of white roses, with one red rose in the center. There were ribbons and lace and some complimenting flowers stuck here and there, but the main flowers were roses. I opened the box to find a pair of diamond earrings in the shape of teardrops. I opened the card and read the inside. *I hope you like your bouquet. Thanks for letting me pick the flowers. The earrings are in the shape of a teardrop to tell you I caught all your tears and put them in these diamonds. From now on all you're going to have is smiles. My prayer is that I will never be the cause of your tears. I'll see you at the altar to collect my kiss. All my love, Daniel*

He said he had planned all kinds of surprises, I guess he was right. Daniel's aunt was going to come by to do my hair and put on my make up. I was going to lie down but changed my mind. I couldn't rest anyway. I heard a knock at my door.

"Are ya ready to put yer gown on?"

"Come in, yes, I'm more than ready."

"My sister should be by soon and help us with our hair and your veil. I hope you didn't mind her comin'. I'm just playin' mama," she said with a chuckle.

"Anything is welcome. Just feel free to do whatever."

"Did ya like yer bouquet?"

"Yes, I love it. Did you see the earrings he sent?"

"No, he told me he was gettin' some, but I didn't see 'em."

THE MOUNTAINS CALL MY NAME

I opened the box and showed them to her. Her eyes misted with tears as she held them in her hand.

"He loves ya so much, 'Lis'beth."

"I know," I said, hugging her.

"Me and you gotta decide what ya gonna call me and Mr. Scott. Now as far as I'm concerned you can call me 'Mama' if ya want to, or 'Mama Scott', but no 'Mrs. Scott'. Or maybe 'Mom Scott', whatever ya want to. We just want ya to feel like we're yours."

"You're the only mom I have left. I would be honored to call you 'Mom'," I said, giving her a big hug.

"Let's get that gown on. I cain't wait to see ya."

We got it down from the hanger where Charlotte had put it after she steamed it.

"I think if we start from the bottom and let ya step in it, it will work better."

After I had wiggled into it she pulled it up to my shoulders. I held the dress up over my breast while she buttoned the buttons up the back and connected the row of beads from one side to the other. Three strands of pearls were strung across the back from above the last button up toward the neck.

"You know what? I shoulda waited till ya put on yer veil before I put this gown on ya," She said, laughing.

"Maybe I can kneel," I said, laughing with her.

THE MOUNTAINS CALL MY NAME

I took the strand of pearls Grandmother Scott had given me and handed them to Mrs. Scott to put around my neck. She took the earrings that Daniel had sent and handed them to me to put on.

"You look just like a princess, 'Lis'beth. Thank ya fer lettin' me be part of all this. Danny's gonna cry when he sees ya. I just know he is."

Her sister got to the house about the time we finished with everything. She worked with deft hands setting my veil in place. When I finally looked at the total picture I couldn't believe my eyes. She brought makeup from her salon and proceeded to help me apply it.

I hardly recognized myself. This was a far cry from my first wedding, I thought.

My first wedding... I had hoped the thoughts of that time would stay far away from today. I had tried to push David completely aside, but for some strange reason his memory just kept creeping into my thoughts. I felt that when I saw Daniel all of it would vanish. I didn't doubt my love for Daniel. This was what God wanted for me, but there was just a tiny bit of sadness. Today, when I became Mrs. Daniel Scott, I would put him completely to rest. Mrs. David Mason would be gone forever.

"Its time to go, 'Lis'beth. Are ya ready?"

"Yes, I'm ready."

I made my way to the living room. Grandmother Scott was waiting for me to come out. She looked at me with tears in her eyes. I knelt beside her wheelchair and gave her a hug and kiss.

THE MOUNTAINS CALL MY NAME

"See how pretty the pearls look," I said, holding them out a bit so she could get a good look at them. "They go perfectly with my dress."

"Ya look like one of my angels," she said.

"Well, let's see if we can get her and all this dress in the car," Mr. Scott said, holding the door open for me to exit.

Mrs. Scott got my coat and put it across my shoulders and the little procession made its way toward the rest of my life. After much positioning, we all made it into the car. I held my bouquet in my lap while I sat quietly listening to the chatter among the three Scotts. I was getting more nervous by the minute. What was wrong with me? I thought, this was going to be the happiest day of my life.

"You're mighty quiet back there 'Lis'beth," Mr. Scott said. "Are you okay?"

"Yeah, just a little nervous."

"I talked with Danny earlier and he was a wreck. Wonder what it is about a weddin' day that does that to people?" he said, grinning at Mrs. Scott."

"It's been so long I don't remember," she said, looking sweetly at her husband.

When we pulled up to the little white chapel, the small graveled parking lot was already full of cars. Some were already parked along the road. Grandmother must have gotten the word out pretty well.

THE MOUNTAINS CALL MY NAME

"Look at all those cars here fer Danny and 'Lis'beth. It just about makes me cry," she said, dabbing at her eyes.

"I'm going to go get mother in and ready fer George and me to push her down the isle. I'll be right back to help you, and George can go check on Danny," she said, scurrying out of the car.

I was left alone to collect my thoughts.

"Oh, God," I prayed, "be with me. Take away all thoughts of the past. Just help me concentrate on Daniel. Bless us and help me not forget my vows. Amen."

The door to the car opened on my side and Mrs. Scott was there to help me out.

"You should see Danny. He's more handsome than I've ever seen him. And he's as nervous as a cat in a room full of rockin' chairs," she said, laughing. "Sharon's waitin' fer you in the little anteroom in the vestibule. The doors are closed to the sanctuary so Danny won't be able to see ya as you go in."

It was a beautiful day. The sun was shining brilliantly. The little chapel was ready to accept another offering. Today the bells would toll for joy, not sadness. That's what Daniel promised me. Maybe Mama could hear them up on the mountainside. Again my mind went back to her little house up the road and around the bend, and of the box I needed to find. The ringing of emptiness surged through me, she is gone... she is gone. I commanded myself not to cry. Stop being foolish I chided, you're about to see Daniel.

THE MOUNTAINS CALL MY NAME

A gentle breeze caught the skirt of my gown, lifting it as if with unseen hands. My veil blew out behind me in a long tulle and lace train. Mrs. Scott was trying to subdue both. We laughed in unison as we were wind-tossed into the vestibule. Sharon met us at the door and helped me into the room with her.

"Okay, sweetie, they said as soon as I got you in they was gonna start the music. I gotta go so they can seat me." She gave me another hug. "Don't be nervous, it's gonna be beautiful. The church is packed."

"Thanks for letting me know that," I said, smiling at her.

Sharon and I walked out into the vestibule after we were sure the doors were closed. Sharon lifted my gown and fluffed it to its fullness. Satisfied that I was proper, she nodded to let the usher know we were ready.

The doors opened and she went through. The music continued to draw Sharon to the altar and then it stopped. In just a moment the wedding march would begin.

Suddenly the doors opened wide for all to see how the bride was adorned for her husband. I was frozen in my space, unable to move forward. The music played and played, and I knew I should start. Every eye was on me, and waiting for me to make my entrance. For a moment I thought I saw David standing there, waiting for me to come to him, a dazzling smile on his face. But no, it was Daniel and Chris not David and Daniel. I closed my eyes to clear my head.

THE MOUNTAINS CALL MY NAME

Please God, clear my mind, take these memories away I can't handle them today.

The music kept playing and the people kept looking and I couldn't move. All I have to do is take one step and the rest will follow, just put one foot in front of the other, I thought to myself. I looked up and tried to focus on Daniel. I saw him smile at me and start in my direction, but his father put his hand on his arm and came down the aisle to me. God had sent me an angel. He stepped beside me and offered me his arm.

"Are you ready, little girl," he said, smiling at me.

I nodded and began my journey to meet my groom. I could almost hear a collective sigh when we started down the aisle. When I got close I could see tears coming down Daniel's cheeks, and I melted into his gaze.

"We are gathered together today to unite in marriage Daniel Scott and Elizabeth Mason. Who gives this bride in marriage?"

I gave Daniel a panicked look. Preacher Simon had forgotten I had no family there. There was no one to give me away. An awkward silence filled the sanctuary.

"I do." A strong voice resonated through the church. The voice came from the man standing beside me. "I give her to our family."

A look of pride washed over Daniel as he smiled at his father.

He took my hand and placed it into his son's hand. Daniel looked at me with more love than I'd ever seen on his face. His father put his arm around him and patted him on the shoulder as he took his place beside him.

"We are gathered here this afternoon to join Daniel and 'Lizabeth in holy matrimony. I have known these two since they were younguns. I was the one what baptized them in the river. I have seen them grow mightily in the Lord since that time. I think they have something they want to say to each other."

I handed Sharon my bouquet and turned to face Daniel. He took my hands in his, and his crystal blue eyes looked into the depth of my soul. His look held me captive as he spoke to my heart.

"Elizabeth..." he said, with tears swimming in his eyes. "I love you with my whole heart. It is said, if you love something set it free and if it is meant to be yours it will return to you. God returned you to me. You are my life and my sunshine. You are my joy in the morning. All the love that I'm capable of giving, I give to you. I promise to care for you according to God's will, and I promise to be to you what God would have me be. I promise to keep you from sadness when at all possible. To shield you and protect you from any harm that might come your way. To be a godly leader in our family. To seek God's wisdom for you and our home. To always cherish you and hold you dear to my heart. I will love you until the day that I die. I will always treasure the gift of your life, and will be eternally grateful that God gave you to me to love."

I raised my hand and wiped the tears from his cheek.

"Daniel..." I said with a shaky voice. I cleared my throat to make my voice stronger.

THE MOUNTAINS CALL MY NAME

"Entreat me not to leave thee, or to return from following after thee. Whither thou goest I will go, and whither thou lodgest I will lodge. Your people will be my people and your God my God.

"I promise to love you with my whole heart. I will follow you and the ways that God leads you. I will honor you and cherish you and you only for the rest of the days of my life. Your family will become mine. I vow to always try to make you happy, and will share with you in your times of sadness. As we complete these vows before God, our hearts and souls will unite into one. Only death will separate me from you. I will be eternally grateful that God gave you to me to love. You made me live again. You brought me from a deep chasm, and took me to the mountaintop. God brought you to me in my darkest hour. I was living in the land of the dead and you made me live again. The light of my days had departed. The Bible tells us that right before the dawn comes it is the darkest time of the night, but our joy comes in the morning. You were there at the breaking of the dawn. My soul is bathed in the light of your love. You called me from the brink of death and I came back to you. I give myself to you body, spirit, and mind." I smiled at him through tear-brimmed eyes.

"Daniel, will you take Elizabeth to be your wife, and take care of her during the good times and the bad, during health and during sickness, during rich times and poor times. You can respond by sayin' 'I will'."

"I will," he said, looking into my eyes.

"Elizabeth, will you promise to love Daniel in good times and in bad times, in sickness and in health, for richer or poorer." You can answer by sayin' 'I will'."

"I will," I said, smiling at him through my tears.

"If you would join right hands and repeat after me.

"I, Elizabeth, take thee, Daniel, to be my lawfully wedded husband."

I repeated the vow to Daniel,

"I promise to love, obey and cherish you. I take you for richer, for poorer, in sickness and in health, till death shall part us."

He turned to Daniel and said,

"I, Daniel, take you, Elizabeth, to be my lawfully wedded wife, I promise to love you, to honor you, and to cherish you. I take you for richer, for poorer, in sickness and in health, till death shall part us. I thereto pledge thee my troth. In the name of the Father, the Son and the Holy Spirit. Amen.

"May I have the rings please?" Preacher Simon said to Sharon and Mr. Scott.

"These rings make a circle." He held them up for all to see. They have no beginnin' and no end. That is the way your love should be," he said, looking at Daniel and me.

He took the rings and held them in the palm of his hand. He raised his hand toward heaven and asked God to bless them.

THE MOUNTAINS CALL MY NAME

"This is a symbol of Daniel and 'Lizabeth's love for one another. Let us pray over the givin' and the receivin' of the rings.

"Dear Lord, bless these two precious children, bless these vows they make before you today in an eternal promise to you.

"Elizabeth, I give you this ring as a symbol of my faith, love and fidelity, and thereto I pledge thee my troth. In the name to the Father, the Son, and the Holy Spirit. Amen

He placed the gleaming golden band on my hand.

"Elizabeth if you would repeat after me.

"Daniel, I give you this ring as a symbol of my faith, love, and fidelity, I thereto pledge you my troth. In the name of the Father the Son and the Holy Spirit. Amen.

I placed the shiny band of gold on Daniel's finger. I felt peace and joy flow over me. The haunting memories fled, and all I could see was my new husband smiling at me through his tears of joy.

Chris had taken his place by the piano as we knelt on the prayer bench. His voice was strong and melodious, and resonated throughout the rafters of the little chapel. I could feel the spirit of God as he sang the Lord's Prayer.

Then Pastor Simon concluded with his own prayer. "Lord, bless your children that now bow before you. Take this union and use it for your honor and glory. Amen."

THE MOUNTAINS CALL MY NAME

The two candles beside the unity candle were lit and waiting for us to join our light together in one. Daniel lifted mine and placed it in my hand, then took his. While the piano played we lit our candles. Afterward, we again stood before Preacher Simon.

"Now by the power vested in me by the state of Virginia, I now pronounce you husband and wife. Daniel you may kiss your bride."

He turned to me and looked into my eyes.

"I love you so much." He lowered his lips to mine and kissed me long and tenderly for all to see.

"I love you, too," I mouthed silently to him.

He pulled me close to him and kissed me again.

"For the first time ever, I get to present to you Dr. and Mrs. Daniel Scott."

As the presentation was made, the bells of the little chapel began to ring. They resounded from the little valley to the top of the mountain where Mama and Daddy lay in their graves. The bells rang forth the joy that I felt in my heart. Daniel promised me the bells would ring for joy again and not sadness, and today his promise came true.

Sharon handed me my bouquet, and straightened my gown behind me. Daniel and I proceeded down the church aisle accepting the accolades that were given. We were greeted by smiles and tears of happiness. There were handshakes from those that were seated near enough to grab our hands. They clapped as we walked past, showing us their approval of our union. Daddy John and the twins were seated near the back. I stooped down when I reached him and kissed him on the cheek.

"Joy comes in the morning, Daddy John, Joy comes in the morning."

"That's right, baby girl, joy does come in the mornin'," he said, smiling up at me. "The angels are smilin' down today."

Anna Belle was there, and greeted me as we ended the aisle.

"Yer mama woulda be mighty proud of ya," she said, giving me a hug.

Daniel and I headed for his car. We planned to meet all our friends and family at the local community center. Mrs. Scott came running to me with my coat, and draped it around my shoulders.

She put her arms around me and said, "Welcome to our family, sweet 'Llizabeth."

"Thanks for making me feel so welcome," I said. returning her hug.

Mr. Scott was close behind her and came to Daniel and me with a broad smile on his face.

"Thank you for my rescue," I said with tears in my eyes.

"Well, I couldn't let my daughter walk down the aisle by herself, now could I?" he stated, taking me into his arms for a welcome hug.

THE MOUNTAINS CALL MY NAME

"You've helped make my day perfect."

He just smiled and went on to hug Daniel.

"Thanks, Dad, thanks for everything."

"Well, let's get her in the car before she freezes," Mrs. Scott said, helping me get my full dress and flowing veil into Daniel's little car. Finally, after all of me was inside the car, we shared our first moment alone as husband and wife. He pulled me to him once again and kissed me.

"My wife, how I like those words. I was beginning to wonder if you were coming down the aisle. I thought, 'Oh God, don't let her change her mind,'" he said, smiling at me. "I was concerned for a moment, though. I didn't know what to do. I started to come and drag you kicking and screaming...no, just kidding, to get you, myself, and Dad touched my arm and went for you."

"I was so relieved to see him come for me. I was kind of frozen to my spot. I was just..."

"Thinking of another day?"

"Only, for a moment, and not just that, but I was thinking about my mom and dad not being there. It had nothing to do with my not loving you."

"I know," he said, taking my hand in his. He raised my hand with his wedding band to his lips. "I told you a long time ago, whatever happens with your memories or flash backs, I will help you through them. I'm not threatened by your memories, for today, my princess, we start our own memories."

THE MOUNTAINS CALL MY NAME

"Today, and all the days of our lives are ours to make memories."

We had a train of cars behind us with horns blowing and lights flashing. Thank God, it was just a short distance to the community center. There were already many cars in the parking lot waiting for us to arrive.

"Daniel, I think the whole community turned out for this reception."

"If Grandmother has anything to do with it they did," he said, laughing.

"I've never seen you look more handsome. I can't believe you're all mine forever."

"I was thinking the same thing. When those doors opened and I saw you, my heart was racing in my chest.

"I thought, 'Oh God! Look what you've given to me. That is surely how Adam felt when he woke up and saw Eve'. I was so nervous; and Chris had been giving me a rough time. You know, 'best man' kind of encouragement. Then when the music played, and played I switched from being captivated by your beauty to becoming worried about you. Talk about rollercoaster emotions. Out of the corner of my eye I saw Chris start to move toward you, and then Dad touched my arm and he went to meet you. It would have been funny if all three of us men came to walk you down the aisle," he said, smiling at me.

"Chris could have been the train bearer," I said, laughing.

THE MOUNTAINS CALL MY NAME

"I can just see Chris doing that," he returned.

"It was just bridal nerves. Everything went smoothly after that. I felt, rather than heard, a collective sigh from among the congregation as I started my walk to you. After I got started, all I could focus on was how incredibly handsome you were standing there."

We pulled up to the front door to find "Mom Scott" already there. She was the first to make it to my car door. She truly was being motherly for me today. She helped me out and fluffed my wedding gown. Sharon was there to hold the train of my dress as we made our way inside. As Daniel and I marched in to our awaiting party, everyone stood and gave us a round of applause. They had a head table set up in the front of the room. But first we had to do the receiving line. Once we were arranged in the correct order we began to receive those that came to honor "baby Daniel" and his new bride. The one they all had watched grow from an infant to become their very own doctor. Some, I'm sure, hoped it would have been their daughter whom he would have chosen.

I knew a lot of the people, but there were many I didn't know. Grandmother was in her element. She glowed with joy and pride. She looked beautiful in her pink chiffon dress. She had a white rose corsage on her tiny little wrist. She looked like a shining little angel.

What seemed like hours of hugs, kisses, and handshakes finally ended. We made our way to our table for some food. I felt a tug on my arm and turned to see Chris standing with his arms open.

"Do I get to kiss the bride?"

THE MOUNTAINS CALL MY NAME

"Oh, Chris, of course. Come here."

He lightly kissed my lips and gave me a close hug.

"Are you okay? I got worried about you when you froze up before coming down the aisle."

"Wedding jitters. I just couldn't get my feet to move."

"I thought now was my chance, you had chosen me over Daniel," he said, grinning at Daniel.

"Not a chance," Daniel said, pulling me close.

"I actually was coming to get you and Mr. Scott beat me to it."

"You really would have done that, wouldn't you?"

"I really would have done that. You have so many people here today that love you. Even though you felt all alone standing up there, you had a room full of people praying for you."

"I forgot about the tradition of giving the bride away. I didn't have anyone to give me away. The silence was deafening. And then Mr. Scott, bless his sweet heart, saved me again."

"I've seen some of the people I treated in the clinic last week. I guess this is good public relations," Chris said, taking his seat at the head table with Daniel and me.

THE MOUNTAINS CALL MY NAME

I saw Mrs. Scott coming our way with two plates filled with food. As she reached our chairs, Daniel rose to meet her. She sat the plates down before us.

"Mom, thank you so much for arranging all this. It has turned out great," he said, hugging her.

"It's been so much fun, and I wanted to show off my son and his new bride. How did you like her weddin' gown?"

"She's more beautiful than words can express."

"I thought you would like what ya saw. I told her I bet you would cry."

"And I did. They were tears of joy. I thought, 'look what God had given us, the Scott family, but most of all what he has given to me.'"

I saw Mandy and Charlotte at a table with friends. They were both laughing. I wanted to get a chance to talk to Mandy before Daniel and I left for our honeymoon. The cake she made was one of the most beautiful I had ever seen. She was such a multi-talented lady. How precious she was to Daniel and me, and she would be staying on with us as a member of our new family.

It was time to cut the wedding cake. Mandy was there to tell us how to cut it. I took the knife in my hand and Daniel placed his hand over mine. We cut a small piece to share. Flash bulbs went off as we proceeded with our project.

"Lets not do the 'smash the cake in the face thing', okay?" I asked Daniel.

"If you won't, I won't," he said, lifting a bite to my mouth. We managed to do it without getting it all over our faces. Then we had the toast with the wine glasses. We intertwined our arms with the crystal goblets and drank to our future. Now the only thing left was the garter throwing and the bouquet toss. Mrs. Scott had a small bouquet made for me to throw so I could keep mine.

"Daniel, this sounds like something you would do at a church picnic. The garter throw and the bouquet toss," I said, laughing at him.

Someone brought me a chair to sit in so Daniel could hunt for my garter. He made some show of it, with hoots and hollers from those watching. After he had procured it, he got all the bachelors in a group.

"Are we ready?" he said, looking at the men and little boys lined up before him.

"Here goes, the one to catch it is the next one to marry."

He turned his back to the group and shot the garter into the crowd. It landed in the hands of Chris.

"Way to go, buddy. You're next."

I heard a cheer from the girls waiting to catch my bouquet.

"See, they're waiting for you," Daniel said, grinning at him.

"Okay girls, it's your turn."

THE MOUNTAINS CALL MY NAME

The girls jostled for position. I turned my back and threw the small bouquet. It landed in the hands of Karen Fowler, one of Daniel's nurses at the clinic.

"There you go Chris. It's all set up."

They both were blushing as Daniel continued to make a big deal out of it.

"Karen, you told me you were looking," he said, shrugging his shoulders at her.

"Daniel, I can make life miserable for you," she said, shaking her fist at Daniel.

"I know you can," he said, laughing at her.

"And I *really* can," Chris said, looking at Daniel with a devilish grin.

"Okay, you guys, I retreat, just don't hold grudges," he said, looking apologetically at them. "But, she's not bad, Chris," he said smiling.

"Are you ready to go?" he whispered into my ear.

"Now?" I asked.

He nodded his head at me.

"I need to go change out of my wedding gown."

"No, you don't. I want you to leave your gown on."

"Okay, but what about my luggage?"

THE MOUNTAINS CALL MY NAME

"It's all taken care of."

"Where is it?"

"This will be my last major surprise for you. I've had people working night and day so this would be ready for you. I'm going to show you, I'm not going to tell you."

Mrs. Scott had everyone line up with their handfuls of rice, waiting outside for our departure. I would be picking rice out of my hair for weeks. I had it in my ears and down my dress. The boys had our car a mess with shaving cream messages, streamers, and tin cans dangling from the bumper. We made a quick exit and were on our way to see my last surprise. There were a few persistent revelers on the tail of our car, blowing their horns and flashing their lights. Finally, after a couple trips through town, they were satisfied to let us be.

"Okay where's my surprise?"

"I'm taking you there right now."

We drove out of town back toward the little chapel where we were just married, and on past his house. He was smiling from ear to ear.

"Daniel, when are you going to tell me what it is? How much further? I can't wait."

"I told you I'm not going to tell you, I'm going to show you."

Just a little way down the road we turned into a lane that led to his grandfather's property. I remembered it from Thanksgiving when we hunted trees. There was a sign at the beginning of it. He slowed down so I could read it.

"Blackberry Ridge," I read. That's my surprise you named this place Blackberry Ridge? That's what I told you would be a good name for it, and you remembered. How sweet."

He kept driving down the little lane. We broke through the clearing where we had parked to look for a Christmas tree. The road kept going right on up the side of the mountain. It was no longer dirt, but well graveled.

"You've done a lot of work since we were here last."

"I've had a lot of work done since we were here last," he said, correcting me.

We drove on up the side of the ridge to the top of the mountain. There, right past the top in a cluster of trees was a beautiful two story house. It was made of a dark brick, trimmed with cream color paint. There were four large columns across the front of the house, connecting to an upper balcony.

"Whose house is this? I thought you were going to build here one day," I said, a little disappointed.

"Let's go see who's home."

"Daniel! I'm in my wedding gown," I exclaimed.

"They're expecting us," he said, as he opened my door.

THE MOUNTAINS CALL MY NAME

"Do we have to?" Can't we go another day?"

"Your surprise is here, come on," he said, going to my side of the car.

After I had wiggled and wormed my way out of the car again, I stood in front of the massive house with Daniel, a little disappointed we had to share our day with someone else.

"Are you sure about this? I don't see any cars and no one seems to be here," I asked, still wondering what he was up too.

"I'll quit teasing you. Elizabeth," he said, turning me to face him. "This is your new home, or should I say, our new home."

"You're kidding me again. Right?"

"Come; let me give you a tour."

"A home… this is ours?"

"Do you like it?"

"Do I like it? Do I like it? You're asking me if I like it?"

"You're repeating yourself," he said, smiling at me.

"It's so grand and elegant. I love it. How did you hide this?"

"I had already started on it when I first met you. Even when we came to hunt trees, the house was well underway. You just couldn't see it from the meadow. I wanted to keep it a surprise."

"Daniel, it's a mansion. The columns in front are so stately."

"Let's go inside. I want to show you all the surprises I have for you."

He took a key out of his pocket and opened the door. He picked me up in his arms and carried me over the threshold.

"Welcome home, my princess," he said, taking me into his arms and kissing me.

"You've outdone yourself." I said, giddy with joy.

"The best is yet to come," he said, kissing me again and again.

"Do you mind spending your wedding night here?" he asked, a little concerned.

"It doesn't matter where." He took me in his arms and kissed me passionately, once more.

"I hope you like all the decorating. Anything you don't like, I'll change. I didn't want to take any of the planning away from you, but you got so sick I had no choice but to proceed and hope you liked it."

I walked in awe from room to room. The furniture and decor were exactly like I would have done it myself.

THE MOUNTAINS CALL MY NAME

"Dad took care of so much stuff while you were sick. He kept on the contractors day and night. I couldn't have done it without him and half of the community. Your luggage is upstairs in the bedroom. Come, let me show the rest of it to you."

We climbed the winding staircase to the second floor. We had four bedrooms upstairs and one downstairs. The one on the ground floor, he had decorated for Mandy. He had let her choose all of her favorite colors.

"Close your eyes," he said as he led me into the master bedroom. "Now open them. Happy Valentine's Day."

I caught my breath in surprise. "Daniel... did you do this?" I said, whirling around the room with my arms spread wide.

"I had some help, but it was my idea. I tried to remember all the things you liked. Your colors from your old house, your taste in furniture, everything I could remember."

"And you did it in grand style. You remembered how I love the fireplace. And the four-poster bed with the canopy is so beautiful."

"Open the closet," he said.

Inside a large walk-in closet were all my clothes and personal items from home.

"When did you have time to do all this?" I asked in awe.

"Chris worked on it. He had the people that moved him go by your house and pick up your stuff. They packed it and everything."

"You're an angel," I said, kissing him. "Where did you put all the stuff from my house?"

"I put it in storage. I thought when you felt better you could choose some of your personal things to put in our house. Whatever you want changed is okay. It's your home now. My gift to you."

"What about your other house?"

"Chris is buying it. Everything just came together like clockwork. It's God's blessings, what can I say."

"Daniel, I'm just speechless. When we were hunting Christmas trees, they were up here working on this house?" I said, smiling at him.

"Well, maybe not that day. But yes, I was already working on this house."

"Why didn't you tell me then?"

"It just wasn't the time. And after we got more involved, the idea of a surprise seemed better everyday."

"You've really pulled this off."

I went to the French doors that opened to the outside and pulled them open. They opened out onto a balcony. There was a white wicker loveseat and a rocker there, with cushions made of a soft blue and white fabric. The view out over the mountain was spectacular.

THE MOUNTAINS CALL MY NAME

"I wish I had my camera," he said, looking at me standing on the balcony. "What a splendid picture this would make of you with your dress sparkling in the sun and your veil blowing in the breeze."

"It's chilly; maybe you should come inside," he said, leading me back into the master bedroom. "You haven't seen the bath yet," he said, leading to the other side of the room. Another set of French doors opened into a room with a built-in vanity. There was a white chair sitting at it. Around the mirror were clear lights for me to see to put my makeup on. There was a single door that opened into another room. I opened it, and there was a white sunken garden tub on the far side of the room. I saw candles everywhere, interspersed with ivy and other greenery, sitting on the short wall around bathtub. On the other side of the room was a walk-in shower big enough for two people. It was enclosed with clear glass doors. A big double sink with lights surrounding the mirror was at the end of the room near the tub. I couldn't find the commode, at first, because it was located at the end of a short hall behind the shower stall.

"I don't think I can stand many more surprises like this one. You promised me a day of them, and you didn't fail me. I love everything you've done for me today. But most especially, becoming my husband. All of the grand things you've done pale in comparison to our becoming as one."

He lifted my face to him and kissed me.

"I love you so much. You are grander than anything I could possibly give to you. You complete me. You make a half a whole. I don't have words fancy enough to describe how I see you."

THE MOUNTAINS CALL MY NAME

He kissed me again and pulled me close.

"I think I would like to get out of this dress and put on something more comfortable," I said, gazing lovingly into his crystal blue eyes.

"Your suitcase is in the closet. I'll get it for you."

"I don't need it right now," I said, turning my back to him.

I took the pins from my veil and lifted it off my head. I took my fingers and fluffed the hair that was flattened.

He brushed my hair aside and kissed my neck. My breath caught as shivers ran through me.

"Daniel, could you unbutton my dress."

"I think I can manage that."

He fumbled with the hooks that fastened the beading from side to side.

"It's amazing. I can do delicate surgery and have so many problems with these hooks."

"I'm glad you haven't had experience with dress buttons."

He undid the strands of beads going across it, and started on the buttons going down my back. The more he undid the buttons, the looser the top became. I held the dress up so it wouldn't fall down over my breasts. When he finished the lower section of buttons, I felt his lips as he kissed my bare back. His touch took my breath away. His hands moved the dress down off my shoulders and it fell in a soft heap to the floor. I turned around and faced him and unbuttoned his shirt. I could tell his reaction to me was as moving as mine had been to him. He pulled me to him as we stood together flesh touching flesh. I stepped out of my wedding gown into his arms. He showered me with kisses. His hands and lips touched parts of my body that he hadn't touched before. Ripples of sensation shot through my being.

The sunset cast a golden glow over our bedroom. We finished undressing, and climbed into our big king size bed.

"Are you happy?" he asked, pulling me close to him.

"Daniel, I've never been happier than I am at this moment," I said breathlessly. "It's okay for you to end your vow now."

"Are you sure it's okay?" he asked hoarsely, as his lips sought mine.

"Believe me there couldn't be a better time than right now," I said, trying to catch my breath from his last kiss.

We let ourselves be swept away in the ocean of passion that had previously been held at bay. It rippled over us, consuming us and rendering us helpless to its power. Our union would now be completed in flesh as well as spirit.

THE MOUNTAINS CALL MY NAME

Part Two

Searching for my Mountain

THE MOUNTAINS CALL MY NAME

Part Two

Chapter One

It had been a month since Daniel and I were married. The time had passed by so swiftly. We had taken a week and a half honeymoon in Hawaii and our time together had been marvelous. I had totally recovered from all my health problems stemming from the blood clot. I had never felt stronger. I could have stayed here in my new house and been just as happy as I was in Hawaii. Not that Hawaii wasn't wonderful, but anywhere with Daniel would have been perfect to me. Mandy is like a kid in a candy shop with the new house. She spoils Daniel and me so much. She lets me do all the cooking I want to, and tries very hard to let me have the run of the house. She's always asking me how I want things done.

When we got back I found a realtor and put my house on the market. It wasn't doing me any good sitting there empty. I was back to the mountains for good. Chris decided to go ahead and sell his home, so both of us were using the same agent. He had fallen in love with the mountains and the people he had begun to call his patients. I was surprised that my home had sold so quickly.

Two of the doctors that helped Daniel when I was sick were also coming on board, as expected. Daniel had been so busy since coming back. He tried his best to be home early but sometimes it was just impossible. We had begun our marriage in the little white chapel, and we became members right after we returned from our honeymoon. We had grown up going to church there. Who would have thought we would be coming back as husband and wife. Daniel took time every morning to have devotions with me. Our prayer time was so precious.

I hadn't gone to my mother's house since she died. I knew I had to, but for some reason I hadn't been able to. I wanted to wait until Daniel could go with me. Anna Belle had gone over and cleaned out the refrigerator, and had thrown out all the perishable food. So now the hard part was up to me. I must go through her personal things and decide what to do with them. I guess I just wasn't strong enough physically or emotionally until now.

We tried to make time on Sunday afternoon to visit with Daniel's family. Mom Scott always had a big dinner after church and we were always invited to come by. Chris would join us sometimes. We became his extended family. The Scotts adopted him along with me.

Grandmother Scott gave us a running assessment of how the population viewed the new health care for the community. There were mixed reviews, of course. Some were more easily convinced than others. Grandmother Scott remained in excellent health. She was faithful in her checkups with Daniel.

I had a surprise in store for Daniel when he came in from work that day. I was going to offer him the profit from the sale of my house to further the health care here.

THE MOUNTAINS CALL MY NAME

I thought a long time about converting a recreational vehicle into a mobile medical clinic. It didn't seem like a farfetched idea. I'm sure with all the input from Chris we could make a real impact. With all the hidden hollows in the mountains there were so many not willing or able to come to the clinic to get needed help.

They continued on with the roots and herbs passed from generation to generation. Some worked well, but some not only couldn't cure, but could kill. With the clinic well staffed now, I thought we could travel together, doctor and nurse, to those isolated places and take the care to them. I hadn't mentioned this to anyone except the Lord.

Daniel had a gazebo built behind our house with a swing inside. There was a path winding down the hill to it. We would sit there sometimes in the evening and listen to the birds sing in the trees around us. It had a beautiful view of the valley below us. We could see wisps of smoke curl up from the chimneys. I would sit sometimes and try to imagine the wood cook stove preparing the evening meal or perhaps a wood stove warming the home itself.

I would let my mind wander back to the times I had sat by the fire while Mama cooked supper. The wonderful dinners she would prepare brought pleasant memories. She could make a perfect cake in that old wood stove.

I was waiting for Daniel in the gazebo. I told Mandy to send him down as soon as he came in. I had set there and rehearsed what I was going to say. I went over and over it in my mind. I had the envelope in my hand with the check in it from when I sold the house. I was so excited I could hardly wait. I closed my eyes and willed myself to calm down. I heard the birds sing and the rustle of the wind through the woods, but it still didn't calm my anxiousness.

I felt two hands come over my eyes and I knew it was Daniel.

"Guess who?" he asked.

"I hope it's my husband," I returned.

He came around and set down beside me. He leaned over and gave me a sweet kiss. I looked forward to this time of day when I would feel his lips on mine again. I still couldn't get enough of him. What sweet times we had together.

"What's wrong?" he asked, taking a seat beside me.

"Why?"

"Well you don't usually ask me to meet you in the swing. Do we have a problem?"

"I hope you don't think of it as a problem," I said, smiling at him.

"Let's see, are we pregnant yet?" he said, looking at me expectantly.

"I don't think so," I said. It's something just as special, I think."

"Okay, I'm through guessing."

THE MOUNTAINS CALL MY NAME

I handed him the envelope. He took it and held it for a moment before he opened it up. He took the check out and held it in his hand.

"This is from when you sold your home. I knew it was due to come."

"I want to give it to you," I said.

"Elizabeth, it's sweet of you to offer me money, but I have enough for the both of us to live on, and more."

"Well, it's not exactly for us to live on, but it's far more special. Let me tell you what I've been thinking about."

"Oh no, you've been thinking! That could be dangerous," he said, teasing me.

"As I was saying, I was thinking maybe we could get a recreational vehicle and equip it as a mobile clinic. We could travel into the remote places of Virginia and West Virginia to care for those people that wouldn't come to us. What do you think?" I asked excitedly.

He put his arm around me and pulled me close to him and kissed me.

"This is all kind of sudden, but I think it is a great idea. I've thought about the same thing from time to time, but I wasn't sure how we could do it. With this we could do a great deal. I've been so busy trying to get the clinic established I haven't been able to give it my attention. Who would run this mobile hospital?" he said, turning to look at me.

THE MOUNTAINS CALL MY NAME

"Well, that's my next idea. I thought the two of us could. I could be your nurse. You've told me often enough that you would be the doctor and I would be the nurse."

"You? This is a surprise. I kind of thought you might start back, but I didn't want to rush you. You know you don't need to work."

"But I want to. I have all this training and people need me."

"I think we could pull this off. Let me sleep on it, and tomorrow I'll run it by Chris. Come here and give me a kiss."

We sat for a long time swinging and kissing. I could never get tired of his love. I remembered the key that Mama had given me and decided to bring it up to him.

"Daniel, do you remember the key Mama gave to me the night she died?"

"Yes, I was waiting for you to bring it up. I figured when you were ready we could go over to her house and see if we could find something this key will fit."

"I've been thinking about it, and I think I'm ready to see whatever it is. Maybe we could go tonight. We haven't turned off the electricity yet. Would you like that?"

"Yeah, I think I would. Let's go eat supper, then we can go over."

He got to his feet and pulled me to mine. He drew me close to him and kissed me long and tenderly.

THE MOUNTAINS CALL MY NAME

"I look forward to you all day. I can't wait to get home to you and this," he said, kissing me again.

"I hope this honeymoon stage never ends," he said, smiling at me.

"We better go, dinner will be cold."

We made our way up the hill to the house. Mandy had dinner ready and waiting.

"I'll be right there," he said, heading for the stairs. "I want to go change right quick."

As soon as we had finished dinner we headed to my mom's house. I really dreaded this trip and had put it off as long as possible. It would be the first time I had been back since my Thanksgiving trip. That seemed a lifetime ago.

"I really dread this. You remember me telling you about the feeling I've had about this place?"

"Are you talking about the unknown fear?"

"Yeah, it's something I've felt here for as long as I can remember. I think that's why I wanted to get away. This is it Daniel," I said, holding up the little brass key.

"I'm holding my fear in my hand. It's like holding a hot coal. I would like to throw it away but I know I have to face whatever it is that this key fits."

THE MOUNTAINS CALL MY NAME

"We'll do this together. If you want me to, I'll look first and tell you what I find."

"No, we'll look together," I said with a weak smile.

We got out of the car and walked hand in hand to the front porch.

The last time Daniel walked me to this door we weren't even engaged, I thought. He put the key in the door and it opened easily.

"Here we go," he said, going in before me.

He fumbled inside the door for the light switch. I slipped under his arm and easily found it. I had used it a million times. The overhead light came on and illumined the room. The big clock no longer ticked. It was eerily quite. I don't know why, but I felt that I had to wind the clock. I had never heard it be silent. It's as if it had died along with its inhabitants. There was no one else to stand sentry over. I had the door opened to wind it, but decided to let "him" remain mute.

I wandered into the kitchen. The room that once seemed so bright and cheery now seemed to be cold and uninviting. The refrigerator door was left open so it wouldn't mildew. How precious Anna Belle had been to have taken over the things that I should have done.

I walked over to Mom's chair by the window and sat down. I reached over and turned on the table lamp. Its light seemed to soften the harshness of the overhead ceiling light. Tears escaped my eyes and ran down my cheeks.

533

THE MOUNTAINS CALL MY NAME

"She loved this chair," I said, wiping my eyes.

"Sweetheart, do you want me to go into her room and look for something this key will fit?" he said tenderly to me.

I shook my head and extended my hand toward him. He reached out and pulled me to my feet and into his arms. He held me close.

"There's nothing here that can hurt you."

He took my hand and led me down the hall to the bedroom. I noticed Anna had made Mama's bed and everything was neat and in its place.

I opened her closet and saw all her clothing hanging just as she left it. Waiting for her to come and wear them. I pulled one of her sweaters to my face catching a faint sent of her lavender sachet. I held it to me just as I had David's clothing, hoping to feel her closeness once again. But in both cases, it was merely a garment, their lives were gone. My mind went back to the day I saw her in heaven. How happy she was there. I must make myself remember that day and not the emptiness of this house.

"I think I need to get a light and a stepstool so I can check back in the corner of the closet."

I walked about the room while he went in search of a stool. Her Bible lay on the simple table beside her bed. The cover was worn from countless hours of holding it and reading it. How often she must have held it as she prayed for my healing from all the grief I was suffering. She needed me and I wouldn't come to her. How selfish of me, I thought. I picked it up and pressed it to my chest as if to somehow feel the prayers she had prayed.

"Honey, I finally found a flashlight that worked. I couldn't find a stool, so I brought the next best thing, a chair," he said, pulling it up to the closet.

"Do you need me to hold the light?" I asked.

"That would help."

I stood on my tiptoes and shined the light in the direction he was looking.

"It would help if I knew what I was looking for," he said, stretching on his toes and reaching toward the far corners of the closet.

"Did she say closet?" he asked.

"I can't remember." I replied.

"It's not on the top shelf." he said, removing the chair.

I got down on my hands and knees to look in the back. I removed shoes and various other items on the floor, but there was nothing with a key hole.

"Maybe it's under the bed," Daniel said, getting on his hands and knees to look.

"I don't see anything that a key would fit in." he said, sitting on the floor beside me.

535

THE MOUNTAINS CALL MY NAME

"The clock uses a key, but it has its own," he muttered to himself.

"Maybe it would be in one of her drawers. She could have hidden it under her clothing," I said, getting to my feet.

I started checking in her chest of drawers, slowly and meticulously moving things. I didn't have time to mourn as I handled her things. We searched all the drawers to no avail. Daniel had gone through one of her other dressers while I was going though another.

"How big do you think this thing is?" Daniel asked me.

"Your guess is as good as mine," I returned.

"Where do we look now? Unless she has it in a secret chamber, it isn't in this room," Daniel said.

"Oh Daniel, I don't have a clue," I said, exasperated. "I don't think she would have put it in my room, but where would she have put it?"

"Maybe it could be in the guest room, let's start looking there," I said, heading down the hall.

The room was neat as a pin. It was a beautiful little room. Mama always called it 'Jonny's room. I assumed it was his nursery during his brief life here.

The furniture in the room was sparse but pretty. There was a large closet in the room with clothing still hanging there. She would transfer seasonal clothing from one to the other for the convenience of it.

"Well, I guess I need to get the chair and flashlight from the other room," he said, heading out of the room.

There was a small chest of drawers in the corner. I would go through it if he couldn't find what we were looking for in the closet.

Once again, Daniel climbed on the chair to investigate the contents of the closet.

"Libby, I'll be darned if I see anything that looks like it has a lock. Think like your mom, and see what pops up."

"That's a hard one." I said, smiling at him.

"Okay, Lord, you know what this thing is, so impress on my mind where to look." I prayed out loud.

"I think He is the only one that knows right now. Maybe He will send it floating through the air and right into our hands."

"Daniel, be serious!"

"I am," he said with a chuckle.

"You'll be surprised if God sends me an answer."

"Actually, I wouldn't be. I've seen Him do some mighty miraculous things, like bring you to me."

"Yeah, that was a miracle, wasn't it?" I replied.

THE MOUNTAINS CALL MY NAME

"I'm going to go out and check the shelves on the porch. Sit in your mom's chair and see if she sends you a message," he said.

I sat there with my eyes closed, trying to imagine where in the world she could have put this locked item. I suddenly felt lips on mine, jarring me to the present.

"Boo! Daniel said, laughing and startling me.

"I was trying to think. Don't do that!" I said, irritated with him.

"I'm sorry; I didn't mean to scare you. I just couldn't help it. Well, I guess I did mean to, didn't I. Let me make up for it," he said, kissing me tenderly."

"I'll forgive you this time. I gather you didn't find anything with a keyhole in it."

"Nope, I came up empty. She sure knew how to keep a secret. I guess she wouldn't put it somewhere you would accidentally stumble onto it," he said, thinking out loud.

"What about the attic where she kept the Christmas decorations? Maybe it could be there," Daniel said.

"Let's go look," I said, getting up.

"But how will we know when we find it?" Daniel asked, pulling down the steps to the attic.

"The key will fit," I said, laughing at him.

"Don't be a smarty pants," he replied.

THE MOUNTAINS CALL MY NAME

There was one light swinging down at the end of a long electrical cord. Daddy had it put in so he could see where to work up there.

There was stuff spread everywhere. Where would we start looking? I wondered.

"Daniel, look, over there in the corner! It's a trunk," I said, climbing over Christmas decorations to get to it.

It was an old humpback trunk, with tin arched over the top. There was a design in it made by a tin punch. Leather bands were stretched over the top, holding it in place. The locking system was rusted and I couldn't budge it.

"Let me see if I can pry it open," he said, working on it with his bare hands.

"I think I'm going to need something that can give me leverage. Look around and see if you see anything I could use," he said, still trying to get it to loosen.

I found an old screwdriver that had been discarded many years ago.

"Here, maybe this will work," I said, handing it to him.

He took the old rusty implement and began to push it in the lock. It slipped and jammed into his knuckle.

"Ouch!" he said, slinging his hand in the air. "That hurt!"

THE MOUNTAINS CALL MY NAME

"Hold still and let me see," I said, taking his hand in mine. "That's what you get for scaring me awhile ago."

"What, sticking a rusty screwdriver in my finger? That doesn't seem like an even trade to me."

"When did you have your last tetanus shot, Dr. Scott? You just might have to have one."

"Don't go getting medical on me, Nurse Scott," he said, taking his right hand in his left.

"Let me see," I said, taking his hand back in mine. "Look, it's just a scratch, a Band-Aid and a kiss will make it all better. I promise. See, it's barely bleeding."

"Kiss it now," he said, holding it to my lips.

"No! It has blood on it. I'll kiss it when the Band-Aid's on."

"Good friend you are," he said with mock pain.

"Does it hurt as bad now?"

"No, not now," he said, taking inventory of his wound."

"Then can you try again?"

"Woman, don't you have any mercy?"

"I love you sweetheart," I said, giving him a little kiss on the cheek.

THE MOUNTAINS CALL MY NAME

"I want you to kiss my finger," he said, teasing me. "I'm not going to work again until you do it."

"Give it here." I said in exasperation.

I kissed his finger above the wound that was now turning purple. Is that close enough?"

"Yeah, that'll do," he said, smiling at me.

He proceeded to pry the lock a little more gingerly this time. It finally gave way through the rust that had gathered over the years.

"No one has been in here for ages," Daniel said, opening the lid.

Inside was a menagerie of things. I gently picked up the articles one by one to look at them. On top, in tissue paper, was the suit that Daddy had worn at my wedding. It was the first and only time I saw him in a suit. I knew he wasn't buried in it, but I never had asked her what she did with it.

"Look, Daniel, this is the suit Daddy wore for mine and David's wedding." Mama had packed it away with such care. I laid it aside and proceeded to look further for the mysterious item which the little gold key would fit.

"Look, Daniel, I found a box in the bottom of the trunk," I said excitedly.

"Does it have a key hole?" he inquired.

"No, it's tied with a ribbon."

"Then I know that's not what we're looking for," he said.

"I know, but it may hold treasure," I said, picking it up.

I gently pulled the bow and released the ribbon from the box. Inside was a long gown and a tiny bonnet. I held up the garment that, on closer inspection, looked like it was hand-stitched. The once-white linen now was spotted yellow.

I held it close to me and remembered the little boy I saw in heaven. Now I could put a face to my little brother. His birth certificate had been neatly placed in bottom of the box. There was a little spray of brown hair tied with a ribbon, and taped to it.

"These were Jonathan's things," I said. "I'm surprised she left them in this old trunk."

"Maybe they were too painful to look at," Daniel replied.

"I wonder if Daddy went to his christening. He hated the church at the time Jonathan was a baby," I said quizzically.

"Maybe he did. He seemed to love him a lot, from what your mom said."

"Daniel, can we move this trunk to our house? I would like to refinish it someday."

"Sure, but does it have to be tonight?"

"No, you don't have to tonight, but sometime soon."

"Well, we need to keep searching for the elusive thing with a small key hole."

We continued to search the attic, but to no avail. We went back down the steps to hear knocking at the kitchen door.

"I wonder who that could be," I said, going to answer it.

Anna Belle was standing there, looking in the window pane of the door. I opened it and invited her in.

"I saw some lights on up here and wanted to make sure there weren't no haints in here," she said, looking at me wide-eyed.

"Do you mean to tell me you would actually come up here to find out? I think I would have just stayed at my house and wondered," I said with a chuckle.

"I ain't never been afraid to go see what things are, thata way you don't have to be afeared of what ya don't know."

"I think that makes sense," I said, still a little perplexed.

"I'm glad it was only you, 'Lis'beth." she said.

"Me too!" Daniel injected.

THE MOUNTAINS CALL MY NAME

"I'm glad to see yer doin' better from you sickness and all. You and Doctor Daniel sure looked purty at yer weddin'. Yer mama would'a been so proud."

"We're going through some of Mama's things. We just came down from the attic. Actually, we're looking for something this key fits."

Her eyes widened. "She showed me that key one day. She said, 'One day 'Lis'beth is gonna want to know things I cain't tell her now, and this here key will unlock the box.'"

"So it's a box?" I asked excitedly.

"Yeah, I've knowed about it, but I ain't never seed it," she said, scratching her head.

"Do you know where she kept it?" Daniel inquired.

"This ole' brain just cain't call up things like it used to."

"Think, Anna Belle, think!" I interjected.

"Well, a long time ago she showed me a place in one of her drawers she kept 'portant stuff in."

"Could you show us?"

"I don't know if I can, but I'll try."

We all traipsed single file down the narrow hall, Daniel leading the way, stopping in Mama's room.

"Let me think. Wher' was that thing?" she murmured to herself. "I think it was in that chester drawer right there," she said, pointing.

I felt downcast. "Anna, we've already looked through there. Are you sure though?"

"I think I am. I'm almost positive it's the one. She brung me back one day and showed me. She took a little key on a ribbon and opened it."

"What did the box look like?" Daniel and I asked in unison.

"It was a wooden box, much like one of them jewe'ry boxes."

"Was it tall or flat?" Daniel inquired.

"I think it was long and flat, so's it would fit the drawer good."

"Is that all you can remember?" I asked her, trying to will her to recall.

"Maybe if'n I go look, maybe it would jar this ole noggin." She said with a chuckle. "If ya don't mine, that is."

"No, please, go look all you want," I said, encouraging her to go ahead.

"Ya got to remember, "Lisbeth, it's been nigh on twenty year since I seed it. She kept tellin' me it was to be a deep secert where she put it. She said you musn't find it till she was…"

THE MOUNTAINS CALL MY NAME

"I know, passed. Keep thinking, Anna this is so important," I said, encouraging her further.

"I'm tryin', I'm tryin'." She said with a perplexed look crossing her brow. I jest cain't 'member what it was she did."

She went through all the drawers one by one.

"I guess she done put it som'ers else. I'm sorry I couldn't he'p more. I sure wanted too."

"It's okay," I said, hugging her. "I'm sure Daniel and I will find it. At least we know it's a flat box," I said with at sigh.

"Well, I guess I'll head on down the holler since I know there ain't no haints up hyer."

Her snaggled teeth were prominent as she threw her head back to laugh.

"No haints, just saints," Daniel added with a hearty laugh.

"I know what ya mean, Doctor Daniel, I know what ya mean," she said, still chuckling to herself.

"Bye," I said as she headed out the door.

"Be careful and don't fall," Daniel called after her.

"I got my flashlight, I'll be okay. I walked these hollers fer years. Bye now."

"I'm sorry, honey; I knew you had your hopes up high. But you know God will show us where it is," he said, comforting me.

"Why don't we go home and get some rest. We can come back over here tomorrow and look some more," he said hugging me. "We'll get the trunk then, too."

I went into the bedroom to turn off the light. It hadn't been long ago since I lay in bed with her and shared with her about mine and Daniel's first intimate moments.

We had everything turned off and ready to leave when we heard a knock on the door again.

"It's sure busy here tonight," Daniel said, going to see who was there.

"Its jus' me again," Anna said. "I was a goin' down the holler and I kinda remembered sumpthin' about the bottom movin'. I don't know if it will he'p any, but I thought I better come tell ya."

"The bottom of the box moved?" I implored.

"No, not the box, the drawer," she replied.

"Oh my God!" Daniel said, running down the hall. "It has to be a false bottom."

I ran after Daniel, with Anna close on my heels.

"Anna, which drawer was it?" Daniel said hurriedly.

"I'm sorry, I don't 'member. Ya got to 'member how long ago, it was," she said, scratching her head and looking puzzled again.

"Just dump the things on to the bed," I said to Daniel.

We started with the top one. Having dumped it, he pecked all around to see if it sounded hollow.

"It's not this one," he said, proceeding to check the others.

"Say a little prayer, sweetie, this is the last one," he said, dumping its contents onto the bed.

He began his pecking process, being careful of his bruised knuckle.

He looked at me with a wide grin. "This is it. We've found the treasure."

"How do you get it open?" I asked.

"I was just getting ready to ask you the same question," he returned.

"Don't go lookin' at me," Anna snapped, "I's sure don't know nothin' 'bout it."

Daniel worked and worked to no avail. Sweat was poring down his brow.

"I've never seen one of these before," he said, in exasperation. "One would think it would be much simpler."

"Maybe that's why they call it a secret drawer," I said, smiling at him childishly.

"Are you being a smarty pants again, Mrs. Scott?" he asked.

"I'm just kidding."

"Who would know how one of these things works?" he murmured as he worked.

"Maybe someone that grew up in the era that Mama did."

I saw a little light go off in his head. His eyes brightened. "My dad or mom might know."

He went into the living room to call his dad.

"No phone hookup," he said dejectedly.

"I guess we could take the drawer by their house," I said.

"It's getting late. Maybe we could take the drawer to our house and call him in the morning," he replied.

"That's a good idea. I'm getting tired and I'm sure you are. Plus we have to fix your war wound," I said, smiling at him.

"Anna, thanks a million. We couldn't have done it without you."

"I jus' wish I coulda knowed how that thing worked."

THE MOUNTAINS CALL MY NAME

"Do you want us to drop you off by your house?" Daniel asked.

"No sir, I jus' walk. Thanks anyway. I be prayin' ya get that thing fixed," she said as she went out the door.

Part Two

Chapter Two

It was well after midnight when we returned home. Daniel took the drawer and put it in the garage.

"We'll get it open tomorrow even if we have to cut the thing in two," he said reassuringly.

I went into the bedroom and changed into my night clothes.

"Honey, I'm going to take a quick shower. I feel grimy after the venture into the attic. I need to wash my cut out, too," he said, examining it again.

"I'll kiss it after you get the Band-Aid on it."

"I won't be long. Don't go to sleep before I get there," he said, kissing me on the tip of my nose.

"I have to clean my face and brush the dust out of my hair. I'm sure I'll still be awake by the time you're through."

I had just slipped into my side of the bed when Daniel finished. He held his newly bandaged finger up for me to kiss. I took his hand gently in mine and kissed his finger.

THE MOUNTAINS CALL MY NAME

"Is that better, sweetheart?" I said, looking into his eyes.

"I think I need a few more kisses."

He reached over and turned off the lamp by his bed.

"Come here, sweetie, let me hold you a little. Have I told you today how much I love you?"

"Umm, I think you might have, but tell me again. I love to hear it."

"I love you more than the stars in the sky and the sand on the seashore."

"I love you that much and more."

"You can't love me more than I love you. I have to think up something else."

"We love each other the same." I said, kissing his neck.

"Oh, Mrs. Scott, show me how much you love me," he said, pulling me close to him.

"I think I showed you once before, that should be enough," I said, teasing him.

"I have short term memory loss. I need to be shown often. In a lifetime I couldn't get tired of this."

"A lifetime is a long time."

THE MOUNTAINS CALL MY NAME

"I know, isn't that great?"

"Yeah...Daniel?"

"Shhh, no more talking, just love me," he said, claiming his love from me once again.

I felt Daniel gently shaking me, and calling my name.

"Daniel... what do you want?" I said, rubbing the sleep from my eyes.

"Look...! Set up and look at what I have."

"I know what you have, now let me sleep."

"Silly girl, wake up, I've got something to show you."

I roused on one elbow, shielding my eyes from the light he had turned on.

"What time is it?" I said, straining to see the clock.

"It's five o'clock."

"What are you doing? It's Saturday, you don't work."

He held his hands out in front of me. Lying in them was a long brown box.

"Is this 'the box'?" I asked.

"Yes, my darling, it is 'the box'," he said. "I couldn't sleep thinking about that false bottom. So I got out of bed and I've been working on it ever since. Finally, I worked it out, and here it is."

"You couldn't stand it, could you? You were always like that, you know. You couldn't stand to be defeated, and I'm so glad you couldn't. Come here and let me thank you."

I kissed him as he handed me the box. My fingers traced the chiseled carving on the top. Here it was: my past, present and future, closed up in this wooden box, no longer than twelve or thirteen inches long and maybe two inches deep. Perhaps it held the secrets of my life, possibly the name of my grandmother whom I needed to find. I held it on my lap, wanting to, but yet afraid to use the key.

"What are you thinking?" Daniel asked, as he crawled back into bed beside me.

"I have a myriad of thoughts. Once I open this box there is no turning back, and there will no more Elizabeth Ann Edwards. I'll know the truth, and the truth shall set me free. Then again, maybe there isn't anything in there that will help me find the grandmother that gave me away.

"Do you really want to find this grandmother? After all, she sent you away," Daniel said tenderly.

"Daniel, I've got to tell you a story," I said, still caressing the wooden box with my fingertips.

"Okay, but do you have to tell me before you open the box?"

"Yeah, it has to do with opening this," I said, looking at the box. "I've wanted to share this with you for a long time, but the right moment hadn't come."

"It's five in the morning, are you sure this is the time?" he questioned.

"I've been working all night to find this, and you're not going to open it?" he said disappointedly.

"First, I've got to tell this to you. Remember the time when I was in a coma, and I told you I had been with David?"

"Yeah, but what does this have to do with the box," he said quietly.

"It has everything to do with this box."

"Your dreams have something to do with what is in here?" he inquired.

"Oh, but Daniel, it wasn't a dream! That's why I need to tell you what happened before I open this box. It will be a validation to where I was when I was in my coma. If what I *think* is there, really is, I'll know for sure where I was."

"You're confusing me. All I remember you saying was that you were with David, so silly me, I thought you must have been dreaming, after all you just said you were with a dead man."

"There was so much more that happened while I was there. I saw David, yes, but I also saw…" I was almost

THE MOUNTAINS CALL MY NAME

afraid to go on. "Promise me you won't think I'm stupid or crazy," I interjected.

He turned my face, so I was looking directly into his eyes.

"I would never, ever think that. I'm ready to hear whatever it is you feel you need to tell me at…what time is it now?" He squinted to see the clock by my bedside, "5:30 it is now. Even though I've worked all night to get that puzzle drawer open, I'm ready."

"Before I open this, I feel I know some of the things I will find.

"When I was in my coma, it seemed as if I just woke from sleeping and was in a bright, beautiful place. I was in this field of flowers, and I turned and saw my mom and dad walking toward me. They had a little boy with them and they introduced me to him as my baby brother.

"They were so glad to see me. They held me in their arms, and kissed my face. I felt their touch. I could physically feel their arms around me. They were so young looking and healthy.

"I walked in the meadow, I swam in the River of Life, I met my brother, Jonathan, and my mother and twin sister."

I stole a look at his face as he understood what I had just told him. He just looked tenderly at me.

"I'm telling the truth, Daniel. It was as real as lying here beside you in bed. The reason I didn't stay with them is the silver cord never broke."

"A silver cord," he repeated. "Everything is still just a little bit fuzzy, but I'm listening."

"It seems that we are all tethered to this earthly body we live in by a silver cord. When the cord breaks, that's when we can't come back to earth. My cord never broke. I kept checking to make sure, but I couldn't see it. Only those that had crossed over could see it."

"I'm glad neither one of us can see it," he said, smiling at me.

"How come I feel like you're not taking me seriously?" I asked.

"Come here, sweetie," he said, pulling me closer to him. I do, or am *trying* to understand, if I sound like I'm not, forgive me," he requested.

"All right," I responded.

"Okay, let's take this one person at a time. You saw your brother? The one we saw the clothes for in the trunk? Is that right?"

"Right," I replied.

"See, I was listening."

"He was with my mother, and daddy. He was so cute, and seemed to be about eight years old. I can't remember him saying anything to me though, he just smiled at me. There was another woman with my mother, and she had a little girl with her. She seemed to be about the age of Jonathan. My mother told me she wanted me to

THE MOUNTAINS CALL MY NAME

meet my mother, my real mother," I said, hurriedly trying to get it all out.

"Slow down just a bit and sort the mother thing out for me."

"My mother that raised me, Mary Margaret, introduced me to my birth mother and my twin sister Abby."

"Go on I'm following you," he said, taking my hand in his.

"Okay, my mother's name is Rose and the little girl she had with her was Abby, my twin sister."

"Your mother mentioned that right before she died?"

"My mother, the real one, said she loved me very much and prayed for me the whole time she carried me in her womb. When she was in childbirth, things went badly and she and Abby died, and I lived. Why, Daniel? Why was I chosen to live and Abby die? Why did God let me live and take their lives?"

"If I had that answer I wouldn't be on earth. I'm so glad he left you for me," he said gently.

"It seemed each one of them had their special time with me. When it was time for another to come, the one that was there disappeared somewhere. I wasn't with anyone of them very long except for..."

"Let me guess... could it have been David?" he said, shifting away from me.

THE MOUNTAINS CALL MY NAME

"Yeah, it... I was so happy to see him. This is so difficult for me to tell you because I don't want to hurt your feelings."

"I'm the one that has you in the flesh, and I'm the one in bed with you right now, and I'm the one who made love to you a few hours ago. Look, I don't feel threatened by David. If I react sometimes, it's just because I know he shared with you the one thing I wish you had only shared with me, and I feel a little jealous. Then I remind myself that we will always share the same heart. Tell me whatever you need to, okay? I'm here for you.

"I told you before we married that anything you needed to say about David I was okay with. He was an integral part of your life. You loved him, and now you love me. I'm still adjusting, but I'm okay with it."

"He told me when he died in the emergency room, he was aware I was with him, and he saw me right before he...before he died." Unbidden tears slipped down my cheeks remembering the horrific scene.

Daniel drew me near to him and held me a little closer.

"Its okay, sweetie, you don't have to finish."

"But I do. He said he felt no pain; he wanted me to know that. He was there with me the night I dreamed he asked me to release him. Daniel, he was there just like I told you it happened in my dream!"

"I don't doubt that, because it was then that you felt free to be mine."

"My mother was so precious. She was beautiful. Her hair fell in cascades down around her shoulders. It was brunette just like mine. She told me she loved me." I said, letting my tears flow freely. "She loved me, Daniel, my mother loved me."

"She would have to of loved you, that's why you're so sweet. Her loved rubbed off on you," he said, smiling at me.

"There was something so sad that she said to me. She told me my grandmother wasn't saved and I had to go find her. She said her mother's life was filled with abuse and bitterness. She, her mother, Ruth, never knew what happiness was; as a result she was a very bitter and angry woman."

"So the grandmother has a name?" Daniel inquired.

"She told me that right before she left me. David came up and whisked me away before I found out. He said I would have time with her later, but that was the last time I saw her until the bridge."

"What happened at the bridge?"

"I first need to tell you what happened at the water."

"Under the bridge?" he inquired.

"No, not the water under the bridge, the water in the meadow."

THE MOUNTAINS CALL MY NAME

"So we're not at the bridge anymore, we're in the meadow?"

"Right, are you with me now?" I asked.

"I'm right with you. Go ahead," he returned.

"There was a river there in the meadow called the 'River of Life'. We sat beside the crystal water for a while with our feet dangling in. Then David suggested we go into the water, which we did. When we got out where it was getting really deep, I was afraid to go under. So he told me to try it, that in heaven we didn't have to breathe under water. I followed his lead and went under, and found that I felt very comfortable not breathing. Daniel, it was so wonderful. The temperature was perfect. We floated around in the water for a while then when we got out, we were perfectly dry."

"It sounds like it was something to behold. Then, what happened after you got out of the river?"

"He said he wanted to walk with me. We left the meadow and wandered through a forest. There was a path that ambled through it. Light filtered down through the limbs of the foliage and made beautiful patterns on the forest floor. The path we followed through the forest came out into a clearing and that was when I saw the bridge. It was white marble and arched over a body of water."

"Did you see your mother again, your birth mother, that is?" he asked.

"She stood on the other side of the bridge with my family and little sister, Abby. They were all waving and smiling at me.

THE MOUNTAINS CALL MY NAME

"He said, 'it's time now for you to choose what you're going to do'. I said, 'you mean I can come with you?' And he answered, 'yes', that it was my decision to make. I threw my arms around him and said of course I would go with him, because I loved him so much." I looked at Daniel and he had a pained expression on his face.

"You chose David?" he asked, with a hurt sound in his voice. "You chose not to come back to me?"

"Well, at first I did. You have to remember how much I loved him."

"Evidently you wanted him more than me," he interjected.

"Who am I with, Daniel?" I said, becoming irritated with him.

"Me, but you wanted to stay with him. Didn't you?"

"Let me finish the story. As I was starting across the bridge, my mother called out to me, 'Lis'beth don't' forget your grandmother'. Then I thought, if I don't go, who will. I knew if I crossed to the other side of the bridge, my cord would be broken. And then I heard you calling my name. You commanded me to look at you. So I turned and looked into your beautiful blue eyes. You told me not to look back, but to come to you. You said, 'don't take your eyes off mine, Libby', and I didn't. When I ran into your arms you held me very tight to you. I did look back, but only once, and they all had gone. It was right after that, that the horrible pain rushed back into my body. I woke up to you calling my name. I came back to you, Daniel, I could have stayed, but I came back to you."

Daniel had his fingers pressed to his eyes holding back the tears that were forming.

"I begged God for you, Elizabeth. Every day, I was in that chapel, asking God to give you back to me. It's funny that wherever you were, I was transported there to bring you back, and never knew. When you opened your eyes, I couldn't believe it for a moment. I thought I was dreaming."

"Neither of us was dreaming. I was transported to heaven for a time. I don't even know how long I was there, but I know I was there, and when I open this box I will find something there that will tell me all of this was not a dream."

"Are we ready to open this?" he said.

I nodded my head. "I'm ready now. I just had to tell you those things before we looked."

"Libby, I will never doubt what you tell me is true. I don't think you're silly. I know something happened to you when you were in the coma. Even when we can't explain things, it doesn't mean it isn't legitimate."

"Thank you, Daniel. I've been concerned about telling you. The experience was so astounding that I couldn't find the words to convey it to you. So tonight..."

"...this morning," he corrected.

"This morning I could wait no longer."

THE MOUNTAINS CALL MY NAME

I reached over and took the little key on the red ribbon and held it tight in my hand.

"I'm scared, Daniel."

"Do you want me to do it?" he said tenderly.

"Yeah, I think I do."

He took the key and put it into the lock on the front of the box. He handled it as if it were a sacred artifact. It turned silently in the lock.

"It's open," I exclaimed to Daniel.

"Now, all I have to do is lift the lid," he said, looking directly into my eyes.

"I know," I replied. We need a drum roll or something," I said, smiling through my nervousness.

"I feel like I'm a tomb raider or something," he said, returning my smile.

Inside, on top of some papers, laid a letter with my name on it. He gently lifted it out of the box and handed it to me. It wasn't sealed, just tucked inside the back part. I slipped the flap out, took the letter out and unfolded it. I recognized it immediately as her handwriting. As she aged, her hand had become shaky, and affected her writing.

"*My Precious Elizabeth,*

"*It will soon be Christmas time. It was wonderful having you home with me over Thanksgiving. It's been a long*

THE MOUNTAINS CALL MY NAME

time since I saw you happy. Daniel sure lit up your face. You're moving on and that is so good. I'm sorry I didn't tell you how sick I was when you was in. I just couldn't ruin your happy days. I've kept things from Daniel about what was happening with me, but I thought it would get better, but it just got worse. I feel like I need to get this down before I get too sick to rite. So I set down and rote things you shoulda knowed. If you're reading this, then I have gone on to be with Jesus."

I wiped the tears from my eyes so I could see the words. Daniel reached over to the side table and handed me a tissue, and I continued reading.

"Daniel, I hope you will fergive me fer making you be the one to tell her about her mama. I just couldn't. I'm so sorry. I kept this on my heart fer her hole life but not fer me, fer her. I just couldn't have her feel bad growing up. I put you through so much and again. I'm sorry but there weren't no one else I could trust.

"In the bottom of this box you will find a gold locket. Your grandmother gave it to your father the day we picked you up. She said the day might come and we...we...

"I can't make out that word. Can you?" I said, holding the letter up for Daniel to see.

"Let's see," he said, rereading the section I had just read. "I think she means would, instead of woud."

"You're right." I continued.

"woud want you to see it. Inside is a picture of your mother. Her name is Rose Ann Ross.

"Ross was her name. We have a name to go hunt.

THE MOUNTAINS CALL MY NAME

"*She died giving birth to you at age 17. Your birth certifcate is in the box. I arranged for you to have one after I got you. Since your daddy was your real daddy he filled in all the things they needed. The last I knowed about your grandmother she was in West Virginnie. I think the name of the place was Craggy Rock. Her name was either Rachel or Ruth. I'm sorry, years have kinda fogged my mind some. I never seen or spoke to the woman. If you want to find her, I don't have a problem with it. As you look at the picture of your mama you will see you look just like her.*"

"Oh, my goodness! You do look like her." Daniel said, holding the locket in his hand. "Here, look at this."

"*I think the good Lord did that as a punishment to your daddy. Ever time he looked at you he was reminded of the sin he done with her. God forgives but sometime we have to pay the price. Your daddy loved you child. He never blamed you for nuthin and I didn't either. I loved you from the minet I layed eyes on you. I just have a feling that Daniel will ask you to marry him one day. He is a wonderful boy, Elizabeth, I hope you say yes. I just wish I could be there to see it happen, but I don't think I will. Just take care of each other and always be faithful to each other.*

"*You will find yer daddy's wedding band in there. I kinda wanted you to give it to Daniel to wear but it ain't no fancy thing. But it is yourn to do with what you want.*

"*Well my sweet child be good to Daniel and I hope you have some purty babys. Maybe God will let me see you from heaven.*

"*I will always love you*

"*Mama*"

THE MOUNTAINS CALL MY NAME

I picked up the birth certificate and read the words that had been printed on it.

"Elizabeth Ann Edwards, mother Rose Ann Ross. Two female children, one still born, and one alive. Mother died in childbirth, no other children. Attending doctor, Ad... Here Daniel you're a doctor, see if you can make out his signature."

"Oh, no, not the dreaded doctor's signature. Let me see." He took the document from me and held it so he could get a better view. "Actually it isn't as bad as some. It looks like Adam Waterhose."

We both started laughing and couldn't stop.

"I think we're both punchy. Look again it couldn't be Waterhose." I said, still laughing. "No wonder they died."

"Waterhouse, that's what it is, it's Waterhouse. I've never heard that last name before, either." Daniel said, still laughing about the other name.

"It also says you were born in Morgantown, West Virginia. That gives us an area to look in. Let's just pray it isn't a big county. This is really a great clue, though, because we have the doctor's name. All we have to do is look in the archives in that county and see where he had his office. Then we can do our snooping in that area.

"Daniel, do you think we will be able to find her on so little information?"

"It is God that will guide us. We will both search until there is no other place to look."

THE MOUNTAINS CALL MY NAME

"Look, Daniel, this is Daddy's ring that she was talking about." I held it up between my fingers. "She wanted you to wear it."

"Let me see," he said, taking it from me.

He slipped it on his finger to see if it fit. It fit perfectly.

"I know this was special to your mother, but I could never replace the one you gave me on our wedding day. I think we can do something special with it, though. If you would trust me with it, I would like to take it."

"Of course I would," I said, taking it from him to hold.

"This is the sum of your fears, my precious Libby. There was nothing here for you to worry about. Maybe this weekend we could start looking. I'll ask Chris to hold down the fort while we're gone. What do you think of that?"

"I think you're the most precious gift God could give to me."

"Other than your life," Daniel said, pulling me close to him. He took the box from my lap and placed it on the night stand. It's been a long, long night. How about snuggling with me, and maybe we could even take a little nap."

"Are you sure napping is all you want to do?" I asked, sliding down under the covers close to him.

THE MOUNTAINS CALL MY NAME

"I didn't think these words would ever escape my lips, but yes, my sweet wife, all I want to do right now is sleep beside you."

"Honeymoon's over, I guess," I said, fluffing my pillow under my head.

"Honeymoon's just resting, we have the whole day to stay in bed if we want to, it's Saturday."

It was only a few minutes until I heard his deep breathing. He still had his arm over me holding me close to him. This was the way he went to sleep every night. I'm sure if I had moved it would have awakened him, so I just laid still and let my mind wander over the past few hours.

I held Daddy's ring in my hand. I wondered what Daniel had in mind to do with it. I pressed it to my lips. Did he wear this ring the night I was conceived; this ring that was a token of eternal devotion. Could one be so easily pulled into adultery? I looked at my own ring, knowing in my heart that it would stay pure forever. I guess Mama felt that sure one time, too. Then the gold turned to brass, but the blood of Christ turned it back to gold. Mama had asked me to not hate him. If I hadn't taken my trip to heaven, maybe it would be harder to forgive. My angel mother took this orphaned little girl and raised her and made her believe she was a princess. The burden she must have carried on her small shoulders. What a price sin had paid, but at least the last half of their marriage was happy.

Now my thoughts have to go from the past to the present. I have an angry, bitter grandmother somewhere in West Virginia that I have to find. Wonder what she would think of this grown woman she handed so carelessly to another? Maybe she had mellowed over the years. Perhaps she has gotten saved by now. Maybe she would even be glad I have come to find her. I know our steps are ordered by the hand of God.

I loved these times when I could lie in Daniel's arms. He had become my protector, my lover, my best friend, and ordained by God to be mine. How could I be blessed twice with such love? I felt the arm Daniel had stretched over me relaxing as he went into a deeper sleep. I felt myself relaxing, slipping into dreamland with him.

Part Two

Chapter Three

Daniel and I got the things from Mama's house that I had requested. Mandy and I got Jonathan's christening gown and bonnet washed and put away. Some day, I thought, if God gives me a child, I would like to have him or her to be dedicated to the Lord in this little outfit. A new week had come and almost gone. Daniel and I had planned the trip we would make to West Virginia. We had planned to go as soon as he got off work that day. He was hoping to be a little early, but we know how doctors' offices are. I had everything packed and ready to put into the car. We would stay overnight somewhere on the way. The weather forecasters said it was supposed to be a beautiful spring weekend, with the promise of sun with no rain. We had located Morgantown, but didn't see Craggy Rock anywhere. Daniel had mapped out the route he would take. It was up in the northern part of West Virginia, so it would take a few hours to get there. He said we would stop and ask people about the area we were looking for there.

I was so excited I could hardly contain myself. He called from the office and said he was on his way. Mandy had fixed us a small picnic supper that we could eat on the way. I felt like a kid at Christmas time. I was in the bathroom when he came home.

THE MOUNTAINS CALL MY NAME

"Hello, anyone home?" he said, as he came into the bedroom.

"Here I am," I said, coming out of the bathroom.

"Umm, you smell so good," he said, planting a kiss on my lips.

"I just finished taking a shower and fixing my hair and makeup."

"Darn, just a few minutes earlier and we could have showered together," he said, pulling me closer.

"We don't have time for hanky panky. We have a trip to make."

"There's always time for hanky panky," he said, nuzzling my neck.

"Okay, I'm going to go take a shower. I think I need one right now," he said, moaning as he went.

By the time he got out of the shower, I had already put our suitcases and picnic lunch in the car. I went up to the bedroom just as he was finishing.

"Umm...come here you smell so good," I said to him.

"Stay away from me. You had your chance," he said, holding me at arms length.

"I bet you'll change your mind later."

THE MOUNTAINS CALL MY NAME

"You're probably right," he said, pulling me in his arms for a long kiss.

"I have everything in the car ready to go," I said, leading the way down the stairs.

"If I don't miss my guess, you're awfully excited. It's good to see you so happy," he said as he followed me.

"You make me happy, Dr. Scott. You've helped me face a lot of fears. There is no fear in this only adventure."

"Maybe we'll find her this weekend, maybe not," he said.

"Are you feeling lucky?" I asked him.

"Not today," he said, smiling at me.

"I didn't mean *that* kind of lucky. I meant like really lucky."

"Oh, you mean that kind of luck. Yeah, I feel lucky. I tell you something that's better than lucky, and that is being blessed. We've prayed about this, and I think God will answer, if not this weekend then we'll go again."

"I know we're blessed. Every day I have with you I'm blessed."

We were finally on the road at four o'clock. It was a beautiful afternoon. The time had changed, and the days were longer. Things were beginning to bloom and the leaves were putting out.

THE MOUNTAINS CALL MY NAME

"Honey, I called about the mobile thing. They said we could order it. They said it will take a few weeks, but we get to pick out all the things we want in it. They said they have equipped several of them to be used in the field. I want you to help me and Chris pick out and design the thing. We've also found a federal connection that will subsidize part of the money because we are going to be using in it in Appalachia."

"What did Chris think about the idea?" I inquired.

"He was real excited. He was wondering how we would work out the schedule, since I will still be at the clinic. I told him we would figure out all the details later."

"Did you tell him I was going to be your nurse?" I said, smiling.

"Yeah, he couldn't believe his ears. He said he would rather have you in the office with him than in the other place. He said you actually belonged in the ICU area. That you were an excellent nurse."

"I didn't know he paid that much attention. We nurses felt so used sometimes."

"Believe me, sweetie, we noticed."

"He also said you need to come in for a checkup. You're long overdue."

"I'm doing great," I returned.

"But he just wants to be sure. You were terribly ill."

"Daniel, I was thinking, since the money is coming from the sale of mine and David's house, do you think we could dedicate the mobile in his memory?"

"Sure, but I don't think I could stand seeing his name on the side of it all the time. Can you understand that? I think I could go with a plaque or something."

"I'm sorry, Daniel. That was thoughtless of me. We don't have to do anything like that."

"Don't be sorry, after all, that's why we'll have one isn't it, because he died"

"What I was thinking is that we might go to community centers or churches and have someone preset the appointments. At least they could tell people we're in the area, and when. If we found some that were real sick we could send them to the local hospital for further testing."

"You've really thought this through, haven't you?"

"Yeah," I said smiling at him, "I've been working on it."

"I tell you what, you make the plans and then you can meet with me and Chris and we'll all go over it together."

"You mean you trust me enough to design this thing?"

"Why shouldn't I? You're a brilliant woman. You need a chance to show what you can do. I think you know exactly what you're doing."

THE MOUNTAINS CALL MY NAME

"It makes me feel good that you trust me."

"I think you could order all the supplies and Chris and I could take care of ordering the medicine. We should be pretty well set up."

"I'm so excited about this, Daniel. Just think that you and I will be working together to make a difference to these people."

"I think some of the pharmaceutical companies might donate some of the medicine."

"That would be great," I exclaimed.

"You caught my dream didn't you?" he said, reaching for my hand.

"When you first mentioned me coming back here, I couldn't believe you were even asking me that question. I was kind of offended that you would want me to come back after all the years we fought to leave it."

"It was hard for you to understand that, wasn't it?"

"Very much so."

"Isn't it amazing how God puts things together?"

"I'm hungry. How about some of that food Mandy made?"

We traveled on for three hours and decided to spend the night at a hotel. We would finish our trip in the morning. Hotels were few and far between, so we decided to take the next one we came to, as long as it wasn't a flea bag. Daniel spotted a Holiday Inn and pulled in. He went to register while I sat in the car. He was soon back with our key and we went to find our room.

"I got us a king size bed," he said, taking the suitcase out of the car trunk. "I don't know why I did. I think a twin would be sufficient. We don't get that far away from each other," he said, grinning at me. "But it's there in case we need it."

"I guess we could roll from side to side." I said, returning his smile.

The room seemed a little cramped with the king size bed, but was nice enough. We went to the restaurant that was in the hotel, and ate a late-night snack. After getting back into the room we undressed and climbed into the big bed. He turned the T.V. on and I cuddled up in his arms. Before I knew it, I was sound asleep. I woke up early in the morning with the T.V. blaring. Daniel was sound asleep; as usual, he was curled up close to me. I found the remote under the sheet and turned it off.

I eased myself out of bed to go to the bathroom and made my way back to the bed in the dark. I tried to quietly slip back under the cover so I wouldn't wake him. As I slipped under the cover, he reached for me and instinctively pulled me close to him.

"I love you," he whispered in a sleepy voice, as he drew me even closer.

"I love you, too," I whispered back to him.

THE MOUNTAINS CALL MY NAME

David was the opposite of Daniel. He wanted all his space and couldn't stand to have arms or legs thrown over him. He loved to be cuddled, but not while he was sleeping. I loved feeling Daniel's closeness as I drifted off to sleep. I sighed deeply and drifted into a dreamless slumber.

We didn't have a wakeup call on purpose. Daniel had to be up and out very early in the morning to do his rounds at the hospital and to get to the clinic for regular hours. It was always good to sleep in for a while. We had a late breakfast at the hotel restaurant and hit the road. We were still a ways from Morgantown. The day was sunny and lovely but the air was still cold enough that we had to wear jackets.

We talked most of the way about the new medical mobile we were planning. Daniel told me he was planning to put a small surgical suite in the very back of the trailer, just in case there were some small procedures he could perform there. The more we talked, the more excited I became.

"You know you're going to have to get your license to practice in Virginia, don't you?" Daniel asked.

"Yeah, I've been thinking about that. I was wondering if I will have to take some classes to get caught up on procedures," I inquired.

"Honey, if there's anything you need to know I'll teach you," he said, smiling at me.

"Are you being condescending to me? I have flashbacks to my childhood and you always having to be the doctor."

"Would you like to be a doctor?" he implored.

"No thanks, when would we ever see each other? I'll settle for being your nurse."

"How prophetic our childhood was. Could we have ever dreamed it would be reality?"

With the conversation, it seemed no time until we were at the town limits of Morgantown. Daniel planned to stop at one of the older stores and ask one of the locals if they knew of a place called Craggy Rock. I was hoping our search would be profitable.

We saw a store not far from the city limits. I went in with Daniel so I could get a soft drink. The workers behind the counter seemed too young to remember anything very far back in history.

"Hi, we're looking for a place that is supposed to be in the area, it's called Craggy Rock. Would you happen to know where it is?"

"No, I don't think I have ever heard of it," the young girl said. "I haven't lived here long. Maybe somebody else could help you."

"Thank you, we'll check around town," Daniel said, taking his change from her.

"It's about time for lunch," I suggested. "Maybe we could look for one of those little family restaurants. Usually those are run by locals who would know the area."

THE MOUNTAINS CALL MY NAME

We drove through town and spotted a little restaurant called 'The Blue Plate Special'. There were four or five cars in the lot. White ruffled curtains decorated the big plate glass window. The large rocking chairs that lined the porch looked very inviting. There was half of a whiskey barrel filled with the remains of last summer's flowers.

A strap of leather with bells on it hung on the door and announced our arrival as we entered. The waitress greeted us and had us follow her to a booth that was located in front of the big window. Each table had a small juke box sitting at the back of it, and for a quarter you had a choice of a variety of country songs.

"What can I get you two to drink?" she asked.

"Do you want tea?" Daniel asked, looking at me.

"Sure, tea would be fine," I returned.

"I'll be right back. Ya'll take ya time lookin'. The specials are on the inside sheet. The vegetables are right under the specials."

"Thank you," we said in unison as we looked at our menus.

She was back in just at few minutes. After sitting down our drinks, she was poised with pen in hand, ready to take our order.

The name "Susie" was printed in large black letters on her handmade name tag. Her hair seemed to have been bleached one time too many, and was pulled up in a ponytail on top of her head. The permed curls cascaded down over her forehead.

Her nails were short and painted a bright red. Faint smears of polish were here and there around her cuticles where she had tried unsuccessfully to remove the mistakes.

Her eyes were outlined with black, and her eye lids donned a brilliant blue eye shadow. Her cheeks had vivid red rouge apples painted on each one. The deep wrinkles that formed around her mouth and eyes seemed to belie the image of youth she tried so hard to convey. When she smiled, her whole face lit up, and softened the harshness of her makeup.

My mind wandered back to my teen years. Looking at Susie reminded of all the things I worked so hard to avoid. I could see the ruggedness of what life in the mountains could do. Now my vision was tempered with kindness on those that chose, or should I say, ended up living a life of poverty. Maybe at one time I did look with disdain on the mountain people. I guess I saw the hardness of their life, and wanted an easier one for myself and my children.

I observed a seemingly happy person, despite the difficulties that the mountains had delivered. Supposedly my grandmother didn't fair so well, if my dream or vision held any truth to it at all. The roughness became a dagger in her heart that slowly and surely killed her spirit.

I'm one of them, I thought. My heritage and my roots started right here in this quaint little town, or somewhere close by. I was jogged from my daydreaming by the return of Susie.

THE MOUNTAINS CALL MY NAME

While she was pouring our tea, Daniel asked her about Craggy Rock.

"Excuse me, is it Susie?" he asked, looking at her name tag.

"Yep, that's me," she said proudly, looking down at her tag.

"Do you happen to know of a place around here called Craggy Rock?"

"Well now, that sounds familiar, but I just cain't seem to place it. We have all kinds of places around here stuck off in the back roads. Sometimes only the people that live there know what it is." She said laughing, "Mama's been here a lot longer'n me. Let me go ask her."

She disappeared through the swinging door at the back of the restaurant. She came bumping back through with an older grey-haired lady in tow.

"Hello, my name is Judy Watson," she said, extending her plump little hand to Daniel. "Susie says you want to know wher' Craggy Rock is?" she asked in her mountain drawl.

"That's right; do you think you can help us?" Daniel asked.

Susie came with the food we had ordered and sat it on the table in front of us wielding the platter of food with expert hands.

THE MOUNTAINS CALL MY NAME

I believe ther's a place down near a dairy farm that's called that. It aint' a very big place, but I'm sure it's the one you'll be lookin' fer."

"Would you mind giving us directions there?" Daniel asked.

"I'll go write 'em down fer ya." she said. Not waiting for a reply, she waddled back through the swinging doors.

Daniel and I ate our food. Susie made several stops by our table to make sure we were well taken care of. Toward the end of our dinner, Judy came to our table with a sheet of paper in her hand.

"Well, if I 'member right here's the directions. It's about six or seven mile down Blackbird road. You'll find that road at the end of town. Take a left at the stop light and go as far as ya can, and it'll stop, there you'll have to go right or left. Go left till ya come to a sign sayin' 'Till Farm Road'. Turn left again and about three mile down the road you'll see a little community there and that will be Craggy Rock. There might be a store or two, but not much more'n that."

"Thank you so much," Daniel said politely, taking the paper from her extended hand.

"What ya goin' there fer?" she asked.

I was taken aback a little by the directness of her question.

"We're going to look for a lady who used to run a tavern there many years ago."

583

THE MOUNTAINS CALL MY NAME

"What's her name? I used to go to the taverns some when I was younger."

"Her name is Rachel Ross, and we aren't sure what the name of the tavern is."

"There weren't all that many taverns around here, so I could name ya off a few. Maybe that would help."

"Sure," Daniel said.

"Well, there was Billy's Place, and there was The Thirsty Traveler, and Rooster Rest. They's all I recollect bein' around here. Oh, and I do 'member one more, The Waterin' Hole."

"Which one was the closest to Craggy Rock?" Daniel asked.

"I believe that would have been Rooster Rest. That was the one the coal miners used to flock to all the time. I used to go there some, and it was a rough place."

"Did you happen to know the owner's name?" I asked.

"Well, like I said, I didn't go there much, and I was much younger then. If my thinkin's right she was one rough lookin' tough talkin' lady. I guess you'd have to be to put up with them rough miners," she said with a chuckle. "But I don't 'member no name."

"Thank you, it's really nice of you to try to help us."

THE MOUNTAINS CALL MY NAME

"I hope ya find who ya lookin' fer," she said, shaking our hands.

The jangling of the bells said goodbye the same way it said hello, as we exited the restaurant.

When I got in the car I studied the directions she offered to us.

"We go straight down the street to find Black what Road?" he asked, pulling out into the street.

"Blackbird Road," I returned. After that, you turn left at the stop light and go as far as you can and then you will have to turn right or left, go left until ya come to Till Farm Road. Turn left again." I said, smiling at the way she had written the directions.

"I just need to remember to always go left and I'll always be right." he said, laughing.

After turning at the stop light in town we drove several miles and came to the dead end intersection.

"I go left, correct?"

"Correct."

"How far is it until we see this 'Till Farm road'?" he inquired.

"It doesn't say, it just says 'go until you find it'."

"That could be several hours, or five minutes," he said.

"I have a feeling it won't be very long," I said.

"The country is really pretty back in here, isn't it? Look up there at the garden on the hillside," I said, pointing out the landscape.

"To harvest, all you would have to do is let the vegetables roll down to you," he observed. "How in the world did they get a plow up there?"

"Daniel, look, we're coming to another intersection. Maybe it's Till Farm Road," I said, squinting, trying to see the road sign.

Sure enough, as we rolled toward the sign I saw the lettering and it was Till Farm Road.

"I know, another left," Daniel said as he turned the wheel. "So according to what's her name this should take us to Craggy Rock?"

"Yeah, Judy. That was her name. And that's what it says. We should go right to it."

"Or left to it," Daniel said, still laughing about the directions.

About four miles down the road we could see a few more houses than usual. I felt that we were coming into a little settlement. I saw a store coming into view.

"I think this could be it, Daniel. It seems to have a store."

THE MOUNTAINS CALL MY NAME

Daniel pulled up beside the gas pump. We both got out and went inside together. There was an elderly man behind the counter.

"Howdy, folks, what can I do you fer?" he said with a big toothless grin.

"I'd like to get some gas," Daniel said.

"Would ya like it filled up?" he asked, heading outside to the car. "And do ya need the oil checked?"

"Just fill her up and you don't have to check the oil," Daniel said.

I got Daniel and me a Coke out of the machine and proceeded down the aisle to get a candy bar for us. I took my items to the counter to purchase. By the time I had collected them, the old man had returned to the store. There was an old fashioned cash register sitting on the counter. He slowly and methodically totaled the sale.

"Will this be all?" he asked.

"We need to ask you some questions about this place."

"Fire ahead," he said, smiling at us. He turned his head slightly toward us and cupped his hand behind his ear so he could hear better.

"What is the name of this place?" I asked, as he most intently listened.

"Blake Mountain," he returned.

THE MOUNTAINS CALL MY NAME

I felt my heart sink a little.

"Could you tell us if you've heard of a place called Craggy Rock?" Daniel asked.

"Yes, indeedy," he said proudly. "You would miss it if you didn't know what ya were lookin' fer." He gave a little chuckle as he continued. "It ain't no town. It's just a spot in the road. You won't find no signs. It's just what people around here call it cause of the rocks near the coal mines. They used to do some strip minin' up there. It left the rocks bare, so they called it Craggy Rock."

"How far is it from here?" Daniel asked the little old man.

He rubbed his bearded chin while he was thinking. "It's about six miles, as the crow flies," he said.

"How far is it in people miles?" Daniel asked.

"Well, they's a workin' on the bridge that goes over Fox Creek, so it's closed. That used to be a short cut through there. But they ain't one now. So you just have to go without the short cut, and that'll take you about eight miles, 'cause you have to circle back. I could take you another way but I'm sure you'd get lost, so I won't tell that way."

"Does this road circle back, or do I have to take a turn off?"

"You'll turn off this road after about five miles. The road you want to take is Mine Shaft Road. There'll be a sign fer it, but you have to keep yer eyes open. It's right after you cross over this big hill. You'll come right up on it, real quick."

"Will there be any place where we might ask for directions once we get there?" I asked.

"If I 'member right there'll be a store like mine, and maybe a small rester'nt where ya can eat a bite."

"Maybe we better get some more snack food in case we can't find this place. We might get pretty hungry before we find a restaurant."

We wandered through the store, picking up various things we might like to munch on. Once we made our purchase, we walked back to the car to continue our journey.

"I didn't think he would ever get the directions out. He took us all the way by the short cut to tell us it didn't work," I said, smiling at Daniel.

"One thing we know we don't want to do is go over Fox Creek," Daniel said.

"Definitely not Fox Creek," I added, smiling at him.

We drove over several hills, thinking each one may have the illusive Mine Shaft Road on the other side. Daniel had tuned in some music on the radio and we were enjoying that. The scenery was beautiful and changed at every turn in the road. There were tiny houses with monster TV dishes in the yards. It seemed in this poverty stricken area that these expensive satellite receivers were a necessity of sorts. There wasn't much to brighten their dreary lives, I guess. Maybe the TV shows they watched carried them to a place away from their pain and misery, and the sacrifice seemed somehow worth it.

"A penny for your thoughts," Daniel said, reaching over to squeeze my hand.

"I was just thinking about these people. What they must go through living in poverty and squalor. What kind of dreams do they have; what hope and aspirations do they have? What do the young people do with their lives?" I answered.

"Those are worth more than a penny." He returned. "To answer your question, they have dreams just like we did, and do. Some are very wise and intelligent. Their dialect and dress sometimes makes us think they aren't. We were cut from the same cloth, sweetheart."

"I know, but some get out of poverty, and some don't. What makes the difference?"

"That's a million dollar question. If I had the answer, I would be a *very* rich man."

"Maybe they don't see themselves as being in poverty," I stated.

"I never knew what poverty was. We always had whatever we wanted. Maybe God blessed us because he used Mom and Dad to help supply the needs of the community. They were so freehearted with everyone, and in turn, the customers responded by being faithful to pay back what was extended to them."

"We grew up in a wonderful place, didn't we, Daniel?"

THE MOUNTAINS CALL MY NAME

"As I get older and wiser I can see more clearly what I had growing up. I never was made to feel superior to anyone. Mom and Dad never acted like that to anyone. I thought everyone grew up with maids until I was older."

"You never made me feel like you had more than I did."

"Maybe it was because I didn't think I did.

"Did I ever tell you how we came to have Charlotte and Mandy?"

"No, I don't think you ever did."

"Mom told me this after I was grown. Charlotte was a young woman in her twenties when she got pregnant out of wedlock and her family disowned her. She came by the store one day, hungry and with no place to go. Mama got to questioning her and finally learned the story. She took Charlotte home with her that day and gave her a place to live and took care of her while she had her baby. Unfortunately she lost her baby at birth. Mom told her she could continue to live with her as long as she wanted to. All that she wanted in return was someone to help her care for the household while she ran the store. A deal was made, and Charlotte became one of our family. She was like a mother to me."

"How did Mandy come into the picture?"

"That's a sad story, too. Her mom and dad were killed in a house fire. A neighbor happened by and rescued Mandy from the house but couldn't save her mom and dad. There weren't any relatives in the area to take her in. The story was circulated around the store. Mom just couldn't stand the thought of no one wanting this girl. She talked it over with Dad and Charlotte about her coming to live with us. She was about twelve at the time. So after the family meeting it was decided that Mandy would become part of our family, too. Mandy became the child Charlotte lost. She mothered her and cared for her. I don't know who needed who more, Charlotte or Mandy."

"And I thought you were just spoiled," I said, shaking my head.

"That just goes to show what happens when you assume things. What we did was give two precious people a life. They always had the opportunity to go or stay. We never held them at our place. But they loved us, and we them. Charlotte and Mandy wielded a heavy hand where I was concerned. I didn't get by with anything. I respected their authority, and if I hadn't, Mom would have set me straight."

"We were doomed from the start, Daniel. My mother took this little stranger in to rear as her own. And your mom and dad took people in to give a home and job to. We inherited this need to help these people. God knew when He took us away that He would bring us back. We were destined to come back for these wonderful people. I wouldn't doubt that our moms prayed us back here."

"You were a stubborn little thing. God almost had to knock you in the head to get you back here."

"You forget, He did knock me in the head," I said, laughing.

"You're right, how could I forget that?"

THE MOUNTAINS CALL MY NAME

"When God lifted the shades from my eyes so I could see, it saddened my heart. Mama died because she was embarrassed to tell you she was bleeding. There are hundreds of people just like her that are ashamed of the things happening to them. We need to educate them some way. I'm hoping the medic mobile will help them."

"I love you more all the time. I never thought that would be possible, but it is. I can't believe it sometimes how God not only gave me my first love, but also placed in her the same dreams I have," he said tenderly.

We had just crested another hill and were headed down the other side when it dawned on me we had just passed Mine Shaft Road.

"There it was, Daniel; it's the road we're looking for," I exclaimed.

"I'll find a place to turn around and we'll head back," he said, slowing the car.

He got the car headed back up the hill to the turn off. It seemed such an odd place to have a road. It looks like the builder could have placed it at the bottom of the hill instead of the top," I said.

"You'll turn right from this direction," I reminded him.

"No kidding, I wouldn't have known that if you hadn't told me," he said, teasing me.

He slowed the car to exit onto Mine Shaft Road.

593

"I guess from here on out we don't know exactly what we'll find," he said.

"What do you think the chances are of finding her on our first try?" I said wistfully.

"I don't know," he said, taking my hand in his. "But if we don't this time, we'll keep looking."

We had driven about three miles when we saw a gas station looming on the horizon. It looks like we'll get to investigate some more.

The area we entered into was a little more populated than the area we came from. The houses were rundown and shabby looking.

We entered the station and approached the counter where and older lady was sitting.

"Hiedy," she said in a warm and friendly voice. "What can I do fer ya?"

"We're looking for a place called Craggy Rock. Do you happen to know where that is?"

"Yer standin' in it, or what's left of it," she said with a chuckle.

"We're looking for a lady that used to live here. Her name is Rachel Ross. She used to run a tavern. There was a lady in Morgantown that said there used to be a tavern here called Rooster Roost," I said.

"I think ya mean Rooster Rest," she said, smiling at Daniel.

THE MOUNTAINS CALL MY NAME

"What ya want to know fer?" she asked, squinting at us, as if to size us up. "Is she in trouble?"

"No, I'm a relative of hers and would like to see her," I answered.

"I reckon the onliest ones that would want to see her would be kin. I don't reckon she has many of 'em left. Ya sure she ain't in no trouble?"

"I'm sure."

"I don't want to get her riled up at me. Ya don't want to be on the wrong side of Rachel. I figgered she done run off all the people that would of keered fer her. She was a hard woman, she was. Didn't have a kind word fer nobody.

"I guess I'm one."

"Rachel ruled that old tavern with an iron hand. She's the onliest one that ever run that place."

"How well did you know her?" I inquired.

"Ya sure ya ain't the FBI or sumthin'? she asked again.

"No, honestly I am her relative," I said, smiling at her.

She seemed to relax as she talked. "I figgered she done run off anybody that was a kin to her."

"And you don't know where she lives?" I asked.

"I know 'xactly wher' she lives. She wanders in sometimes, but she don't say much. She's gettin' purty old, and cain't get around much, but you still don't want to get her riled up. She can cut ya sixty ways to Sunday, and spit on ya as she walks away," she said, still keeping a keen eye on me.

"I ain't never been to her place. Only one person I know of goes to see her. She lives way back in the woods somewher' purty close.

"She used to have a friend named Hazel Jones that lived up in Spring Holler."

"How do we find her?" Daniel asked.

"I might need to give her a holler and see if she's still close to her. Let me go in the back room and see if I can find her phone number in the phone book. I'll be back, Ya'll make yerselves at home," she said, leaving the room.

"Daniel, we're getting so close," I said excitedly.

"Don't get your hopes up too high. Okay?"

"Okay. I'll try not to, but it's going to be hard to do."

It seemed like we waited forever before she returned.

"Well, I talked to her and she agreed to meet ya. She said she don't know if she will be able to help ya or not."

"Where do we meet her?" Daniel inquired.

"Well, ya just keep goin' down this road your on and she will be out at her mail box. You won't be able to miss her. She said to tell ya she'll have a yeller dress on."

"Straight down the road, yellow dress," Daniel said to make sure he had the right directions.

"Yep, right straight down the road."

"Thank you so much," we said as we left her quaint store.

"I love it," Daniel said, chuckling. "The directions she gave are so unique. Keep you eye out for the little lady in a yellow dress."

We drove a short distance down the road, and true to her word, there stood a small-framed lady dressed in yellow standing at - you guessed it, the mail box. Daniel slowed to a stop where she was standing.

"Hello," I said after rolling down my window.

"Hiedy, are ya'll the ones I'm supposed to meet?"

"I guess we are. We're looking for Rachel Ross."

"Don't nobody look fer Rachel. Who might ya be?"

"Well, it's a long story, but I'm her granddaughter."

"She ain't never mentioned no grandchild."

"I know, I only found out myself a short while ago."

THE MOUNTAINS CALL MY NAME

"Would ya'll like to come in and visit awhile?"

"Sure," Daniel said.

"Come and park your car down by the house," she said, motioning in that direction.

Daniel slowly pulled our car down the little dusty drive to her house. By the time we had parked and had emerged, she was waiting for us on the front porch.

"You children come on in."

Daniel and I made our way into her humble living room. Everything was neat and in order. She was such a gracious little lady.

"Y'all can call me 'Hazel'. What can I call you?"

"Excuse us for not introducing ourselves earlier. I'm Daniel Scott and this is my wife, Elizabeth," he said as we extended our hands to her.

"Can I offer ya'll a glass of tea or sumpthin'?"

"No, we're fine," Daniel and I answered in unison.

"Well, tell me about how ya come to know Rachel."

"I just learned from my mother on her death bed that the one I called 'Mama' all my life was not my real mother. My mother died giving birth to me. She was Rachel Ross's daughter."

"I knowed Rachel when Rose died. She was real quiet about the whole thing. At first she told me Rose had a baby and they both died during the birth, but she never mentioned there was another baby. Not at first, anyway."

"I understand she had twins and one died and one lived. I'm the one that lived (of course). My father, the one that fathered us girls, was a miner here and I guess he got drunk at the tavern one night and that's when he got with her daughter, Rose."

"I didn't know for a long time that Rose was in the family way. It was when she died that Rachel came to me and wanted to know if I had any burial land. I thought for a long time that Rose had gone to live with an aunt somewhere in Norf Ca'liner. Then I found out she was here all the time. Rachel kept her shut up in the back room. It was then my heart broke fer that little girl."

"How did you find out about how she was treated?"

"Stories get around, and I think the midwife was the one what told the real story. I did find out right before she was due that she was pregnant. I knowed she didn't have no doctor. I kept tellin' her to let Dr. Adam check her, but I think she was just ashamed and said the midwife could take care of her. So I let it drop. You know, you just don't go wher' ya ain't invited. Ya just got to respect other people's privacy. Anyway, she said that Rose was doin' good, and was real healthy.

The story goes that she was in labor fer about three or four days runnin'. I think the midwife just up and left when things went bad. She didn't say a word, just left that little girl in a real bad way. Rachel finally got Dr. Adam to come. His last name was Water sumthin'. We just called him Dr. Adam. When he got there, one baby was already born and dead, and you was stuck sideways in her. Rose was already dead when he got there. It was told she bled to death. So all Dr. Adam could do was get you out. He took a knife of sorts and cut you out of her stomach. Yer a miracle, that's all I can say, is yer a miracle. Like I said, I never saw you or even knowed you were in the world.

"She didn't say anything to you about a second child."

"No, she just said she needed to bury her daughter and grandchild."

"You never saw her other child?"

"No."

"Wher' did you go?" she asked, looking at me quizzically.

"My father came and took me to his home, and his wife became my mother."

"Rachel don't know you're lookin' fer her?" she inquired.

"No, I just found out not too long ago what her name was. So this hunt to West Virginia came out of some records my mother left me in a box."

"I don't 'xactly know how to tell her. What do you say to someone?"

"Well, at least she knows I didn't die. Does she have a phone?"

THE MOUNTAINS CALL MY NAME

"No, she don't."

"Well, can you take me to her?"

"Maybe I need to go see her first and tell her about ever'thing."

"I don't have much time. Daniel and I have to get back to Virginia tomorrow."

"If you could just give me today to go see her, and prepare her, that would be good. You know she ain't in real good health. I would hate to kill her with the surprise."

"I wouldn't want to kill her either, but I don't think it would. My husband is a doctor and would be ready to take care of her if something happened."

"What do ya want her fer? If ya just want to find her and ya gonna be mean to her, then I'm not sure it would be good."

"Hazel, why in the world would I be mean to her, she's the only blood family I have. I just want to get to know her."

"But because she give you away you just might jump on her fer that."

"Hazel, I can't begin to understand what happened when I was born. I know without a doubt I was raised exactly where God wanted me to be. I don't know why things happen the way they do, but I was raised to love God and to love others. My father made a terrible mistake by getting Rachel's daughter pregnant. But he lived the remainder of his life going to church and raising a Godly family. I guess he paid for his mistake over and over throughout the years."

"I didn't go up to the tavern much. I kept Rose Anne fer Rachel when she was little. Rose was three when her daddy died. He was killed in a drunken brawl at the tavern. She could never remember him.

After his death Rachel changed. She was hard, with her words and her life. She could cut ya to the bone by her words if ya done her wrong. She loved little Rose, but had a hard time showin' it. She was a good-looking little girl. She had shiny brown hair, jest like yers. Beautiful, she was. After Rose got on up in age, Rachel kept a hard hand on her and she wasn't seen much. I think all she did was go to school and come home and stay in the back room. As she got a little older, her mama let her wait on customers some."

"So you knew my mother well?"

"Oh, yes, she was a lovely little girl. She was as sweet as she could be. Her smile would light up the whole room when she walked in. Always quiet, never loud, she just evidently got caught up in drinking one night, and you were conceived. I think she was a lonely little thing."

"I guess that's why she was attracted to my father, because she was so lonely. She wasn't a bad girl was she?"

"A bad girl? Heavens, no. Not Rose Anne. She just wanted some love and affection and got it in the wrong place. How old was ya when yer Daddy took ya home?"

"Not more than two or three weeks old."

"I knowed it couldn't 'a' been too long. I don't think she coulda kept ya a secret for long. Course like I said, I didn't go up there to the tavern, but ya must 'a' been a good baby or she couldn't a kept the tavern open."

"I think that's why she was so desperate to get rid of me," I mused.

"Your mama must 'a' been an angel to take you and raise you, bein' you was the other woman's baby."

"Yes, she was an angel. I didn't know how much so until recently. The reason she kept the secret was that she was afraid I would feel like I was only here because of an accident. She also said she didn't want me to be called a... a bastard," I said hesitantly.

"No one's here because of an accident. You were created by the Master. He doesn't accidentally create something, He creates everything on purpose."

"You're a wise woman, Hazel," Daniel said.

"Do you two have children?" she asked, smiling at first one, then the other.

"No, but we're working on it. We hope to soon," Daniel replied.

"What line of work do ya'll do?" Hazel asked.

"As Elizabeth said, I'm a doctor, and she's a nurse."

I saw her eyes light up with the information Daniel had given her.

"I don't think I been this close to a real doctor before."

"You don't have a doctor?" Daniel asked.

"No, I've been blessed with good health, just an ache or two here or there. I wish I could say the same thing fer Rachel. She looks awful bad." A cloud of sadness crossed over her face as she thought of her friend.

"How did you two become friends. Was it just because you kept Rose Anne for her?"

"Nah, me and Rachel go back a ways. We were friends in school. We always were doin' things together. Those were happy days fer Rachel. She weren't always hard and bitter then. It was only after she married that she became so mean with people. I married right after she did, so we just kinda went our separate ways. I would see her around and we would talk about gettin' together, but she was busy with the tavern and my husband didn't want nuthin' to do with that place. Church people didn't hang around places like that. But me and Rachel stayed friends. I think she knew why I didn't come around."

"Where is your husband?" I asked.

"He died about twelve years ago. He had a heat stroke out in the hay field. He didn't live to say goodbye," She said wistfully.

"I'm sorry."

"I didn't remarry. So Rachel and I kinda took up a closer friendship after our husbands died. Her little Rose filled up a lot of lonely hours fer me."

THE MOUNTAINS CALL MY NAME

"Do you see her often?"

"Neither of us drive, so it's been a while since I seen her. It's been about a month since I seen her last, I reckon"

"Does she live close by?"

"Just down the road around the corner. There used to be a road goin' down to her house, but it's kinda growed up now with weeds and stuff. There's a little creek ya have to cross over with a foot bridge."

"Maybe we could go with you and wait in the car while you talk to her."

"Well, maybe, I just don't know."

"We won't go in unless you say it's okay," Daniel offered.

"Okay, let me get my coat. It's kinda chilly today."

We waited while she gathered her things and made our way out to the car. My stomach was churning with the prospect of seeing this woman. I didn't know what to feel or how to act. I tried to rehearse what I would say, but the words wouldn't come. Daniel reached over and squeezed my hand.

"You won't have to do this by yourself. I'll be right by your side," he quietly said only for my ears to hear.

"Right around this curve you will see a mail box. That's the lane to Rachel's house. I don't know if you dare drive there. You might could make it to the spot where we cross over the bridge. You could wait fer me there.

Daniel drove slowly over the rutted driveway. It was a long drive. By the time we reached the place where the foot bridge was, we could no longer see the mail box.

Across a little stream on a small rise was the house of my grandmother. It was a depilated shack that had a porch going completely across the front. There was some kind of seat that reminded me of one from a school bus. Three or four large dogs ran down to the bank of the water, growling and barking at our car. I saw a large-framed woman standing in the open doorway. Hazel was proceeding across the bridge when I heard her call out to Rachel.

"It's just me, Hazel. I came to see how you're doin'. Call yer dogs."

I heard her call out several names, and the dogs came running to her. Hazel slowly made her way up the worn path to the porch. Rachel never moved toward or away from her approaching friend. Our car was partially hidden by the overgrowth of brush and trees. I'm not sure if she saw the car, but she didn't seem to.

Daniel pulled me over to him and kissed me.

"How do you feel?" he asked, looking tenderly into my eyes.

"I feel nauseated and nervous."

"I won't let her bite you," he said, smiling at me.

"I know, it's just that this is all so unnerving." I returned his smile weakly.

It had been such a long time and still no Hazel. We listened to the radio and talked about one thing after the other. She had been in there an hour, but it seemed so much longer.

"I wonder if she has told her yet. I wonder if she's refusing to see me. Then what will I do?" I asked nervously.

"Sweetheart, you're driving yourself nuts. Just don't think about it."

"That's easy to say, but hard to do," I said, taking a deep breath.

We waited about ten more minutes before we saw Hazel cross the bridge. I got out and approached her as she was walking toward me.

"Well, she will see ya."

"What did she say?"

"It's hard to tell how she feels, she don't show much emotion. The reason I was so long I just couldn't get up my nerve. I finally just blurted it out. She said to come on over. She was going to chain the dogs."

Daniel, Hazel and I trudged across the bridge and up the hill toward the house. Rachel stood on the porch.

THE MOUNTAINS CALL MY NAME

"Ya'll come on up and have a seat," she said.

We sat down on a make-shift bench. They were indeed old bus seats. Daniel sat beside me, and Hazel sat on the far end in an old rocker. Rachel took her place directly beside mine and Daniel's. She didn't fit the description I had been given of her. She didn't look or act mean at all.

"My name is Elizabeth Anne, and this is my husband, Daniel Scott," I said, putting my hand out to shake hers.

She hesitantly took it and gave me a stiff little shake.

"So you're Rose Anne's baby," she said, clearing her throat.

"Yeah, that's what they told me. I only found out a few weeks ago."

"What do ya want from me?" Rachel said, still not looking at me.

"I don't want anything in particular. I just wanted to get to know you. You're all I have left, and I felt like I needed to find out more about the family I never knew."

"You ain't missed nuthin'. What ya see is what ya get."

She finally lifted her head and looked at me. I saw an empty shell of a woman. Her face was lined with heavy wrinkles.

THE MOUNTAINS CALL MY NAME

Ya look just like her, ya know. She had hair the same color as yers. It's been a long time since I 'llowed myself to think back. Is yer daddy dead?"

"Yes, he died a few years ago, and my mother died..." I hesitated for a moment realizing that my real mother was her daughter. "My mother died a few weeks ago. It was then that I found out she wasn't my real mother, but your daughter, Rose, was my mother."

"My daughter Rose was yer mother. For a few brief moments she was yer mother."

"She will never cease being my mother. Time doesn't alter the fact that she is who she is. I had a wonderful woman that took me and raised me as her own, but she isn't the one that gave me life, she just sustained my life. Rose would have been so happy to know this lady. She couldn't have loved me more if she had given birth to me."

"Do you want me to feel guilty for givin' you away?"

"No, I didn't come here to make you feel bad. I came here to get to know the grandmother I've never known. I would never come to make you feel bad. You did what you had to do. God made it all turn out right. I had my father. He changed after I was born. At least that's what Mama said. She said she wouldn't take me if he wouldn't quit drinking. So, true to his word, he started going to church and never drank again. He was a good man, he just ..."

"I know what he did, and it cost me my girl's life." I could hear the pain in her voice.

THE MOUNTAINS CALL MY NAME

"I know it won't bring Rose back, but the reason my dad would drink so badly was because he lost a little baby boy. He just couldn't get past the pain. He tried to run from it, but it haunted him, I guess."

"My Rose wasn't no angel. I guess they both found what they was a lookin' fer, but couldn't see the price they would have to pay."

"Do you think we could have some kind of relationship? Maybe I could come and see you, and we could get to know each other."

"Maybe, I ain't gonna promise. I don't know much about havin' family. Maybe that's why God took all of 'em away. God might take you away if ya get too close."

"Well God and I will work that out," I said, smiling at her tentatively.

"I'm tired now; if ya don't mind, I think I need to lie down," she said, getting slowly to her feet.

I guess that was the signal to say goodbye.

"Daniel and I will be in the area until tomorrow. Can I come back and see you one more time before I leave?"

"You can do whatever ya want to. It don't matter none to me."

"What should I call you?"

"I guess whatever ya want to."

THE MOUNTAINS CALL MY NAME

"Well, I guess I'll call you 'Grandma Rachel'. Would that be okay?"

"If that's what ya want."

I went to her and gave her a hug. She was stiff and awkward as I put my arms around her.

"You better go now," she mumbled.

"I'll come back tomorrow and you can tell me about my mother," I called to her as she ambled into her house.

Daniel, Hazel and I made our way back down the dirt path we had come in on. I wasn't sure what I was feeling at the moment. I don't think victory would be the word I'm looking for, maybe relief, perhaps pity.

"She seemed fairly mellow," Daniel said, patting my knee.

"I'm glad ya'll let me go in first, I think it holp some," Hazel added from the back seat.

"Well, I guess we need to go find a place to stay for the night," Daniel said.

"There's a place out on the main road. It's a small place, but it clean. I know the family that runs it. If I'm not mistaken the name of it is called the 'Midnight Serenade'," she said.

"Umm, sounds like a good place to me," Daniel said, winking at me then pursing his lips.

THE MOUNTAINS CALL MY NAME

I punched him in the ribs and laughed at him. We slowed to turn into Hazel's driveway.

"Ya'll can just let me out at the mailbox. I can walk."

"I'm already turning now. I insist on taking you to your door," Daniel said.

He got out of the car and opened her door for her.

"You're such a nice boy. I ain't never had nobody open my door fer me," she said, grinning up at Daniel with her toothless little grin.

He walked her all the way to her front door, and when he left her, she was still grinning.

"You made her day," I said to him as he got back in the car.

"I think I'm ready to take you to the 'Moonlight Serenade', and let you make my day," he said, leaning over to give me a kiss.

"You think you can handle me?" I said, smiling at him.

"I think I'd like to try, Mrs. Scott."

I always liked it when he teased with me.

"What did you think about your grandmother?"

"I'm not sure. Do you think she liked me?"

THE MOUNTAINS CALL MY NAME

"I know she did. What's not to like. She said you looked just like Rose. That's why I know she liked you."

"She felt so stiff when I tried to hug her."

"She probably hasn't been hugged in a long time, and doesn't know what to do."

"What will we talk about tomorrow?"

"Maybe she will tell you about your relatives. You might want to find out about health issues to see what runs in the family. You may be susceptible to diabetes or something. You never know."

"Yes, Dr. Scott."

"I think these curves are making me nauseated. I'm feeling a little sick to my stomach."

"Probably from all the excitement. We might need to get something to eat. When we find our hotel we'll look for a restaurant."

It didn't seem to take as long getting back to the main road as it did coming in. We followed Hazel's directions and came right to the hotel. There was a small café across the street. We registered, got our key and walked to dinner. The people there were very friendly, just like all the other places we'd been to on our trip. We ordered the Saturday special.

We talked throughout dinner about our trip thus far. It seemed our steps had been predestined. It wasn't as hard as I thought it might be to find Rachel. Having a name and place sure did help the hunt. There were a lot of things I needed, or I should say wanted, to ask my grandmother. Would she be willing to answer? I thought to myself.

After dinner I was still a little nauseated. Daniel suggested that I take an Alka-Seltzer, and proceeded to try to find some at the little drug store down the street. He asked me to rest in the car while he got something to ease my nausea.

Our hotel room was small and smelled musty. The scent of the carpet suggested that some heavy smokers had visited the room prior to us.

Daniel found a glass in the bathroom and brought the bubbling concoction to me where I was stretched out on the bed. I hated the taste of Alka-Seltzer, and shivered as I drank the last of it.

"This may help if I can keep it down. I think I'm going to go take a quick shower," I said, grabbing my train case and pajamas.

"I'll go after you, or we could shower together," he hinted.

"I don't think we would both fit, it's so small in there."

"Okay, I'll be waiting for you."

I got the water as hot as I could stand it and let it cascade down over my tired body. I let my mind wander back over the day. I still was trying to sort through my feelings of the past few hours. Before the day began I wondered what would happen when I saw her. I

THE MOUNTAINS CALL MY NAME

wondered how I would feel knowing she was my grandmother; looking at her for the first time. I also pondered about what she thought of me. I felt sorry for her in one way. She must have been a very lonely lady. Would tomorrow bring more unanswered questions or would I come away satisfied? For now I needed to get out of the shower and let Daniel have his turn.

"I was about to send a search party to hunt you," he said, smiling at me as I rounded the corner to the bedroom.

I put on my pajamas and snuggled down under the cover to wait for Daniel. I must have fallen asleep, because when I woke up it was dark and Daniel was asleep beside me. So much for the Midnight Serenade Hotel, I thought, smiling to myself. I would make it up to him tomorrow.

Tomorrow, Lord, go before me and prepare my way; I pray things will go well for both my grandmother and me.

Part Two

Chapter Four

Daniel and I slept late. There was a soft rain falling on the hotel roof and the room was darkened by the drawn curtains.

I felt his kisses on my neck as I was waking up.

"Good morning, my princess," he said, still nuzzling my neck.

"Good morning, yourself," I returned. "Sorry I fell asleep last night. I was trying to stay awake for you."

"Yeah, I hurried through my shower, just thinking about you waiting for me. And you were sound asleep," he said in mock disappointment.

"I'm sorry. I'm not a very good wife am I?" I said, turning over to face him.

"I guess I'll have to trade you in for a new one." he teased.

"Please, Dr. Daniel, I promise not to fail again."

"Okay, one last chance, but if you fail me again you're a goner," he said, pulling me to him.

THE MOUNTAINS CALL MY NAME

It didn't take me long to respond to his arduous ovations. Our departure could wait awhile longer, I thought, as I snuggled even closer to him.

At breakfast I felt the nagging nausea return. I hoped I wasn't coming down with something. I managed to eat breakfast and it seemed to settle everything down.

We made plans for our last day there. We calculated that we could head back home late in the afternoon and still get home at a decent hour. It was almost eleven by the time we finished breakfast. We figured Grandma Rachel would be up and about by the time arrived. We headed back down the winding roads we traveled the day before. The twist and turns in the highway seemed to bring back the reoccurring nausea.

"You look a little green, are you okay?"

"I've never had problems with car sickness before, but the curves sure do seem to bother me today," I said, holding my hand on my stomach."

Tell me if you need to stop. I'm a little concerned. I remember the last time we went through with the nausea thing. Is your head hurting?" he asked, with concern rising in his voice.

"No, no headache this time, just this queasiness. Eating seemed to help though."

I think there are some crackers in the basket that Mandy packed. Let me stop the car and see. I know

617

crackers help morning...morning sickness," he said more slowly.

We suddenly looked at each other with full realization of what might be wrong. My breath caught with excitement.

"Do you think we could be pregnant?" he asked, grinning from ear to ear. "When did you have your last period?" he questioned.

"Well, let me think," I said, my mind trying to calculate the last time I had a period. "Let me see, if I'm right, I *am* late, but I do this sometimes. But I don't usually have the nausea, but it could be the curves in the road."

"And you had it last night and this morning."

"Yeah, but let's not get our hopes up yet. Maybe it's just the curvy roads."

He pulled over to the side of the road and stopped the car. He went to the trunk and retrieved the crackers and a soda we had in the cooler.

"Libby, let me get excited," he said, as he opened my car door. Just think, you could be carrying our baby right now."

"I just don't want you to get your hopes up and my not be pregnant."

We instinctively put our hands over my stomach. We just couldn't keep the smiles from our faces. He pulled me to him and kissed me.

THE MOUNTAINS CALL MY NAME

"Tomorrow you're coming to my office and we are going to find out for sure."

"But for right now, we need to go see my grandmother."

It was around 12:30 when we arrived back at her little cottage. The dogs were still on the loose running up and down the creek bank barking at us. I could see Grandma Rachel standing on the porch as we exited the car.

"Come on boys, get back under the porch," she hollered at the dogs. They obeyed like loyal soldiers.

When they were safely under the porch, Daniel and I started over the little foot bridge.

"Come on up to the house, they ain't gonna bite. They jest like to bark."

I could have sworn I saw a little smile at the corner of her mouth.

There was still a slight drizzle in the air. Fog shrouded the surrounding mountain. I felt in my heart of hearts that today would be a good day.

She stood at the porch railing as we walked up the dirt path. I saw a toilet peeping out from behind the house, so I assumed she didn't have a bathroom. We walked up the rickety old porch steps. Daniel had a firm grip around my waist.

THE MOUNTAINS CALL MY NAME

"Be careful with your step; we don't want you to have any accidents," he said softly, smiling at me. "The first trimester is the trickiest."

"Daniel, we don't know yet."

"But I don't want you hurt either."

"You two come on in the house. It's kinda' chilly out today. I've got a fire a goin' in the stove," she said, leading the way into her little home.

When I walked in, it reminded me of Bessie's house the night we went up for her viewing. It hit me fully as we entered the room. I took off my sweater and held it in my lap. She motioned for Daniel and me to sit on the sofa. Thank God, it was at the far corner, away from the stove.

She was the first to break the awkward silence.

"I didn't think I would ever see ya again. I told ya goodbye the day ya left and that was that."

"Did you ever wonder about me, Grandma Rachel?"

"Oh, I wondered about ya all my life. I couldn't let myself get too caught up in it though. It hurt too bad. Fer when I would think of you, I would think of my little Rose."

"I felt yer Daddy would love ya, he seemed like a decent man."

"I wanted to tell you my mother named me after your daughter. She asked my daddy what my mother's name was and she said it was only right that I carried on a small part of her. I don't know if I could have done the same if I were in her shoes."

"Ya musta' had a good mama to do that."

"I had a wonderful mother. You see what happened was, Mama and Daddy had a little boy. He was just a few months old. Daddy ran away from his pain to West Virginia and Mama was left behind. He buried his pain in a bottle, and Mama took hers to the Lord. I was born out of his loneliness and pain. He found solace in Rose. I can't apologize for him, but I can say he turned out to be a good man."

"Rose was lonely, too. I guess I kept too tight a grip on 'er. I was afraid she would turn out wild, and I kept her holed up in the back of the tavern, and it happened anyway. She was a beautiful girl. I guess she took after her daddy. He was a looker, he was. He had a tough time with the bottle and it ended up killing 'im,"

"I'm so sorry you lost so much. It must have been very painful."

"I tried to push it all to the back of my mind, but it didn't stay there."

"I wish I could have been there for you over the years, but as it was I didn't know who you were."

"I was cursed all my life. I was meant to be lonely and sad. It came because I operated the tavern. My grandmother told me no good would ever come of me because I put the bottle to people's mouth. I guess she was right. All I ever knowed was pain and suffering."

THE MOUNTAINS CALL MY NAME

"It doesn't have to be like that always," I assured her.

"It's too late fer me. I'm gonna' die here a lonely old woman."

"You don't have to stay a lonely person. There's got to be some joy that will come your way."

"I had some joy yesterdey when you came to see me. You look so much like Rose. It took me aback how much. I thought fer a minute I was seein' a ghost."

"No, I'm for real, and if you'll let me, I would like to be the granddaughter to you that I am. Your giving me away didn't change the fact that I'm your family."

"You're the only family I have. I don't have another livin' soul to call mine," she said, wiping at her face.

I could tell she was embarrassed at the unbidden tears that were falling down her cheeks.

"I fixed ya'll a little bite of dinner if ya want some."

She got up and headed to the kitchen. Daniel and I followed her. She had three plates set at the small dining table in her kitchen. She had fried some chicken, and I could see it piled in a platter on the counter. She made her way around the kitchen, putting things into dishes. She had green beans and mashed potatoes, and some corn-on-the-cob. I could see a pan of cornbread sitting on the back of the stove.

THE MOUNTAINS CALL MY NAME

"It's so nice of you to fix lunch for Elizabeth and me. We really appreciate it. Elizabeth was just commenting on the fact food might settle her stomach."

"Are ya with child, Elizabeth?" she asked pointedly.

"Well," I said smiling, "I don't know. I have to have a checkup when I get back home and I'll know for sure. Daniel sure hopes so."

"Make sure ya have a doctor. I learned my lesson with Rose," she said sadly.

"I'll see to that," Daniel interjected.

"Did I 'member ya sayin' you were a doctor?"

"Yes, that's right. Elizabeth and I grew up together in Virginia. Then she went away to become a nurse and I went away to become a doctor and here we are at your doorstep."

"You listen to him," she said, looking at me.

"I will," I said, smiling at him.

"Is there anything I can help you do?" I asked as she piddled around the kitchen.

"No, I have everything under control," she returned.

"Are you sure? I really don't mind."

623

THE MOUNTAINS CALL MY NAME

"Well, if ya really want to you can put the food on the table. That would help."

"I can help, too," Daniel said.

"No, you just stay put. We'll wait on you." She returned.

We had an enjoyable dinner. I tried not to think about how clean her cooking was. I figured God would take care of everything and not let me get sick.

It was getting late and by the time we finished dinner and I helped her with the dishes it was time to leave.

"Grandma, it's time for us to go, but we'll be back to see you real soon."

She reached out to me for the first time. I felt her give a little this time when I placed my arms around her. We had a lot of time to make up and we wouldn't do it in one day. We bade her goodbye and made our way down the footbridge to our car. She had even given Daniel a hug goodbye.

We turned around, and were headed back to the world we came from. But I wouldn't return the same. My grandmother had become an integral part of our lives now. We would make sure we didn't forget her. She gave Daniel and me Hazel's phone number and said if we ever needed her, Hazel would get a message to her.

Part Two

Chapter Five

I was at Daniel's office early on Monday morning to visit with Dr. Roger Stanley, the new gynecologist. I don't know who was more excited, Daniel or me. I had continued the nausea and still hadn't seen a period. My appointment was for 10:00 o'clock. I arrived a little early so I could see Daniel before I went in.

"Honey, we should have the test results soon. I'd be willing to bet money that you are pregnant, if I was a better, that is," Daniel said, patting my tummy.

"Would you like to go have this pelvic exam?" I asked him.

"No, I don't think I can help you there, but I'll pray for you while you're in there.

"You don't mind my being examined?" I teased him.

"No, not from a doctor's point of view, but I would mind if it was Chris, since we are such good friends, and he wants to marry you if I die. Yeah, I would mind if Chris was doing a pelvic."

THE MOUNTAINS CALL MY NAME

"You silly man, what if Chris was the only one here?"

"I guess I would just have to get over it."

"Well, it's time for me to go. I'll see you in just a few minutes." He kissed me and told me to go find out about our baby.

Dr. Stanley was both very young and professional. If he was ill at ease because Daniel was my husband, it didn't come across in the exam.

"Well it feels like you're pregnant. Your uterus seems to be a little larger than the time frame you've given me. Could it be possible you're further along than you think?"

"That's one thing I'm quite sure of. Daniel and I married Valentine's Day and he's the only man in my life."

"I didn't realize you had just gotten married. I didn't mean to imply that..."

"I was just teasing you."

"Is there a problem with the early enlargement?"

"No problem, it could and I want to stress *could* mean that you're carrying more than one."

I took a sharp intake of air.

"You're kidding, aren't you?"

"No, I wouldn't kid you about this."

After finishing a pap test, he told me to get dressed and he would meet me back in his office. When I arrived, Daniel was already there.

"Have you told him anything?" I asked Dr. Stanley.

"No, I was waiting for you to join us. You tell him," he said, smiling at me.

"They're going to do a urine test to make sure, but he really thinks we are going to have a baby."

"And what else?" Dr Stanley said, raising his eyebrows at me.

"Is something wrong?" Daniel asked, suddenly concerned.

"I want you to tell him," I said, looking at Dr. Stanley.

"Will *someone* tell me?"

"Like I was telling her, I'm not totally sure, but from my exam, her uterus seems to be a little larger than it should be for the time frame we're talking about. Think, Daniel…" he said, smiling.

"Oh, my God! Twins, it could be twins?" He grabbed my hand and his mouth fell open. For once the good doctor was speechless.

"We'll know more when we can hear heartbeats. But I just want you to know it still could be just one. What am I doing? I'm sitting here telling this to a doctor that does this every day," he said, laughing at himself.

"Are you okay? Is she okay? He redirected his question to Dr. Stanley.

"She is in perfect health. She needs to get vitamins and rest; you know how to take care of her, doctor," he said, smiling at Daniel.

"I can't believe this, two..." Daniel exclaimed.

Dr. Stanley got up from his chair and came around to where we were sitting.

"I've got another patient I have to see. You can use my office to regroup. You know, Daniel, I didn't say twins, what I said was it could be more than one." He patted Daniel on the back and walked out of the room, not waiting for his last comment to hit Daniel and me.

"I'm just letting the word 'twins' sink in, but what if it were three?"

"Oh, man, was I ever thrown for a loop. I was all ready for the pregnant thing, but I didn't let myself think multiples," Daniel said in shocked disbelief.

"We've got to remember, he said 'could be', not 'is'."

"Yeah, we need to hang onto that thought. What if it is? Are you okay with that?" Daniel asked me tenderly.

"I was barren for so long, whatever God gives me, I will be happy with. I have a wonderful husband that will take care of me," I said, leaning over to kiss him.

THE MOUNTAINS CALL MY NAME

We heard a light tap on the door. His nurse poked her head into the room.

"Dr. Scott, you have a patient that is ready to be seen in room five."

"I'll be right there," he said to her. "I've got to go, baby, but stick around and we'll talk in just a minute. I hate to leave you," he said, pulling me into his arms. He kissed me warmly and tenderly.

The nurse had left the door ajar and Chris entered the room catching us off guard.

"That's not allowed during office hours. I've told him over an over not to hit on our patients," he said, laughing at Daniel.

"Hey, Chris, it's good to see you," I said, giving him a hug.

"Since you're here, Mrs. Scott, I need to see you in my office. You're long overdue."

"I hope those words don't ring true," Daniel and I said, laughing.

"What did I say?" Chris asked.

"'Long overdue', I hope those aren't prophetic words. You tell him, Daniel."

"We just found out you're going to be an uncle, Chris."

"No way! Congratulations. When will you be due?"

"Sorry, I forgot to tell you that important information. We got sidetracked on another issue," Dr. Stanley said, entering the room.

We all said in unison, "When?"

"If what Elizabeth tells me is true, and I don't doubt that, and I emphasize, *don't doubt that*, it should be the end of December."

"Wow!" came from all of us again in chorus.

"Chris, are you an integral part of this pregnancy? You seem so excited about Daniel's baby," Dr. Stanley said.

"We've promised Chris he can be an uncle," Daniel explained.

"You see, Chris was going to marry her but he didn't know she was single and by the time he found out I had already asked her to marry me. So we've kind of adopted him into our family."

"You guys confuse me," he said, shaking his head.

"He also saved my life. I would have died if the good doctor hadn't done emergency surgery on me. I had a blood clot on my brain," I said, smiling at Chris.

"Chris, there's something else we need to tell you about her pregnancy," Daniel said seriously.

THE MOUNTAINS CALL MY NAME

"Is there a problem? After all, I'm you're doctor, too, and I need all of the information."

"It's possible that we will have more than one."

"No way! Boy, you must be fertile," he said, smiling at me. "No kidding, I do need to see you even more now," Chris said, his voice changing to a more serious tone.

"Will you have time for me now?"

"Yeah, I'll fit you in. I'll tell Karen to put you in a room."

"Okay, I'll see you guys later," Dr. Stanley said, walking away.

"Daniel, I want to see you as soon as you finish with your patient," Chris called out. "Meet me and Elizabeth in my office."

"Okay, I'll see ya," Daniel answered.

Karen told me to follow her.

"You need to come in here and give a urine sample."

"Okay."

As soon as I was finished, she came and took me to the exam room to wait for Chris.

"I'm going to go get your chart and put it outside for the doctor," she said, exiting the room.

Chris wasn't too far behind her.

"How you doin'?" he asked, looking at my chart.

"I've been doing great. I just have this nausea that seems to have an explanation. Pregnancy does that to some women."

"You're glowing, I think that's what they say happens when you're pregnant. You seem very happy and content."

"I couldn't be happier. I'm just flabbergasted about the possibility of having more than one baby."

He took his light and looked into both eyes.

"Have you had any dizziness, double vision, anything I should be aware of?"

"Nope, I'm feeling wonderful."

He felt of the scar where he did the surgery.

"I'm happy for you and Daniel. God not only spared your life but he has given you another one to bring into the world."

"I will never be able to thank you enough for what you did for me," I said, giving him a hug.

"Just take care of yourself. Come, let's go into my office. Daniel is supposed to meet us there."

We had no sooner seated ourselves when Daniel came in.

"How is she doing?" Daniel asked.

"There is one small thing I want to discuss with the both of you," he said, looking from one to the other of us.

"You sound so serious Chris," Daniel said.

"It's about the baby, I don't want to burst your bubble right now, but I do foresee a possible problem."

"And...?" Daniel questioned.

"Knowing what I know about you, and having done your surgery, I don't think you will be able to have a vaginal delivery. I think it will put too much pressure on the area of the surgery. There is a tremendous amount of pressure during the pushing stage of delivery, and I don't want to take a chance on you rupturing something."

"But you said I had healed so well," I stated.

"You have, but there is a big question mark about a lot of pressure. You may deliver fine, but I would strongly suggest C-section."

"Wow, I didn't think about that. But I can see where you're coming from," Daniel interjected.

"I just don't want you to get to the end and have to have emergency surgery. You two are very special to me, and you know I wouldn't tell you something that wasn't true."

"I know, I didn't even think about my surgery in the context of having a baby."

"C-sections aren't all that bad, your recovery is a little slower, but all in all, I think you would do great."

"Thanks for the advice, we will proceed with caution," I told Chris.

"Multiple babies, how about that. I'm going to have to rest up; it looks like I'm going to have a busy Christmas," he said, smiling at Daniel and me.

"We're going to go have lunch and digest all our news. She didn't keep a lot of her breakfast down, so I want to make sure she has an early lunch," Daniel said protectively.

"Keep in touch with me, Elizabeth. I'll talk to Roger Stanley and tell him my concerns. He's a great doctor to be so young. He will take excellent care of you," he said, hugging me. "Don't worry about what I just told you. But I felt as your doctor I needed to. See you guys later."

Since getting back from West Virginia, Daniel and I had been very busy. The medical mobile had come in from the factory and we were so excited at its arrival. I had ordered all the supplies except the medicine and Daniel had ordered that. Daniel and I would take turns with the other doctors going on the mountain trips. They seemed more than glad to share the adventures. Daniel and I would have first shot, since it was our dream. We would go the first and third Thursdays in every month. We had already designated places to go. They would be divided among church fellowship halls and community centers. Daniel's and my first two assignments were ready to work.

THE MOUNTAINS CALL MY NAME

There was a nurse with the health department that was more than willing to go ahead and spread the word that we would be coming. Her name was Sharon Light and she was a real top-notch, caring worker. She said she knew just the way to get the word out. She was going to set up radio spots, announcements on Sundays, and mailbox flyers.

She would have the people there, signed in and ready to be seen when we arrived. She was allotted a small staff from the health department, so she had all the help she needed. The next Thursday was d-day. I couldn't wait to get started.

The nausea was abating and my appetite was ferocious. I could tell that my waistband was getting snugger. Daniel was pleased with the fact that I could eat again, and keep it down. He was so protective of me, and I cherished every moment of it. His mom and dad were beside themselves with joy concerning the baby or babies. We hesitated telling them about the possibility of twins, but decided to let them in on all aspects of their future grandchild. Grandmother Scott had broadcast the information all over the county by that time. My next visit with Roger, he said we should be able to hear the heartbeat. Daniel had been listening everyday with his stethoscope trying to hear them himself, but hadn't yet. He said he was going to bring home a special listening device that Roger had so we might be able to hear it. We had a nightly ritual of listening for the heartbeat. He thought he heard it one night, but decided it was gas. I was having so much fun watching Daniel watch me.

Early in the week that we would take our first trek into the hills and hollows of Virginia, Daniel, Chris and I met at the medic mobile and had prayer over it; asking

THE MOUNTAINS CALL MY NAME

God to bless all that came into its doors. When we went to our little dedication, Daniel had a surprise waiting for me. He had had the manufacturer place a small plaque on the entry door in memory of Dr. David Mason. I was moved to tears that it came voluntarily from Daniel and not my pushing for it. He *had* remembered my asking him. I thought he'd likely forgotten it altogether.

I was anxious to go over and do another recheck of everything, but Daniel put his foot down. Between him and Mandy, I was going to have a rough time getting to do stuff, especially if it was strenuous at all. I might have to get Chris to talk to him about chilling out some. He was concerned about my traveling with him, but I assured him it was perfectly normal to work during pregnancy. Some women work right up until they deliver, but I was sure that wouldn't be the case with me. One more day and we would have our first trip.

Part Two

Chapter Six

The next day would be the beginning of our mission. I doubted I would be able to sleep. I just had finished my shower when Daniel came up from downstairs. He went back to make sure he had locked the door to the medic mobile. He had brought it home from work so we could start from here. Chris came over and had dinner with us. I guess we were like kids with a new toy. Chris had really caught hold of our dream for the mountain mission. He was chomping at the bit for his turn. We had a rotating staff to go with the doctors, so I only had to travel with Daniel.

"Do you think you will be able to sleep tonight?" Daniel asked.

"I hope so. I'm so excited, I feel like it's my first day of school," I returned.

"I know what can make you rest," he said teasingly.

"But you don't want me overly tired, doctor. You yourself told me not to overdo it."

"It's been proven that it is very healthy for pregnant women to have sex."

THE MOUNTAINS CALL MY NAME

"I know it's very healthy for the husband of the pregnant woman to have sex," I said mockingly.

"Oh, I just about forgot." He raced out of the room and down the stairs. "I'll be back in a minute," he called over his shoulder."

I turned the cover down on the bed and was just crawling in when Daniel hurried back into the room.

"Look what I have," he said, holding up a small black case.

"Oh no, doctor, what are you going to do?" I said in mock horror.

"This, my little princess, is what I'm going to hear my little baby's heartbeat with. Or should I say *try* to hear my little baby's heartbeat."

I pulled my top up so he could get to my tummy and he put the sensitive device in place. I lay in absolute stillness while he moved it over my stomach. There was a volume button that would amplify the sound, if he found it.

"There it is. I can hear it, sweetheart, I can hear it. Listen..." he said, turning up the sound.

I heard the swishing of the little heart. Tears began to flow at the beautiful sound we heard. Daniel leaned down and kissed my stomach twice where he heard the beating.

"That was from Mommy and Daddy," he said.

THE MOUNTAINS CALL MY NAME

"Did you just hear one?" I questioned.

"I guess I need to keep checking, don't I?" he said, as he continued to listen.

"What do you want Mama? Do you want me to hear two or three?"

"I'm not even going to answer that. I'll be happy with whatever you find."

"Okay, here goes." He continued to move the device up and down my stomach.

"Oh, my goodness, I hear another one, here, down at the bottom." His eyes were wide with amazement.

"Don't tease me, Daniel, not about this."

"I'm not, sweetheart, listen." He turned up the volume and there was the soft swishing sound of another baby. He took an ink pen and marked the first sound and did the same with the second one. He went back and forth, from one to the other listening to the sweet beats of their hearts.

"God is making them as we speak. He's knitting their little bones together," I commented.

"This is awesome, honey, we found it together. It's like hunting treasure. I've got to call Roger."

He reached for the bedside phone and dialed his private number. I could only hear one side of the conversation, of course.

THE MOUNTAINS CALL MY NAME

"Hey Roger, this is Daniel. We've got two."

"Yeah, I definitely heard two."

"Three, I don't think so. I just heard two. Do what? Okay, thanks for letting me use this. I can't tell you how good it sounds. Okay, I'll see you day after tomorrow. I will be out of the office tomorrow. Do you need me to drop this by? Will do, goodbye."

"He said for you to turn over on your side. We might find three."

"This isn't an Easter egg hunt," I said, turning on first one side, then the other."

"Well, I guess I only hear two," he said disappointedly.

"Only hear two!" I exclaimed. "That's quite enough, don't you think?"

"I was kind of excited about three."

"But you're not the one carrying them," I said, laughing at his remark.

"Can I listen again?" he pleaded. "Just once more?"

"Sure," I said, "but you know you're taking away from daddy time. I have to try to get some sleep."

"I tell you what I think I'll listen more tomorrow," he said, grinning at me.

THE MOUNTAINS CALL MY NAME

"What did Roger say about getting that thing back?"

"He said for me to keep it, he had another one at the office, and mentioned that I might need it on our trip. That's one thing we forgot to put in."

Daniel reached over on his side of the bed and turned out the lights. We snuggled close together under the cover. He caressed my stomach lightly.

"Libby, we heard the heartbeats. I'm one happy man, and I'm about to be just a little bit happier. What better way to celebrate than by making love to their mama?"

"You can say some of the most unusually romantic things, and this is one of them."

Later, as I was lying in Daniel's arms, the full impact of what had transpired really hit me. We were going to have two babies. How incredible that was. I placed my hand over Daniel's, the one that was resting on my stomach; I wondered what his thoughts were as he drifted off to sleep. My excitement was ebbing, and finally I could feel myself drifting off to where Daniel had already gone.

The clock alarm jarred me as it sounded its wake-up call.

"Daniel, are you awake?" I mumbled.

THE MOUNTAINS CALL MY NAME

"Umm..."

"I guess that's a yes." I said.

"Are you going to shower first or am I?"

"I will let you catch a little extra sleep. I'll wake you when I get out of the shower."

"Okay, I mumbled."

I drifted in and out of consciousness. It seemed like he took an awfully short shower, I thought as he gently shook me.

"Time to get up, princess. Our day is awaiting."

I threw the covers off and made my way into the bathroom. Morning showers are more for waking up than getting clean, I thought to myself.

It didn't take long for my shower. Daniel was ready and waiting in the kitchen when I came down.

"Don't we look cute? This is the first time I've seen you in your nurse's uniform. You look awfully sexy. Come here and let the doctor give the nurse a good morning kiss.

"I hope the patients don't think you're as sexy as I do."

"Daniel, Daniel, Daniel, we have to get on the road," I said, smiling up at him.

"We're going to work together, can you believe it?"

THE MOUNTAINS CALL MY NAME

"It's kind of neat, huh? I returned.

"How about some breakfast?" he asked, handing me a cup of coffee. He knew exactly how I liked it and had it perfect that morning.

"Too early, I'll just have coffee, thanks. I'll eat later in the morning. I'll throw up for sure if I eat now."

"You'll eat later, promise?" he said, intently listening for my response.

"I promise I will, but how about you?" I asked him.

"We'll stop at Hardee's and get something later."

"Okay, then let's get going."

We traveled for about forty-five minuets before coming to a Hardee's. Daniel went in and got a couple of sausage biscuits and some coffee to go. We were almost there, so we decided it would be a good time to stop and regroup.

"How are you feeling now?" he asked.

"I feel good. I'm not having any nausea at all. The little guys seem to be doing okay today," I answered.

"Little guys, wow, it still hasn't sunk in. We're going to have two little ones. What will we name them?"

"I haven't got that far. I'm still trying to get used to the thought of carrying two."

"Does the thought of a C-section scare you?"

643

THE MOUNTAINS CALL MY NAME

"No, I've seen them before. I think I can get a spinal and actually be awake for the delivery. I want to see them when they are born."

"Are you sure about that?" he quizzed me.

"Yeah, I am right now. Why, do you think it isn't a good idea?"

"It's not a bad idea; I just want you to be sure. It does cause some residual back pain sometimes."

"I'll take my chances, just to see them born, and plus, I don't want them to have any extra sedation."

"It 'll be done real fast, so they won't get much, if any."

"I guess we can do some research. I still might try for a vaginal birth."

"You know what Chris said, honey; it could be bad for you. I couldn't take another time like I had at Christmas, and neither could you."

From what our directions said, that must be our rendezvous place. I could see the church steeple rising above the ridge in the road. I was anxious to see what the day would bring.

Sharon said she would be here waiting on us. From all the information I had received from her, we would have about fifteen patients to see that day. I knew that we would just have to wait and see how it all would play out.

THE MOUNTAINS CALL MY NAME

We pulled into the graveled church parking lot, undid our seatbelts and stood to stretch our legs.

"Honey, can we pray? Daniel said, hugging me.

"Please," I returned.

"Our Dear Heavenly Father, bless our endeavors, give me wisdom as we see these patients. Bless Libby's and my babies today." I heard a catch in his voice as he continued. "Take care of them and keep them safe. Help us to be a blessing to the people that pass this way today. Amen."

"Amen," I echoed.

We heard a light tap on the side door. We opened it to a smiling Sharon.

"Hi, I'm Sharon," she said, looking up at us.

"Come in," Daniel said, motioning for her to come into the trailer.

"I'm Dr. Scott and this is my wife and nurse assistant, Elizabeth," he said, extending his hand to shake hers. I followed suit.

"I've been looking forward to this day for a long time. Everything has come together so smoothly," she said, grinning from ear to ear.

"It's nice meeting you, too," I said.

"Are you all ready to go? We already have people here. So far we don't have any cancellations from anyone. I have an assistant inside and she has already done the preliminaries on those who are here, like temperature, blood pressure, and the history.

"I have them coming pretty steady until four. Our fifteen patients have turned into thirty. But barring any unforeseen problems, we should be through by 5:00."

"I like a take-charge woman," Daniel said smiling at her.

"Was that a complement?" Sharon asked.

"It was definitely a complement. You don't know what inefficiency can do to a doctor's day."

"Actually I do. My husband is a doctor also." She winced. "I've kept supper warm many evenings because of that one thing."

Daniel nodded. "Then I don't have to tell you."

"Tell me how this setup is going to work?" she said, waving her arm to the back of the trailer.

"Follow me. This first room is where we will do intake. I will talk to them a little before I do an exam."

"What is at the end of the hall?" She asked curiously.

"This is a miniature operating suite. We can take care of minor surgical procedures here. I'm really proud of this area. It was given to us by the State of Virginia, as a grant of sorts. They offered, and we took it. We have a doctor on staff that has more connections than you could

THE MOUNTAINS CALL MY NAME

imagine. His name is Dr. Chris Thomas. You will really like him when he comes."

"Well, I guess I'll go get your first patient. His name is Jake Sowers. He's seventy-five, and says he doesn't have any problems," she said, smiling at Daniel. "He said he only came along with his wife, Ida, because she needs to see a doctor, and she says she coming so he can see the doctor."

"Well, this is going to be interesting," Daniel said, shaking his head.

Sharon left us and went to get the Sowerses.

"Do you want me to stay up front while you interview them? You probably want some privacy."

"Good idea, when I'm ready, I'll call you. Go put your feet up," he said, giving me one last kiss.

Daniel had the door open for them. Both were feeble and had to be assisted up the steps. Daniel seated them in two chairs across from him.

"Hi, my name is Dr. Scott, what's yours," he said, shaking hands with each of them.

"My name is Jake Sowers, and this is my wife, Ida," he said.

"What can I do for you today?" Daniel said, looking at the fresh chart.

"He is... she is..." they said in unison.

THE MOUNTAINS CALL MY NAME

I saw a little smile on Daniel's lips as I watched him from the front of the trailer.

"How about I give you both a check up?" Daniel said, smiling at the sweet little couple.

"How about my wife taking you into the exam room and I will be in, in just a minute?"

I took my cue from Daniel, and came and stood by him.

"This is my wife and nurse, Elizabeth. She will take very good care of you. If you will follow her, she will show you where to go."

I took Ida by the arm and led her down the hall.

"Jake and I will compare hunting stories until you get back."

I knew by the smile on Jake's face that Daniel had hit his hot button.

"You ever hunt, Dr. Scott," I heard him ask Daniel as we made our exit.

"Ida, I'm going to ask you to put this gown on so Dr. Scott can listen to your lungs and heart."

"Are ya sure? There ain't nuthin' wrong with me 'cept my ole joints hurt. See, the reason I come was fer Jake. He ain't been feelin' so good. I figered since ya'll was a comin', it would be good to get him to the doctor."

THE MOUNTAINS CALL MY NAME

"Do you want me to help you into the gown? It can be kind of hard to close in the back."

"If ya don't mind."

"I get a bit swimmy-headed. Not ever' day, but sometimes I jest go stumblin'," she said, laughing at herself. "I go right over on my head sometimes."

I opened the door to signal to Daniel that she was ready.

"Do you want me to stay or go?" I asked Daniel.

"Stay, please," he said.

I stood out of his way, and watched as he gently and modestly examined Ida.

"Ida, do you check your breasts for lumps?"

"Well, Dr Scott, I don't have any."

"Ida, you've got to have breast," he said, trying hard not to laugh.

"Well, I did at one time. They's now not much there."

"Do you mind if I check you to see if you have any lumps?"

"I think I would know if there was one, but ya can look."

649

THE MOUNTAINS CALL MY NAME

Daniel checked her for lumps and felt around on her stomach.

"How 'm I doin', doc?"

"You're doing great. Sit up and let me look in your eyes and ears."

He continued to give Ida a once-over. This was the first time I had ever seen Daniel with a patient. I was overcome with love for him. God had given me such a wonderful man as a husband.

"Your blood pressure is high. Did anyone ever tell you that?"

"I ain't been to no doctor to see."

"You've never been to a doctor," he asked in amazement.

"Well, there's one that would come to the house when the babies was born. But we always just doctored ourselves with herbs and stuff.

"Do you know what I mean when I say 'high blood pressure'?"

"Yeah, I know."

"When your blood pressure is high you can have a stroke, or heart attack. So what we need to do is get it to come down, and one way is by medicine. Then you will have to adjust your diet."

THE MOUNTAINS CALL MY NAME

"We only have one kind o' food. It's the kind I always eat."

"It's the salt that you're going to have to cut out, or down, anyway."

"I do like the salt shaker," she said, smiling at Daniel. "But food tastes so bad without it."

"What kind of meat do you eat?"

"Mostly pig, you know, we kill 'em ever' fall. I can it and salt cure it. I can all my vegetables. I make my own bread. So I don't know rightly what you want me not to eat."

"Okay, let's do this, don't add extra salt at the table and cut back on some of the pork you eat. I'll give you some pills to take until I come back again and we'll see if it gets better."

"I'll try."

"That's all I can ask. You have some cataracts on your eyes," he said, shining a light in them. "You really need to have them removed. I bet you could see a lot better."

"I thought that was sumpthin' old people lived with."

"You don't have to live with them. It isn't painful to have them removed."

"Have you had them, too, Dr. Scott?" she inquired.

651

THE MOUNTAINS CALL MY NAME

"No," he replied.

"Then how do ya know?"

"Well, Ida you got me there. I just read somewhere that it didn't hurt. It might be uncomfortable, but not painful."

"You can get dressed now, and I will give Jake the once-over, okay?" he said, shaking her head.

"I need for you to draw a little blood to get some tests done for Ida. I've written on her papers what I want ordered. Okay?" he said as we left the room.

"Yeah, I can do that."

"After that, she can get dressed, and then we can let Jake have his turn."

As Daniel started to leave the room, Ida called him back.

"Dr. Scott, Jake probably won't tell ya this but..." she hesitated shyly and continued in a hushed voice.

"He's been a bleedin' down there fer a while."

"Would that be his urine or his bowels."

"It's his pee. He can't hardly go sometimes and the pain gets bad."

"Thanks for telling me. I'll check it out for you. Okay?"

"Thank ya." she said, smiling at him.

Ida and Jake changed places.

"Elizabeth, Jake is going to have his prostate checked, so have him take everything off."

"Ever'thing?" he questioned as we made our way to the exam table.

"Yes, I'm afraid it has to be everything, so he can get *everything* checked."

"But I wasn't the one with the problem, it was Ida."

I almost laughed out loud at his comment.

"Here is the gown, do you think you could get it on by yourself, or do you need help?"

"Well, I'll do the best I can, then what I cain't get done, I'll let you do. Ain't nobody ever seed me without clothes on."

"Dr. Scott does these every day, and I promise he will respect your privacy.

"If'n I have to, I guess I can."

"Okay, I'll be right outside the door, just call me when you need me."

My heart went out to them. They were so embarrassed to have anyone look at them. But Daniel seemed to handle it so well. I could tell that he was going to win over these mountain people.

THE MOUNTAINS CALL MY NAME

I was about to go in and check on him when he called for me.

"You can come in," I heard him say.

I entered to find him sitting on the table with the sheet wrapped tightly around him. His clothing was piled on the chair in the corner.

"I'll go get Dr. Scott," I told him.

Daniel stopped me before we entered the room.

"While I check his prostrate you can stay outside. I'm sure he'd be embarrassed with you in the room. It'll be hard enough with me. But I want you in there until then."

"Okay, but do you want me to go in now or later?"

"Come in with me now."

"How are you doing?" Daniel asked him.

"I'm a little bit cold right now."

Daniel checked his eyes and ears, and listened to his lungs and heart.

"You have a strong heart, and your lungs sound good. Do you smoke?"

"I smoke a pipe. That's all I ever smoked."

"If you will lie back on the table, I'll feel around on your stomach a little bit."

THE MOUNTAINS CALL MY NAME

He swiveled around and I pulled the extension out at the end for him to put his feet on. He was a short little man and barely needed it. As Daniel examined him, I saw him wince with pain.

"Does that hurt when I push there?"

"That hurts purty powerful right there," he responded.

Daniel was pushing down near his bladder area, and into his side.

"Do you have any problems urinating?"

"Is that like peeing?"

"Yes, it's the same thing."

"I do pretty much all the time."

"Have you noticed any blood?"

"Well, now that you mention it, sometimes when I empty the slop jar I see something that might be blood. We use it at night so we don't have to go to the outhouse."

"How long have you noticed it?"

"Well, let me think, it seems about five or six months, off and on. I thought it would go away, and I didn't have no way to the doctor, so when they mentioned you was a comin' by, I wanted to get Ida looked at. She's been kinda stumbly lately."

THE MOUNTAINS CALL MY NAME

"I'm going to ask my pretty little wife to step out and I'm going to check your prostate."

"What is the prostrate?"

"The prostate is what produces semen when you ejaculate."

"Oh, that's what does that?"

"Yep, that's what it does, and sometimes it can become enlarged. This is caused by infection, and sometimes a cyst or a blockage. It can cause burning, flu-like symptoms, bleeding; it can affect your sleep, and may make your legs become restless at night."

"But what if you don't do it?"

"That could be some of the problem. Men need to 'do it', to help the prostate stay flushed,"

"Do you do it, Jake?" Daniel asked without cracking a smile.

"I'll tell ya in private," he whispered to Daniel.

"I think that's my cue to leave. I'll go check on Ida," I said, smiling at Daniel.

I waited outside the door for Daniel to call me back in.

"Elizabeth, can you get some blood work on Jake?" And also I need for him to give us a specimen."

"Okay, will do."

When the tests were done, the two of them were seated back where they started. I would walk them back over to the church and bring someone else over, I thought. If all of them took this long I couldn't see how we could possibly be done by 5:00.

"Well, Ida, I'm going to give you some medicine for your high blood pressure. I have written exactly how you're supposed to take it. Don't miss any doses. When you come back to me, I'll give you some more. You won't have to buy it. And Jake, I'm going to give you a prescription for an antibiotic for your prostate. There was an enlargement there, and it could just be an infection. Remember what we talked about. When you come back to see me, we'll do a recheck and see if it's better."

"Okay, we'll be back."

I walked them back to the church. When they left, Ida gave me a hug and thanked me for all I had done.

"You just follow what Dr. Scott said to do and we'll see you in about two weeks."

I told Sharon's assistant, Lori to make them an appointment for our next visit, and to make sure they would be picked up.

The day was a long and arduous one. We didn't finish until almost seven o'clock. By the time we reached home and did all the paperwork, it would be past midnight. We had stopped long enough for lunch, and Daniel insisted I put my feet up and rest awhile. Sharon came over while I rested and helped Daniel. She was an RN, so she could do all that Daniel required be done for his patients.

THE MOUNTAINS CALL MY NAME

The ladies of the church fixed lunch for us and boxed us up some food for supper. They provided snacks for the people that came to see Daniel. I felt really good about the response we had.

We were just finishing cleaning up the trailer when we heard a knock on the back door where the patients had come in all day.

"Sharon or Lori must have forgotten something." I started to get up, but Daniel motioned for me to stay seated.

"I'll get it," he said, already half way to the door.

"What did you..." he stopped in mid sentence realizing it was neither Lori nor Sharon.

"Is there something we can do for you?" I heard him ask.

My curiosity got the better of me and I joined Daniel at the door.

A woman that looked not much older than Daniel and me stood at the door.

"My name is Iona Lewis. I live close by and I really need to speak to Dr. Scott. They said he would be here today."

"I'm Dr. Scott, but we are through seeing patients for the day."

"Ya see, I couldn't come till it was a gettin' dark, 'cause I didn't want nobody seein' me. I'm real sceert."

THE MOUNTAINS CALL MY NAME

"Come in and have a seat," Daniel said gently.

The last thing Daniel and I needed was another patient, but hadn't we just prayed that morning that God would send people to us that needed us? Well, here she was.

She sat down in the chair opposite Daniel and me. She seemed to be visibly shaken and nervous. She kept wringing her hands together.

I went over and knelt down in front of her and took her hands in mine.

"It will be okay. Just tell us what we can do to help."

"I don't rightly know wher' to start. It's the baby; it's been cryin' fer three days a runnin'."

"How old is the baby?" Daniel asked.

"She's six months old, almost seven."

"Why didn't you bring her with you?"

"Oh, she ain't mine. She's my sister's baby. I don't know what it is, but there's sumpthin' bad. I just know."

"Is she running fever?"

"Hot as a poker at times, then it'll break, and she'll be cool fer a little bit. I've been after Essie to get her to somebody, but all she says is 'mind my own business', that she be taken care of it. She says it's just a teethin' and that's all. But, Dr. Scott, I ain't never heared no baby cry that hard all the time from just cuttin' teeth.

"Essie's the baby's mother?"

"Yeah, she is."

"It sounds like she doesn't want you involved. There's nothing I can do to change that. I can't make her bring the baby to me."

"Don't ya see, it ain't her, it's that man of her'n. She's sceert to death of him. He beats her and the younguns all the time. He's mighty mean. 'Specially when he's been on the bottle, which is about all the time."

"How many children does she have?"

"She has the baby, Melissa, and a little boy, Ronnie, that's almost three, and another little boy, Andrew, five, and a little girl, Hannah, who's twelve."

"You know, Iona, that we just can't go up there and check their baby unless they ask us," Daniel lamented.

"I was thinkin' maybe ya could go and say yer givin' shots to the babies or sumpthin', and ask to give the baby a shot."

"What makes you think they would even let me see her?" he asked.

"We can't go tonight. I've got to get my wife home. She's having a baby and needs to get her rest. We'll go home and talk about a plan."

THE MOUNTAINS CALL MY NAME

"Please, Dr. Scott, I don't think the little girl can stand much more," she said with tears in her eyes.

"Could you give us a few minutes to talk?" I asked Iona.

"Sure."

We went into the examining room and shut the door.

"What are we going to do, Daniel? This is a real crisis."

"I've got to get you someplace to rest."

"There was a hotel back on the road. We could stay over and go see this baby tomorrow?"

"I'll have to call Chris and see if I could get it worked out for him to take my calls tomorrow. This was just supposed to be a one day thing," he said, running his hand through his dark curls. "I don't know when I've been this tired."

I went to the back of his chair and rubbed his shoulders. He took my hand and pressed it to his lips.

"What are we going to tell her?" I asked gently.

"There is a baby out there that could die, and I'm a doctor, we've got to try, Elizabeth."

"Let's go talk to her," I said, opening the door.

THE MOUNTAINS CALL MY NAME

"We'll be back over here at the same place about ten o'clock in the morning. Can you meet us here to show us the way?"

I saw new fear appear in her eyes. "No!" she said empathically. "You don't know what you're askin'. If Bob knowed I was here I would be dead. I've got to not be with you, but I could give you directions to their house. It'll be easy to find."

"Are you close enough to see their house?"

"Yeah, I'm right on the same side of the road."

"Could you call the police if there is trouble?"

"Ani't nobody got no phones up there."

"Great!" Daniel exclaimed.

"Honey, we have the two way radio in here, couldn't you call the emergency channel with that."

"Yeah, that would work, but if we can't get to it, it won't do us any good." he interjected.

"Daniel, we're just going to have to trust God to take care of us."

"Honey, would you get Iona some paper and pencil, and let her write the directions down."

I got some paper off his work station and handed it to her. She took it tentatively.

THE MOUNTAINS CALL MY NAME

"I can't write," she said, hanging her head with shame.

A tear escaped down her face. Her rough, calloused hand was quick to wipe it away.

"That's okay, sweetie, you tell me and I'll write it down," I said, trying to hide the emotion I felt for her.

"Do you know anything about these hills around here?" she asked.

"No, I'm afraid we don't."

"You go out here in front of the church and go up the road. You'll go about three mile, then you'll come to a store called County Line Store, ya turn right there. You won't go far 'til ya come to a bridge, go across it and turn up the next road. It'll wind up around this mountainside. You'll pass a big white farm house, and that un's mine, you can see Esther's house right next to mine. That's Essie's full name. I gotta go. I been gone way too long."

She got up and started to the door. I arose before her and put my arms around her. The tears she had tried so hard to fight back now were released into sobs. As I held her to me, the odor of her unkempt body hit my pregnant condition. Nausea attacked me with a vengeance. I pushed by her to try to make it to the little bathroom in the back of the trailer, and reached the commode just in time. After getting everything settled down again, I made my way back toward them and met Daniel coming down the hall.

"Are you okay, sweetie?"

THE MOUNTAINS CALL MY NAME

I nodded my head as he pulled me into his arms. "I'm so embarrassed. I lost it when her body odor hit me. You know how smells get to me quicker than anything. I wanted to comfort her and look what I did. She must think I'm terrible. It was obvious what happened."

"No, she didn't think that. I reminded her about your pregnancy, and I prayed for her safety. She felt better when she left."

"I feel better now, too." I said smiling at him.

"We just need to go to the hotel and eat supper. Then I'm calling Chris."

We got buckled into our seat and headed out to the hotel. It was nine o'clock by the time we got into our room. The cold plate they fixed for us was good. My nausea had abated and I was famished.

"I'm asking Chris to come," Daniel said.

"Here?" I asked in amazement.

"I'm asking him to go with us to these people's house. I don't want you involved, because you and the babies could get hurt."

"I don't think that will be necessary," I said curtly. "I'm not sick, Daniel; you're treating me like a child. I can do this job! You don't have to call Chris."

"I'm not saying you aren't capable, I'm just saying this could be a very dangerous situation. God gave you and these babies to me, and I have to protect you the best way I know how. I am calling Chris!" he said, reaching for the phone as he spoke.

I knew from the sound of his voice he was going to be as stubborn as I. I flipped over with my back to him and pulled the cover up around my head. This was the closest we had ever come to actually being mad at each other. Unbidden tears slipped down my cheek. This pregnancy had made me so emotional. I quickly wiped them off with the corner of the sheet so he wouldn't know I had been crying.

"Chris, it's Daniel here."

"We're still here at Mount Laurel. We ran into kind of a problem..." I listened as he conveyed what had happened and asked him to come.

I heard him in the shower and tried to go to sleep before he came back in, but couldn't. I was too upset to calm down. I knew he was right. I needed to think about the babies. I was just so used to going long hours and being efficient. I felt like a failure.

He turned out the light and slipped under the cover beside me. I wanted him to hold me, but I wasn't going to make the first move. For the first time in our marriage, he turned his back to go to sleep. Evidently he wasn't going to disturb my pouting. I lay there in the darkness, suddenly very lonely in our king size bed. A new wave of tears started. I turned over on my back and reached out for Daniel. He turned toward me and without a word took me into his arms. He just held me until my tears were dried.

"Daniel?"

THE MOUNTAINS CALL MY NAME

"Huh?"

"I just wanted you to be proud of me and see that I could handle whatever it was we would have to face, and all I managed to do was throw up on one of our new patients."

I heard him chuckle as he pulled me closer. "Honey you did a great job. I saw how professional you were with all the patients today, and I saw your gentleness. I haven't worked with anyone as good or as cute as you are."

"You're just saying that because you have to," I mumbled into his chest.

"I can't win. So you'll just have to believe me."

"Daniel?"

"Huh..." he returned sleepily.

"I was so proud of you today. It's the first time I've seen you be a doctor."

"Thank you, but you're only saying that to make me feel good."

"Okay, you got me," I said, laughing at him.

"Daniel, I don't like it when we're mad at each other."

"I wasn't mad, were you?"

"Yes you were. You've never gotten into bed and turned your back on me."

"I didn't think you wanted to be bothered. You had your back turned to me and your head covered up."

"But you knew I wanted you to hold me."

"I can't read your mind. Give me a break I'm really new at this. So if I'm right, when you get in bed and turn your back to me, I'm supposed to know that you really want me to hold you. That makes a lot of sense to me."

"I'm sorry; I did get frustrated with you, but not mad. There's a difference."

"Okay, I was frustrated with you too, but not mad. I think we were upset over different things. I was upset because you were going to put you and the babies in jeopardy, and you were because you didn't think that I thought you could do the job. Am I right?"

"You're right."

"And I will tell you this right now, I will protect you and my babies until the day I die," he said, pulling me closer to him.

"I'll try hard to not resist. I've been on my own so long I forgot how it was to have a protector."

"When we said our vows at the altar, God transferred you into my hands, and I take that very seriously."

THE MOUNTAINS CALL MY NAME

He placed his hand on my stomach above our babies. "That was why I hesitated about going up there. If I went into something that made you lose our children, I would die."

"I know, and I won't do anything stupid. I love you so much, I felt so lonely awhile ago over on the other side of the bed. Would you have gone to sleep and not have hugged me?"

"No, I knew you would turn over."

"Why were you so certain?"

"I knew that I just needed to give you some space, so I gave you some."

"I don't need space, I need you," I said, shifting my body closer to his.

"And I need you, Elizabeth," he said, smothering me with kisses.

We were lost in the sweet ocean of love that God made so beautiful. All the tiredness and frustrations of the day ebbed away as we were swept along in the current of its flow.

Later, as we lay in each others arms, all seemed right with the world.

The sound of Daniel's breathing told me he was sleeping. I had gotten used to those comforting sounds. His hand rested on my stomach where he liked to lay it as he went to sleep.

THE MOUNTAINS CALL MY NAME

"You're daddy loves you, little ones," I silently told my babies. "He will always be there to protect you and care for you." I wondered how my mother felt when she found out she was pregnant. How she must have loved me as she carried me. I had thought often of her since I found out I was pregnant. I had Daniel; she didn't have anyone. I would rather have him overprotective than not have anyone. I drifted off to sleep, content in the arms of my love.

Daniel had already showered and was ready to go before he woke me. I opened my eyes to feel his kisses on my face.

"Good morning, my princess," he said, pushing my hair back from my face.

"What time is it? Am I late?"

"No, you're fine. I got up early to read the Bible and pray. I figured we might need an extra measure of grace today."

"I'm so tired this morning."

"I know, that's why I let you sleep. We had a busy day and night."

"I'm barely into my fourth month with this pregnancy and I'm already tired. I hope this isn't a bad sign."

"In the first three or four months you are more tired because your body is adjusting to such an awesome task. There is a miracle taking place in your womb. As you sleep, God is doing some awesome things with our babies. I was just reading in the scripture about how God works in the secret parts of the womb to do marvelous and wonderful works. He knew our children before we conceived them." he said, his eyes filled with the emotion of it all.

"I love you so much, Dr. Scott."

He didn't say another word, just climbed in bed beside me and held me for a long while.

"I need to get up soon and hop in the shower. Maybe it will wake me up."

"We might need to rethink your doing all this until the babies are born," he said gently.

I knew he might be right. I got silently out of bed and headed to the shower. The thought of my dream going to someone else seemed so unfair, and I didn't want someone else sharing all of this with Daniel. I pushed it to the back of my mind and let the hot, steamy water flow over me. I suddenly felt something that seemed like a flutter in my stomach. I turned off the shower so everything would be totally quiet. I waited and felt nothing again, I was about to give up and call it gas when it happened once more. I screamed for Daniel to come into the bathroom.

"What? What's the matter?" he said, visibly shaken as he reached me. "Answer me, what's wrong?" He took me by my shoulders and looked deep into my eyes.

"I just felt one of the babies move," I said with tears running down my face. "I just felt life inside me."

He grabbed a towel and put it around my shoulders. "You scared me to death. I thought you had a problem. I feel weak as a kitten," he said, leaning up against the bathroom wall.

"Daniel, did you hear what I said?" I asked. "I felt one of our babies move".

"I heard what you said. I'm just trying to switch from being scared to death to being overjoyed. You're going to kill me before the babies get here," he said, holding his hand over his heart.

"This is the first time I've ever felt this. It's like a little kiss from heaven," I said, with water dripping down out of my hair.

"What does it feel like?"

"It feels like a butterfly fluttering around," I said, smiling.

"Do you think I could feel it?" Daniel asked excitedly.

"No, it's too deep, but you can listen to the heartbeat later," I said, kissing him.

"You get all the fun," he said. "Run along and get dressed. I need to go pull the trailer around."

THE MOUNTAINS CALL MY NAME

I hurried and dried my hair and dressed. I was ready to go in no time. I told Daniel I would put some make up on in the trailer while he found a place for breakfast. We found the Hardee's where we got our food the morning before.

"What's our plan, Daniel?" I asked between bites of my sausage and egg biscuit.

"Chris will be at the church at 9:00. I guess we'll make final plans when he gets here. How do you feel today?"

"I feel great, no nausea this morning. I just hope I don't barf today. Do you think it's early for me to feel the babies move?"

"Not with twins. They take up more space, so you would feel them sooner."

"Today has been a good day," I said, smiling at him.

"I hope that's the way it ends," he said on a serious note.

We pulled into the church parking lot to wait for Chris. It was ten till nine, so if he was on time he should be here any minute.

"I'm going to work on some of the paper work from yesterday," I said, heading to the back.

"We didn't get much done last night, did we?" he said with a smile.

"Actually, we did. We had our first fight, and made up. That took up most of the night.

"It wasn't a fight, it was a discussion." he added.

"Okay, whatever it was, it was fun making up afterward," I said, smiling.

"Okay, here's file one, Jake and Ida Sowers," I added, handing the folder to him.

"I didn't have time to talk to you about these two. I have a feeling Jake is in for some heavy duty problems. His prostate is way too large. I'm hoping antibiotics are going to work for him, but I think it could be cancer. I didn't want to hop into radical treatment too quickly, but in two weeks if I don't see change I'm going to have to send him to the hospital. I guess if I send him, Ida will have to go with him. Those two make such a cute couple."

"What did he whisper to you about doing it?"

"That's patient privacy. You know that."

"Do they?"

"Actually they do. Isn't that good to know? I hope when we get that old we still do it."

"Oh, Daniel, you embarrass me sometimes."

Chris came in just as I was finishing my statement.

"I can embarrass you all the time. Want me to try?" he said, leaning over and kissing my cheek.

THE MOUNTAINS CALL MY NAME

"How's the little mama?"

"The little mama felt one of the babies move this morning," Daniel said, smiling up at Chris.

"No way, isn't this early to be feeling movement? I'm not up to snuff on my obstetrics, but isn't it?"

"That's right, I haven't talked to you lately to tell you our other news. I counted two heartbeats the other night."

"No way!" he exclaimed grinning from ear to ear.

"Way, he was trying to find a third one and was so disappointed he only found two. I told him he acted like he was hunting Easter eggs." I said, laughing.

"Do twins run in your family?"

"Well believe it or not, I'm a twin of a sister." I held my hand up before he could say it. "I know, no way."

"You took the words right out of my mouth. Where is she, are you keeping her from me?"

"You can date her when you get to heaven. She died during childbirth."

"Oh, I'm sorry, I didn't know."

"Neither did I until right before Christmas."

"No way," we all said in unison.

"You are loaded with info today, girl."

THE MOUNTAINS CALL MY NAME

"My mother died in childbirth and I was raised by another woman."

"So, don't twins skip a generation?"

"Evidently not." I said, smiling at him.

"You know what, putting all kidding aside; we seriously have to talk about your health. You know that I think a C section is the only way to go."

"Daniel thinks so, too."

"And what does Elizabeth think?" Chris asked, looking directly at me.

"Elizabeth thinks she has some mighty good doctors and she ought to take their advice," I said, smiling at Daniel.

"How do you feel?" Chris questioned.

"You and Daniel are going to drive me nuts before they get here."

"You ain't seen nothin' yet, baby."

"I was really tired last night. How many patients did we see yesterday, Daniel?"

"Elizabeth said fifty some, but I only counted forty folders."

"Man! That was a good turnout for the first visit. What kind of patients?"

THE MOUNTAINS CALL MY NAME

"Old, young, pregnant, you name it, we saw 'em. I was pleased with the number of pregnancies that came through. At least they're seeking early prenatal care," Daniel said.

"What's going on with this case today? Talk to me, do you have a gun?"

"I'm a doctor, not a sheriff. To answer your question, no, I don't have one with me."

"I think maybe you better start carrying one. Just make sure it's out of sight and away from any kids."

"I know how to care for one, I just never thought of needing one. Now, I think I'm about to change my mind.

"What happened last night?"

"There was a knock about seven or so and the lady looked upset. So we invited her in and she said her niece had been crying incessantly. I think she said about three or four days. She has been running fever off an on. The problem is the parents don't think she needs to see a doctor. Iona (the aunt) says the father is very abusive when he drinks. He evidently beats the crap out of his wife and kids, and threatens to kill the relatives. There are four children ranging from six or eight months to twelve. There's two little boys."

"So maybe this won't be as bad as Iona thinks it will be."

"Iona suggested we go to the house and tell them we're out and about giving kids their shots."

THE MOUNTAINS CALL MY NAME

"That sounds good. It just might work."

"Do you have the directions?"

"Yeah, here they are." I said, handing them to him.

"Well, let's go do it."

"Let's pray first," Daniel suggested.

"Good idea."

"Father, protect us as we go. Go before us and prepare the way. Help us be a blessing today. Amen."

"Chris you can set up front with Daniel and read him directions. I'll sit back here and do records."

It didn't take long for us to reach the place where we turned at the store to go up the mountainside. Iona's directions were distinct, and we didn't have any problems.

I cleared away the folders and stored them for transfer. Everything looked neat and tidy. I hoped the visit was smooth for everyone.

I looked out the window and saw the white farm house that Iona lived in. I thought I saw a curtain move in what appeared to be the kitchen window. The house we pulled up to was a rundown, dilapidated old shack. The boards that were once white hung with peeling and blistered paint, and some windows were missing. An old sofa and lounge chair sat on the front porch. Chickens were pecking around in the barren yard. Where a picket fence used to be, slats were lying here and there, all the way around the yard. The front gate was still closed, with no fencing on either side. It seemed the only thing that was fully intact was the front gate.

I heard the barking of several dogs. I didn't see any, so I supposed they were tied.

"Libby, now that I have thought about it, maybe it would be good for you to go in with me. It would be less alarming for them. And you're so cute, who would want to hurt you."

"So you're going to make me walk in front?" I exclaimed.

"You don't think I would want to be first, do you?" he said, winking at Chris.

Daniel got his doctor bag and we proceeded to the front door. I could still hear the dogs bark, but didn't see any. Mountain dogs scared me the most because they were trained to hunt and protect rather than be cuddly companions. I saw the ragged curtain pull back and two dirty little faces peer out.

Daniel knocked on the door. We waited and no one came. He rapped again and we waited some more. Finally the door cracked open just about two inches.

"We don't want nuthin'," I heard her say.

"Ma'am, my name is Dr. Scott, and this is my wife, Elizabeth. We're not selling anything, we're just checking to see if any of the children are in need of their baby shots. I see you have children," he said.

THE MOUNTAINS CALL MY NAME

We could hear her baby crying all the way out on the porch.

"My babies don't need nuthin'."

As she shifted the baby in her arms, the door came open a little farther.

"You sure do have a pretty little baby there. She seems to not be feeling well. Do you think she might need for me to check her? It won't cost you anything."

I saw her demeanor soften some as I talked to her. The baby continued to scream as she patted her back.

"I wouldn't mind stepping in for just a minute since we're here anyway."

I could see her waffling as she stood there. I prayed she wouldn't turn us away. Just looking at the baby, I could tell she was in distress. Her face was flushed and looked feverish. Esther appeared frightened, but reluctantly invited us in.

"Has your baby been sick very long?" Daniel quizzed her.

"It's just her teeth fixin' to come in. They'll be in soon and she'll be better.

We were working our way up to checking the baby when we heard a piercing scream come from the back room. Our heads jerked around toward the direction of the eerie sound. I caught Daniel's eye and saw the alarm that crossed his face.

"Don't pay no 'teniton, it's just them kids fightin' agin. They do that all the time."

About the time she finished her sentence, a young girl came stumbling into the room holding her stomach and screaming in agony.

"Mama he'p me I'm hurtin' bad," she said, holding tight to her stomach as she fell. She lay writhing on the wooden floor.

Daniel rushed to her side. He told her that he was a doctor and could help her. "Turn over and let me see what this pain could be," he said gently.

Her pain seemed to lessen after a minute or so. I could tell that she was no more than eleven or twelve, at the most, a skinny little girl with a protruding stomach. I knew this had to be Hannah. He was trying to feel of her belly when she grabbed Daniel as if he could free her of this demon that had gripped her body. Terror filled her little eyes as the pain gripped her again.

"He'p me, please, please he'p me," she screamed again.

"We're going to help you, baby. Just hold on until I can see what's happening, okay?" Daniel smoothed the hair from her sweaty face, talking calmly as he tried to do a visual exam.

"I'm going to take you to our trailer outside so I can check you better. Okay?"

As he lifted her off the floor there was a circle of blood where she had lain.

"Elizabeth, go tell Chris I'm coming, and to get ready for me. We have a problem."

I rose to go and heard a booming voice behind me.

"Move her ya die."

We heard the cocking of a gun and as we turned toward the sound we looked up into the end of a double-barrel shotgun.

"Sir, is this your little girl?" Daniel asked calmly.

"What's it to ya?" he slurred.

I could tell he was very drunk.

Suddenly the scream came again, piercing the air around us.

"Daddy, Daddy, please let him he'p me, I'm hurtin'. I'm gonna die, I know it, I'm gonna die," she yelled at him.

Daniel lifted the little girl in his arms and stood to face the drunken man.

"Elizabeth, I want you to slowly move in behind me. We are going to walk to the door," he said, as much to the man as to me.

My heart was racing as the adrenalin pumped through my body.

Daniel kept staring at the man as he backed out of the house. Their eyes were locked on each other. The little girl had fainted in his arms. Her once ridged body was now limp in his arms.

"I have a trailer right out side. I can take care of her there. I'm not going to hurt her. She's real sick; I've got to help her."

The man didn't say whether we could go or not. We just backed out of the house. Once we were outside, Daniel and I ran into the trailer with the little girl.

"What the hell?" Chris exclaimed as we rushed in with the little girl.

"I don't know what we have here, but she's bleeding and screaming with pain." Daniel said, headed to the rear operating suite.

I grabbed the scissors and began cutting her clothing off. All of my trauma training just seemed to kick in. I hooked up the blood pressure cuff and got an IV started. The room was small, so I stepped back to give Chris and Daniel room to work.

She came out of her fainting spell as the pain gripped her again and the screaming started over. With terror still in her eyes, she looked helplessly at Daniel, begging him to stop the pain.

A gush of water came from under her.

The horror of what was wrong with her hit us all at the same time.

"Damn! Chris said. "She's having a baby.

THE MOUNTAINS CALL MY NAME

I had exam gloves ready for Daniel and Chris to slip into. I helped them get her legs into the stirrups at the end of the table.

Daniel examined her internally as he pressed gently on her stomach.

"She's about seven centimeters. Elizabeth, go get me the stethoscope that I listened to the babies with. It's in the front of the trailer. I need to see if I can get a heartbeat."

"Doctor?" the little girl moaned. "What's wrong? Can you make the pain leave?"

"What's your name, sweetie?"

"Hannah," she said through the snubbing of her crying.

"Hannah, honey, do you know what having a baby means?"

About that time another contraction started.

"It's coming again! It's coming again!" she screamed, grabbing Daniel's hand.

Chris slipped some of the pain medication into her IV.

"This should help in just a second, sweetheart," Chris crooned to her.

"The contraction is going away now. Your pain is going back down now."

THE MOUNTAINS CALL MY NAME

"Hannah, do know what's happing to you?" Daniel asked as he listened for a heartbeat.

She shook her head. She still had the wild look of an animal getting caught in a trap.

"You're going to have a baby. We can't make the pain go away, but we *are* going to help you through it."

New sobs gripped her body.

"You can put some valium in with pain meds," Daniel told Chris.

"I've already done that."

"I should have known that," Daniel said, forcing a smile.

"Are you a doctor, too? Hannah said, looking at Chris.

"Yeah, I come along to make sure Dr. Daniel treats you right," he said, winking at her.

"Will you help me keep him straight?" Chris asked her.

"I want my mama," she said, holding her hand tight over her eyes.

"We'll get her in a little bit, okay?"

"I get a faint heartbeat way down low. I think we're going to be in for a breach," Daniel said, shaking his head. "We need her mama. We may have to do a C-section

THE MOUNTAINS CALL MY NAME

Chris, and we can't without permission from someone." He removed his gloves and threw them into the trash can. I thought I had seen him angry before, but never had I seen him like this.

"Daniel, he has a gun, you know. You can't risk going in there again," I shouted at him out of sheer panic.

"That little girl is going to die if I don't," he said as he started out the door.

"And my baby's father might if he goes out there." I said, my voice getting quieter.

He hesitated for a second and slammed the door as he went to get Esther.

"Oh God, send your angels to protect him," I prayed.

I saw out the window that Esther had met Daniel in the yard and was coming to the trailer with him.

"Bob is gone; he's not in the house anymore. We're safe right now," Daniel said, coming into the trailer.

He came to me and gave me a reassuring hug. "I'm sorry, but I had no choice. I desperately need your prayers."

We heard a scream coming from the back room again.

"Esther, Hannah is having a baby, and you need to go say something to her. She wants you."

Daniel headed full speed back to where Hannah lay on the table. He and Chris both were trying to help her through the contraction.

"What'll I say?" Esther sobbed.

"Did you know she was pregnant?" I questioned.

She nodded her head.

"Didn't you tell her anything?" I asked.

"I didn't know what to do."

"Stop crying!" I demanded, shaking her shoulders. "You've got a baby back there that doesn't have a clue what's happening to her. You dry those tears and go back there and help her."

The latest contraction was beginning, and tension was high as we entered the room.

"Mama!" she cried out when she saw her.

"Did what daddy did make a baby?" she questioned her mother.

"I'm so sorry, honey. I was afraid of 'im too," she said, leaning down to hug her. They sobbed in each other's arms.

"He won't hurt ya no more. I promise. He ain't comin' back, sweetie. You rest now, I gotta go get Melissa Ann, she's a sleepin', and the boys."

"Don't go, Mama, I'm sceert."

THE MOUNTAINS CALL MY NAME

"I'm takin' the kids to Iona's, and I'll be right back." She said, kissing her forehead.

Daniel followed her into the hallway.

"Dr. Thomas and I may have to do surgery to deliver the baby. We talked it over and we're sure we have everything to do it. Do we have your permission? If we don't, she may die."

She nodded her head and left the trailer.

Daniel had just finished with another internal exam when I entered.

"She's a ten and can push if we let her. We've got to make a decision, Chris. I say let her try pushing some and see if she can do it. We would be in much better shape if we didn't have to do a C section."

"You're the doctor," Chris said, yielding the choice to Daniel.

"Hannah, when your next pain comes, I want you to push down like you do when you go poop."

"I like your medical terms," Chris said, smiling at him.

"I figured she wouldn't have a clue what a bowel movement was," Daniel returned.

"Elizabeth, would you get Chris and me set up for surgery. We will need it as sterile as possible. You remember the procedure we went through the other day?"

"Yes, it's already done."

"I told you she was good," Chris said to Daniel. "I've seen her in action, you haven't.

"I beg to differ," Daniel said.

The contraction was starting. Daniel positioned himself at the end of the table to watch the progress. She pushed for over an hour with no success.

"I cain't do it no more, Dr. Daniel. I cain't do it no more," she wailed. "Just pull it out, please, just pull it out."

"Daniel, her blood pressure is unstable," Chris said.

"Sweetheart, just close your little eyes. We're going to let you rest. When you wake up from your sleep, it will all be over," Daniel said, patting her arm.

"Promise?" she said, grabbing his hand and staring into his eyes to see if he was telling the truth.

Chris was already administering the anesthesia.

"Are you getting sleepy?" Daniel asked.

She looked up at him and smiled the sweetest little smile.

"Thank you," she said as her eyes fluttered. "No more pain," she mumbled weakly.

THE MOUNTAINS CALL MY NAME

"That's right, honey, no more pain," Daniel answered, struggling to keep the emotion from his voice. He stroked her hair as she went into a deeper sleep.

I already had her stomach scrubbed and ready for the procedure by the time she was totally under.

I put my gown and mask on and helped the guys with theirs.

"Would you like to cut?" Daniel asked Chris, since he was a surgeon.

"If you want me to, but I think you're more than capable."

"Elizabeth, you watch her meds and vitals and Chris will help me. When we deliver the baby you're going to have to help with it. Okay?"

"Right." I nodded as he pulled the bright light down and positioned it above her stomach.

I had already gotten the other exam room ready for the little one.

All was quiet except for the banter between the doctors as they worked to get to the baby.

"She is so small. There isn't much space to work in here," Daniel said, trying to wiggle the baby out.

"How's she doing, honey?" Daniel asked.

"Her blood pressure has come down some since she's asleep. But everything looks stable," I answered.

689

THE MOUNTAINS CALL MY NAME

They birthed the butt first. "It's a little boy," Daniel said, lifting him the rest of the way out.

There was a gasp from Daniel as he turned the baby over. His little face was grotesquely deformed. By the time he had cut the cord, there was no heartbeat. There was no life in the little baby. His tiny limbs flopped as Daniel moved him.

"Elizabeth, you need to leave the room. Chris and I can finish. You don't need to see this," he demanded.

He didn't have to tell me twice. Nausea hit me full force and I headed to the bathroom down the hall.

After throwing up all I had on my stomach, I just sat down on the commode and sobbed. I held my hand over my stomach where my own babies lay, and begged God to make them healthy.

After he was finished, Daniel carried Hannah into one of the other exam rooms that had a more comfortable bed. Chris was right behind with the IV bag. She was waking up some from the anesthesia, and was beginning to moan.

I looked in the intake room of the trailer and saw that Esther was back and sitting quietly with her hands folded in her lap. I went to her and told her that Hannah was okay, but they had to do a C-section. Her eyes were red and swollen from crying. "Can I see her?" she asked quietly.

"I'll go ask Daniel," I said, and patted her hand as I went into the other room.

THE MOUNTAINS CALL MY NAME

I closed the door behind me. Daniel was sitting beside her taking her vitals as I came in.

"How is she? Her mom wants to know."

"She's trying to wake up, but we're going to keep her pretty sedated until we can get her to a hospital. Chris went up front to call a rescue squad and the police," he said quietly. I could see that he was totally drained. "Her blood pressure is still on the high side, but considering all she's been through it isn't surprising."

"Are you okay?" I asked, putting my hand on his shoulder.

He reached up and put his hand on mine. "They don't teach this stuff in med school. I'm sorry you had to see the baby. I tried to send you out before you got a good look at him."

"I'm fine, down a meal or two, but other than that, I'm fine."

"Libby, you did such a superb job today," he said, smiling at me.

We heard a light tap on the door and Chris entered.

"How's the patient?" he inquired.

"I was telling Elizabeth that her pressure is still up, but it's nothing I didn't expect. I'm going to keep her pretty much out until we can get her outta here," Daniel told him.

"I thought you might want to know that the other lady that is the sister to Hannah's mom, she's out in the waiting room with a crying baby."

"I forgot about the other kids..." he exclaimed and jumped up. "Bring her back to the other exam room. I wonder where her boys are."

"Libby, could you watch Hannah for me while I go check the baby?"

"Sure."

I went and got Hannah's mother to come in and sit by her.

"She will rest comfortably until the rescue squad comes," I told her. "Your sister said you had two boys. Where are they?"

"Iona took them over to her house. Her teenage daughter's there with 'em. Wher's Hannah's baby?" Esther asked.

"The baby died," I said gently.

"Oh," was all she said aloud. "It's prob'ly just as well," she muttered to herself.

I went in to check on Daniel and Chris. The little girl had cried so much that her cry was raspy. They had all her clothing off except her diaper.

"What did you find?" I asked.

"Nothing so far." They said in unison.

THE MOUNTAINS CALL MY NAME

"Your two big guys look cute with that little baby." I said smiling at them.

"Okay, let's take the diaper off and I'll check her stomach area. It could be appendicitis."

Daniel removed her diaper and saw dried blood.

"Oh God, don't let this be what I think it is." Daniel moaned.

He spread her little legs and she cried out in pain. He separated her as much as he could.

"She's swollen badly. There's blood caked around her genitals. See, Chris?" Daniel said.

"It looks like she could be infected. No wonder she's crying. An animal wouldn't do this," Chris returned.

"Honey, there's some numbing solution in that drawer, could you hand it to me?"

"Sure." I looked over his shoulder as he doctored the little girl.

"What was her temp, Chris?"

"103 point two."

"Chris, could you get her some pain meds ready for an injection and a syringe of penicillin? She's going to love us," Daniel said to no one in particular. "That will keep her comfortable until we can get her to a hospital. She's probably ripped inside."

THE MOUNTAINS CALL MY NAME

"You know she is," he said, shaking his head.

Our heads jerked up and we all jumped at the sound of the shotgun going off.

"Was that a gun?" Chris asked.

"I hope he's not coming in here. Go lock the door Chris." Daniel demanded. "The police should be here soon."

"Esther, would your husband come in here shooting?" I asked her from the hall.

"He won't be botherin' nobody. He just kilt hisself'. He told me was a gonna do it. I told him go ahead, then me and the kids would finally be free. I told him he better do a good job, 'cause I would finish it if he didn't. He knowed what was happenin' to the kids and he knowed he did it," she said with all emotion gone from her face.

Daniel took the sleeping baby and gave her to Iona to hold.

"She's very sick. I gave her some medicine to help her rest until we get her to a hospital. Her fever was spiked and I gave her something to bring it down. I also gave her a big shot of antibiotic for her infection. She didn't like Dr. Scott too much by the time I finished with her." Daniel said smiling.

"I knowed sumpthin' bad was wrong with her. What was it, Dr. Scott?"

"She was raped," Daniel said with his voice breaking.

THE MOUNTAINS CALL MY NAME

Iona drew the little sleeping girl close to her and sobbed into her blanket.

"I wasn't soon enough. I wasn't soon enough!" She repeated as she sobbed.

"If you hadn't had the courage to come to me when you did there would have been three dead children today. As it is we have only one, Hannah's."

"She had a youngun? Little Hannah had a youngun?" she said, confused at Daniel comment.

"You didn't know?"

She shook her head in disbelief. "They quit lettin' me come around. When I'd try, Essie wouldn't let me in."

"Did Essie know Hannah was gonna have a baby?" Iona questioned.

"Yeah, I guess she was scared to death to tell anyone, even Hannah..." he hesitated for a moment. "Even Hannah didn't know what was happening to her. She was terrified."

"We kinda suspected he was messin' with 'em, but you just don't jump in wher' ya ain't invited. You get mad, but just keep yer mouth shet. We all been messed with by somebody, Dr. Scott. Me and Esther both lived through things that would make you sick to yer stomick. We didn't have nobody to turn to. Nobody woulda believed us anyhow. We was just lucky we didn't have no younguns. People are jest like animals up here on this mountainside. They don't care who they hop on and ride: animals, kids, boys, girls, it never mattered. When they'd be drunk you knowed ya better hide till they get over it, but sometime there weren't no place to hide. Then you jest have to make yer mind take ya someplace wher' ya cain't be hurt."

"I'm sorry, Iona, I'm so sorry," Daniel said.

"Did you hear the shotgun, Dr. Scott? I came a runnin' when I heared it."

"Chris has gone to check, but Esther thinks he might have committed suicide."

"He did," Chris said, coming into the trailer. "Esther was dead on, pardon the pun," Chris said.

"You look like you saw a ghost," Daniel told Chris.

"It wasn't a pretty sight. I had to get close enough to see if he was living. There wasn't much left of his head." Chris grimaced at the thought.

"I was so skeert. I thought fer sure he kilt somebody." I woulda prayed if I was a prayin' person, Iona said.

Esther was sitting by Hannah in silence, just staring at her. We heard the ambulance coming up the road to the house. Hannah and the baby were still sleeping. Both finding respite from the awful pain they had suffered. Chris had prepared the dead baby for transport.

The police came in and took a report from all of us. Daniel explained that the children had been raped, supposedly by the father. The policeman let out an oath that would make a sailor blush. "He won't rape any more," Chris said. "He blew his face off with a shotgun."

THE MOUNTAINS CALL MY NAME

He's back behind the house. I guess things caught up with him and he couldn't face it."

The policeman told his partner to go check it out.

"What a mess," the officer said, shaking his head as he continued to write.

"I need to ask Mrs. Luke some questions. Where is she?" he said curtly.

"Right this way. She's sitting with her daughter," Daniel said.

He showed him the way to the exam room where they were.

"Mrs. Luke, do you know what happened to your girls?" the policeman said, towering above her as she sat with her hands folded in her lap.

She barely nodded her head, never looking his way.

"So you knew that he had sex with both them?"

"He said he would kill me if I told. Then they woulda had nobody to hold 'em when he hurt 'em. I'm all they had." She said emotionless.

"I'm sorry to have to do this but you're going to have to come down to the office with me and answer some more questions."

She rose in robot fashion and walked to the waiting room. She didn't focus on anyone or anything.

THE MOUNTAINS CALL MY NAME

Iona got to her feet and put her arms around her. "I'm so sorry Esther. I wish I had been sooner," she said, trying to control the sobs that had started in her throat. "I'll take care of the kid fer ya, and I'll be over to see ya." She sobbed as she held her sister.

She stood stiff and motionless in Iona arms, never acknowledging her presence.

Daniel mentioned to the police officer that he was concerned about her mental state. She seemed to have retreated to a place in her mind where the pain couldn't reach her anymore. She had become totally unresponsive by this time. There were no signs of life as Daniel shown a light into her eyes. She had shut down the line to wherever she had gone.

"Sometimes when the trauma is more than we can handle, it will just shut a person down. We have a lot to learn about the mind and how it works. She may never heal from this one. Maybe it's because she doesn't have to protect the kids anymore. She can finally take care of Esther. I just hope it isn't too late."

"You know we're going to have to take her in. She allowed this to happen to these little girls, so we've got to charge her with child neglect."

"You won't be able to communicate with her. The real criminal is dead, you know? She was a victim as much as the children were," Daniel said, taking her pulse.

"She's in a catatonic state right now. You aren't going to get any statement from her."

"We'll see that she gets taken care of. We'll probably carry her on down to the mental hospital."

Chris helped load Hannah and the baby, Melissa. He filled the paramedics in on all we had done and gave them instructions for the ride to the hospital. Hannah hadn't roused enough to ask about the baby. She mumbled a couple of times for her mama.

The coroner took Bob Luke and the dead baby to the morgue. Iona still was trying to regain her composure.

"Dr. Scott, are you a prayin' man?" she asked.

"Yeah, we prayed a lot today, all three of us."

"Wher' was he at?" she asked, concentrating on the wringing of her hands.

"Where was who at?" Daniel responded.

"That God ya pray to, wher' was he at when this happened to the girls? Wher' was he at when me and Esther was raped all our lives. Does he even care about us hill people?"

"He was here, and still is here. If I could tell you why God allowed it to happen, I would, but I won't even pretend to know the answer. I do know what caused it to happen."

"I know what caused it," she returned. "It was that bastard, Bob Luke and his drinkin'."

"But what made him that way?"

"The bottle," she answered.

"It's sin, Iona, we are all born sinners. Satan controls people and they end up doing just what Bob Luke did."

"How come I ain't ever felt 'im, Dr. Scott? Am I so bad that he won't come to me?"

"No, it's because we are all bad that He came. Allow me to tell you a story, Iona. A long time ago, in the Garden of Eden, Adam and Eve sinned, and after that, every child that has ever been born has been born a sinner. The wages or payment of this sin is death. That death is not dying like we die physically, but it's a spiritual death, an eternal separation from God. Then God sent His only son from heaven to come to earth to die on an old rugged cross. By doing this, we would have a payment for our sin that we were born into. Do you understand what I'm saying?"

She nodded to let him know she did.

"There could only be one sacrifice for us, it had to be someone perfect without blemish. The only one that could do that was God's son, Jesus. He took all our sin on him the day He died on Calvary, and made a way for us to go to heaven. That's a gift from God to us. If I were to give you a gift, what would you have to do for it to be yours?"

"I guess I would have to take it from ya."

"That's the way salvation is. It's a gift to you from God. But for you to have it, you must accept it. If you never take it to yourself, it will never become yours. If I were to buy you a gift and you never took it from me, it would never be yours, even though it had your name on it. So even though Christ died for our sins, unless we take it, or ask for it, it will never be ours."

"So what yer sayin' is, if I want to have this gift of salvation all I have to do is ask fer it?" she said, nodding her head.

"That's what I'm saying. God makes it so simple that a child can understand."

"Why ain't nobody ever told me this before?" she said with a tear running down her cheek.

"I don't know the answer to that, but I do know that God sent me today to tell you about how much He loves you. All you have to do is pray and ask Him. In Romans it says if you will confess with your mouth the Lord Jesus and believe in your heart that God has raised Him from the dead, you shall be saved."

"What's Romans?"

I had gotten Daniel's Bible from the front of the trailer and handed it to him with the page open to the book of Romans.

"It's a book in the Bible. Look, it's right here," he said, turning it so she could see it.

"I ain't never had one of them. So does that mean I have to confess my sins? I have so many I cain't 'member 'em all," she said with an embarrassed little chuckle.

"No, what it means is that you confess that Jesus is your Lord, you tell people with your mouth that Jesus is your Savior. And if you believe that He died and rose again, and is in heaven with His Father, his word says He will save you. And that salvation is forever. He won't ever take it from you, because all your sin is covered by the blood of Christ."

"You mean that's all I have to do to know the Jesus you know? Will God hear my prayers then?"

Her eyes lit up with the news Daniel was telling her.

"Yes, He promised us He would, and He has never broken a promise."

"Would ya help me, Dr. Scott, to know your Savior?"

"We can pray right now. Would you like to?" Daniel asked expectantly.

"Yes," she said with tears running down her cheeks.

Daniel went through the sinner's prayer with her while Chris and I watched. I stood and listened in amazement as my husband led her to the Lord. A miracle took place as the two of them, on bended knee, asked for her salvation. I stole a look at Chris, and saw the tenderness in his eyes as he looked on the scene before us. We had melted into the background as the Holy Spirit worked in our midst. On that day, this gentle husband of mine had physically saved lives and had led a soul to the saving knowledge of Christ. This truly was a ministry that God could use to further the kingdom.

Chris and I knelt beside them in the small waiting room and rejoiced together in prayer for her new spiritual life.

"I feel so light inside. It's like I got butterflies goin' around my insides," she said as we got to our feet.

"You're now our sister in Christ," Daniel said as he hugged her.

"The sister of a doctor, who could imagine?" she said, smiling.

"But better still, you are a sister to Christ and all that is His is yours to share with Him when we all get to heaven."

"Maybe this will be a start of healin' here on this sin-cursed mountain," she said, wiping the tears from her eyes.

"The girls are going to need a lot of love as they get better. And Esther's boys have also been affected. Their father is dead and it's hard to say when their mom will come home. All they've known has been ripped from them. You will be able to tell them that Jesus loves them. They are so young to have suffered so much. Melissa Ann probably won't remember much, but Hannah is going to need a lot of help from you. Find you a good church so you can grow in the Lord."

"I guess I better git on down to the house. The kids will prob'ly be needin' me. My daughter, Susan, is a watchin' 'em. I'll never be able to pay ya fer all ya done fer me, but I guess now I can be prayin' fer ya. Mrs. Scott, ya take keer of yerself and them younguns ya got growin' inside ya."

"I will, Iona. Maybe after they're born, Daniel and I will bring them to see you."

"You would do that fer me?"

"We sure would," Daniel added. "After all, we have to keep tabs on the girls to see how they are mending."

"Bye now," she said, going down the steps.

"Iona, wait. I have something for you." Daniel turned and got his Bible off the table and handed it to her.

"Oh, Dr. Scott, I cain't take it, it yers."

"I have another one. I think you might want to read some of the stories in here. It will help you get to know about Jesus."

With tears in her eyes, she accepted the gift Daniel offered her. She hugged it to her and walked silently down the dusty road toward home. Freer than she'd ever been in her life.

The three of us just sat and looked from one to the other.

"It's been one helluv a day," Chris piped up, breaking the silence.

THE MOUNTAINS CALL MY NAME

"That's exactly what it's been, directly from hell. That's how all of this happened. Because of Satan and the hell he came from. It gets into people and they do things like what has happened here today," Daniel said. "And we saw hell defeated when Iona accepted the Lord as Savior."

"I've never witnessed a soul being saved before, except mine, that is," Chris said.

"I never expected to be doing that. It just started in an innocent conversation and the Holy Spirit took over. I haven't led a soul to Christ in a long time. It's a humbling experience."

"I've never led a soul to Christ. I'm ashamed to say. I guess I've never known how. Of course I haven't been close enough to Him over the years to be of any service. If I had, my marriage would not have ended. I put my work ahead of everything and I lost a lot."

"But it isn't too late," I added.

"The experience I had with you and almost losing you was what turned my life around. I witnessed a miracle, and I recognized it as such. There was nothing I could do to save you, and I knew it. When I operated on you, it was really for Daniel, because I knew he loved you so much. I knew in my heart of hearts you were as much as gone. Not that I didn't give it one hundred percent. It was when I knew there was no hope and God healed you that I was changed forever. I saw Daniel never give up. He prayed all the time and let me know that. When things were so bleak, he was still begging God for you. And I kept seeing you hang on, and he kept praying and you kept hanging, and then it happened, you opened your eyes. That was the moment I knew I had to be with you guys, and have what you have. I had to make something count for someone other than myself."

"And here you are witnessing some more miracles."

"I'm glad you called me last night. It's been a horribly wonderful day."

"I couldn't have expressed it any better," Daniel added.

"Guys, we need to go home," I interjected.

"You're right. Let's get this baby home," Daniel said.

"Don't say baby," Chris said.

"I've got three babies to get home, two little ones and the one carrying them," Daniel said, smiling at me.

"I'll help you get the trailer cleaned up and back in shape tomorrow after I sleep in. I've had them transport Hannah and the baby to our hospital," Chris said.

"So that means one of us is going to have to go by the hospital before we go home, Daniel surmised.

"No, what I did was, I told them to call Roger. He's the one that could handle this better than we can. The baby is probably going to have to have surgery." Chris said.

"Great, now we can go home." I sighed.

THE MOUNTAINS CALL MY NAME

Daniel came and hugged me.

"Yeah, I think that's a good idea."

We took Chris back to the church to get his car and we headed home. It seemed like we had been gone for several days. I couldn't wait to get home to my bed.

Part Two

Chapter Seven

We arrived back at our house at 10:00 o'clock. We drug ourselves out of the trailer and up the stairs to our room. After a quick shower we snuggled down under the cover. I felt a baby move, and took Daniel's hand and placed it over the area where I felt it.

"I know you can't feel it but I want you to know where the little flutter is," I said, moving his hand to the area.

"I wish I could feel what you're feeling," he said wistfully.

"When I saw that little baby today, I thought for a moment..."

"Shhh...Don't even think that, sweetheart. Our babies are going to be beautiful just like their mother. We can't worry over things that are beyond our control. Hannah's baby was probably deformed from incest. I've read some studies on that."

"Our first trip will be a memorable one."

"I hope and pray this isn't an omen," he said with a chuckle.

THE MOUNTAINS CALL MY NAME

"I was so proud of you today. You made me feel so safe. Your decisions were made without hesitation. You were so sure of yourself."

"If you only knew what went through my brain today. The last thing I wanted to do was to operate on that little girl, but I knew she would never push it out. I wanted to at least give her a chance to deliver."

"She was just a baby, herself. At twelve, pregnancy shouldn't even enter her mind, especially *her* pregnancy," I lamented.

"She didn't even know what was happening to her. I'll never forget the terror I saw in her eyes. Oh, and honey, little Melissa was horribly brutalized by that monster. She was so swollen and bruised. It must have happened in the last three or four days."

"I can only imagine how horrible it was for her. No wonder she cried so hard."

"How are you feeling? Tell me the truth. How hard was this for you?"

"I really don't want to answer your question. I'm afraid you'll make me quit."

"That bad, huh?" he returned.

"I promise you I won't harm our babies. I'm exhausted, and I just made it to the bathroom before I threw up, after seeing that little baby. I threw up from Iona's peculiar odor. So I haven't faired so well on my maiden voyage."

THE MOUNTAINS CALL MY NAME

"You did remarkably well. When we were working with Hannah, you anticipated our every move, and had things ready when we needed them. I couldn't have asked more of you."

"I was surprised how much of my training came back right when I needed it."

"What I'm going to say next I want you take the right way."

I knew it was going to be something I didn't want to hear by the way it was worded. I could feel myself stiffen for the next sentence.

"I can't worry about you and take care of crises. We made it through today by the grace of God. So..."

He softened his voice as he continued.

"I would like for you to wait until after the babies are born to continue doing this."

My tears came unbidden and I couldn't control them. Daniel pulled me close to him.

"Honey, I didn't mean to make you cry."

"You didn't make me cry. The reason I'm crying is because I know what you're saying is true."

"Maybe we could take some shorter trips and you could go with me on them."

"You think so?"

THE MOUNTAINS CALL MY NAME

"Yeah, I think that would be a good idea."

I glanced over Daniel's shoulder at the clock. It was a quarter till midnight. I could tell Daniel was already drifting off when the phone rang. He rolled over with a moan and took the call.

"Dr. Scott."

"Yeah, just now? How is she doing?"

"Oh man, I figured it was going to be a mess. Will she be okay?"

"How is Hannah?"

"Thank you. Chris helped me."

"Badly deformed, he was stillborn."

"I didn't tell her anything. I kept her pretty much out after the surgery. She probably won't remember anything. Her mother? Tell her that her mother is very sick and won't be able to visit, but her aunt, Iona will be there tomorrow."

"I agree with you, she doesn't need to know about Melissa."

"Okay, I'll see you tomorrow at the hospital."

"Goodnight."

"I presume that was Roger."

"Yeah, he thanked me for sending him some work," he said with a chuckle. "He just got out of surgery with Melissa. I guess he figured if he couldn't sleep, I couldn't either."

"How's Melissa?"

"He took her straight to surgery. Let's see," he said, turning to look at the clock, she was in surgery for four hours. She was really damaged, he had to reconstruct her vagina, and also her rectum was torn. She was just ripped apart inside. The infection had traveled all around her insides, but he thinks everything will work okay one day."

"How's Hannah?"

"Hannah is crying for her mama. She still hasn't asked for her baby, but that doesn't surprise me. I think it all is probably like a bad dream to her. He isn't going to tell her what happened to Melissa. He said we did a good job on her. She is stable and comfortable."

"On that good note, I think I'm going back to sleep," he said, kissing me on the forehead.

"Me, too." I mumbled, as I scooted up close to him.

THE END

There will be a sequel.

www.ingramcontent.com/pod-product-compliance
Lightning Source LLC
Chambersburg PA
CBHW060357230426
43663CB00008B/1298